Continuous Integration, Delivery, and Deployment

Reliable and faster software releases with automating builds, tests, and deployment

Sander Rossel

BIRMINGHAM - MUMBAI

Continuous Integration, Delivery, and Deployment

First published: October 2017

Production reference: 1271017

Published by Packt Publishing Ltd.
Livery Place
35 Livery Street
Birmingham
B3 2PB, UK.

ISBN 978-1-78728-661-0

www.packtpub.com

Credits

Author
Sander Rossel

Reviewers
Wen Gu
Oleksandr Tkachuk
Rui Vilão
Olga Filipova

Commissioning Editor
Ashwin Nair

Acquisition Editor
Shweta Pant

Content Development Editor
Roshan Kumar

Technical Editors
Bharat Patil
Sachin Sunilkumar
Harshal Kadam

Copy Editor
Akshata Lobo

Project Coordinator
Devanshi Doshi

Proofreader
Safis Editing

Indexer
Pratik Shirodkar

Graphics
Jason Monteiro

Production Coordinator
Shraddha Falebhai

About the Author

Sander Rossel is a professional developer with working experience in .NET (VB and C#, WinForms, MVC, Web API, and Entity Framework), JavaScript, Git, Jenkins, Oracle, and SQL Server. He has an interest in various technologies including, but not limited to, functional programming, NoSQL, Continuous Integration (and more generally, software quality), and software design.

He has written two e-books so far: *Object-Oriented Programming in C# Succinctly* and *SQL Server for C# Developers Succinctly*, which you can download from Syncfusion for free. He seeks to educate others through his articles on his CodeProject profile, and through his book writing.

I would like to thank my parents for their support and advice. Also, of course, I would like to thank the people at Packt, and especially Shweta Pant, Johann Barretto and Roshan Kumar, for making this book possible.

About the Reviewers

Wen Gu has worked at several industry leading technology companies. He led the effort to create large-scale Continuous Integration and Continuous Delivery platforms and solutions to drive the adoption of Continuous Integration and Continuous Delivery.

I would like to thank to my wife, Annie, and my daughter, Tiffany, for their inspiration and love. I would also like to thank my colleagues at work for their encouragement and advice.

Oleksandr Tkachuk has more than 15 years of experience. He has been working as a software engineer and is responsible for full life cycle development of next-generation software, from initial requirement gathering, planning, and analysis to design, coding, testing, documentation, and implementation.

He graduated from Lviv Polytechnic National University, Ukraine, with a master's degree in computer systems and networks.

He worked as a Senior Developer, Team Leader, Solution Architect, Solution Architect, and also worked in Ukraine, UK, and Germany IT companies.

This is his first reviewed book.

Rui Vilão and **Olga Filipova** are a happy couple of software engineers and travelers currently living in Berlin. Rui is originally from Coimbra, Portugal, and Olga is from Kiev, Ukraine.

Both Rui and Olga are technical cofounders of a non-profit online education project called EdEra based in Ukraine. Besides that, Olga is a lead software engineer at a fintech company called OptioPay based in Berlin, and Rui is a lead software engineer at an online fitness company called Gymondo based in Berlin.

They live in Berlin since 2014; before that, they lived in Portugal, where both graduated as masters in computer science and worked for 5 years at Feedzai--the most successful Portuguese startup that prevents fraud all over the world.

Olga is author of *Learning Vue.js 2* and *Web development with Vue.js, Bootstrap, and Firebase*, and Rui unofficially reviewed both these books.

www.PacktPub.com

For support files and downloads related to your book, please visit `www.PacktPub.com`. Did you know that Packt offers eBook versions of every book published, with PDF and ePub files available? You can upgrade to the eBook version at `www.PacktPub.com` and as a print book customer, you are entitled to a discount on the eBook copy. Get in touch with us at `service@packtpub.com` for more details. At `www.PacktPub.com`, you can also read a collection of free technical articles, sign up for a range of free newsletters and receive exclusive discounts and offers on Packt books and eBooks.

`https://www.packtpub.com/mapt`

Get the most in-demand software skills with Mapt. Mapt gives you full access to all Packt books and video courses, as well as industry-leading tools to help you plan your personal development and advance your career.

Why subscribe?

- Fully searchable across every book published by Packt
- Copy and paste, print, and bookmark content
- On demand and accessible via a web browser

Customer Feedback

Thanks for purchasing this Packt book. At Packt, quality is at the heart of our editorial process. To help us improve, please leave us an honest review on this book's Amazon page at https://www.amazon.com/dp/1787286614. If you'd like to join our team of regular reviewers, you can e-mail us at customerreviews@packtpub.com. We award our regular reviewers with free eBooks and videos in exchange for their valuable feedback. Help us be relentless in improving our products!

Table of Contents

Preface

A problem that a lot of developers face is that software is complex and becomes only more complex over time. A single change to the software can lead to numerous unexpected bugs that may not be discovered in time. Using Continuous Integration, we can automatically test software before it is released. Using other tools, such as SonarQube, we can ensure that our code adheres to the latest standards. Unfortunately, getting started with testing and automation requires various tools and all of those tools take time and effort to learn.

In this book, we will start a project from scratch and use Continuous Integration techniques to guarantee a certain software quality. Tools such as Git, Jasmine, Karma, Selenium, Protractor, Gulp, Jenkins, SonarQube, and Postman are introduced and used to ensure that our software is up to par.

Finally, to further reduce the chances of human error, we will automatically deploy our software to another environment so that we can go from Git commit to production deployment fully automated and still sleep easy at night.

What this book covers

Chapter 1, *Continuous Integration, Delivery, and Deployment Foundations*, starts by exploring some of the theory covering Continuous Integration, Delivery, and Deployment, as well as the differences between the three.

Chapter 2, *Setting Up a CI Environment*, teaches us how to install our environment. We will set up a Linux Virtual Machine and install some of the tools we will use throughout the book, such as Jenkins, PostreSQL, and SonarQube.

Chapter 3, *Version Control with Git*, source control is a necessity for any software project and is also a prerequisite for CI, so this explores Git and how to work with it, both from a command line as well as from a graphical tool.

Chapter 4, *Creating a Simple JavaScript App*, says that before we can continue, we need a project, so we will create a simple web shop using only frontend technologies. Throughout the rest of the book, we will use this app and expand on it.

Chapter 5, *Testing Your JavaScript*, informs us that we can start writing tests for our project using the project from Chapter 4, *Creating a Simple JavaScript App*. For our unit tests, we will use Jasmine and Karma, and for our End-To-End (E2E) tests, we will use Selenium and Protractor.

Chapter 6, *Automation with Gulp*, begins with automating our tests and adding other tasks, such as linting and other frontend work, to our automated build using Gulp.

Chapter 7, *Automation with Jenkins*, takes our automation a step further with Jenkins. With Jenkins, we can run tasks automatically on any Git commit so that no code is left untested.

Chapter 8, *A NodeJS and MongoDB Web App*, informs us that moving our app forward, we will add a Node.js and MongoDB backend for our web shop. This presents us with some new challenges that are best automated.

Chapter 9, *A C# .NET Core and PostgreSQL Web App*, repeats Chapter 8, *A NodeJS And MongoDB Web App*, but with C# .NET Core and PostgreSQL. Additionally, we will add SQL database tests.

Chapter 10, *Additional Jenkins Plugins*, explores Jenkins further now that our apps are pretty much done. We will see plugins that will make your life easier and your options greater.

Chapter 11, *Jenkins Pipelines*, dives deeper into Jenkins to explore Jenkins pipelines, which are basically Jenkins configuration in code. This opens up new possibilities in Jenkins.

Chapter 12, *Testing a Web API*, is a little unrelated to the rest of the book, but not unimportant; here, we will take a look at Postman and API testing.

Chapter 13, *Continuous Delivery*, takes us near to the end of the book, and all that is left is to deploy our apps. First, we will do a manual deployment, and then automate this task using Jenkins.

Chapter 14, *Continuous Deployment*, concludes with completely automating our entire deployment process. The goal of this chapter is to get a Git commit to production without any manual intervention.

What you need for this book

For this book, we will need various software, but everything is explained in the chapters of this book. A computer with at least 16 GB memory is advised.

Who this book is for

The audience will typically be the developer. Developers tend to lose themselves in their code while missing the bigger picture. Continuous Integration, for many developers, is something that must be done, but is not truly understood by many. This book will get developers, but hopefully also team leads, into Continuous Integration and Continuous Deployment, and show them the added value it brings.

Basic knowledge of at least JavaScript and HTML/CSS is required. Knowledge of C# and SQL comes in handy. Most programmers that have programmed in a (compiled) C-like language should be able to follow along.

Conventions

In this book, you will find a number of text styles that distinguish between different kinds of information. Here are some examples of these styles and an explanation of their meaning.

Code words in text, database table names, folder names, filenames, file extensions, pathnames, dummy URLs, user input, and Twitter handles are shown as follows: "A thousand-line function with multiple nested if and while loops (and I've seen plenty) is pretty much untestable." A block of code is set as follows:

```
public static class MyMath
{
    public static int Add(int a, int b)
    {
        return a + b;
    }
}
```

When we wish to draw your attention to a particular part of a code block, the relevant lines or items are set in bold:

```
<!DOCTYPE html>
<html>
    <head>
        [...]
    </head>
```

```
      <body ng-app="shopApp">
  <%- include navbar.ejs %>
        <div class="container" ng-controller="productController">
          [...]
        </div>
    </body>
</html>
```

Any command-line input or output is written as follows:

```
sudo apt-get update
sudo apt-get install ubuntu-desktop
```

New terms and **important words** are shown in bold. Words that you see on the screen, for example, in menus or dialog boxes, appear in the text like this: "Git will rewind your work until it finds the master, which is after the **Added weapons** commit."

Warnings or important notes appear like this.

Tips and tricks appear like this.

Reader feedback

Feedback from our readers is always welcome. Let us know what you think about this book-what you liked or disliked. Reader feedback is important for us as it helps us develop titles that you will really get the most out of. To send us general feedback, simply e-mail feedback@packtpub.com, and mention the book's title in the subject of your message. If there is a topic that you have expertise in and you are interested in either writing or contributing to a book, see our author guide at www.packtpub.com/authors.

Customer support

Now that you are the proud owner of a Packt book, we have a number of things to help you to get the most from your purchase.

Downloading the example code

You can download the example code files for this book from your account at `http://www.packtpub.com`. If you purchased this book elsewhere, you can visit `http://www.packtpub.com/support` and register to have the files e-mailed directly to you. You can download the code files by following these steps:

1. Log in or register to our website using your email address and password.
2. Hover the mouse pointer on the **SUPPORT** tab at the top.
3. Click on **Code Downloads & Errata**.
4. Enter the name of the book in the **Search** box.
5. Select the book for which you're looking to download the code files.
6. Choose from the drop-down menu where you purchased this book from.
7. Click on **Code Download**.

Once the file is downloaded, please make sure that you unzip or extract the folder using the latest version of:

- WinRAR / 7-Zip for Windows
- Zipeg / iZip / UnRarX for Mac
- 7-Zip / PeaZip for Linux

The code bundle for the book is also hosted on GitHub at `https://github.com/PacktPublishing/Continuous-Integration-Delivery-and-Deployment`. We also have other code bundles from our rich catalog of books and videos available at `https://github.com/PacktPublishing/`. Check them out!

Downloading the color images of this book

We also provide you with a PDF file that has color images of the screenshots/diagrams used in this book. The color images will help you better understand the changes in the output. You can download this file from `https://www.packtpub.com/sites/default/files/downloads/ContinuousIntegrationDeliveryandDeployment_ColorImages.pdf`.

Errata

Although we have taken every care to ensure the accuracy of our content, mistakes do happen. If you find a mistake in one of our books-maybe a mistake in the text or the code-we would be grateful if you could report this to us. By doing so, you can save other readers from frustration and help us improve subsequent versions of this book. If you find any errata, please report them by visiting http://www.packtpub.com/submit-errata, selecting your book, clicking on the **Errata Submission Form** link, and entering the details of your errata. Once your errata are verified, your submission will be accepted and the errata will be uploaded to our website or added to any list of existing errata under the Errata section of that title. To view the previously submitted errata, go to https://www.packtpub.com/books/content/support and enter the name of the book in the search field. The required information will appear under the **Errata** section.

Piracy

Piracy of copyrighted material on the Internet is an ongoing problem across all media. At Packt, we take the protection of our copyright and licenses very seriously. If you come across any illegal copies of our works in any form on the Internet, please provide us with the location address or website name immediately so that we can pursue a remedy. Please contact us at copyright@packtpub.com with a link to the suspected pirated material. We appreciate your help in protecting our authors and our ability to bring you valuable content.

Questions

If you have a problem with any aspect of this book, you can contact us at questions@packtpub.com, and we will do our best to address the problem.

1

Continuous Integration, Delivery, and Deployment Foundations

Continuous Integration, Delivery, and Deployment are relatively new development practices that have gained a lot of popularity in the past few years. Continuous Integration is all about validating software as soon as it's checked in to source control, more or less guaranteeing that software works and continues to work after new code has been written. Continuous Delivery succeeds Continuous Integration and makes software just a click away from deployment. Continuous Deployment then succeeds Continuous Delivery and automates the entire process of deploying software to your customers (or your own servers).

If Continuous Integration, Delivery, and Deployment could be summarized with one word, it would be Automation. All three practices are about automating the process of testing and deploying, minimizing (or completely eliminating) the need for human intervention, minimizing the risk of errors, and making building and deploying software easier up to the point where every developer in the team can do it (so you can still release your software when that one developer is on vacation or crashes into a tree). *Automation, automation, automation, automation... Steve Ballmer*, would say, while stomping his feet on the ground and sweating like a pig.

The problem with Continuous Integration, Delivery, and Deployment is that it's not at all easy to set up and takes a lot of time, especially when you've never done it before or want to integrate an existing project. However, when done right, it will pay itself back by reducing bugs, making it easier to fix the bugs you find and producing better quality software (which should lead to more satisfied customers).

The terms Continuous Integration, Continuous Delivery, and Continuous Deployment are often used incorrectly or interchangeably (and then I've also seen the term Continuous Release). People say Continuous Integration when they mean Continuous Deployment, or they say Continuous Deployment when they mean Delivery, and so on. To make matters more complex, some people use the word DevOps when they mean any of the Continuous flavors. DevOps, however, is more than just Continuous Integration, Delivery, and/or Deployment. When talking to people about any of these subjects, don't make assumptions and make sure you're using the same definitions. DevOps is outside the scope of this book.

Continuous Integration

The first step to delivering consistent and high-quality software is **Continuous Integration (CI)**. CI is all about ensuring your software is in a deployable state at all times. That is, the code compiles and the quality of the code can be assumed to be of reasonably good quality.

Source control

CI starts with some shared repository, typically a source control system, such as **Subversion** (**SVN**) or Git. Source control systems make sure all code is kept in a single place. It's easy for developers to check out the source, make changes, and check in those changes. Other developers can then check out those changes.

In modern source control systems, such as Git, you can have multiple branches of the same software. This allows you to work on different stages of the software without troubling, or even halting, other stages of the software. For example, it is possible to have a development branch, a test branch, and a production branch. All new code gets committed on development; when it is tested and approved, it can move on to the test branch and, when your customer has given you approval, you can move it into development. Another possibility is to have a single main branch and create a new (frozen) branch for every release. You could still apply bug fixes to release branches, but preferably not new features.

Don't underestimate the value of source control. It makes it possible for developers to work on the same project and even the same files without having to worry too much about overwriting others' code or being overwritten by others.

Next to code, you should keep everything that's necessary for your project in your repository. That includes requirements, test scripts, build scripts, configurations, database scripts, and so on.

Each check into this repository should be validated by your automated build server. As such, it's important to keep check-ins small. If you write a new feature and change too many files at once, it becomes harder to find any bugs that arise.

CI server

Your builds are automated using some sort of CI server. Popular CI server software includes Jenkins (formerly Hudson), **Team Foundation Server** (**TFS**), CruiseControl, and Bamboo. Each CI server has its own pros and cons. TFS, for example, is the Microsoft CI server and works well with .NET (C#, VB.NET, and F#) and integrates with Visual Studio. The free version only has limited features for only small teams. Bamboo is the Atlassian CI server and, thus, works well with JIRA and BitBucket. Like TFS, Bamboo is not free. Jenkins is open source and free to use. It works well for Java, in which Jenkins itself was built, and works with plugins. There are a lot of other CI servers, all with their own pros and cons, but the thing they all have in common is that they automate software builds. For this book, we will use Jenkins as the CI server of choice.

Your CI server monitors your repository and starts a build on every check in. A single build can compile your code, run unit tests, calculate code coverage, check style guidelines, lint your code, minify your code, and much more. Whenever a build fails, for example, because a programmer forgot a semi-colon and checked in invalid code or because a unit test fails, the team should be notified. The CI server may send an email to the programmer who committed the offending code, to the entire team, or you could do nothing (which is not best practice) and just check the status of your build every once in a while. The conditions for failure are completely up to the developer (or the team). Obviously, when your code does not compile correctly because it's missing a semicolon, that's a fail. Likewise, a failing unit test is an obvious fail. Less obvious is that a build can fail when a certain project does not have at least a 90% test code coverage or your technical debt, that is, the time it takes to rewrite *quick and dirty solutions* to more elegant solutions grows to more than 40 hours.

The CI server should build your software, notify about failures and successes, and ultimately create an artifact. This artifact, an executable of the software, should be easily available to everyone on the team. Since the build passed all of the teams, criteria for passing a build, this artifact is ready for delivery to the customer.

Software quality

That brings us to the point of software quality. If a build on your CI server succeeds, it should guarantee a certain level of software quality. I'm not talking perfect software that is bug-free all of the time, but software that's well tested and checked for best practices. Numerous types of tests exists, but we will only look at a few of them in this book.

Unit tests

One of the most important things you can do to guarantee that certain parts of your software produce correct results is by writing unit tests. A unit test is simply a piece of code that calls a method (the method to be tested) with a predefined input and checks whether the result is what you expect it to be. If the result is correct, it reports success, otherwise it reports failure. The unit test, as the name implies, tests small and isolated units of code.

Let's say you write a function int Add(int a, int b) in C# (I'm pretty sure every programmer can follow though):

```
public static class MyMath
{
    public static int Add(int a, int b)
    {
        return a + b;
    }
}
```

The first thing you want to test is whether Add indeed returns a + b and not a + a, or b + b, or even something random. That may sound easier than it is. If you test whether Add(1, 1) returns 2 and the test succeeds, someone might still have implemented it as a + a or b + b. So at the very least, you should test it using two unequal integers, such as Add(1, 2). Now what happens when you call Add(2147483647, 1)? Does it overflow or throw an exception and is that indeed the outcome you suspected? Likewise, you should test for an underflow (while adding!?). -2147483647 + -1 will not return what you'd expect. That's three unit tests for such a simple function! Arguably, you could test for +/-, -/+, and -/- (-3 + -3 equals -6 and not 0), but you'd have to try really hard to break that kind of functionality, so those tests would probably not give you an extra useful test. Your final unit tests may look something like the following:

```
[TestClass]
public class MathTests
{
    [TestMethod]
    public void TestAPlusB()
```

```
    {
        int expected = 3;
        int actual = MyMath.Add(1, 2);
        Assert.AreEqual(expected, actual, "Somehow, 1 + 2 did not equal 3.");
    }

    [TestMethod]
    [ExpectedException(typeof(OverflowException))]
    public void TestOverflowException()
    {
        // MyMath.Add currently overflows, so this test will fail.
        MyMath.Add(int.MaxValue, 1);
    }

    [TestMethod]
    [ExpectedException(typeof(OverflowException))]
    public void TestOverflowException()
    {
        // MyMath.Add currently underflows, so this test will fail.
        MyMath.Add(int.MinValue, -1);
    }
}
```

Of course, if you write a single unit test and it succeeds, it is no guarantee that your software actually works. In fact, a single function usually has more than one unit test alone. Likewise, if you have written a thousand unit tests, but all they do is check that true indeed equals true, it's also not any indication of the quality of your software. Later in this book, we will write some unit tests for our software. For now, it suffices to say your tests should cover a large portion of your code and, at least, the most likely scenarios. I would say quality over quantity, but in the case of unit testing, quantity is also pretty important. You should actually keep track of your code coverage. There are tools that do this for you, although they cannot check whether your tests actually make any sense.

It is important to note that unit tests should not depend upon other systems, such as a database, the filesystem, or (third-party) services. The input and output of our tests need to be predefined and predictable. Also, we should always be able to run our unit tests, even when the network is down and we can't reach the database or third-party service. It also helps in keeping tests fast, which is a must, as you're going to have hundreds or even thousands of tests that you want to run as fast as possible. Instant feedback is important. Luckily, we can mock (or fake) such external components, as we will see later in this book.

Just writing some unit tests is not going to cut it. Whenever a build passes, you should have reasonable confidence that your software is correct. Also, you do not want unit tests to fail every time you make even the slightest change. Furthermore, specifications change and so do unit tests. As such, unit tests should be understandable and maintainable, just like the rest of your code. And writing unit tests should be a part of your day to day job. Write some code, then write some unit tests (or turn that around if you want to do Test-Driven Development). This means testing is not something only testers do, but the developers as well.

In order to write unit tests, your code should be testable as well. Each `if` statement makes your code harder to test. Each function that does more than one thing makes your code harder to test. A thousand-line function with multiple nested `if` and `while` loops (and I've seen plenty) is pretty much untestable. So when writing unit tests for your code, you are probably already refactoring and making your code prettier and easier to read. Another added benefit of writing unit tests is that you have to think carefully about possible inputs and desirable outputs early, which helps in finding edge cases in your software and preventing bugs that may come from them.

Integration tests

Checking whether an `Add` function really adds `a` and `b` is nice, but does not really give you an indication that the system as a whole works as well. As said, unit tests only test small and isolated units of code and should not interact with external components (external components are mocked). That is why you will want integration tests as well. Integration tests test whether the system as a whole operates as expected. We need to know whether a record can indeed be saved in and retrieved from a database, that we can request some data from an external service, and that we can log to some file on the filesystem. Or, more practically we can check whether the frontend that was created by the frontend team actually fits the backend that was created by the backend team. If these two teams have had any problems or confusion in communication, the integration tests will, hopefully, sort that out.

Last year, we created a service for a third party who wanted to interface with a system we wrote. The service did not do a lot basically it took the received message and forwarded it to another service that we used internally (and wasn't available outside of the network). The internal service had all of the business rules and could read from, and write to, a database. Furthermore, it would, in some cases, create additional jobs that would be put on a (asynchronous) queue, which is yet another service. Last, a fourth service would pick up any messages from the queue and process them. In order to process a single request, we potentially needed five components (external service, internal service, database, queue, and queue processor). The internal service was thoroughly unit tested, so the business rules were covered. However, that still leaves a lot of room for errors and exceptions when one of the components is not available or has an incompatible interface.

Big bang testing

There are two approaches to integration testing: big bang testing and incremental testing. With big bang testing, you simply wait until all the components of a system are ready and then start testing. In the case of my service, that meant developing and installing everything, then posting some requests and checking whether the external service could call the internal service, and whether the internal service could access the database and the queue and, not unimportant, give feedback to the external service. Furthermore, of course, I had to test whether the queue triggered the processing service and whether the processing service processed the message correctly too.

In reality, the processing also used the database; it put new messages on the queue and sent emails in case of errors. Additionally, all the components had to access the hard drive for logging to a file (and do not assume the filesystem is always available; the first time on production I actually ran into an Unauthorized Exception and nothing was logged). So that means even more integration testing.

Incremental testing

With incremental testing, you test components as soon as they are available and you create stubs or drivers (some sort of placeholder) for components that are not yet available. There are two approaches here:

- **Top-down testing**: Using top-down testing would mean I would've checked whether the external service could make a call to the internal service and, if the internal service was not available yet, create a stub that pretends to be the internal service.

- **Bottom-up testing**: Bottom-up is testing the other way around, so I'd start testing the internal service and create a driver that mimics the external service.

Incremental testing has the advantage that you can start defining tests early before all the components are complete. After that, it becomes a matter of filling in the gaps.

Acceptance tests

After having unit tested our code and checked whether the system as a whole works, we can now assume our software works and is of decent quality (at least, the quality we expect). However, that does not mean that our software actually does what was requested. It often happens that the customer requests feature A, the project manager communicates B, and the programmer builds C. There is a really funny comic about it with a swing (do a Google image search for `how projects really work`). Luckily, we have acceptance tests.

An acceptance test tests whether specific functionality, as described in the specification, works as expected. For example, the external service we built made it possible for the third party to make a call using a specific login method, create a user, update the user, and finally, deactivate that user. The specifics of the updates were described in the specifications document. Some fields were specified by the third party and some fields were calculated by the service. Keep in mind that the actual calculations had been unit tested and that we knew all the parts worked together as we had done some integration testing. This test was all about testing whether the third party, using their Java technology (our service was written in C#, but communication was XML), could indeed create and update a user. I probably tested that manually once or twice. The problem with testing this manually was that it was a web service; the input and output was XML which is not that easy to read and write. The service only returned whether or not the user was successfully created (and if not, why) so in order to test whether everything had gone well, I needed to look up the user record in the database, along with all other records that should have been created. I knew how to do that at the time, but if I needed to do it again now, I'd be pretty frustrated. And if I do not know how to properly test it, then how will my coworkers who need to make changes to the service know? Needless to say, I created something like 30 automated tests that check whether specific use cases work as intended.

Another one of our applications, a website, works pretty much the same. A user can create a record on page A, look it up on page B, and update it. Obviously, XML is not going to cut it here; this is not a web service. In this case, we used GUI tests (that is, Graphical User Interface tests). Our build server is just going to run the application and click on the buttons that we told it to click. If the button is not available, we've got ourselves an error. If the button is available, but does not take us to the requested page, we've got an error. If the page is correctly loaded, but the record is not visible (for whatever reason), we've got an error. The important thing here is that the tests do more or less exactly what our users will do as well.

There is some confusion on the difference between integration tests and acceptance tests. Both test the entire system, but the difference is that integration tests are written from a technical perspective while acceptance tests are written from the perspective of the product owner or business users.

Smoke tests

Of course, even when all of your tests succeed, a product can still break in production. The database may be down or maybe you have a website and the web server is down. It is always important to also test whether your software is actually working in a production environment, so be sure to always do an automated smoke test after deployment that gives you fast and detailed feedback when something goes wrong. A smoke test should test whether the most important parts of your system work. A manual smoke test is fine (and I'd always manually check whether your software, at least, runs after a release), but remember it's another human action that may be forgotten or done poorly.

Some people run smoke tests before doing integration and acceptance tests. Integration and acceptance tests test an entire system and, as such, may take a bit of time. A smoke test, however, tests only basic functionality, such as *does the page load?* When a smoke test fails, you can skip the rest of your tests, saving you some time and giving you faster feedback.

There are many types of tests available out there. Unit tests, smoke tests, integration tests, system tests, acceptance tests, database tests, functional tests, regression tests, security tests, load tests, UI tests... it never ends! I'm pretty sure you could spend an entire year doing nothing but writing tests. Try selling that to your customer; you can't deliver any working software, but the software you can't deliver is really very well tested. Personally, I'm more pragmatic. A test should support your development process, but a test should never be a goal on its own. When you think you need a test, write a test. When you don't, don't. Unfortunately, I have seen tests that did absolutely nothing (except give you a false sense of security), but I'm guessing someone just wanted to see tests, any tests, really bad.

Other quality gates

Next to tests, you want other measurements of code quality. For example, code that has many nested `if` statements is hard to test and understand. Writing an `if` statement without curly braces (for single statements) will increase the chances of bugs in the future. Not closing database connections or file handles may lock up your system and cause other processes to fail. Failing to unsubscribe from (static) events may cause memory leaks. Such errors may easily pass unit tests, but will eventually fail in production. These sort of errors can be very difficult to find as well. For example, a memory leak may cause your application to run slowly or even crash after a day or two. Good luck finding bugs that only happen to some users, sometimes, because they haven't closed the application in two days. Luckily, there are tools that find exactly these kinds of issues. SonarQube is one such tool. It will show you where you can improve your code, how important it is that you fix this code, the time it will probably take to fix it, and a trending graph of your technical debt.

It is important to note here that these issues, unlike unit tests, may or may not be actual bugs. For example, the following code is completely valid, but may introduce bugs that are not easy to spot:

```
if (valid)
    DoSomething();
```

Now the specifications change and you, or a coworker, have to change this code so something else is also executed when valid. You change the code as follows:

```
if (valid)
    DoSomething();
    DoSomethingElseIfValid(); // This is a bug as it's always executed.
```

Tools such as SonarQube, will recognize this pattern and they will warn you that the code is not best practice including an explanation on what's wrong with it and how to change it. In this case, the original code should be changed, so it's clear what happens when valid:

```
if (valid)
{
    DoSomething();
}
```

We will have a look at SonarQube later in this book and see both C# and JavaScript issues that may or may not be bugs.

Automation

Depending on what you're used to, I've got some bad news for you. When doing CI, the command line is your best friend. Personally, I see the need for a command line, but I don't like it one bit. It requires way too much typing and memorization for my taste. Anyway, Linux users rejoice and spoiled Windows users get ready for a trip back to the 80s when user interfaces had yet to be invented. However, we're going to automate a lot, and that will be the computer's job. Computers don't use user interfaces. So, while you hit *F5* in Visual Studio and compile your code, your build server needs to know it should run MSBuild with some parameters, such as the location of your solution or the `msbuild` file.

Luckily, most tools have some form of command-line interface. Whether you are working with .NET, JavaScript, Java, SQL Server, Oracle, or any language or tool, you can always run it using a command line. Throughout this book, we will use various tools and I do not think we will use any of them without using the command line as well. In fact, the command line seems to be back (although, was it ever really gone?). Various tools, such as NodeJS, npm, and MongoDB, are used through the command line. Furthermore, we will see tools, such as MSBuild, MSTest, and NuGet, that all work from the command line (or from a single click in your IDE).

Teamwork

Imagine doing all this locally on your own computer. For simplicity, let's say you've got some code that has to compile and some unit tests that have to run. Easy enough, everybody should be able to do that. Except your manager, who doesn't have the developer software installed at all. Or the intern, who forgot to kick off the unit tests. Or the developer, who works on a different OS making some tests, that aren't important to him, fail (for example, we have an application developed on and for Windows, but a complimentary app for iOS developed on a Mac). Suddenly, getting a working and tested executable becomes a hassle for everyone who isn't working on this project on a daily basis. Besides, the people who can get a working executable may forget to run tests, creating a risk that the executable is compiling, but not actually working. As you can see, a lot can go wrong and there are only two steps. I've intentionally left out all the other tests and quality gates we might have. And that's the biggest benefit to CI. The software is compiled and fully tested automatically, reducing the chance of human errors and making it considerably easier to get a working executable that is more or less guaranteed to work. By testing on a server that closely or completely resembles the production environment, you can further eliminate hard to find bugs.

As you might have guessed, CI is not something you just do. It's a team effort. If you're writing unit tests to make sure everything works as best as it can, but your team members commit large chunks of code, never write tests and ignore the build status, your build becomes untrustworthy and quite useless. In any case, it will not lead to the (increase in) software quality you were hoping for.

Having said all of the above, it's crucial that you, and your team, take your automated build environment very seriously. Keep build times short, so that you get near-instant feedback when a build fails. When someone checks in code that makes the build fail, it should become a top priority to fix the build. Maybe it's that missing semi-colon, maybe a test fails, or maybe more tests have to be added. The bottom line is, when the build fails, it becomes impossible to get an executable with the latest features that's guaranteed to pass your tests and other quality criteria.

 When your build passes, it guarantees that the software passes your tests and other quality gates for *good* software, which should indicate that it's unlikely that the software will break or, worse, produce erroneous results in that part of the system. However, if your tests are of low quality, the software may still break even though your tests pass. Parts of the system that are not tested may still break. Even tested parts can still produce bugs. As such, Continuous Integration is not some magical practice that will guarantee that your code is awesome and free of bugs. However, not practicing it will almost certainly guarantee something somewhere sometime will go wrong.

Continuous Delivery

The next step towards successful software deployment is Continuous Delivery (which doesn't have an abbreviation, as it would be the same as that of Continuous Deployment and the difference between the two is already confusing enough). With Continuous Delivery, the artifacts that are produced by your CI server are deployed to the production server with a single button click. Continuous Integration is a prerequisite for successful Continuous Delivery.

Let's first take a quick look at what you are probably doing now or have done in the past. You implement the feature, compile, run tests, and when it all works, decide to release the new version of the software to your customer. You need to copy/paste some files to their environment manually. You need to check whether the specific configuration is correct (so your customer will not be targeting your local database). By the way, did you make a backup of the current version of their software in case your fix breaks something else? When a database update is involved, you probably need to stop some services that read and/or write to the database. Oops, you forgot to turn on the **maintenance** page for your customers, website. Now, they'll see this wonderful *This site can't be reached ERR_CONNECTION_REFUSED* page. Ah well, update the database, copy those files, and getting it back up as soon as possible. And now, you have to test if everything works as expected. Also, don't forget to restart that service you had to stop in order to update the database. Those are quite a lot of steps for a single deployment and each of those steps can go wrong. And even if you do it right, will your coworkers know what to do as well? Will you still know next month when you need to do another release? So, you've just finished this release and now the customer calls again, *looks good, but can you make that button green?* Yes, you can make that button green. That's like three seconds of work and then another thirty minutes sweating and swearing while you release it to production. And who will do all of this when you're on vacation?

But we have documented our entire delivery process, I hear you say. Be that as it may, people could still skip a step or execute it incorrectly. Documentation needs to be written and updated, which is, again, a time-consuming and error prone task. Sure, it helps, but is by no means fail-safe.

The benefits of having an automated deployment soon become visible. Less obvious, but most useful, is that automated deployment makes it so much easier to deploy that you can (and will) deploy more frequently as well. When a release takes an hour of your time and has considerable risks of failure, not to mention frustration, every time you do it, you tend to postpone a release as long as possible. That also means that the releases you make probably have many changes, which increases the risk that anything breaks the software and which makes it harder to find the bug. Making the release process easier, by automating it, is important, since you will now deploy smaller changes more often. That means that it is easier to roll back any deployments in case of failure, but it will also reduce the risk that any failures occur in the first place. After all, the changes relative to the old version of the software remain small.

You should be able to deploy your software to a production (like) environment at any time. To achieve this, your software must always be in a deliverable state, meaning your build succeeds, the code compiles, and your tests succeed. The advantages should be obvious; your customer calls and asks for a new feature, or maybe he has found a bug in the software and wants you to fix it. You can now simply implement the feature or fix the bug and have it on production just minutes later. Your CI server builds the software and you know it is probably alright because it compiles and your tests succeeded.

Unfortunately, Continuous Delivery is not always (completely) possible. For example, when your customer has a database administrator (the dreaded DBA) that prevents you direct access to the database, you could still automate the delivery of the software, but not the database. In one case, I even had a customer where only the system administrator had internet access. All other computers in the company (or at least, at that specific site) were not connected to the internet. As a result, each software update was done manually and on site (a one-hour drive single trip, no matter how small the update). Even then, the more you can automate, the better, so get that CI server up and running, get that tested artifact, drive to the customer, and deploy that artifact (using a local script if possible). If you do it right, which we didn't at the time, you could email it to the system administrator and tell him *just run that script*, saves you a two hour drive!

Not everyone is keen on having their deployments automated, especially not customers. When, at one time, my manager mentioned that we were looking at automating deployments as it would be faster, easier, and less likely to go wrong, the customer actually responded that they did not want that as we, and they, could not check on, or control, automated deployments. That's a pretty absurd statement as if anything is controllable, it's a script, and if anything isn't, it's a person who can ignore protocol or make honest mistakes. Still, people aren't known to be rational about stuff they don't understand. So, if you are looking to implement any of the above expect some initial resistance. On the flip side, customers are never around when you deploy anyway, so they will not even notice when you automate it (you did not get that from me).

Continuous Deployment

The final stage of automating your software development process is Continuous Deployment. When practicing Continuous Deployment, every check into your source control is deployed to a production (like) environment on a successful build. The rationale behind this is that you are going to deploy the software to production sooner or later anyway. The sooner you do this, the better the chance you'll be able to fix bugs faster. It's easier to remember what you did yesterday that might have caused the bug than it is to remember what you did two months ago that might have caused the bug. Imagine checking some code into source control and get error messages from your production environment five minutes later. You'll be able to find and fix the bug immediately and, five minutes later, the production software is up and running without bugs again. Unfortunately, most managers and software owners I know get pretty nervous at the thought of automated deployment, let alone automated deployment on every check in.

Again, as with Continuous Delivery, Continuous Deployment is not always possible. All the issues with Continuous Delivery still apply, except now when a DBA doesn't give you access to the database, Continuous Deployment is pretty much out of the question. After all, you can't automatically deploy software multiple times a day while your database is only updated when some DBA has time. Currently, I'm working on a website for a customer who in turn has a customer who needs three days' notice before any changes to the website can be made. It's a contractual obligation and whether it makes sense or not, it is what it is. So in that particular case, Continuous Deployment is obviously a no-go. Still, we use this technique on our own test environment and automate as much as possible while still giving three days, notice.

The difference between Continuous Integration, Continuous Delivery, and Continuous Deployment may still be a bit vague. Consider the following image (I apologize for my poor MS Paint skills) which indicates where the three types start and stop:

Code	Build	Test	Release	Deploy

Continuous Integration

Continuous Delivery

Continuous Deployment

Does all of this mean we have no more manual tasks? Not at all. For example, the only way that you're going to know if what you build is actually what the customer wanted is by having the customer see it and, ideally, use it. So the customer should validate any changes manually. Even if it's just a bug fix, your customer probably wants to see that it's fixed with his own eyes before you can release to production. Likewise, exploratory testing is a typical manual task. Other tasks, such as making changes to your firewall, (web) server, or database may (or even must) be done manually, although preferably not.

Summary

Continuous Deployment helps in getting software out to your customer as soon as it is written. Continuous Delivery is a good alternative if you need more control over your deployments. To minimize the risk of deploying bugs, your software should be thoroughly tested using Continuous Integration. Continuous Integration is all about making sure your software is tested and deployable. In the next chapter, we are going to set up an environment with some tools that are necessary for Continuous Integration.

2
Setting Up a CI Environment

In the remainder of this book, we're going to implement Continuous Integration, Delivery, and Deployment. However, before we start, we must choose some software to work with. As I have mentioned, we have multiple choices for our source control and for our CI server and, of course, we can use a ton of programming languages and databases. Additionally, we need to create some project to work with. This chapter will lay out the technologies that are used in the remainder of the book, as well as a high-level overview of how they all work together. For the test project, we'll create a simple to-do list web app. We'll implement it in Node.js with a MongoDB database and in C# Core with a PostgreSQL database. That way, we'll see CI in action in both frontend and backend development, as well as the popular JavaScript language, the compiled C# .NET Core language, SQL, and NoSQL.

We'll start by building a frontend using JavaScript and the npm package manager, creating unit tests and UI tests in Selenium and Jasmine, and automating these using Karma and Gulp. After that, we'll hook it up to a JavaScript-driven Node.js and MongoDB backend.

With the same frontend, we can build a C# .NET Core and PostgreSQL database backend. We'll use NuGet and Microsoft's unit testing framework as well as MSBuild and MSTest.

Chapter 1, *Continuous Integration, Delivery, and Deployment Foundations*, starts with source control. For this book, I have chosen Git, as it is a widely used source control system. As for the CI server, we are going to use Jenkins. Both Git and Jenkins are free and can be downloaded and used privately and professionally at no cost. In a real-world scenario, you would install Git and Jenkins on one or two servers that your entire team can access. Likewise, your database may get a separate server as well. However, since you and I, as poor programmers, probably do not have an idle server (or two) laying around, we will make use of Virtual Machines (which is like a computer on your computer). Later on, we will also need an environment to deploy to, so that could be a second or third **Virtual Machine** (**VM**). For our VMs, we are going to use Oracle VM VirtualBox. This software is also free to use. Of course, any VM is going to need an operating system, just like a *normal* computer. I may have given it away earlier, but I am a Windows user. Unfortunately, I don't have some spare Windows licenses laying around and I am guessing you haven't either. Luckily, there is another popular operating system that is free to use and can run Git, Jenkins, JavaScript, and anything we are going to use throughout this book. You have probably guessed that the operating system is Linux. As for the Linux distribution, I am using Ubuntu Server, as it is one of the most used Linux distributions out there (if not the most used). Do not worry, I expect no prior knowledge of any of the tools I mentioned, so I will be taking you through the installations step by step.

I should mention that running a VM is pretty heavy work for your computer, let alone running two. After all, your computer will be running multiple operating systems and all the programs in it. If you have less than 8 GB RAM memory, I recommend not installing everything on your VM (it is possible, but it will not run very smoothly). There is one tool in this book, GitLab for Git, that really needs Linux to run on. You will also need some space on your hard disk. The minimum recommended size for a new VM is 8 GB, but that is not enough for our environment. I would use 30 GB just to be safe (especially if you plan on installing a user interface). We are going to install some other software as well, so reserve at least 40 GB to be on the safe side (for two VMs).

My own system runs Windows 10 and has 16 GB RAM memory, so all of the examples in this book are guaranteed to work on Windows 10 (probably 8 and even 7 as well). The examples may work on Linux and even Mac, but I have not tested them. Some of the explanations are Windows-specific, but most of it is pretty generic.

You may have noticed that we are going to use C# .NET Core. C# .NET traditionally only works on Windows (unless you use Mono), but, with the recently released .NET Core, that is all in the past. With .NET Core, an official light version of .NET, you can code C# and run it everywhere. Of course, it would be nice if we could also develop that application everywhere. The Visual Studio flagship editor from Microsoft still only works on Windows. Luckily, Microsoft realized that too and created Visual Studio Code, a lightweight editor for all your .NET code.

Installing a Virtual Machine

As mentioned, we will need a Virtual Machine. We are going to use Oracle VM VirtualBox to host our VMs, which you can download at: `https://www.virtualbox.org` (I have downloaded the VirtualBox 5.1.12 platform package for Windows). Download the version that is applicable to you on the downloads page and install it on your computer. I've left all the defaults as they were, but you can change them as you see fit (at your own risk). If all goes well, you should soon see the Oracle VM VirtualBox Manager, as follows:

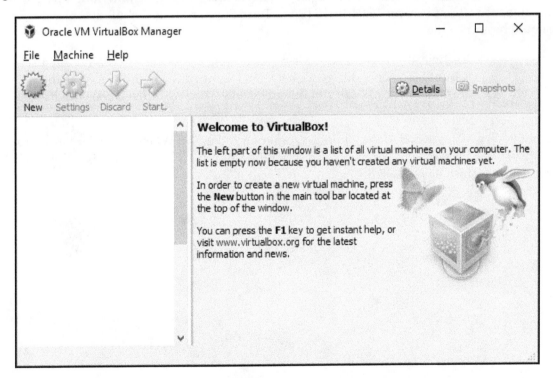

To create a new VM, click the **New** button. You then get to pick a name (I have called my VM `CI server`), a type (**Linux**), and a version (**Ubuntu (64-bit)**, which is the default). The next window lets you specify the amount of memory. The default is 1 GB, but I recommend making that 4 GB (4096 MB), unless you are only going to run GitLab on it, in which case you can do with less. After that, you have to actually create the virtual HD. You can pick **Create a virtual hard disk now** (which is selected by default). The next two windows let you specify the type of file you wish to create and whether you would like to dynamically allocate space or have it fixed. I recommend leaving the defaults. After that, you get a summary and you can create your VM.

The VM is now added to the list of VMs in the VirtualBox Manager. You can start it by either double-clicking or by selecting it and clicking **Start** (don't do this just yet).

Installing Ubuntu

When you start your VM for the first time, VirtualBox will ask for a startup disk. The startup disk should install our operating system, but we don't have one yet. Head over to `https://www.ubuntu.com/` and find the server download. At the time of writing this, I downloaded Ubuntu Server 16.04.1 LTS (Long Term Support). The default download should be an `iso` file.

 Technically speaking, there is no such thing as Ubuntu Server. It is all just Ubuntu. The only difference between Ubuntu and Ubuntu Server is the installation procedure and the preinstalled packages that come with it.

Once you have downloaded the Ubuntu `iso` file, start the VM. When it asks for the startup disk, you can browse your computer and select the Ubuntu `iso` file. Once it is selected, click **Next** and the installation will begin.

If you ever lose your mouse cursor in the VM and you cannot deselect, minimize or close your VM, use the right-*Ctrl* key to get your VM out of focus. If, for some reason, you did not follow my tutorial and backed out of the installation, you may find that your VM gives you the error message *FATAL: No bootable medium found! System halted*. If this is the case, you can close your VM (using VirtualBox, like using the off button on your physical computer) and then go to the settings of your VM to select a bootable medium, which is your Ubuntu `iso` file:

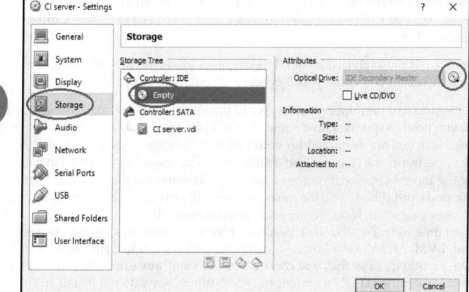

When you select the `iso` file and restart your VM, it will now take you to the installer again and you can follow the steps as explained.

First, you have to choose the language (you can navigate using the up and down arrow keys and select using the *Enter/return* key; use the left and right arrow keys to select **<Go back>**). I have chosen English and I suggest you do too, so you can follow along with the tutorial (and the rest of the book) without translating everything. In the menu that follows, pick the top option, **Install Ubuntu Server**. Next, you have to pick a language for your installation. Again, I picked English. The next step is to pick your location, which will, among other things, determine your time zone. I've actually picked **The Netherlands** here and I suggest you look for your own location as well. If you are lucky, you will be taken to the keyboard configuration. However, if, like me, you picked a language that is not spoken in your location (and we don't speak English in the Netherlands) or your locale is not preinstalled, you will be prompted to pick a locale first. I have picked **United States (en_US.UTF-8)**.

So, next up is the keyboard layout. I recommend following the automatic keyboard detection, unless you know your keyboard layout (there are loads of them).

After you have determined your keyboard layout, you will see some progress bars. After that, you need to specify a host name. Again, I picked `ciserver` (no spaces or capitals this time). Next, you are prompted for your real name (`Sander Rossel`), and after that, you can make up a username (`sander`). After that, pick a password (`1234` or whatever; you will only use this on your local computer anyway). Re-enter the password. If your password is a weak password (like `1234`), the next question will be if you are sure that you want to use this weak password. Next, do not encrypt your home directory. You can just accept the chosen time zone. For your disk partition, choose the default, **Guided - use entire disk and set up LVM**. An LVM is a Logical Volume and allows you to dynamically create, resize, or delete partitions. After that, just choose **Yes** and **Continue** until a few more progress bars appear. Leave the HTTP proxy empty and continue. Also, do not install automatic updates. After that, the installation will prompt you to pick some software to install. Leave the **standard system utilities** selected, but do not select any of the other software. We can always install other software manually later. After that, choose to install the GRUB boot loader.

Hooray, you have now successfully installed Ubuntu Server. The VM will now restart and you can log in with the credentials you chose during installation (for me, that is the username `sander` and the password `1234`):

```
Ubuntu 16.04.1 LTS ciserver tty1

ciserver login: sander
Password:
Welcome to Ubuntu 16.04.1 LTS (GNU/Linux 4.4.0-31-generic x86_64)

 * Documentation:  https://help.ubuntu.com
 * Management:     https://landscape.canonical.com
 * Support:        https://ubuntu.com/advantage

109 packages can be updated.
58 updates are security updates.


The programs included with the Ubuntu system are free software;
the exact distribution terms for each program are described in the
individual files in /usr/share/doc/*/copyright.

Ubuntu comes with ABSOLUTELY NO WARRANTY, to the extent permitted by
applicable law.

To run a command as administrator (user "root"), use "sudo <command>".
See "man sudo_root" for details.

sander@ciserver:~$
```

You would do well to make frequent backups of your VM. It is as easy as copy/pasting some files. VirtualBox stores the VM files in the folder specified under the **Preferences** | **General** | default machine folder. Simply copy/paste the folder of the VM your want to backup. Restoring is as easy as replacing the VM files with your back up files. Doing this allows you to play around and mess up your VM without having to worry about going through the entire installation again. Backup after each of the subsequent steps, so you never lose work.

You will notice that Ubuntu gives you nothing more than a command line. We have just installed a server, and servers do not really need fancy user interfaces. User interfaces do come in handy, especially when you are not used to doing everything through a command. Luckily, Ubuntu does actually have a user interface (multiple actually); it is just not installed. In this book, I am not going to use the Ubuntu desktop, but if you want, you can install it by simply running the following commands:

```
sudo apt-get update
sudo apt-get install ubuntu-desktop
```

When the installation is done, you can restart either by using the `reboot` command or by using, `poweroff` command and then restarting from VirtualBox again.

If you are not familiar with Linux terminology, these terms are **superuser do** (**sudo**) (so you are running the commands as an administrator) and **Advanced Packaging Tool** (**apt**). `apt-get update` makes sure your packages source is up to date (it does not update packages!). You should run this before installing a package to make sure you install the most recent version. `apt-get install some-package` installs a package.

The next thing we will need to do is to make sure we can access our Ubuntu server running in the VM from our host. To do this, we first need to close our VM. After that, go to the settings of that VM and go to the **Network** tab. Select **Adapter 2** and select the **Enable Network Adapter** box. After that, pick **Host-only Adapter** in the **Attached to** dropdown. Save your changes and start up the VM again. It gets a little tricky from here. Log in to your VM and execute the command `ls /sys/class/net`. This will list your available network devices. You should be seeing something like `enp0s1 enp0s2 lo` (the numbers of `enp0s#` may vary; I actually had 3 and 8). The next thing we need to do is add one of those `enp0s#`'s to your network settings. First though, open your VirtualBox preferences (under the **File** menu) and go to the **Network** settings. There, select the **Host-only Networks** tab and select the network you used for your VM's second adapter (there should be only one). Now check out the **DHCP Server** tab, specifically **Lower Address Bound**. You will need this IP address (or any IP address between the lower and upper bound). Mine was `192.168.56.101`, so I suspect it will be the same for you. Now, edit your network settings in Ubuntu. To do this, open the `/etc/network/interfaces` file in vi; you can do this by executing the command `sudo vi /etc/network/interfaces`. Now, press *I* to edit and add the following lines to the file:

```
auto enp0s8
iface enp0s8 inet static
address 192.168.56.101
netmask 255.255.255.0
```

Once you have made the changes, hit *Esc* to stop editing and run *:wq* to exit and save (or *:q!* to exit without saving). Restart your VM again (using poweroff or reboot), log in to Ubuntu, and use the `ifconfig` command. If everything went well, you should now see your three network devices listed.

> While the default **Network Address Translation** (**NAT**) network adapter gives your VM access to the Internet through the host, the *host-only adapter* is a method that actually makes your VM visible to the host. The settings for this network adapter roughly translate as follows:
>
>   - `auto enp0s8`: Automatically brings up the enp0s8 device when Ubuntu boots
>
>   - `iface enp0s8 inet static`: Gives the enp0s8 network interface a static (as opposed to dynamic, or dhcp) IPv4 address (inet6 for IPv6)
>
>   - `address`: The actual IP address
>   - `netmask`: The netmask

Using this VM, we are trying to mimic a real-world server. In the real world, security is of utmost importance. It is possible to run all the tools we are going to install on SSL (HTTPS) and even restrict the login to specific IP addresses. However, since this is not the real world, the VM will only be available from the host, and additional security is more work before we can actually get to writing code and using tools, I will leave such security to you for practice.

> Remembering your IP address every time you need to access your server (for applications such as Git, Jenkins and others) is rather tiresome. Unfortunately, it is not easy to map your IP address to a human-readable host name, such as `ciserver`. Luckily, in Windows, we do have a little workaround. Find the `C:\Windows\System32\drivers\etc\hosts` file and open it in Notepad (as administrator). Add the following line at the bottom of the file: `192.168.56.101 ciserver`. Be sure to replace the IP address with your own. You can now access your server by navigating to `ciserver[:port]`.

Installing Git

The first thing we have to do is install Git. As I said at the start of `Chapter 1`, *Continuous Integration, Delivery, and Deployment Foundations*, CI starts with a shared repository and this is it. Git is the immensely popular **Source Control Management** (**SCM**) tool from the creator of Linux. It shows that everything is done through the command line, and the only official user interface is so bad you might as well use the command line. Luckily, there are some third-party tools available. Aside from the tooling, Git is a really good source control system that has some benefits over its competitors. As I mentioned earlier, we are going to use GitLab (`https://gitlab.com`) on Ubuntu, which gives you a nice GitHub-like portal.

A good alternative for hosting your own Git server is to look for an online host. The most popular, by far, is GitHub (`https://github.com/`). Personally, I use GitHub for all my personal projects. It is free but everything is open source, meaning everyone may browse and download your code. There are priced plans for private projects though. Another popular alternative is Atlassian's BitBucket (`https://bitbucket.org/`), which I (am forced to) use professionally. Like GitHub, BitBucket has free and priced plans. Another benefit to using BitBucket is that it works well with other popular Atlassian products, such as SourceTree, JIRA, and Bamboo. You may skip this section altogether and use one of the online providers if you wish. If you do, be sure to follow their tutorials, as I am not going to discuss them further here.

Installing GitLab

Installing and setting up Git (with **Secure Shell** (**SSH**)) authentication in Ubuntu is a pain when you are not a Linux veteran. Once you have installed everything, you are left with a plain, bare, command-line Git. Luckily, there are third-party providers that do all the heavy lifting and give you a neat portal with all your projects and commits as an added bonus (making it look like GitHub)! The one we are going to use is GitLab. Again, the docs are pretty explicit on how to install GitLab (`https://about.gitlab.com/downloads/#ubuntu1604`).

The first thing we have to do is install some necessary dependencies:

```
sudo apt-get update
sudo apt-get install curl openssh-server ca-certificates postfix
```

The installation of postfix will give you an install window (kind of like when you were installing Ubuntu) that will let you choose a default configuration. Just pick the default (**Internet Site**) and hit *Enter*. After that, it will ask for the system mail name. The default is your server name, so just go with it. After that, the installation will continue.

After that, we need to add the GitLab package so we can install it:

```
curl -sS
https://packages.gitlab.com/install/repositories/gitlab/gitlab-ce/script.de
b.sh | sudo bash
sudo apt-get install gitlab-ce
```

The curl program is a well-known program (also available in Windows) to transfer data from command lines or scripts. According to the curl website (https://curl.haxx.se/), it is used in your car, television, and practically everything you own. The -s switch is the silent mode, meaning it will not output errors or progress. The S (from -S) makes sure any error messages are still printed (despite the silent mode). The resulting script (which you can also view on your browser by simply browsing to the URL) is given as a parameter to Bash. Bash is a shell program, or a command-line program, that executes commands. Kind of like what we were doing the entire time, but with different commands. After the script runs, we can install GitLab.

I have mentioned it before, but a lot of programs run on port 8080. GitLab uses port 8080, which is a problem for us, since Jenkins also runs on port 8080. You can pick either to change the Jenkins port (and reboot) or change the GitLab port. You can change the Jenkins port by changing the /etc/default/jenkins file (simply find the port and change it) or you can change the GitLab port by adding a line to the /etc/gitlab/gitlab.rb file. I would recommend changing the GitLab port, since we are installing and configuring it right now anyway. Just a reminder, sudo vi /etc/gitlab/gitlab.rb opens the file, *I* let's you edit, *Esc* gets you out of edit mode, :wq saves and quits, and :q! quits without saving. Under the line external_url 'http://ciserver', add the line unicorn['port'] = '8081'.

Now, you need to reconfigure GitLab (which you always need to do after changing the gitlab.rb file):

```
sudo gitlab-ctl reconfigure
```

This can take a few minutes. GitLab may also need a minute or two to boot, so do not be alarmed when it does not show right after booting your VM. Now, in your host, browse to `ciserver` (or `192.168.56.101`, the IP of your VM) and you should get the GitLab login page:

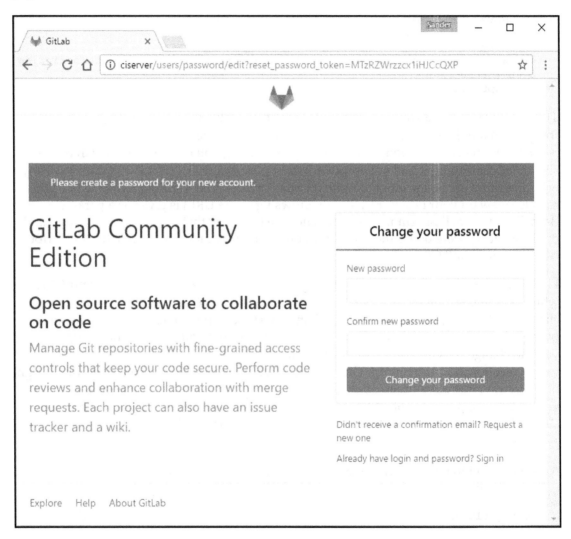

Configuring GitLab

Configuring GitLab is a breeze. The first thing you need to do is provide an administrator password. This can be done on the first page you get after starting it for the first time. After that, you get a **Register** or **Sign In** box, just like when you were visiting an actual website. Just create an account (the account will be stored on your VM, not on gitlab.com). You will not receive a confirmation email; apparently, this is a known issue at GitLab. From here on, you can create projects, collaborate with your team, and do everything Git was designed for.

Now, let's take her for a test drive! In GitLab, create a new project (it should be on the page right after you create an account). Pick a project name, such as **test**, and hit **Create project**. Notice that you can make your projects **Private** (default), **Internal**, or **Public**. We have just created a free private project.

Creating free private projects is awesome, but you probably want your project to be a little less private. In the settings of your project (in the top-right corner), you can grant access to other members and groups and even give them access to separate actions, such as read and write.

Speaking of groups, log out and create a new account for John or Alice or whatever. Log out and log in with your first account again. You can now create a group (from the menu at the top left) and invite your second user. This time, you will get an email about getting access to a group (it might go straight to spam). Create a new project in the group and now you and your second user have access to this repository (and any repository that is created in this group in the future).

In the following section, we are going to install Git on Windows so that we can test if we can actually put something in our repository.

Using Git

Installing Git on Windows is easy enough. Simply head over to their website (https://git-scm.com/) and download the Windows installer. Run it and leave all the defaults. This will also install the Git GUI and the Git Bash.

Open up a Command Prompt. First, we need to identify ourselves to Git. Git has settings on three different levels, system, global, and local. The system settings are system-wide and apply to all Git repositories on the computer. The global settings apply to all the repositories for the currently logged in user. The local settings apply to a single Git repository. More specific settings override less specific settings, so system settings can be overridden by global and local settings, and global settings can be overridden by local settings. To identify ourselves, we are going to set the global settings `user.name` and `user.email`. After that, we can clone our Git repository (meaning we are copying it to our computer):

```
git config --global user.name "Your Name"
git config --global user.email "your.email@provider.com"
git clone http://ciserver/user/test.git desktop\myrepo
```

The link to your Git project can be found on the project page of GitLab. The `desktop/myrepo` part is optional and specifies a custom folder for your project. The default folder is the name of the Git repository in your current folder. Add a file to the folder `Git` just created. A simple text file will do. Now move to your repository with `cd desktop\myrepo` (or whatever folder you cloned to). The next thing we need to do is add the new text file to the repository; you can do this with `git add .` (the `.` means we are just adding all the files). You can now check out the status of your repository using `git status`. You will see that the text file needs to be committed. We can commit our changes using `git commit -m "Some commit message"`. Because Git creates a local repository, we still need to push to commit to the server. We can do this using `git push`:

```
cd desktop\myrepo
git add .
git status
git commit -m "Added a text file."
git push
```

Here is output of the preceding commands:

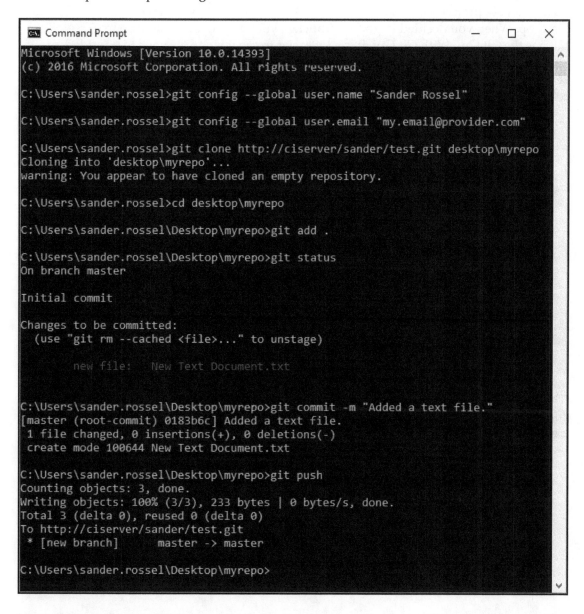

Now, if you go back to GitLab, you should see your commit. If everything worked, you have successfully installed Git and GitLab!

Working from the command line is doable, but not very practical. Especially when you have got a big project with many files. When you use GitHub, you can use their GitHub Desktop. When you decided to go for BitBucket, you are probably using SourceTree. Well, Git has the Git Gui. With Git Gui, it is a lot easier to see which files need to be added, are changed, will be committed, and so on. When you open it, you can create, clone, or open a repository. Go for **Clone Existing Repository**, enter the repository URL and a non-existent folder, and the repository will be cloned to your computer:

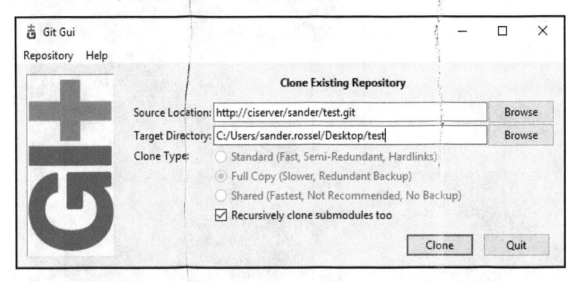

The next window will show you your changes. When you make some changes to your text file, add another text file, and hit **Rescan**, you will see the files in the upper-left corner. You can click the icons to add or stage the files, after which you can commit and push:

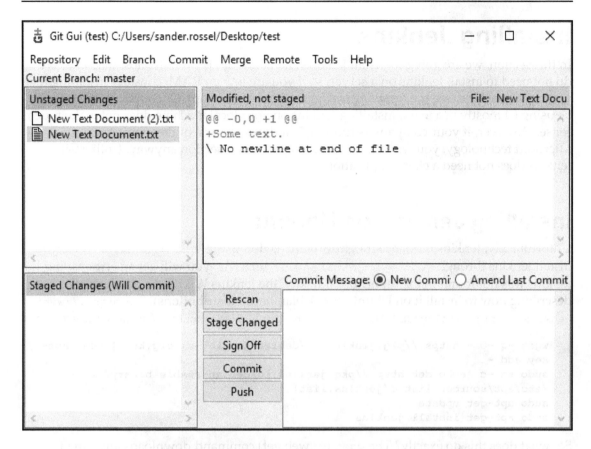

The Git GUI, while functional, does not give you all that much. The GitHub Desktop and SourceTree clients give you so much many options and are a lot prettier to look at. Another one that is worth checking out is GitKraken (`https://www.gitkraken.com/`). GitKraken is completely multiplatform (it works on Windows, Mac, and Linux) and integrates with both GitHub and BitBucket. Unfortunately, GitKraken is only free for open source, education, non-commercial, and private projects.

Installing Jenkins

In this section, we are going to install Jenkins and configure it from the host machine. We do not need to install Jenkins on a server, so if you are low on RAM, consider installing it on your local machine (see the *Installing Jenkins on Windows* section). Of course, since you will be using CI mostly in a team, installing Jenkins on your local machine does not make much sense. However, if your company is running Windows servers, or developing using Microsoft technology, you will want to read the Windows section anyway. Unlike Git, Jenkins does not need a client application.

Installing Jenkins on Ubuntu

Unfortunately, Jenkins is not as straightforward as doing `apt-get install`. If you try to install Jenkins through `sudo apt-get install jenkins`, you will get an error saying Jenkins was not found in the repository. Luckily, the Jenkins Wiki did a good job of describing how to install it on Ubuntu (or Debian-based distributions). See: `https://wiki.jenkins-ci.org/display/JENKINS/Installing+Jenkins+on+Ubuntu`, for more information:

```
wget -q -O - https://pkg.jenkins.io/debian/jenkins-ci.org.key | sudo apt-key add -
sudo sh -c 'echo deb http://pkg.jenkins.io/debian-stable binary/ >
/etc/apt/sources.list.d/jenkins.list'
sudo apt-get update
sudo apt-get install jenkins
```

So, what does this do exactly? The `wget` (or web get) command downloads anything from the web. That could be a file or a web page, or even an entire folder. In this case, we are going to download: `https://pkg.jenkins.io/debian/jenkins-ci.org.key` (you can download it using a browser as well). The `-q` switch means there is no logging (*q* is for quiet). The `-O` switch is a little more complex and ensures that all downloaded content is concatenated and written to a single file. Since `-` is used as the name of the file, the document will be written to the standard output, instead of an actual file. Next, the resulting output is passed as input (with the pipe `|` character) to the `sudo apt-key add -` command. `apt-key add` simply adds a key to the `apt-get` repository (so we should update that!) and the `-` at the end means the key is written from the standard output (where we put the key download) instead of a file. Simply said, we are downloading `apt-get key` and adding it to `apt-get` repository.

The next line starts with `sudo sh`, meaning that we are going to execute a shell command as the root user. The `-c` is actually a parameter to the `sh` and means the following is the shell to execute. Within the shell, we are going to write the contents of the deb URL to the standard output, which is what echo does. The deb URL gets a Debian software file from the URL. We are then redirecting the output to the file `/etc/apt/sources.list.d/jenkins.list` using the > character. This adds the Jenkins package to the `apt-get` sources.

`sudo apt-get update` and `sudo apt-get install jenkins` should be familiar.

After you have installed Jenkins, you will notice you cannot use the `poweroff` and `reboot` commands anymore. Ubuntu will tell you that the Jenkins user is still running and that you can use `systemctl poweroff/reboot -i` instead. Easier still, you can simply use `sudo poweroff/reboot`.

If all of that worked, you have just installed Jenkins! Now go back to your host, open up a browser, and browse to: `http://ciserver:8080` (or `http://192.168.56.101:8080/` (the IP address you added to the interfaces file earlier on port `8080`, which is the default Jenkins port)). You should see the following page with instructions on how to unlock Jenkins:

You know what to do: run `sudo vi`
`/var/lib/jenkins/secrets/initialAdminPassword` in your VM, enter the code in that file on your browser, and hit **Continue**. From here on, the installation is the same as the Windows installation, so skip the *Installing Jenkins on Windows* section and head over to the *Configure the Jenkins admin* section.

Installing Jenkins on Windows

If you chose not to use a VM, you can easily just install Jenkins on Windows. Head over to `https://jenkins.io` and find the downloads page. At the time of writing this, there is a big red button in the center of the page that says **Download Jenkins**. Even if it is not there, I am pretty sure you will find it. I downloaded Jenkins 2.32.1 for Windows; it is a zip file containing an `msi` file. Simply run the `msi` file and the installation will start. Upon completion, Jenkins will be started on your browser under `localhost:8080`:

The directions on the page are pretty clear. Open C:\Program Files
(x86)\Jenkins\secrets\initialAdminPassword, copy the password, paste it into the
Administrator password field, and hit **Continue**.

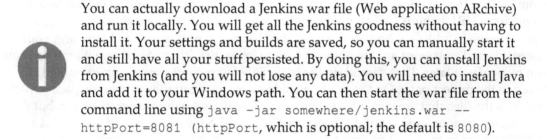

Jenkins installs to port 8080 by default, just like a lot of other applications.
If Jenkins does not start or localhost:8080 does not show Jenkins,
chances are port 8080 is in use by another application. To change the
default port used by Jenkins, go to the installation folder (C:\Program
Files (x86)\Jenkins) and look for jenkins.xml. Open the file as
administrator in Notepad and look for --httpPort=8080. Change 8080
to something else, such as 8081, and save it. Head over to your services
(under **Administrative Tools** under **Control Panel**) and look for Jenkins.
If it is not running, start it; otherwise restart it. Open up your browser and
browse to localhost:8081 (or whatever port you chose) and you should
see Jenkins.

You can actually download a Jenkins war file (Web application ARchive)
and run it locally. You will get all the Jenkins goodness without having to
install it. Your settings and builds are saved, so you can manually start it
and still have all your stuff persisted. By doing this, you can install Jenkins
from Jenkins (and you will not lose any data). You will need to install Java
and add it to your Windows path. You can then start the war file from the
command line using java -jar somewhere/jenkins.war --
httpPort=8081 (httpPort, which is optional; the default is 8080).

Configuring Jenkins

The next page will ask you if you want to install suggested plugins, but you do not want
that. In fact, you do not want anything at this moment, so just close the popup (on the
Jenkins website, not the browser). Jenkins will inform you that it has created an admin user
with the password you used earlier and then take you to the Jenkins home page (logged in
as admin, as seen at the top-right). On the homepage find **Manage Jenkins** (in the left side
menu) and, from **Manage Jenkins**, go to **Manage Users**. You should see your admin user,
so you can either select it and then go to **Configure** on the left-hand side menu, or you can
click on the cog on the right-hand side of the admin user to be taken to the configuration
screen directly. On the configuration screen, you can enter (and re-enter) a password you
can actually remember (like 1234) and save your settings. Try logging out (in the top right
of the screen) and logging back in without your new password.

The next thing we are going to do is try and get our Git project pulled into Jenkins. Jenkins alone does not do a lot. Luckily, there is a Jenkins plugin for practically everything. Go to **Manage Jenkins** and from there to **Manage Plugins**. Many plugins require other plugins to be installed too, but Jenkins will handle that for you. You can browse through all the different plugins at your leisure, but for now we are interested in just one plugin, which is the Git plugin. You can filter for Git in the upper-right corner (NOT the **Search** bar, quite confusing). You will find GitHub, GitLab (which we will look at later), Git client, Git server... just a whole lot of Git really. We want the *vanilla* Git Plugin. So check it and hit **Install without restart** at the bottom. This will install the Git Plugin and thirteen other plugins that are needed to run the Git plugin.

Now, we can create a job. Go back to the Jenkins homepage and either click **New item** on the left-hand side menu or click on **Please create new jobs** to get started right in the middle of your screen. Choose **Freestyle project** and a name such as `Test` or whatever. The next screen is the job configuration screen. What you see here depends on your kind of job and on the plugins you have installed. The only thing we will do right now is get our source from Git and into Jenkins. Under **Source Code Management**, select Git. You can find the **Repository URL** in your GitLab project; mine is `http://ciserver/sander/test.git`. Then, choose to add a credential. We want the **Username with password** kind and your username and password are the ones you use to log in to GitLab. Also, give it an ID so you can recognize it later. That should do the trick. Save your configuration and you will be taken to the project page. On the left-hand side menu, you can view the workspace (which includes the files that are currently in your job). You do not have a workspace yet, but that will change as soon as you build the job. So click **Build Now** and you will notice that a build is added to the build history and that, when you refresh your workspace, you will see your text files.

If a build fails (for now because you misspelled your Git repository or you used the wrong credentials), you will see that the build *ball* in the build history turns red, indicating failure. That is what we expected. However, when a build succeeds, the ball turns blue when you probably expected green. It has to do with the Jenkins creator, *Kohsuke Kawaguchi*, being Japanese. In Japan, red means stop and blue means go. Apparently, it is an issue for a lot of people so the *Green Balls Plugin* is pretty popular (as is the Chuck Norris Plugin!). You can read about the blue ball phenomenon in this Jenkins blog: `https://jenkins.io/blog/2012/03/13/why-does-jenkins-have-blue-balls/`.

Congratulations, you have successfully installed and configured Jenkins! That is all we are going to do with Jenkins for now, but we will be using Jenkins a lot throughout this book.

Installing PostgreSQL

PostgreSQL (`https://www.postgresql.org/`) is a powerful and popular open source SQL database. Even though it has nothing to do with Continuous Integration, we will need it to install the next tool, SonarQube. We will make use of PostgreSQL in the later chapters of the book, so we are not going through all this trouble just for SonarQube (but trust me, SonarQube alone is already worth it!).

Installing PostgreSQL on Ubuntu

First, we need to install PostgreSQL and some popular extensions. Ubuntu has some pretty good documentation on how to install PostgreSQL (`https://help.ubuntu.com/community/PostgreSQL`):

```
sudo apt-get update
sudo apt-get install postgresql postgresql-contrib
```

The installation creates a default postgres user without a password. However, we are going to create our own user with admin rights:

```
sudo -u postgres createuser --superuser sa
sudo -u postgres psql

\password sa
\password
\password
\q
```

The `sudo -u postgres` command means we are going to execute the next command as the postgres user. The command `--superuser sa` command creates a user named `sa` (for system admin). The `psql` command puts us in the PostgreSQL terminal. This means that `password sa`, which sets the password for the user `sa`, is executed by PostgreSQL. You can then set the password for the sysadmin. You have to enter the password twice; the second time is a confirmation. The final command, `q`, gets us out of the PostgreSQL terminal.

In theory, this should be enough. Unfortunately, or maybe it is better this way, PostgreSQL has some pretty strict default settings when it comes to connecting. So, we will need to change some settings before we can connect from our host computer. The first file we need to change is `pg_hba.conf`. The following file path has a version in it. My version is 9.5(.5), but if you have another version (which you could see in the PostgreSQL terminal), change the file path accordingly. So change the file using `sudo vi /etc/postgresql/9.5/main/pg_hba.conf`. You might have to scroll a bit, but you should find a line that reads `host all all 127.0.0.1/32 md5`. In this line, replace `127.0.0.1` with `0.0.0.0/0`. The next file we are going to change is `postgresql.conf`. So, open the file using `sudo vi /etc/postgresql/9.5/main/postgresql.conf` and mind the version number. This file is pretty big, but you can scroll to the bottom pretty quickly using the page down key. At the bottom, add the following line to the file `listen_addresses='*'`.

Last, but not least, we must restart PostgreSQL for the changes to take effect:

```
sudo systemctl restart postgresql
```

Installing PostgreSQL on Windows

Installing PostgreSQL on Windows is as easy as downloading and installing from the PostgreSQL website (`https://www.postgresql.org/download/windows/`), running it, and clicking **Next**, **Next**, **Next**. Be sure to remember the password you use for the `postgresql` user. Also, at the end of the installation, be sure to deselect the Stack Builder installation.

Installing pgAdmin

Now, in our Windows host we will need to install some management tools. There are plenty of management systems for PostgreSQL that run on various systems, but I have chosen the popular pgAdmin. You can download the latest version of pgAdmin (pgAdmin 4 at the time of writing) from the PostgreSQL website (`https://www.postgresql.org/ftp/pgadmin3/pgadmin4/v1.1/windows/`). Simply download the `exe` file and run it. This installation is, again, a matter of clicking next and leaving all the defaults.

Once you have installed pgAdmin, open it, right-click on **Servers** in the top left corner, and go to **Create** | **Server...**. Enter a name for your server in the **General** tab and enter your credentials in the **Connections** tab. If you followed my Ubuntu tutorial, your credentials will be sa and your chosen password. If you did the Windows installation, your username will be postgresql with the password you chose. Also, if you did the Windows installation, your **Host name/address** should be localhost. pgAdmin might find your local database automatically. In that case, just enter your password when opening the server node:

Once you hit **Save**, pgAdmin should connect and you will know whether you did everything correctly during the installation of PostgreSQL.

Installing SonarQube

SonarQube (`https://www.sonarqube.org/`) is a tool that scans your code and does a quality check. A set of rules are applied to your code and every time you break a rule, SonarQube will report it and add it to the technical debt. A rule can be simple, such as a missing semi-colon at the end of a JavaScript line. That should be a few seconds fix. Another rule can be more difficult, such as that the complexity of a function (nested loop and `if` statements and the lines of code add to the complexity) should not be greater than a certain value. SonarQube has a default set of rules, but you can roll out your own. In this book, we are going to see SonarQube with HTML, CSS, JavaScript, and C#, but SonarQube supports many languages, such as Java, VB.NET, SQL, Haskell, PHP, and many more.

Configuring PostgreSQL

The first thing we need to do is create a user and database that SonarQube can use. Just for the record, SonarQube can work with SQL Server, MySQL, and Oracle too, but PostgreSQL is always a good (and free) choice.

On Ubuntu, open the PostgreSQL terminal and run the script to create a sonar user and then the script to create a database, making the sonar user the owner:

```
sudo -u postgres psql
\create user sonar with password 'sonar';
\create database sonar with owner sonar encoding 'UTF8';
\q
```

The `UTF8` encoding is NOT optional, so be sure to include it. Also, don't forget the semicolons at the end of your statements.

On Windows, you can also create a user and database using the command prompt. It only differs from Ubuntu in the first line:

```
cd "C:\Program Files\PostgreSQL\9.5\bin\psql" -U postgres
[enter password]
\create user sonar with password 'sonar';
\create database sonar with owner sonar encoding 'UTF8';
\q
```

If you installed PostgreSQL in another folder, you should change that in the command. You may, of course, also create a user and database using pgAdmin. Just right-click on the **Login/Group Roles** node and create. Same for the new database.

Installing SonarQube on Ubuntu

To install SonarQube on Ubuntu, we must first make sure we are on the correct Java version. You can check your version using the `java -version` command. It should be on 8. If you have followed this tutorial, your Java version will not be what SonarQube expects. So, let us first install Java. The `add-apt-repository` command is new to us. It adds a **PPA**, or **Personal Package Archive**, to the repository, telling Ubuntu it should look for updates from that specific package:

```
sudo add-apt-repository ppa:webupd8team/java
sudo apt-get update
sudo apt-get -y install oracle-java8-installer
[Ok]
[Yes]
java -version
```

Now, we can download the SonarQube package and add it to the `apt-get` sources. You can find the installation steps in the documentation (`http://docs.sonarqube.org/display/SONAR/Installing+the+Server`). After that, we can update `apt-get` and install SonarQube. When prompted, choose to install without authentication:

```
sudo sh -c 'echo deb http://downloads.sourceforge.net/project/sonar-pkg/deb
binary/ > /etc/apt/sources.list.d/sonarqube.list'
sudo apt-get update
sudo apt-get install sonar
```

Now, we need to tell SonarQube how to connect to our database. Open the `sonar.properties` file with `sudo vi /opt/sonar/conf/sonar.properties`. Near the top of the file, you will see `sonar.jdbc.username=` and `sonar.jdbc.password=`. Change them to `sonar.jdbc.username=sonar` and `sonar.jdbc.password=sonar`. After that, scroll further down the file and you will find the settings for PostgreSQL. The only thing you need to do is uncomment the line `#sonar.jdbc.url=jdbc:postgresql://localhost/sonar` by removing #.

Now, we only need to start SonarQube. You can start and stop it as follows, but do not run these commands just yet:

```
sudo service sonar start
sudo service sonar stop
```

Manually starting the SonarQube service whenever the server starts is not an option, so instead, we are going to make sure SonarQube starts at server startup and stops when the server shuts down:

```
sudo update-rc.d sonar defaults
sudo reboot
```

This will run `sudo service sonar start` and `stop` commands automatically at start and shutdown respectively (more specifically, it will run a sonar script with `start` or `stop` as a parameter).

Now, on your host machine, open a browser and browse to `ciserver:9000`. SonarQube may take a minute or two to start, so if it does not show immediately, try again in a minute.

Installing SonarQube on Windows

To install SonarQube on Windows, download the latest version, I got 6.2, from the website (`https://www.sonarqube.org/downloads/`). Unzip the contents of the zip file and put them somewhere. I simply unzipped the `sonarqube-6.2` folder to `C:\`. Now, we need to hook up SonarQube to the database. This is actually exactly the same as in Linux. Open `C:\sonarqube-6.2\conf\sonar.properties` (or wherever you have unzipped it) and change `sonar.jdbc.username=` and `sonar.jdbc.password=` to `sonar.jdbc.username=sonar` and `sonar.jdbc.password=sonar`. After that, scroll further down the file and you will find the settings for PostgreSQL. The only thing you need to do is uncomment the line `#sonar.jdbc.url=jdbc:postgresql://localhost/sonar` by removing #.

Now, if you go to `C:\sonarqube-6.2\bin\windows-x86-64` (replace Windows-x86-x64 with your own OS), you will find some `.bat` files. To start SonarQube, simply run `StartSonar.bat`; to install SonarQube as a service, run `InstallNTService.bat` (with administrative privileges); and to start the service, run `StartNTService.bat` (also with administrative privileges). Using a browser, browse to `localhost:9000` and you should see SonarQube.

Trigger SonarQube from Jenkins

You can log in to SonarQube with the default administrator account; both username and password are `admin`. In a real-world scenario, you should absolutely change those, but we are going to use them as is. If you do decide to change them, be sure to change them in the configuration up ahead as well:

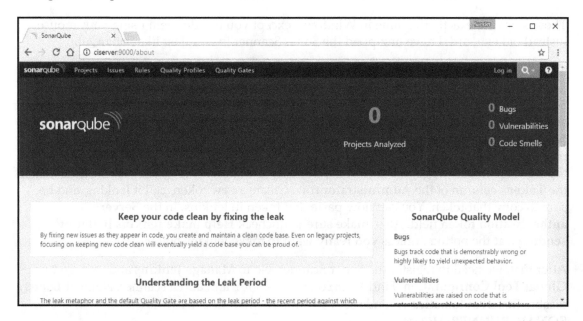

Like Jenkins, SonarQube alone does not do much. It needs a runner that does all of the heavy work. There are specific runners for certain platforms, but the generic runner will suffice in most cases:

```
sudo apt-get update
sudo apt-get install unzip
wget
https://sonarsource.bintray.com/Distribution/sonar-scanner-cli/sonar-scanne
r-2.8.zip
unzip sonar-scanner-2.8.zip
sudo mv sonar-scanner-2.8/ /opt/
rm sonar-scanner-2.8.zip
```

These commands download a zip file containing a runner; unzip it, move the unzipped folder to the `opt` folder, and remove the original zip. We need to make some configuration changes as well. In the `/opt/sonar-scanner-2.8/conf/sonar-scanner.properties` file, uncomment `sonar.host.url`, `sonar.jdbc.username`, `sonar.jdbc.password`, and `sonar.jdbc.url` under PostgreSQL. Also, add the two lines `sonar.host.username=admin` and `sonar.host.password=admin`.

Those steps are exactly the same in Windows, except you can do them using your mouse instead of keyboard. I have unzipped the Sonar Scanner in `C:\`, just like SonarQube.

Now, we need to register SonarQube and the Sonar Scanner in Jenkins. To do that, we first need to install the SonarQube plugin. Once you have done that, you can register the SonarQube server under **Manage Jenkins** and then **Configure System**. Find **SonarQube servers** and add one. The least you have to do is give it a name (such as `ciserver`). Right now, Jenkins cannot connect to SonarQube and you will notice that the username and password fields are disabled. Log in to SonarQube and head over to **Administration** (in the top right menu). Now, go to **Users** in the **Security** dropdown. Now, click on the little icon in the **Tokens** column of the **Administrator** row. Create a new token, call it Jenkins, and be sure to copy that token. You can now paste that token in Jenkins, in the **Server authentication token** field. Also, make sure to uncheck **Help make Jenkins better by sending...** at the bottom, unless you really want to make Jenkins better.

After that, we need to register the Sonar Scanner. Go to **Manage Jenkins** and then go to **Global Tool Configuration**. Find `SonarQube Scanner` and add a scanner. Name it `Local`, disable **Install automatically**, and set `/opt/sonar-scanner-2.8/` as **SONAR_RUNNER_HOME**.

If everything went well, you have now successfully configured Jenkins to work with SonarQube. Of course, we want to test it and see it with our own eyes. First, we will need a little code file that SonarQube can analyze. In your Git project, create a new file and call it `something.js`. Put the following code in it and then push it to Git:

```
var something = 'something'
if (something)
    console.log('something');
```

Now that we have some code that SonarQube can analyze, go back to our Jenkins project. On the project page, click **Configure** to change the configuration of your build (which will be active immediately after saving). Add a build step, **Execute SonarQube Scanner**, and, in **Analysis properties** put the following configuration:

```
sonar.projectKey=test
sonar.projectName=Test
sonar.projectVersion=1.0

sonar.sources=.

sonar.exclusions=*.txt
```

This is basically saying create a project with the ID **test** and display name **Test** on version *1.0*. The sources property includes all the files in the current folder, but we ignore all the files with a `txt` extension. Run the job and head over to SonarQube (you will notice a SonarQube link on your project page; it does not work). In SonarQube, view your projects on the upper-left menu and be sure to filter all (the default is your favorites, which is none at the moment). Click on the project to get a detailed report. You will see one vulnerability issue, bringing your security rating to B. If you click on it, you will get details on what is wrong, why it is wrong, and how you should fix it; that is pretty awesome. In this case, the `console.log` statement is a security risk.

Unfortunately, we had expected at least one more issue. The first line of our code is missing a semicolon at the end. That may prove disastrous if we are going to minify the code! On the top left menu, go to **Quality Profiles**. Here, you can create and modify the sets of rules. Our project used the **Sonar way** profile. Click on the little button behind the profile and choose **Activate More Rules**. Find **Statement should end with semicolons** and activate it. You can set a severity for the issue. I made it a critical issue. Once it is activated, you can return to your project and you will see it now has a code smell and one minute technical debt:

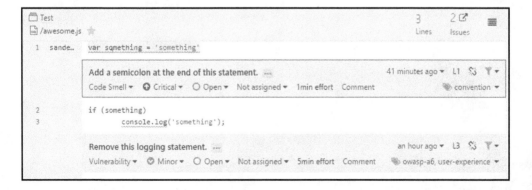

It is possible to make a Jenkins build fail when your technical debt rises or when you write blocking issues (which is even worse than critical). This is what CI is about: check in code and get instant feedback.

You may have noticed that the terms Sonar, SonarQube, Sonar Runner, and Sonar Scanner are being used interchangeably on the internet by Jenkins and even by SonarQube. The reason for this is that SonarQube used to be called Sonar and Sonar Scanners used to be called Sonar Runners. Make no mistake though, Sonar/SonarQube is not the same as a Sonar Runner/Scanner.

Summary

In this chapter, we have installed our CI environment. We have discussed the various tools we are going to use throughout the book. We have also had our first look at Git, Jenkins, and SonarQube and made them work together. In the remainder of the book, we are going to install many more tools on the server and locally. But before we get to that, we will take a closer look at Git in the next chapter, as there is a lot more to Git than we have seen so far.

3
Version Control with Git

Before we continue with an example in the next chapter, we want to take some time to truly get to know Git. Git is an invaluable tool in your tool belt. It helps you and your team to share code, check out each others code, revert to previous code, and keep different versions of the same code side by side. In this chapter, we are going to explore these issues and learn how to make the most of it using Jenkins.

 For some really in-depth Git reading, I recommend the book *Pro Git*, which you can read for free at the Git website, `https://git-scm.com/book`. With almost 600 pages, this is the absolute Git bible. For some practical use, just keep on reading.

The basics

Before we head over to the more advanced stuff, let's go over the basics. You have already done most of this in the previous chapters, but getting a good grasp of what is going on is important if you want to use Git effectively and to the fullest. I recommend creating a new Git repository so you can experiment and throw out your repository when we are done.

Centralized Source Control Management

In traditional **Source Control Management (SCM)** systems, such as CVS and Subversion, which have long been the industry standards, your code was saved to a server. This server kept the entire history of your project. Developers working on the project could check out a snapshot of the project, make their changes, and commit back to the server. It enabled teams to work together and get an idea of what other people on the team were up to.

However, since all code was stored in a single repository, you had a problem if this repository became (temporarily) unreachable (for example, due to network problems) or, worse, when your repository or server became corrupted. Storing the entire history of your projects in a single place comes with the risk of losing everything. This model of version control is called a centralized version control system.

Distributed Source Control Management

Git is a little different. With Git, you always copy the entire repository, including the entire history, to your local machine. That means you can make local commits without actually pushing anything to your server. It also means when your server becomes unreachable, you can still make local commits and push them when your server becomes available again. And, of course, it means that when your server explodes into tiny bits, every programmer on the team still has the entire project history sitting on their computers ready to be restored to a new server. This model is also known as the distributed version control system. While Git is the most popular distributed version control system by far, and actually the most popular source control system period, Mercurial is also a reasonably popular distributed version control system.

The working directory

As we have seen in the previous chapters, getting a Git repository on your local computer is as easy as cloning a repository. The folder that serves as your Git repository is a regular folder like any other and is also known as the working directory. The magic trick is the hidden `.git` folder that has all the data that is necessary for Git to track your files. It allows you to execute commands, such as `git status`, `git add`, and `git commit`. The `.git` file contains your HEAD, which is basically the current state of your branch. Whenever you move commits, branch, cherry pick, or whatever, the HEAD will know your current state and what it once was. Knowing this, resetting your working directory becomes as easy as resetting your HEAD, as we will see later. It also means that you can move your current branch to another commit simply by editing your HEAD. Now, I do not recommend you go around and edit files in the `.git` folder, but this is exactly what Git does for you when you execute command through the command line or through other Git clients.

The staging area

Once you commit your changes, they go out of the working directory and into your history. There is a stage between the two though, called the **staging area**. Whenever you change, add, or delete a file in your working directory and then check out the status using `git status`, it will tell you whether you have new (untracked) files, changes that are not staged for commit, or changes to be committed:

```
C:\Users\sander.rossel\Desktop\test>git status
On branch master
Changes to be committed:
  (use "git reset HEAD <file>..." to unstage)

        modified:   index.js

Changes not staged for commit:
  (use "git add <file>..." to update what will be committed)
  (use "git checkout -- <file>..." to discard changes in working directory)

        modified:   repository.js

Untracked files:
  (use "git add <file>..." to include in what will be committed)

        utils.js

C:\Users\sander.rossel\Desktop\test>
```

From that explanation, it becomes clear that whatever is not staged will not be committed. This allows you to change multiple files, but only commit a few of them. It is even possible to stage only parts of files. It can come in handy when you are working on some big changes and then someone asks you to fix the whatchamacallit. You can alter a couple of lines of code and stage and commit only those.

As we have seen before, putting your files into the staging area is easily done using the `git add .` command. Now, instead of using a dot (for all files), we can specify a single file. For example, `git add repository.js`.

We can stage and commit only parts of files that we changed. Such a part is called a **hunk**. First, create a new file, call it `hunks.txt`, and add four lines to it. You can just number the lines 1, 2, 3, and 4 and commit it using `git add hunks.txt`. Now add two lines, one between 1 and 2 and one between 3 and 4; just put in `1.1` and `3.1` or whatever you like. Your file should now look as follows:

```
1
1.1
2
3
3.1
4
```

Now you can create a patch, or some changes that you would like to stage. You can do this using the `git add --patch filename` command. You can now see the contents of your file and the hunks in green. You will be asked if you want to stage the current hunk and your options are [y,n,q,a,d,/,s,e,?]. Simply type ? and *Enter* to see what they mean:

```
C:\Users\sander.rossel\Desktop\test>git add --patch hunks.txt
diff --git a/hunks.txt b/hunks.txt
index b178657..bfaf5b6 100644
--- a/hunks.txt
+++ b/hunks.txt
@@ -1,4 +1,6 @@
 1
+1.1
 2
 3
+3.1
 4
\ No newline at end of file
Stage this hunk [y,n,q,a,d,/,s,e,?]?
y - stage this hunk
n - do not stage this hunk
q - quit; do not stage this hunk or any of the remaining ones
a - stage this hunk and all later hunks in the file
d - do not stage this hunk or any of the later hunks in the file
g - select a hunk to go to
/ - search for a hunk matching the given regex
j - leave this hunk undecided, see next undecided hunk
J - leave this hunk undecided, see next hunk
k - leave this hunk undecided, see previous undecided hunk
K - leave this hunk undecided, see previous hunk
s - split the current hunk into smaller hunks
e - manually edit the current hunk
? - print help
```

In this case, the command line has both our files in one hunk, so we want to split the hunk by typing s. After that, you see only 1.1 is green and we do want to stage that, so we pick y. After that, we get two more hunks, but we only have one more added line. We do not want to stage 3.1, so pick n. The last hunk might be a Windows thing, I am not sure. Anyway, do not stage it:

```
@@ -1,4 +1,6 @@
 1
+1.1
 2
 3
+3.1
 4
\ No newline at end of file
Stage this hunk [y,n,q,a,d,/,s,e,?]? s
Split into 3 hunks.
@@ -1,3 +1,4 @@
 1
+1.1
 2
 3
Stage this hunk [y,n,q,a,d,/,j,J,g,e,?]? y
@@ -2,3 +3,4 @@
 2
 3
+3.1
 4
Stage this hunk [y,n,q,a,d,/,K,j,J,g,e,?]? n
@@ -4 +6,2 @@
 4
\ No newline at end of file
Stage this hunk [y,n,q,a,d,/,K,g,e,?]? n

C:\Users\sander.rossel\Desktop\test>_
```

Now when you use `git status` you will see that `hunks.txt` is both in the staged part and in the unstaged part.

One more thing I would like to say about `git add` is that there is an interactive commands option. This is probably the closest you get to an actual GUI in the console. You can get it using the `git add -i` command. Here, you can easily select files for staging, apply patches, remove files from staging, and see the changes you have made to files. You should check it out.

Committing and pushing

Once you have staged the changes you want to commit, you can proceed with the actual commit. Committing your changes will write them to the history of your local project. Your changes are more or less cast in stone. You can commit as much as you like, but remember that a commit is only local. To actually push your work to the server so others can get it too, you must push your commits using the `git push` command. When you push your commits, three things can happen. First, your changes are pushed and everything is fine. Second, your changes are pushed, but others have also pushed changes to the same files resulting in a merge conflict that Git can resolve. Third, a merge conflict that Git cannot resolve requires you to manually change your files and pick between your changes or those of your coworker. In case of a merge, an extra commit will be created (on your name) that contains the merge.

Merge conflicts can be a real pain in the behind, so be sure to keep commits small and pull regularly. Whenever you do have a merge conflict, despite all your best efforts, you must edit the file manually and simply stage it when you are done. A conflict looks as follows:

```
<<<<<<< HEAD
These are my local changes.
=======
Remote changes.
>>>>>>> 449d9120c205609132e0983230fa48f5629dc41c
```

To clear that up, I literally typed `These are my local changes` on the same line that someone else typed `Remote changes`. Git cannot decide whether both lines should stay; if so, in what order; or if one should overwrite the other. Besides manually editing your conflicted files, you can also keep your own changes or the changes of them:

```
git checkout --ours filename
[or]
git checkout --theirs filename
git add filename
```

Staging your file will mark it as resolved. After all the conflicts have been resolved, you can continue your push.

Reviewing commits

No doubt, you sometimes need to review some commits or those of others. One thing you can do is look them up in GitLab or whatever Git server you use. You can also view them in Git GUI or any Git client. However, it is also possible to look them up using the command line. The `git log` command lists all commits in your current branch. There are some caveats though. Since the list of commits can be very long, they will never fit in your console window. What Git does to make this manageable is page the results. You can use the *Enter* key to show new lines. When you want to exit the log, you have to type q (Linux style). Usually in Windows, you exit such operations using *Ctrl + C*, but this will not exit the log and will probably mess up your command window and leave you confused and annoyed, and ultimately make you hit the *X* button and restart your console:

```
git log

commit f90cfa90227bf1cb21d8023b03273c991fc2f471
Author: Sander Rossel <sander.rossel@gmail.com>
Date: Sun Jan 29 21:40:16 2017 +0100

  Added xlsx support.

commit 475bb165299b3d85c142b03462be9f82b8fbefb1
Author: Sander Rossel <sander.rossel@gmail.com>
Date: Sun Jan 29 21:38:16 2017 +0100

  Added reporting module.

commit 51eadeab96e1950f5e61273fcb3bbfb24a75e901
Author: Sander Rossel <sander.rossel@gmail.com>
Date: Sun Jan 29 21:37:07 2017 +0100

  Added reporting files.

[...]
:q
[Alternatively]
(END)q
```

As you can see, the latest commits are at the top as those are the ones you most likely want to see. There are a couple of useful switches to log that can be very useful. The `--pretty=oneline` or `--oneline` switches are probably the ones you would use the most. It simply prints every commit on a single line, giving you a much clearer overview of the various commits. The only difference between the two is that `--pretty=oneline` prints the full commit hash whereas `--online` prints the short version. Other `--pretty` formats are short, full, and fuller, but you will need to use the full `--pretty=[format]` syntax for those. The `-p` switch lists all the differences in the commit. It is also possible to limit the number of results using `-[some number]`, for example `-2`:

```
git log --oneline -p -2
```

Other useful switches that can help you sort the results are `--skip`, `--since`, `--after`, `--until`, `--before`, and `--author`. There are dozens of switches for `log`, so if you really need this kind of functionality, I suggest you look it up in the Git documentation.

Pulling and stashing

That leaves us with the final part of the Git basics, pulling code from the server. Whenever your coworkers push code to the server, you want to get it from there on to your own computer. You can pull code using the `git pull` command. Just like when you push, a pull can result in a merge conflict. Whenever this happens, there are two things you can do. You can either commit your current work, pull the code from the server, and then resolve the conflicts. Or you can stash your changes, meaning you put them aside for the time being and reset all the files as they were when you last pulled, and then do the pull and apply your stash over the newly pulled code. A conflict between your current code and the stash will still occur, but you can now resolve it manually before committing your code.

Stashes are an easy way to put some code aside, either because you want to pull from the server or because you want to try some alternative solution to a problem without losing your current solution. It is good to notice here that new files in your repository will not be stashed; they will simply continue to exist in your current working directory. You can create a stash using the `git stash` command. You can optionally give your stash a name. You can then apply any stash you like or apply and delete your latest stash or any other stash by index. Try committing a file, then change and save its contents, and see what happens to it after each of the following commands:

```
git stash
git stash pop
git stash save "My awesome stash"
git list
```

```
git stash apply 0
git stash drop 0
```

If you apply a stash to your working directory and you get a merge conflict, *theirs* is actually your stash. I once lost quite a lot of work that way! Imagine this: you want to pull, but get a conflict. You stash, pull, and then apply the stash. Your stash feels like your code (or *ours*). However, when you pull *their* code, it actually becomes *your* code. Now when you apply the stash to *your* code, the stash is *their* code. It makes sense when you think about it, but usually a stash does not feel like *theirs*. So remember, when you want to resolve and keep your stash, resolve using *theirs*.

Branching

Another major feature of Git is branching. With branches, you can create a copy of your current repository that is isolated from your main branch. So far, we've just committed everything to the default master branch, but you could make a new branch to develop certain features. Think of the many different versions of Linux. They are basically all different branches of the same master branch. Some branches even get their own branch. Ubuntu, for example, is a branch of Debian.

When you first create a Git repository, it will not have any branches by default. You need to add a file and commit it to initialize the master branch. If you have nothing to add to master, because you want to use feature branches, just add a `readme`, `license`, or `.gitignore` file, which can all be added directly from the GitLab project page. Only after you have created your master branch can you create new branches. You can rename your master branch after you have created it if you want, but I really see no reason for that.

While Linux distributions separate from each other and grow in different directions, that probably does not make much sense for your own projects. Ultimately, you probably want to merge your work from one branch with that of another. Imagine working on some administrative software and your client requested a reporting feature and a means to send emails directly from the software. You are tasked with writing the reporting module while two of your coworkers are tasked with writing the email module. The rest of the team continues to work on other stuff.

You can now create two new branches, one for the reporting and one for the emailing module. This way, you and your other coworkers can safely commit any code without having to worry about breaking anything or deploying a half-finished reporting module. When you are finished with the reporting module, you can simply merge it into the main development branch.

You can create a new branch using the `git branch branch-name` command. Your branch name cannot contain spaces and it is generally considered a best practice to start your branch name with a letter, use lowercase only, use hyphens between words, and keep your branch names small. The `git branch` command will show a list of branches and it indicates your current branch with an asterisk (*). Finally, using the `git checkout` command, you can switch to another branch:

```
git branch reporting
git branch
git checkout reporting
```

Here is an example of some branches in Git GUI, found under the menu item `Repository` and then `Visualize All Branch History`:

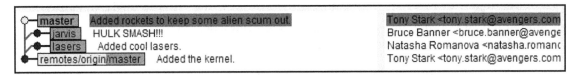

Here, we have the master branch, the code branch, and the `jarvis` branch. In case you are unfamiliar with the Avengers movies (or comics), these are the guys trying to assemble an Iron Man suit. Apparently, Mr. Iron Man himself, Tony Stark, is taking care of the master branch while Black Widow and The Hulk are working on lasers and JARVIS, Iron Man's own really very cool Siri (he actually did it all himself as he is a rich genius, but for the example, let's say they are working together). Git GUI is not the prettiest tool out there, so here is another visualization of the same branch, but this time in GitKraken:

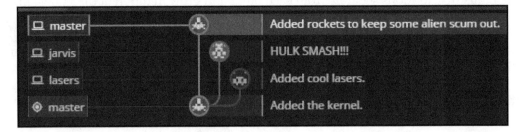

After merging the `lasers` and `jarvis` branches back to master, we get a pretty clear picture of what has happened. We will get back to merging in a minute:

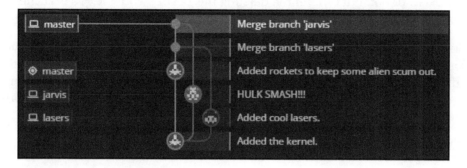

You can also create branches off of branches. Simply check out the branch you want to use as a base and create a new branch there:

```
git branch weapons
git checkout weapons
git branch lasers
git checkout lasers
```

Things could now look as follows:

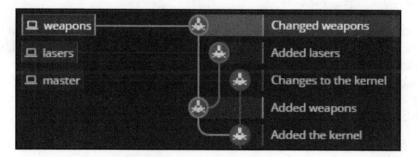

It is possible to remove branches. If a branch is merged into another branch and has no uncommitted changes, you can simply delete that branch using the -d switch. If a branch is not fully merged or has uncommitted changes, you must force delete it with the -D switch:

```
git branch -d branch-name
git branch -D branch-name
```

If you merged the branch with another, still existing, branch, the deleted branch will still show up in your branch overview. That makes sense as it is part of your history, whether the branch exists or not. Put differently, deleting the lasers and jarvis branches will not change the previous picture.

Once you create a branch, that branch only exists locally. That may be enough for your needs, for example, if you want to try out some stuff on a short-lived branch. Creating a branch, making changes, committing, and then pushing will not work. Once you push, you will get an error. Next, we will create a new branch, code (that is the big glowing orb in Iron Man's chest):

```
git branch reactor
git checkout reactor
git push
fatal: The current branch reactor has no upstream branch.
To push the current branch and set the remote as upstream, use

git push --set-upstream origin reactor
```

What --set-upstream origin reactor will do is tell your server to create a new branch where all your commits on this branch will go to. The shortcut for --set-upstream is -u, so that is what you will use:

```
git push -u origin reactor
```

When you go to GitLab and check out the branches tab on the project page, you can now see you have two branches. You will also see whether the branches are merged; you can compare branches, delete branches, and also create branches from here. Keep in mind that if you delete a branch here, it will still be present in your local working directory, but trying to push or pull will result in an error (unless you push with the -u switch, which will recreate the branch on your server).

The advantage of pushing your branch to the server is that you can share your branch with others. You will often have different branches, such as the development, test, and master (or production) branches, that everyone on the team will sooner or later commit to. Creating a branch to develop a single feature is often referred to as a feature branch. Feature branches can also be pushed to the server to have multiple developers working on the same feature. As an added bonus, if something happens to your computer, your branch is still on the server.

The origin is simply a local alias to a URL that Git creates. In this case, the origin points to `http://ciserver/the_avengers/the-suit.git`. So what you are actually saying is push my commits to the Git URL on the specified branch. Every Git repository has an origin by default. You can check your remote aliases using the `git remote -v` command and you can rename your URLs using `git remote rename origin somethingelse`.

Merging

Merging a branch into another branch is easy enough. First of all, make sure you are in the branch where you want to merge to. So, if you want to merge `jarvis` into `master`, make sure everything you want to merge is committed and pushed and then switch to `master` using `git checkout master`. Now, simply use `merge branch-name` and resolve any conflicts that occur:

```
git branch my-branch
git checkout my-branch
[Make some changes]
git add .
git commit -m "Some message"
[optional] git push -u origin my-branch
git checkout master
git merge my-branch
```

A nice option when merging is to merge but not commit automatically. This is the default behavior when you have merge conflicts. That way, you can inspect and edit your changes before committing. To do this, you can use the `--no-commit` flag while merging:

```
git merge my-branch --no-commit --no-ff
```

The `--no-ff` switch stands for no fast-forward. A fast-forward happens when your current branch is an ancestor of the branch you are trying to merge and the current branch has had no changes since you branched it. In that case, your branch is simply a continuation of your current branch. Git will now move your current commit to the last commit of the branch you are targeting.

The difference becomes clear when we do a merge of each scenario:

```
git branch merge-test
git checkout merge-test
[Add a file]
git add .
git commit -m "No FF commit"
git checkout master
git merge merge-test
git log --oneline -2
3d28b26 No FF commit
8bff38e HULK SMASH!!!

git checkout merge-test
[Add a file]
git add .
git commit -m "FF commit"
git checkout master
[Add a file]
git add .
git commit -m "This does the trick"
git merge merge-test
git log --oneline -5
5948c05 Merge branch 'merge-test'
b21e3f3 This does the trick
944321f FF commit
3d28b26 No FF commit
8bff38e HULK SMASH!!!
```

As you see, there is no extra merge commit after the first merge, but there is an extra commit message after the second merge. That is because the `This does the trick` commit is in the way of `FF commit`. This is also what happens when you try to commit while there are still changes on the server that you do not yet have locally. Git will push your changes and, at the same time, pull changes from the server and an extra merge commit will be created. As we know, the merge commit will not be automatically committed if there are any merge conflicts.

Cherry picking

Another form of merging is cherry picking. With a cherry pick, you target a specific commit on one branch and merge just that one commit, as a new separate commit, to another branch. That means you do not have to merge an entire branch all at once.

It also means that when you do cherry pick all the commits on a branch, the branch still will not be marked as merged and so deleting it is only possible by forcing it:

```
git cherry-pick [commit id]
```

You can get the commit ID using `git log` and preferably `git log --oneline`. For example, I have added a reactor branch and created two commits. In the first commit, I added a `reactor.txt` file and in the second commit, I changed some text in that file. Now, on my master branch, I only want the `reactor.txt` file, but not the change. We can use `git log branch-name` to look for a commit on a specific branch:

```
git checkout master
git log reactor --oneline -2
6cc4c08 Changed the reactor.
710a366 Added the reactor file.

git cherry-pick 710a366
[master baefa8b] Added the reactor file.
 Date: Sun Jan 29 14:51:23 2017 +0100
 1 file changed, 0 insertions(+), 0 deletions(-)
 create mode 100644 reactor.txt
```

Notice how the changes of the cherry picked commit are applied to your current working directory and committed with the cherry picked commit's message immediately. It is possible to not commit your cherry picks automatically using the −n switch:

```
git cherry-pick -n 710a366
```

This way, you can cherry pick multiple commits from different branches, make changes, and commit everything at once. Whatever you do, your cherry pick is a separate commit and not linked to the original commit in any way (except maybe your commit message). Whenever you decide to merge the branch later, you may encounter some conflicts.

Cherry picking by ID is a bit of a hassle. The IDs are not exactly easy to remember, let alone type. You can use various patterns to target a specific commit or commits (plural). For example, the `branch-name~index` pattern selects the commit on a specific branch on a specific index (beginning at 0 for the latest commit). The previous cherry pick would then look as follows:

```
git cherry-pick -n reactor~1
```

You can cherry pick multiple commits using IDs or patterns:

```
git cherry-pick -n 710a366 reactor~0
```

Make sure you apply the commits in the correct order. There are ways to cherry pick entire branches and multiple branches, but there are easier ways to do this as we will see.

If you are using Git GUI, or any other Git client, making a cherry pick is as easy as right-clicking on the commit you want and selecting *Cherry pick* or something along those lines.

Rebasing

All these extra merge commits you can get from merging and cherry picking make a mess of your commit history. They are all superfluous commits that only exist because you need to merge some changes. Instead of merging, you can rebase your branches. When you rebase a branch, you are basically saying your branch was not branched from commit A, but from commit B. So, imagine you are working on a feature branch, but you do want to keep up with the master branch so your branch is not left behind on features. Besides, if you do not pull regularly, the chances of conflicts increase and it is easier to solve them as they come. Instead of merging or cherry picking everything your coworkers do, you can simply rebase your branch:

```
git checkout some-feature
git rebase master
First, rewinding head to replay your work on top of it...
Fast-forwarded some-feature to master.
```

Your branch is now an extension of master, so when you merge a feature into the master branch, you do not need an extra merge commit.

You can also use the shortcut, so you do not need to check out your branch explicitly:

```
git rebase master some-feature
```

A more advanced use of rebasing is rebasing commits onto specific other commits. For example, suppose you have a branch that is branched off another branch. In the case of the Iron Man suit, let's say we have the weapons branch and the lasers branch on that branch. Now, if we would rebase lasers to master, the entire history of lasers, which means including the part of the weapons branch, would be rebased to master.

So, here we have our starting situation, the lasers branch was branched off the **Added weapons** commit:

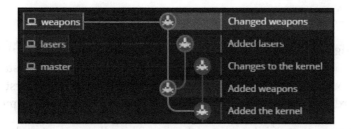

When we rebase lasers to master, `git rebase master lasers`, Git will rewind your work until it finds master, which is after the **Added weapons** commit. Next, Git will replay your commits on master, so the **Added weapons** commit and the **Added lasers** commit will be replayed on master. This will leave you in the following situation:

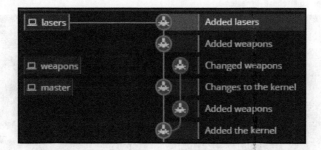

However, we can specify a commit to rebase. In this case, we want the commit **Added lasers** to rebase to master. We can specify a commit using the `--onto` switch:

```
git rebase --onto master weapons lasers
```

In this example, we are telling Git to rebase lasers to master, but only commit after the weapons branch. This will give us the following situation:

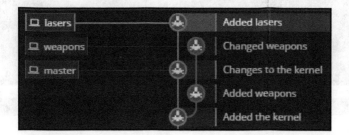

As you can see, the **Added weapons** commit was not replayed on master.

Using `--onto`, it is also possible to remove certain commits:

```
git rebase --onto some-branch~2 some-branch~1 some-branch
```

Here, we are telling Git to rebase to the commit at the top of `some-branch` to the commit that is on index 2 (`~2`), which is the third commit from the top and we start searching from the second commit from the top (`index 1, ~1`). This means the first commit is rebased to the third commit and, as a side effect, the second commit is removed.

Another cool feature is that of interactive rebasing. This allows you to take your commits and edit them before rebasing. You can combine commits, change commit messages, and remove commits. The following example shows what happens when you rebase master using the `rebase -i master` command:

```
Command Prompt - git rebase -i master
pick 4844862 Commit 1
squash 31e4c9d Commit 2
drop_f91ce19 Commit 3

# Rebase 4844862..f91ce19 onto 897dd47 (3 commands)
#
# Commands:
# p, pick = use commit
# r, reword = use commit, but edit the commit message
# e, edit = use commit, but stop for amending
# s, squash = use commit, but meld into previous commit
# f, fixup = like "squash", but discard this commit's log message
# x, exec = run command (the rest of the line) using shell
# d, drop = remove commit
#
# These lines can be re-ordered; they are executed from top to bottom.
#
# If you remove a line here THAT COMMIT WILL BE LOST.
#
# However, if you remove everything, the rebase will be aborted.
#
# Note that empty commits are commented out

~/Desktop/the-suit/.git/rebase-merge/git-rebase-todo[+] [unix] (22:24 30/01/2017)
-- INSERT --
```

This example will drop `Commit 3` and merge `Commit 2` into `Commit 1`, creating a single (new) commit.

Of course, as always, rebasing can end up with conflicting files. If this happens, you should fix the conflicts, add them to your staging area (`git add some-file`), and then use `git rebase --continue`. In case you decide not to rebase after all, you can use `git rebase --abort`.

Unfortunately, there is a caveat to rebasing. *It will destroy your commits!* What Git does is recreate the commits on your new base and discard the old ones. This may be clear in the case of interactive rebasing, for example, when deleting or squashing commits. However, rebasing will always do this. There is a golden rule when rebasing: *only rebase local branches!* If you ever rebase a branch that your coworkers use as well, they will suddenly miss historic commits. Git will not know what to do with those commits. Your coworkers will curse you for it and you will be doing a lot of apologizing.

Reverting changes

Sometimes, you just want to get rid of whatever it is you did. Whether you just want to clean your working directory or you want to actually undo some items you (accidentally) committed, Git makes it possible.

There are a couple of scenarios we can think of that we want reverted. The first is quite simple. We have staged some files and we simply want to unstage everything. The `git reset` command does this:

```
git status
On branch master
Changes to be committed:
  (use "git reset HEAD <file>..." to unstage)

  new file: accidentally added.txt
  modified: kernel.txt
  deleted: lasers.txt

git reset
Unstaged changes after reset:
M kernel.txt
D lasers.txt

git status
On branch master
Changes not staged for commit:
```

```
(use "git add/rm <file>..." to update what will be committed)
(use "git checkout -- <file>..." to discard changes in working directory)

modified: kernel.txt
deleted: lasers.txt

Untracked files:
(use "git add <file>..." to include in what will be committed)

accidentally added.txt
```

It often happens that you do not want to unstage a file, but undo all your changes completely. Maybe you messed everything up; maybe your coworker just committed a fix that you were also about to commit; or maybe you just tried something and now want to revert it. The trick is still `git reset`, but with the `--hard` switch. Make sure you have committed at least two files to some branch. Now, change a file, delete a file, and edit a file. Check your changes using `git status`, reset, and check your status again:

```
git status
git reset --hard
git status
```

This will undo all the changes you made to files as well as restore files you deleted. However, what it will not do is delete untracked files. That behavior is as expected; Git is really careful with deleting your work after all. Once you add your added file to Git, `git reset --hard` will delete it though:

```
git add some_untracked_file.txt
git status
git reset --hard
git status
```

In case you wish to remove all your untracked files as well, you can issue a `clean` command. By default, git clean needs a parameter, either `-i` (for interactive); `-n` (being a *dry-run*, it tells you what it would clean, but does not actually do anything); or `-f` (force). Another useful parameter is `-d`, which specified not only untracked files, but also untracked directories should be removed:

```
git clean -n
Would remove New Text Document.txt

git clean -nd
Would remove New Text Document.txt
Would remove New folder/

git clean -f
```

```
Removing New Text Document.txt

git clean -fd
Removing New Text Document.txt
Removing New folder/
```

As you see, all of them behave slightly differently, but are incredibly useful for cleaning out your working directory.

To wrap it up, to completely remove everything in your workspace, you can do a reset, followed by a clean:

```
git reset --hard
git clean -fd
```

Another feature that is sometimes useful is that of reverting commits. You can revert a commit, keep the changes, and then edit them before committing again, or you can just completely delete a commit, therefore removing it from history. For this, you use `git reset` with the `--soft` or `--hard` switch and the commit, relative to HEAD, that you want to revert. In the following example, I have made four commits, doc1, doc2, doc3, and doc4:

```
git log --oneline
6a4bfff 4
083179b 3
86049c9 2
04e7e80 1
26df795 Add .gitignore
```

We can now revert the last commit, but keep the changes using `--soft`:

```
git reset --soft HEAD~1
git status
Changes to be committed:
  (use "git reset HEAD <file>..." to unstage)

 new file: doc4.txt

git log --oneline
083179b 3
86049c9 2
04e7e80 1
26df795 Add .gitignore
```

We can also revert the last two commits. We get all the changes that were committed in those two commits so we can edit them and recommit them as one commit (or as many commits as you like):

```
git reset --soft HEAD~2
git status
Changes to be committed:
  (use "git reset HEAD <file>..." to unstage)

  new file: doc3.txt
  new file: doc4.txt

git log --oneline
86049c9 2
04e7e80 1
26df795 Add .gitignore
```

Lastly, it is possible to just completely delete commits in this way using the --hard switch:

```
git reset --hard HEAD~2
HEAD is now at 86049c9 2

git status
nothing to commit, working tree clean

git log --oneline
86049c9 2
04e7e80 1
26df795 Add .gitignore
```

Just like with rebasing, *be very careful not to revert commits that have already been pushed to the server!* You may do it, but anyone that already has that commit pulled will now possibly also pull their hair out trying to fix all the errors.

The branching model

Now that you know how to use Git, create branches, merge them, move commits, push, pull, reset, clean, stash, and more, it is time you put this into practice. Any project should have at least two permanent branches, master and development. The development branch is where programmers put their work. When something is ready for release, it goes onto master, which should then be released.

If you do at least that, you are on your way. When a bug arises in production, you can branch from master; fix the bug on that branch, a hotfix branch if you like; and then merge that branch back into master (and release it) and development, fixing the bug for future releases.

Developers should always branch from the development branch. Any new features can be developed on so-called feature branches, sometimes also called topic branches. Once the feature is done, they can be merged back into development.

You probably have some (acceptance) test environment as well. I can recommend creating another permanent branch for each environment you have. The merge flow should then be something like from the development branch to your test branch, and from your test branch to your master or production branch. That way, you can release features to your test environment, independent from the master. You can put features A and B on test, and if the customer only approves feature B, then you can put only that into production.

 This model is actually described really well in a blog post by Vincent Driessen. It is from 2010, but still relevant today. The images he uses to describe the model may also help in grasping what is going on. I recommend you read it as it is pretty good. You can find it at `http://nvie.com/posts/a-successful-git-branching-model/`.

Tagging

One last issue I would like to discuss, which really comes in handy when releasing, is tagging. You can tag a commit for later reference. Tagging is mostly used to give a commit a version tag, so you can find it later. You will know exactly what commit represents version 1.0 or 1.1 of your software as that commit is tagged with that specific version.

There are two types of commits, lightweight and annotated. A lightweight tag is just that, a tag. An annotated tag keeps some extra information, such as a commit message, creation date, and the author of the tag. Creating a tag is really easy. Simply use `git tag tag-name`. For annotated tags, use the `-a` switch and specify a message. This will create a tag for your current commit:

```
git tag v0.1
git show v0.1
commit cf5e5c6af16f90990b2fb439e65973a66ff717aa
[...]

git tag -a v1.0 -m "Tag for v1.0"
git show v1.0
tag v1.0
```

```
Tagger: Tony Stark <tony.stark@avengers.com>
Date: Wed Feb 1 23:55:36 2017 +0100

Tag for v1.0

commit 6a4bfff9386a18f6122bc1e419d35d1e3625b0bd
[...]
```

As you see, using `git show tag-name` reveals the commit that was tagged with the specific tag. The annotated tag also shows information on when and who created the tag. You can list all your tags with the `git tag` command.

Tags are not automatically pushed to the server. When you want to share a tag, you need to explicitly push the tag:

```
git push origin v1.0
 * [new tag]         v1.0 -> v1.0

git pull
remote: Counting objects: 1, done.
remote: Total 1 (delta 0), reused 0 (delta 0)
Unpacking objects: 100% (1/1), done.
From http://ciserver/the_avengers/the-suit
 * [new tag] v1.1 -> v1.1
```

You can also create tags for older commits. Simply specify the commit hash to the `git tag` command:

```
git log --oneline
083179b Added even more files
86049c9 Changed some files
04e7e80 Added some files
26df795 Add .gitignore

git tag v0.5 04e7e80
```

By the way, when you go into GitLab, there is a **Tags** page, where you can view and create tags.

Summary

In this chapter, we have looked at the most used features of Git. You should now be able to effectively control your source. There will be time when you mess up, but at least you still have source control. Git clients, such as GitHub, SourceTree, and GitKraken, all make use of the features discussed in this chapter. Whenever you click a button, one or more of the commands we have seen in this chapter will be performed in the background. Personally, I find it far easier to use a client, but I know some people who would rather use the command line (to each his own). Whatever you choose, this chapter should be a pretty good introduction. It is not until the later chapters in this book, when we are going to use Jenkins extensively, that many of the advantages of using Git and branches become apparent. In the next chapter, we will start with writing some JavaScript that we can set up for CI using Node.js and npm, both locally on your development machine and on your CI server for your entire team to see.

4
Creating a Simple JavaScript App

In this chapter, we are going to create a simple web shop. We will start by writing a frontend using HTML, CSS, and JavaScript. Notice the lack of a backend. What I really like about frontend development is that it is so easy to get started with. We can create a complete app using only Notepad(++) or any other text editor. Of course, the lack of a database will prevent us from storing our results, but for now, that does not matter. The focus of this book is CI, not databases or backend development. The frontend alone will be enough to explore CI. After all, we can do tests and other automated tasks, such as minification. Even Continuous Delivery and Deployment are possible to implement (just copy your files to some server hosting your website), but we will delay that until we have our backend as well. What is really cool though is that we will now build some lame frontend, make the necessary tests, and then later we can connect it to a backend, run our tests, and be confident that everything works. Actually, our first version of the frontend will be so naive, a proof of concept rather than anything else, that we will need to change the frontend later as well without breaking it.

To make our lives a little easier, we will use Twitter Bootstrap for styling our pages, and jQuery (because Bootstrap needs it) and Google's Angular.js to bind our data to our pages. I am keeping the code samples simple because the focus of this book is CI and not frontend (or backend) development. If you have never worked with Bootstrap or Angular.js before, you should still be able to follow all the examples.

Nowhere in this chapter, or the rest of the book, will I give you the complete code in one listing. All code can be downloaded from the GitHub page for this book, `https://github.com/PacktPublishing/Continuous-Integration-Delivery-and-Deployment`. You will find the code for this specific chapter in its respective folder, `https://github.com/PacktPublishing/Continuous-Integration-Delivery-and-Deployment/tree/master/Chapter04`. ;In this chapter, I will explain the more interesting or important parts of the code from GitHub, often before listing the actual code, so expect the following format:

We can see feature x and y implemented in the code:

```
[Actual code sample]
```

Sometimes additional information on the previous code or comments on the next code sample.

The `node_modules` folder is not included in GitHub, so you will have to do an `npm install` to get those (explained in *Creating the project*). This is true for the rest of the book.

The web shop specs

Before we get started, we will have to know what we are going to build. Since we are super agile, we only need a basic outline (I used agile as an excuse not to write specs):

- **Home page**: First, of course, we will need a home page. The home page is very basic and shows us what other people have been buying. These are tiles that show an image, name, and price.
- **Search page**: When you search for a product, you get to the search page where you can filter by category and sort your results. The page will show us images, names, categories, prices, and a short description of all the products that match your criteria. From here, you can place any product in your cart if you are logged in. A user can search for products on any page.
- **Product page**: When you click on a product, either from the home page or the search page, you will be taken to the product page, which is also very basic. It shows an image, the name, category, price, and description of the product. If a user has logged in, they can place a product in their cart from here.
- **Shopping cart page**: Finally, your cart shows the products you want to buy, how many of each, and the price and totals of each product and of your complete order. It will have a checkout button that simply shows a message that says your order is being processed and you cart will empty. When a user is logged in, the cart icon is shown on every page at the top right.

- **Login page**: Any web shop needs some method of logging in. We can log in at any page at the top right of the screen. At this time, it is not possible to log in, since we only have a frontend and it is not possible to keep any session or state on our pages. For now, let's just add the button, but it will not do anything yet. Let's assume you are always logged in.

Installing Node.js and npm

For this project, we are going to use the packages Bootstrap and Angular.js. We can install these through npm. npm is the Node.js Package Manager, so we need to install Node.js and get npm for free. In the next chapters, we are going to use Node.js as well as more npm.

Node.js is a JavaScript runtime. JavaScript, traditionally, could only be executed on your browser. That poses a problem when you want to automate your JavaScript tests. You really do not want a browser every time you test, lint, or minify.

Node.js makes it possible to run JavaScript outside your browser. It starts up a local server (that can be exposed to the outside world) and runs JavaScript. Node.js is currently a popular alternative for Apache, IIS, and Nginx. In order to automate our JavaScript tests, we will need Node.js. Additionally, we will create a web application using Node.js.

npm is the Node Package Manager. Kind of like `apt-get`, we can install (or uninstall) packages in our web projects. It comes bundled with Node.js, so we do not need to do any additional work to install this.

For now, we will need Node.js and npm on our development machine only; in the next chapters, we will need it on our CI server as well, so we can run it in Jenkins.

Installing Node.js and npm is quite easy. Simply head over to `https://nodejs.org` and download the latest LTS version. This should give you an `msi` file. Simply run the `msi` file, leave all of the defaults, and click **Next, Next, Next**. If everything went well, you should now be able to open up a command prompt and check the versions of both the programs:

```
node -v
v6.9.4
npm -v
v3.10.10
```

Creating the project

First, let's create a Git repository that will hold our web shop project. Make sure your VM is running and browse to GitLab. It does not really matter if you create the project under your local account or in a group; you can always change that later. I have called the repository `web-shop`, but you can really name it anything you like. If you go for another name, make sure to change the name of the repository in all upcoming code snippets.

Now that you have a repository, you can clone it to your development machine. We have done this before, so that should not be a problem. I have chosen to clone the repository to my desktop for quick access, but I would recommend cloning it to `C:\Repositories` or your `Documents(\Repositories)` folder, some place where you keep your Git repositories:

```
cd your-folder
git clone http://ciserver/youruser/web-shop.git
cd web-shop
```

Make sure to replace `youruser` with your username and `web- shop` with the name of your repository if you picked another name. If you are unsure about the URL, you can always copy-paste it from GitLab.

After that, we will want to install Bootstrap and Angular.js. We will install this using npm. One of the benefits of using a package manager is that it installs dependencies for you automatically. It can also keep track of which packages you have installed in a separate file. The benefit to that is that you do not need to check your packages into source control and you can retrieve those packages on your build server. Your packages folder can become pretty big, so it is usually faster to download them on your CI server than to check them in to Git. For example, installing a somewhat bigger package, such as Gulp (which we will use in a later chapter), will give you a staggering 1,000+ files. They are only 4 MB altogether, but checking them in and out of Git takes time. In one of my own projects, which is not even that big, I have about 80 MB in 10,000+ files, all npm modules. Think what you want, but that is the reality of JavaScript programming in the year 2017.

Next to the time it saves by not having to check your packages into source control, another benefit is that whenever a package gets pulled from Git, your build will fail (hopefully) and you can immediately take action. You could save the missing locally and use that, but you will know for sure it will never be updated to the latest standards (which may or may not be a problem, depending on the nature of the package), unless you update it yourself, of course.

A downside to not checking in your packages is that your build is now dependent on the actions of third parties. Although, arguably, that is always the case because you are using third-party software. Actually, about a year ago, thousands of programmers worldwide saw their builds failing because a left-pad package with 11 lines of code was pulled from npm. No one knew they depended on the package, but other packages they depended on did depend on it.

That said, when your build succeeds, you should save the packages with your build, whether you keep them in your repository or not, so you can easily deploy the build and it will just work. So, knowing the pros and cons to checking and not checking your packages into source control, I leave you with the final decision whether you want to include them in your repository or not. In this book, we are not going to do it, but it is your choice.

Now, let's actually install the packages. In the command prompt, browse to the folder of your web-shop project. If you have not closed the command after the last example, you are probably already there. Before we install any packages, we will need a packages.json file. The easiest way to create a packages.json file is using the npm init command. The packages.json file holds several properties about your project, such as the ID, name, description, version, license, and which packages it depends upon. You can create one manually, but using npm init lets you specify values for these properties and will put them in the file for you automatically. For the default, between parentheses, you can simply hit *Enter*:

```
cd your-folder\web-shop
npm init
name: (web-shop) [Enter]
version: (1.0.0) [Enter]
description: A simple web shop for the CI example. [Enter]
entry point: (index.js) [Enter]
test command: [Enter]
git repository: (http://ciserver/sander/web-shop.git) [Enter]
keywords: [Enter]
author: Sander Rossel (your name here) [Enter]
license: (ISC) [Enter]

{ example json }

Is this ok? (yes) [Enter]
```

Now, check out the package.json file that was created. The only mandatory fields here are name and version, as they uniquely identify your own project should you ever want to publish them to npm. You can find what other fields can go into package.json in the npm documentation at https://docs.npmjs.com/.

Now, we can install Bootstrap and Angular.js:

```
cd your-folder\web-shop
npm install jquery --save
npm install bootstrap --save
npm install angular --save
```

There is a shortcut for installing multiple packages at once; just list them one after the other:

```
npm install jquery bootstrap angular --save
```

The `--save` switch is optional, but it is necessary for npm to restore your package from the npm repository automatically. Using the `--save` switch updates your `package.json`. It should now contain the following lines:

```
"dependencies": {
  "angular": "^1.6.1",
  "bootstrap": "^3.3.7",
  "jquery": "^3.1.1"
}
```

You will also find npm has created a `node_modules` folder, which contains the Bootstrap, jQuery, and Angular.js sources. Apparently, neither of them have any dependencies because no other packages were installed. You can check out what happens when you install a package, such as Gulp. It will install lots of packages, although it will only add one line to your dependencies in `package.json`. Go ahead, try it:

```
npm install gulp --save
npm uninstall gulp --save
```

The only thing that will leave behind is an empty `.bin` folder in `node_modules`.

The next thing we need to do is make sure Git does not add all of our packages to the repository. Check out the status of your Git repository and you will see the `node_modules` folder and `package.json` have been added:

```
git status
[...]
Untracked files:
  [...]

    node_modules/
    package.json
```

You can create a `gitignore` file, where you can specify which files, folders, or patterns to ignore. Creating this file is a little tricky as the name has to be `.gitignore`, which is not a valid file name in Windows. Instead, simply create a text file and name it `.gitignore`. Windows will automatically remove the last dot and you are good to go. In the `.gitignore` file, put the text `node_modules`. This will tell Git to ignore anything called `node_modules`. Now, check the status again:

```
git status
[...]
Untracked files:
  [...]

    .gitignore
    package.json
```

Time to commit these changes to Git. Lesson number one: when using source control, keep your commits small:

```
git add .
git commit -m "Initialized the web-shop project."
git push
```

Check it out in GitLab and you can confirm `node_modules` really were not pushed to Git.

To test whether we can really restore our packages from `npm`, `clone` the project again, into a different folder. You can check that there really really really are no `node_modules`. After that, use the `npm install` command to restore your packages. After that, you can simply delete this folder:

```
cd your-folder
git clone http://ciserver/youruser/web-shop.git web-shop-test
cd web-shop-test
npm install
cd ..
rmdir -s -q web-shop-test
```

Creating the Home page

On to the actual code. The first thing we will need are some HTML pages. I am trying to keep things as simple as possible so we will not use any HTML rendering engines. As a result, we will have to copy/paste some HTML into every page we have (for now). In your project folder, create three new folders called `css`, `scripts`, and `views`. Also, create a file called `index.html` and put the following code in it:

```html
<!DOCTYPE html>
<html>
    <head>
        <meta charset="UTF-8">
        <title>CI Web Shop</title>

        <link rel="stylesheet" type="text/css"
href="node_modules\bootstrap\dist\css\bootstrap.css">
        <link rel="stylesheet" type="text/css" href="css\layout.css">
        <link rel="stylesheet" type="text/css" href="css\utils.css">
        <script src="node_modules\angular\angular.js"></script>
        <script src="node_modules\jquery\dist\jquery.js"></script>
        <script
src="node_modules\bootstrap\dist\js\bootstrap.js"></script>
        <script src="scripts\utils.js"></script>
        <script src="scripts\repository.js"></script>
        <script src="scripts\index.js"></script>
    </head>
    <body ng-app="shopApp">
        ...
    </body>
</html>
```

This is part of the code that is more or less the same for every page. All the other pages will go in the `views` folder, so the references to the style sheets and scripts will start with `..\` to get back in the main folder first. `ng-app` is an Angular.js notation and designates the root element of your application to Angular.js. Within your app are controllers that can neatly define the properties and functionality of (a part of) a page and so help to keep functionality isolated or "separate your concerns." An app can have multiple controllers and controllers can be re-used.

Inside the `body` tags goes the rest of the page. The first part is reserved for a menu bar that is the same for every page. After that comes the Angular.js controller, which is unique for each page (separation of concerns). The `footer`, which is still in the same `div` as the controller, is the same on all pages:

```
<nav class="navbar navbar-default navbar-fixed-top">
   <div class="container">
      ...
   </div>
</nav>
<div class="container" ng-controller="homeController">
   ...
   <footer class="footer">
      <p>Copyright &copy; 2017</p>
   </footer>
</div>
```

There is quite a lot going on in these few lines. The classes `navbar`, `navbar- default`, and `navbar-fixed-top` are Bootstrap classes which create a navigation bar that is page-wide, fixed to the top, and always visible. The `container` class is the base of Bootstrap's power and is necessary to wrap site content and also houses Bootstrap's grid system. The grid system divides your page in rows and twelve columns. There is a `row` class, which we will see in a bit, and various column classes that you can use to divide your content over a number of columns.

The `ng-controller` bit is another Angular.js notation and indicates your binding context. Since we are using the `homeController` and the `homeController` exposes `topProducts`, we can loop through those products in our HTML. Each looped product has a `name` property that we can bind to, so our binding context is a list of objects (products) with a `name` property. We will see this binding in action in the next few examples. Notice that `navbar` has no explicit controller, but we can still use binding as we will see.

The footer kind of speaks for itself, so I am not going to expand on that.

Before we continue, here is an image of what the page ultimately looks like. It should give you a bit of an idea of what is going on:

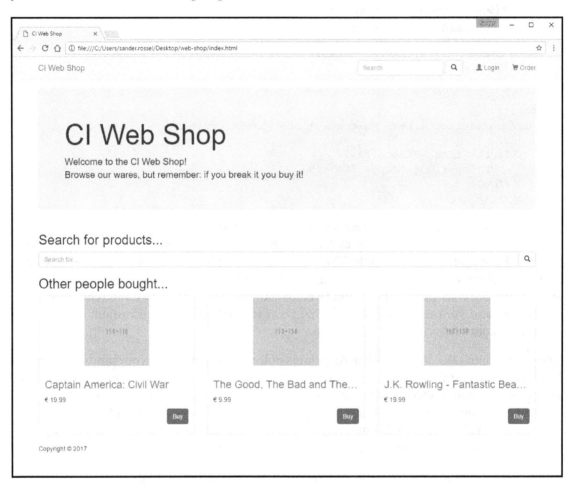

Let's take a closer look at the navigation bar. It is not exactly easy, but it looks cool and Bootstrap still makes it a lot easier than when you had to do it yourself. So, inside `<nav ...><div ...>` goes the following HTML:

```
<div class="navbar-header">
    <button type="button" class="navbar-toggle collapsed" data-
toggle="collapse" data-

target="#menu">
        <span class="icon-bar"></span>
        <span class="icon-bar"></span>
```

```
        <span class="icon-bar"></span>
    </button>
    <a class="navbar-brand" href="index.html">CI Web Shop</a>
</div>
<div class="collapse navbar-collapse" id="menu">
    <ul class="nav navbar-nav navbar-right">
        <li><a href="#"><span class="glyphicon glyphicon-user"></span>

Login</a></li>
        <li><a href="views\shopping-cart.html"><span class="glyphicon
glyphicon-

shopping-cart"></span> Order</a></li>
    </ul>
    <div class="navbar-form navbar-right">
        <div class="form-group">
            <input class="form-control" placeholder="Search" ng-model="query">
        </div>
        <a href="views\search.html?q={{query}}" class="btn btn-default">
            <span class="glyphicon glyphicon-search"></span>
        </a>
    </div>
</div>
```

There are two components here, `navbar-header` and `navbar- collapse`. The button in the header is the so-called `hamburger` menu, when your page gets too small to display the menu (on your phone, for example). The span elements with the `icon-bar` class are just the images on the button. The anchor with `navbar- brand` is the company logo at the top left of the page.

In the `navbar-collapse` part, we find the actual menu. There is an unordered list of menu items, being our login page, and our shopping cart. The span elements with the `glyphicon` classes are just images. The `div` element with the `navbar-form` class is our search bar. What is interesting here is that the input element has the Angular.js `ng-model` set to `query`. This means the value of the input is bound to some `query` property on our implicit model. Since we never explicitly created a model with a `query` property, Angular.js creates the model with a `query` property which can then be used on the page. The `query` property is then used in the anchor tag with the `{{query}}` syntax. This syntax tells Angular.js to place the contents of the query there instead of `{{query}}`. The update is done automatically when the value of the query changes. So, when the pages are complete, if you type `Fan` into the input and then click the link (which takes the form of a button), it will direct you to `view\search.html?q=fan`.

Now for the unique body part of our home page. It starts off with this big square that says `CI Web Shop` and `Welcome....` It is called a Jumbotron and it is actually pretty easy to implement using Bootstrap:

```
<div class="container" ng-controller="homeController">
    <div class="jumbotron">
        <h1>CI Web Shop</h1>
        <p class="lead">Welcome to the CI Web Shop!<br />
        Browse our wares, but remember: if you break it you buy it!</p>
    </div>
```

Then comes the search bar. We put this in `row` so nothing will ever get placed next to it. It is part of the Bootstrap grid system. Here, we also see the `col-lg-12` class. It means the content of the element should be spread out over 12 columns when the screen size is large. If you wanted two elements next to each other, you could specify `col-lg- 6` twice. When the screen gets smaller, you might not want to display two elements next to each other. In that case, you could use the class `col-sm-12` or spread out over 12 columns when small. Putting the two classes on one element is totally valid and will change how the elements are displayed in different screen sizes. This kind of design is called responsive, as the UI responds to the size of the screen, making it readable on all screen sizes (when done right, of course). Again, you see the `ng-model` and `{{}}` syntaxes. This time, we are binding to the `searchTerm` property of `homeController`:

```
<div class="jumbotron">
    [...]
</div>
<div class="row">
    <div class="col-lg-12">
        <h2>Search for products...</h2>
    </div>
    <div class="col-lg-12">
        <div class="input-group">
            <input class="form-control" placeholder="Search for..." ng-
model="searchTerm" />
            <div class="input-group-btn">
                <a href="views\search.html?q={{searchTerm}}" class="btn btn-
default">
                    <span class="glyphicon glyphicon-search"></span>
                </a>
            </div>
        </div>
    </div>
</div>
```

The last part of our page is the popular products section. Here, we see `ng-repeat`, which loops through an array and applies the binding for each item in that array:

```
<div class="row">
    <div class="col-lg-12">
        <h2>Other people bought...</h2>
    </div>
    <div ng-repeat="product in topProducts">
        <div class="col-lg-4">
            <div class="thumbnail">
                <a href="views\product.html?id={{product.id}}">
                    <img src="http://placehold.it/150x150" alt="..." />
                </a>
                <div class="caption clearfix">
                    <a href="views\product.html?id={{product.id}}">
                        <h3 class="wrap"
title="{{product.name}}">{{product.name}}</h3>
                    </a>
                    <p>{{'&euro; ' + product.price}}</p>
                    <p class="clearfix">
                        <a href="views\shopping-cart.html" class="btn btn-primary
pull-

right">Buy</a>
                    </p>
                </div>
            </div>
        </div>
    </div>
</div>
```

In the Bootstrap department, we see the classes `thumbnail`, `caption`, `clearfix`, and `pull-right`. It is all pretty straightforward. You can check out what they do on your browser. The image comes from `placehold.it`, which is a web service that serves images in any dimension you specify in the URL. So `placehold.it/150x150` returns a 150 x 150-pixel image. Really very handy.

The only class you see here that is not Bootstrap is *wrap*. It resides in `css\utils.css` and it makes sure the titles of our products are shown on a single line and show ellipsis when they are too long. The only other CSS file we have is `layout.css` and it adds some padding on the top, so our page starts below the top menu instead of behind it. Here are the contents of both `utils.css` and `layout.css`. We could put it in a single file, but the two files have very separate functions, so we don't:

```css
body {
    padding-top: 70px;
}

.wrap {
    overflow: hidden;
    text-overflow: ellipsis;
    white-space: nowrap;
}
```

That leaves us with the JavaScript code. It is actually pretty simple. In `index.js`, we create the Angular.js app and controller. In the binding model, we specify the top popular products and `searchTerm` for the search field that is not on the menu:

```javascript
angular.module('shopApp', [])
    .controller('homeController', function ($scope) {
        $scope.topProducts = repository.getTopProducts();
        $scope.searchTerm = '';
    });
```

And so most of the code goes into the `repository.js` file. This file has the data we show on the various screens:

```javascript
var repository = (function () {
    'use strict';

    var products = [{
        id: 1,
        name: 'Final Fantasy XV',
        price: 55.99,
        description: 'Final Fantasy finally makes a come back!',
        category: 'Gaming'
    }, {
            //...
    }];

    return {
        getTopProducts: function () {
            return [products[1], products[2], products[3]];
        },
```

```
    getProduct: function (id) {
        return products.filter(p => p.id === id)[0];
    },
    search: function (q) {
        if (q == null) {
            return [];
        } else {
            return products.filter(p =>
p.name.toLowerCase().indexOf(q.toLowerCase()) >= 0);
        }
    }
  };
})();
```

At the top is our array of all the products. The functions at the bottom are an interface to these products. The functions are pretty self-explanatory. It is good to mention that the `search` function returns an empty array when the search string is empty and the search is performed on name only and is case insensitive. The `getTopProducts` function simply returns the first three products, because we cannot actually calculate a most ordered list.

 The `=>` notation is a relatively new EcmaScript 6 notation. It is basically the shortcut for a regular function. Using "arrow functions," as they are called, we can use `p => p.id === id` instead of the much longer `function (p) { return p.id === id; }`. For more information on arrow functions (and ES6 in general), see `https://developer.mozilla.org/en-US/docs/Web/JavaScript/Reference/Functions/Arrow_functions`.

Creating the Product page

Next up is the product page. In your `views` folder, create a new file and call it `product.html`. This is by far the simplest page:

```html
<div class="row">
    <div class="col-lg-12 text-center">
        <h2>{{name}}</h2>
        <p>
            <img src="http://placehold.it/300x300" alt="..." />
        </p>
        <p>{{description}}</p>
        <p>{{'&euro; ' + price}}</p>
        <p>
            <a href="shopping-cart.html" class="btn btn-primary">Buy</a>
        </p>
```

```
     </div>
   </div>
```

That is all there is to it. The `text-center` class, while called `text-center`, will actually center everything.

We can put the scripts for utils, repository, and the product page itself in the header:

```
<script src="..\scripts\utils.js"></script>
<script src="..\scripts\repository.js"></script>
<script src="..\scripts\product.js"></script>
```

The `product.js` file is actually pretty straightforward. We create the app and the controller, we get the product, and we copy the product's properties to our own view model:

```
angular.module('shopApp', [])
    .controller('productController', function ($scope) {
        var id = +utils.getQueryParams()['id'],
            p = repository.getProduct(id);
        $scope.name = p.name;
        $scope.price = p.price;
        $scope.description = p.description;
        $scope.category = p.category;
    });
```

The interesting part is the `utils.getQueryParams()['id']` part. It comes from the `utils.js` file and looks as follows:

```
var utils = (function () {
    return {
        getQueryParams: function () {
            var qs = document.location.search.split('+').join(' '),
                params = {},
                tokens,
                regex = /[?&]?([^=]+)=([^&]*)/g;

            while (tokens = regex.exec(qs)) {
                params[decodeURIComponent(tokens[1])] =
decodeURIComponent(tokens[2]);
            }

            return params;
        }
    };
})();
```

I admit, I got the code somewhere from the internet, but it is easy enough. We get the URL that is on our browser, get the query parameters
(`someurl.com?param1=value+param2=value`) using a regular expression, decode the values (as they are URI encoded), and put the parameter name with the value in an object that we return. So, in `utils.getQueryParams()['id']`, we get the value of the `id` parameter in the URL. Now, we can actually show products with `id=2` when we browse to
file `:///C:/Users/sander.rossel/Desktop/web- shop/views/product.html?id=2`
(or wherever you saved your project).

Creating the Search page

The next page we are going to implement is the search page. This page should have few surprises for you now:

```
<div ng-repeat="product in results">
    <div class="thumbnail">
        <div class="row">
            <div class="col-lg-2">
                <a href="product.html?id={{product.id}}">
                    <img src="http://placehold.it/150x150" alt="..." />
                </a>
            </div>
            <div class="col-lg-9">
                <div class="caption">
                    <a href="product.html?id={{product.id}}">
                        <h3 class="wrap"
title="{{product.name}}">{{product.name}}</h3>
                    </a>
                    <p class="label label-default">{{product.category}}</p>
                    <p class="wrap">{{product.description}}</p>
                </div>
            </div>
            <div class="col-lg-1 clearfix">
                <div class="caption pull-right">
                    <p>{{'&euro; ' + product.price}}</p>
                    <a href="shopping-cart.html" class="btn btn-primary pull-
right">Buy</a>
                </div>
            </div>
        </div>
    </div>
</div>
```

The JavaScript is pretty much what you would expect as well:

```javascript
angular.module('shopApp', [])
    .controller('searchController', function ($scope) {
        var q = utils.getQueryParams()['q'];
        $scope.results = repository.search(q);
    });
```

Creating the Shopping cart page

Last, but not least, is the shopping cart. This page is a little different from the other pages, as it has some logic to it. On this page, we can increment a counter and delete items. If we had a backend, it would be possible to add items, but that is something for later chapters:

```html
<div class="row" ng-hide="lines.length">
    <div class="col-lg-12 text-center">
        <p>There are no items in your shopping cart...</p>
        <p>You should do some shopping!</p>
    </div>
</div>
<div ng-repeat="line in lines">
    <div class="thumbnail">
        <div class="row">
            <div class="col-lg-2">
                <a href="product.html?id={{line.product.id}}">
                    <img src="http://placehold.it/150x150" alt="..." />
                </a>
            </div>
            <div class="col-lg-7">
                <div class="caption">
                    <a href="product.html?id={{line.product.id}}">
                        <h3>{{line.product.name}}</h3>
                    </a>
                    <p class="label label-default">{{line.product.category}}
                    </p>
                </div>
            </div>
            <div class="col-lg-1 clearfix">
                <div class="caption pull-right">
                    <input ng-model="line.number" />
                    <button type="button" ng-click="removeLine(line)">
                        <span class="glyphicon glyphicon-trash"></span>
                        Delete
                    </button>
                </div>
            </div>
        </div>
```

```
            <div class="col-lg-2 clearfix">
                <div class="caption pull-right">
                    <p>{{'&euro; ' + line.subTotal()}}</p>
                </div>
            </div>
        </div>
    </div>
</div>
<div class="row">
    <div class="col-lg-12">
        <p class="pull-right">{{'&euro;' + total()}}</p>
    </div>
</div>
```

The top row has `ng-hide`, which means this element should not be visible when, in this case, `lines.length` evaluates to truthy. So, when `lines.length` returns 0, we display the text `There are no items in your shopping cart....` You will also see we bind to some functions. `ng-click`, which binds a function to the click event handler, invokes the `removeLine` function, and passes in the current `line` variable (from `ng-repeat`) as an argument. Other than that, we see the `line.subTotal()` and `total()` functions being bound. Notice that we need to invoke the function or Angular.js will bind to the string representation of the function:

```
angular.module('shopApp', [])
    .controller('shoppingCartController', function ($scope) {
        var Line = function (options) {
            this.product = options.product,
            this.number = options.number
        };
        Line.prototype.subTotal = function () {
            return (this.product.price * this.number).toFixed(2);
        }

        $scope.lines = [new Line({
            product: repository.getProduct(1),
            number: 1
        }), new Line({
            product: repository.getProduct(3),
            number: 2
        })];

        $scope.total = function () {
            var sum = 0;
            $scope.lines.forEach(function (l) {
                sum += +l.subTotal();
            });
            return sum.toFixed(2);
```

```
    };

    $scope.removeLine = function (line) {
        $scope.lines.splice($scope.lines.indexOf(line), 1);
    }
});
```

So, we are creating a `Line` class, which contains `product` and a `count` property. I am using `prototype` because it has been around for a long time, all browsers support it, and I think most people will understand this better than newer ES6 classes. Anyway, the subtotal of an order line is the price of the product times the number of products you want. We create two lines using `repository.getProduct`. The total of the order is the sum of subtotals of all the lines. The `toFixed(2)` function will round decimals to two (this is a floating point, so before we know it, we get `.000000001` kind of numbers). `toFixed()` returns a string, so we have to cast `subTotal` of a line to an integer before we can add them in `total`. Last, `removeLine` removes a line from the `lines` array. You will see all this binds nicely in the HTML. You can change the number of a line, and both the subtotal and total will update immediately. Keep in mind that we are not checking whether the number is actually a number, so giving it an input of *some string* will give it the subtotal `NaN` (Not a Number), and because anything plus `NaN` equals `NaN`, the total will also become `NaN`.

Summary

In this chapter, we have created the first version of a web shop application that we are going to use throughout the book. To keep it simple, it has no backend yet, but in the following chapters we will add a backend with Node.js, MongoDB, C# Core, and PostgreSQL. But first, let's add various tests and automate those. In the next chapter, we will use Jasmine to write our tests, Karma to automatically run those tests, and Selenium with Protractor to write and run end-to-end tests.

5
Testing Your JavaScript

In this chapter, we are going to test the code we have written in the previous chapters. We will start out with unit tests. We can write unit tests in, and for, JavaScript using Jasmine. After that, we will write UI tests using Selenium. At the end of the chapter, we will have tested our complete application so far and a little bit more.

The obvious advantage to testing your code is that you will be able to catch bugs as soon as they are introduced in any part of the application. How often have you made a change to some page only to find out another page broke because you changed some JavaScript that was shared between the two pages? The more important question: how often did you *not* find out about the other page breaking? Exactly! So that is why testing your JavaScript can really give you an edge in delivering high-quality software.

A less obvious advantage to testing your code is that in order to make your code testable, you need to write it in a certain way. A 1,000-line-long function (and yes, I have seen them) is not testable. Such a function does so much that you would have to write 100 tests just to cover every possible outcome. However, since no one understands a 1,000-line function, no one will understand its tests either, let alone expand on them.

You are also forced to think about separation of concerns within your application. A function that directly inserts into the database is not testable because we cannot write an assertion that checks whether the record was inserted (well, we could, but we shouldn't). So, somehow, we need to create interfaces that we can mock, and implement it twice. One implementation that does a database insert for our production application, and one implementation that uses "inserts" to memory for use in our tests. This has the added advantage that your code becomes more modular, making the different parts properly isolated and thus easier to understand, easier to test, and easier to change.

Again, I will not give you the complete code in one listing anywhere in this chapter. The code can be downloaded from the GitHub page for this book, `https://github.com/ PacktPublishing/Continuous-Integration-Delivery-and-Deployment`. To restore `node_modules`, use `npm install`.

Unit testing with Jasmine

First things first, we will need to install Jasmine. I can recommend going through this chapter to get started with Jasmine. After that, check out the documentation on the website, `https://jasmine.github.io/`. Jasmine is pretty extensive, but the documentation is pretty spot on. Now, open up a command prompt and browse to your project folder. Once there, we can install Jasmine through `npm`. Like with Angular.js and Bootstrap, we want to save Jasmine to our `package.json` file, but this time, as a developer dependency. A regular dependency such as Angular.js and Bootstrap, is necessary to run the code. A developer dependency is only interesting for developers who want to make a build of the software. In other words, software cannot run without the dependencies, but it can run perfectly fine without the developer dependencies. That said, developer dependencies are not less important to the development process. Our website does not need Jasmine to run, but we definitely want to run our unit tests after we have made some changes:

```
cd folder-of-your-project
npm install jasmine --save-dev
```

This adds a new property in your `package.json` file:

```
"devDependencies": {
  "jasmine": "^2.5.3"
}
```

Developer dependencies are installed on `npm install` just like regular dependencies. However, `npm install` has an additional `--production` (or `--prod`) flag that can prevent the developer dependencies from installing.

You can also list your installed dependencies and filter on `dev` or `prod`. In the next example, we will see different ways to install and list dependencies. The `--depth` flag indicates whether to show dependencies of your packages (and the dependencies of your dependencies and so forth). The `rmdir` command is a Windows command and simply removes the `node_modules` folder (`/S` to force deletion of any files and subdirectories and `/Q` to not ask for confirmation):

```
rmdir /S /Q node_modules
npm install
npm list --dev --depth=0
npm list --prod --depth=0

rmdir /S /Q node_modules
npm install --only=prod
npm list --depth=0

rmdir /S /Q node_modules
npm install --only=dev
npm list --depth=0
npm list --dev --depth=0

npm install
```

Now that we have Jasmine installed, we can almost start using it. Jasmine is just some JavaScript library, so it needs a browser to run. Browsers have no built-in support for Jasmine, so we need to create a page to run our tests and show the results. Luckily, Jasmine has a lot of that; we only need to glue some pieces together on a simple HTML page.

In your project folder, create a folder called `test`. In there, create a file named `index.html`. In the `index.html` file, put the following HTML code:

```html
<!doctype html>
<html>
    <head>
        <title>Jasmine Spec Runner</title>
        <link rel="shortcut icon" type="image/png"
href="../node_modules/jasmine-core/images/jasmine_favicon.png">
        <link rel="stylesheet" href="../node_modules/jasmine-
core/lib/jasmine-core/jasmine.css">
    </head>
    <body>
        <script src="../node_modules/jasmine-core/lib/jasmine-
```

```
core/jasmine.js"></script>
        <script src="../node_modules/jasmine-core/lib/jasmine-core/jasmine-
html.js"></script>
        <script src="../node_modules/jasmine-core/lib/jasmine-
core/boot.js"></script>

        <!-- include source files here... -->

        <!-- include spec files here... -->
        <script src="spec/test.js"></script>
    </body>
</html>
```

To be honest, I really do not know what this does. Obviously, we load some Jasmine files and they somehow work their magic. The good thing is we really do not need to know how Jasmine does it; that is the entire reason we use a third-party library instead of writing our own.

The important part in this file is the `spec/test.js` script, which we have not created yet. So go ahead and create a folder called `spec` (within the `test` folder) and put a `test.js` file in it. We can put our tests in the `test.js` file:

```
(function () {
    'use strict';

    describe('sample tests', function () {
        describe('our first Jasmine tests', function () {
            it('should succeed', function () {
                expect(true).toBe(true);
            });
        });
    });
})();
```

There is quite a bit going on there and we will get to it in a second. First, make sure you did everything right. Open up your `index.html` file on your browser. You should see something like the following:

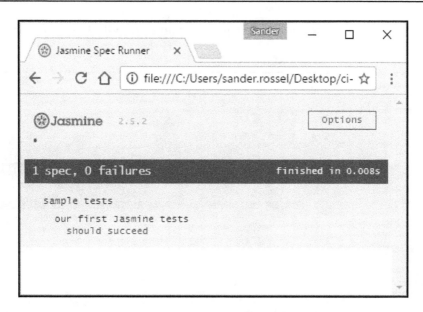

They say a picture says more than 1,000 words and I guess that is true. Looking at the code and the screenshot, it becomes clear what the describe and it functions do. The describe function simply adds a bit of context to your tests, what you are testing, or how you are testing it. You can nest your describe functions to add even more context. Our first describe makes it clear that we are testing the web shop while the second describe makes it clear that we are running our first Jasmine tests. The it function contains your actual test and should contain at least a single assertion. An assertion, in unit testing, is simply checking whether the value you expect matches the actual value in your code. In this example, true indeed matches true. As you can see, the test almost reads as plain language with the expect and toBe functions.

Explaining what you are going to test in this manner is also called **Behavior-Driven Development** (**BDD**) for short. You define and describe the behavior and then test whether your application successfully implements that behavior. The test.js file is in a folder called spec because your tests describe the specs, or specifications, of your application.

Next, let's add a failing test. In your test.js file, add the following test directly under the previous test (included in the example for clarity):

```
it('should succeed', function () {
    expect(true).toBe(true);
});
it('should fail', function () {
    expect(false).toBe(true);
});
```

Refreshing your Jasmine page should now give you an error with the details of what is wrong:

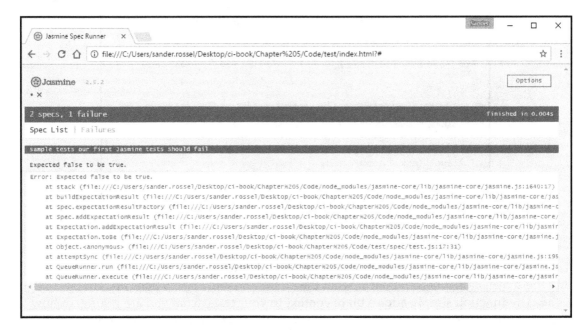

You get the name of your failing test, the expected value, the actual value, and a complete stack trace of your error. When multiple tests fail, or multiple assertions within the same test fail, they are all shown in this overview. Notice that you can still switch your view to the list of all your tests, where you get a better overview of the tests that failed:

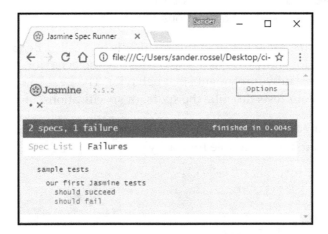

Useful to mention is that `toBe` tests two objects for equality. Quite often, you will want to compare two objects or arrays that are equal in terms of properties and values, but not in terms of reference in memory. In languages such as C#, this is often a problem, as you either need to loop through properties and compare them using reflection or manually, both of which are a hassle. In JavaScript, this is a lot easier. The `toBe` function is not going to cut it here, but the lookalike function `toEqual` will do the job for you:

```
it('should be the same object', function () {
    var o1 = {
        firstName: 'Sander',
        lastName: 'Rossel'
    };
    var o2 = {
        firstName: 'Sander',
        lastName: 'Rossel'
    };
    expect(o1).toEqual(o2);
});
```

Obviously, `o1` and `o2` are not actually the same object, but they do have the same properties and values. Because we use `toEqual` for comparison, this test will not fail unless we add, change, or remove a property on one of the objects. You might be happy to know that `toEqual` also works on arrays:

```
it('should be the same array', function () {
    var arr1 = ['Hello', {}, 1, true];
    var arr2 = ['Hello', {}, 1, true];
    expect(arr1).toEqual(arr2);
});
```

Other functions you can use to create your asserts are `not`, `toBeDefined`, `toBeNull`, `toBeTruthy`, `toBeFalsy`, `toContain`, `toBeNaN`, `toThrow`, and lots more:

```
expect(something).toBeDefined();
expect(something).not.toBeNaN();
expect(something).toContain('a value');
expect(something).toBeGreaterThan(10);
expect(function () {
    something();
}).toThrow();
```

Additionally, there are `setup` and `teardown` functions you may use for every test in your `describe`. The functions `beforeEach` and `afterEach` run before and after each `it`, so your tests may use the same variable and you can reset and reinitialize it between each test. Alternatively, you can use `beforeAll` and `afterAll`, which only runs once before all your tests and after all your tests are finished:

```
describe('setup and teardown tests', function () {
    var something;

    beforeEach(function () {
        something = 'Some value';
    });

    afterEach(function () {
        something = null;
    });

    it('should do stuff with something', function () {
        expect(something).toBe('Some value');
    });
});
```

One of the coolest features is probably that of spies. You can actually track whether the methods are called, how often, and using what arguments:

```
// Intentionally outside the scope of the tests...
var math = {
    add: function (a, b) {
        return a + b;
    }
};

(function () {
    'use strict';

    // ...

    describe('sample tests', function () {
        describe('spy tests', function () {
            beforeEach(function () {
                spyOn(math, 'add').and.callThrough();
            });

            it('should add 1 and 2 and call on the add function', function
            () {
                expect(math.add(1, 2)).toBe(3);
                expect(math.add).toHaveBeenCalled();
```

```
        });
      });
    });
  })();
```

You may not need all of this functionality. For the sample web shop, we certainly won't. But knowing what is available to you now will save you time and trouble in the future. Again, the Jasmine documentation is pretty extensive and describes all of this in more detail. It contains samples on asserts, setup and `teardown`, spies, regular expressions, mocking, and asynchronous testing.

Once you get a few more tests, it is possible to single out a single test or a group of tests in the way. It helps in focusing on fixing a single test. This is very helpful when you have dozens of failing tests, but you know all failures are caused by the failing of some core functionality. You can now focus on just the tests of that core functionality, so you will not be distracted by all the other failing tests. You can simply click on a test or describe to filter them out:

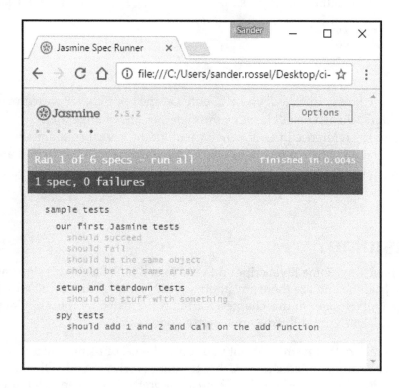

The Yeoman shortcut

Getting Jasmine up and running is quite a hassle, especially if you have never done it before. There is a tool that will set up this sort of project for you, called Yeoman (http://yeoman.io/). Yeoman has all kinds of project templates that it can install for you automatically (including Angular.js). The downside to using Yeoman with Jasmine is that it uses Bower instead of npm. Bower is a package manager that can be installed through npm (yes, you need a package manager to install a package manager). Bower does a couple of things better than npm, most notably keeping track of different versions of the same package that are used by different packages. However, we have chosen npm for this project and we do not want yet another package manager, another tool, or another dependency. You can choose to install Bower, but if you do not, Yeoman will simply set up the project, but fail to actually install Jasmine, which you can then install manually. It is best to install both Bower and Yeoman globally so you can use them directly from the command line. Using the -g switch with npm will install packages globally as opposed to only in your current project. The downside to this is that it is impossible to do npm install on global packages:

```
[optional] npm install -g bower
npm install -g yo
npm install -g generator-jasmine
yo jasmine
```

If you do not have Bower installed, you will only get the test folder with an index.html and a spec folder. You can install Jasmine through npm and change the bower_components reference in index.html with node_modules manually. Additionally, Yeoman will create .yo-rc.json, which you can delete if you are just using Yeoman for this one-time setup. This is actually what I do myself when I need to set up Jasmine.

Why Jasmine?

Now that we have seen some JavaScript unit tests in action, let us take a step back. Why would we use Jasmine and are there any alternatives? Jasmine works well with Karma, a test runner we will use later in this chapter. Karma was created by the Angular.js team, and thus Angular.js, Jasmine, and Karma are a pretty good match.

You do need to realize that Jasmine is not your only choice, but since we are working with Angular.js, it is a recommended choice. Other testing libraries include QUnit, used by the jQuery team, Unit.js, Intern, and Mocha. There are a pretty much a gazillion unit testing libraries out there though, but these ones are pretty popular choices.

I do not wish to confuse you, but you should be aware that some of these libraries have abstracted just about everything. For example, when you use Mocha, you can use different assertion libraries, such as `should.js`, `expect.js`, or `chai`. Likewise, mocking and spies are not a part of all testing libraries, requiring additional libraries, such as SinonJS. Such an approach has pros and cons. Obviously, knowing which libraries to install and how to configure them can be pretty confusing, especially if you have never used a testing framework before. On the other hand, you can configure everything specifically to your needs and preferences. A great example of what some libraries can and cannot do is on the home page of Intern, `https://theintern.github.io/`. The home page has a *What can Intern do that others can't?* section. You may notice not even all testing frameworks can perform unit tests (such as Karma). So you will need a unit testing library for your unit testing library. Which will make sense once we get to the part about Karma.

As with most things JavaScript, picking your testing framework can end up in installing multiple libraries that all do a very specialized thing and sometimes have some overlap. Jasmine just has it all and requires no extra libraries. Ultimately, all testing libraries do the same: test your JavaScript.

Testing the web shop

Let's continue to add some tests for our web shop. The first thing we should ask ourselves is which files we should test in the first place. For now, the most obvious file is the shopping cart module. When we look at the shopping cart module, it seems like it is pretty difficult to test this file. An obvious test would be to add a product and check whether the price is correctly updated. However, the `Line` object is private to the controller and the controller `$scope` represents the entire cart. We have two options here: either we find out if and how we can get access to the `$scope` object in our unit tests or we create an additional file that has the shopping cart object and that we can reuse in our controller (or even non-Angular.js projects). You can already see that we are forced to think about our code in a certain way, because we need to use our code in the application where we really need it. Also, in our unit tests, we need to write more generic code than we might do otherwise.

Luckily, Angular.js has some means to test controllers. We will need an additional package though, `angular-mocks`:

```
npm install angular-mocks --save-dev
```

Next, we need to add Angular.js, `angular-mocks`, and our own `shopping-cart.js` script to the test page or our test will not be able to make use of them:

```
<!-- include source files here... -->
<script src="../node_modules/angular/angular.js"></script>
<script src="../node_modules/angular-mocks/angular-mocks.js"></script>
<script src="../scripts/repository.js"></script>
<script src="../scripts/shopping-cart.js"></script>

<!-- include spec files here... -->
<script src="spec/test.js"></script>
```

After that, we can write a test using the controller:

```
describe('web app tests', function () {
    describe('shopping cart controller', function () {
        beforeEach(module('shopApp'));

        var $controller;

        beforeEach(inject(function(_$controller_) {
            $controller = _$controller_;
        }));

        it('should update the line sub total when a product is added',
function() {
            var $scope = {};
            var controller = $controller('shoppingCartController', { $scope:
$scope });
            $scope.lines[0].number = 2;
            expect($scope.lines[0].subTotal()).toBe('111.98');
        });
    });
});
```

There is quite a lot going on in those few lines of code, so let's break it down. The real trick is in the `module` (short for `angular.mock.module`) and `inject` (short for `angular.mock.inject`) functions that come from `angular-mock`. The `module` function simply registers our module configuration code, so it can be used by Angular.js and, specifically, the `inject` function. The `inject` function is less straightforward. It wraps a function into another function, which can be injected. The object to be injected is the name of the parameter, which is kind of a problem when you are minifying your code.

Anyway, we can name our local variable `$controller` and still pass in `$controller` to the `inject` function by wrapping it in underscores, because `inject` ignores the underscores. This behavior was specifically designed for this purpose. Think of it what you want, this is how it is. So, we can now call our controller and pass our `$scope` object to it, which we can then use in our tests.

We can now create a second test using the same controller:

```
it('should update the order total when a product is added', function() {
    var $scope = {};
    controller('shoppingCartController', { $scope: $scope });
    $scope.lines[0].number = 2;
    expect($scope.total()).toBe('131.96');
});
```

In hindsight, I am not very happy with the choice to return strings instead of numbers. We used the `toFixed(2)` function to round to two decimal points, but that function returns a string. In `shopping-cart.js`, I changed the `subTotal` function:

```
Line.prototype.subTotal = function () {
    return +(this.product.price * this.number).toFixed(2);
}
```

If we save this change (+ was added to convert to a number) and run our tests again, we get the following error: `Expected 111.98 to be '111.98'`. That makes sense: it expected a number to be a string. We can now do two things, fix the code so it returns a string again (after all, we may have broken some other untested functionality) or change our test because we know this is now the new expected behavior. Let's change the test because this is really what we want:

```
expect($scope.lines[0].subTotal()).toBe(111.98);
```

I am going to change the `total` function in the same way. We can remove a + sign and then add one to cast the result. Of course, we need to fix the test as well:

```
$scope.total = function () {
    var sum = 0;
    $scope.lines.forEach(function (l) {
        // Remove a plus on the next line.
        sum += l.subTotal();
    });
    return +sum.toFixed(2);
};

// And in the test check for a number.
expect($scope.total()).toBe(131.96);
```

Speaking of `toFixed` and rounding errors, it is risky to check a floating point numeric (which JavaScript uses) to an exact number. Jasmine has a `toBeCloseTo` function to check for approximate values. In this particular case, we do want to check for an exact number, because we do not want any rounding whatsoever. This is the expected behavior of the `subTotal` and `total` functions and we have now tested that to work.

Let's add a third test:

```
it('should update the order total when a product is removed', function() {
    var $scope = {};
    controller('shoppingCartController', { $scope: $scope });
    $scope.removeLine($scope.lines[0]);
    expect($scope.total()).toBe(19.98);
});
```

You should now get a warm feeling inside that is caused by knowing that your JavaScript code can be modified and any errors are caught by your tests. We are missing a couple of tests though. For example, what happens when we remove a line from `$scope.lines` directly? What happens when we change the product of a line? What happens when we change the price of a product? And since this is JavaScript, what happens when we overwrite or remove some property or pass in a value of the wrong type somewhere (like setting `line.number` to `foo`)?

One word of advice: this is JavaScript and people can mess up your code in ways you cannot even imagine. You cannot possibly test what will happen if people overwrite or remove properties, so do not even bother trying. So, what then when people set `number` to `foo` or a negative number? Personally, I would not test such a scenario as it is improper use of the code. It is really hard to test improper code, as people can really abuse it. You can, however, test what will happen in some cases that do make some sense. Think about testing with `number` set to `undefined`, `null`, or `2`. It is really up to you how far you want to go with this. My advice: do not go too far. Just document and test the cases you wish to support. That way, you know your code will work when it is used as intended and other people can read how you intended it.

At this point, we are able to test our software, which is awesome, but running our tests requires us to open up a web page manually and check the results. If we want to test our code on different browsers, this can be quite annoying. This is where Karma comes in.

Running tests with Karma

Karma, as mentioned, is a test runner (and it is spectacular, according to the Karma team). So a test runner really does what the name implies: it runs tests. So, instead of having to refresh your test page, Karma just runs them for you. Karma can be easily configured to run your tests on multiple browsers, such as IE (or some specific version), Edge, Firefox, Chrome, Safari, and Opera. After running your tests, Karma can generate reports on your tests and your code coverage. You can set minimum coverage thresholds and make your test runs fail when your code is not sufficiently covered. On top of that, Karma is a layer of abstraction. You can configure your test framework, such as Jasmine, and then switch to something else, such as Mocha, and everything will still work. You only have to change your tests, of course, and a single line in your Karma configuration.

Installation

First though, let's install Karma. We are going to install Karma using npm. Karma basically has two components: Karma itself, which uses Node.js, and the Karma **Command Line Interface** (**CLI**). We are going to install Karma in our project folder and we can install the CLI globally for easy access from the command line:

```
npm install karma --save-dev
npm install karma-cli -g
```

Optionally, you can use Yeoman, but we will not use the defaults for now, so that is pretty useless at this point. However, if you really want to, you can:

```
npm install generator-karma -g
yo karma
npm install karma-cli -g
```

Karma is all about configuration. Now that we have the Karma CLI tool installed, we can easily generate a configuration file. Just use karma init and answer the questions that come up, pretty much the same as npm init. Where you want to put the file is up to you; you can put it in your test folder, but putting it in the root folder makes sense too. Since Yeoman puts it in a test folder, I am going to follow that example:

```
cd test
karma init
Which testing framework do you want to use ?
Press tab to list possible options. Enter to move to the next question.
> jasmine

Do you want to use Require.js ?
```

```
This will add Require.js plugin.
Press tab to list possible options. Enter to move to the next question.
> no

Do you want to capture any browsers automatically ?
Press tab to list possible options. Enter empty string to move to the next
question.
> Chrome
>

What is the location of your source and test files ?
You can use glob patterns, eg. "js/*.js" or "test/**/*Spec.js".
Enter empty string to move to the next question.
> ../node_modules/angular/angular.js
> ../node_modules/angular-mocks/angular-mocks.js
> spec/*.js
> ../scripts/*.js
>

Should any of the files included by the previous patterns be excluded ?
You can use glob patterns, eg. "**/*.swp".
Enter empty string to move to the next question.
>

Do you want Karma to watch all the files and run the tests on change ?
Press tab to list possible options.
> yes

Config file generated at "C:\Users\sander.rossel\Desktop\ci-book\Chapter
5\Code\test\karma.conf.js".
```

Now, if you open the generated `karma.conf.js` file, which is just a JavaScript file, and remove all the comments and white space, it should look as follows:

```
module.exports = function(config) {
    config.set({
        basePath: '',
        frameworks: ['jasmine'],
        files: [
            '../node_modules/angular/angular.js',
            '../node_modules/angular-mocks/angular-mocks.js',
            'spec/*.js',
            '../scripts/*.js'
        ],
        exclude: [],
        preprocessors: {},
        reporters: ['progress'],
        port: 9876,
```

```
        colors: true,
        logLevel: config.LOG_INFO,
        autoWatch: true,
        browsers: ['Chrome'],
        singleRun: false,
        concurrency: Infinity
    })
  }
```

The `module.exports` is a Node.js thing and means that when the current module is loaded (with `require`, something we will see in later Node.js modules), `module.exports` is exposed to Node.js. Do not worry about `module.exports` or `require` for now; I just wanted to point it out in case you were wondering about it. The configuration itself is pretty straightforward, especially with all the comments. For now, we will leave it as it is and run our first tests with the current configuration. Note that you will need Chrome to run this example (we will use other browsers in a minute). To run your tests, simply use the `karma start` command. This will start up a Node.js server, open up a new browser window, and run your tests. Karma will pick up your `karma.conf.js` file automatically. Alternatively, if you are in a different folder than your Karma config file or if you have multiple configs, you can specify your file using `karma start path_to_file/my_karma_conf.js`:

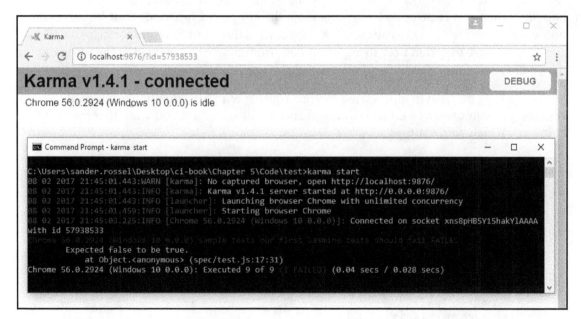

And there you have it. One of our tests is still failing! Luckily, we planned this. So, now is the time to fix this failing test. Fix it however you like; I have opted for `expect(false).toBe(false);`. Now, here comes the good part. Watch what happens when you save the file:

```
Command Prompt - karma start                                                              —   □   ✕

C:\Users\sander.rossel\Desktop\ci-book\Chapter 5\Code\test>karma start
08 02 2017 21:57:09.687:WARN [karma]: No captured browser, open http://localhost:9876/
08 02 2017 21:57:09.702:INFO [karma]: Karma v1.4.1 server started at http://0.0.0.0:9876/
08 02 2017 21:57:09.702:INFO [launcher]: Launching browser Chrome with unlimited concurrency
08 02 2017 21:57:09.702:INFO [launcher]: Starting browser Chrome
08 02 2017 21:57:11.534:INFO [Chrome 56.0.2924 (Windows 10 0.0.0)]: Connected on socket CWO174z21H4vBnZDAAAA
with id 97567384
Chrome 56.0.2924 (Windows 10 0.0.0) sample tests our first Jasmine tests should fail FAILED
        Expected false to be true.
            at Object.<anonymous> (spec/test.js:17:31)
Chrome 56.0.2924 (Windows 10 0.0.0): Executed 9 of 9 (1 FAILED) (0.052 secs / 0.036 secs)
08 02 2017 21:57:19.436:INFO [watcher]: Changed file "C:/Users/sander.rossel/Desktop/ci-book/Chapter 5/Code/t
est/spec/test.js".
Chrome 56.0.2924 (Windows 10 0.0.0): Executed 9 of 9 SUCCESS (0.04 secs / 0.024 secs)
```

Without doing anything but saving the file, your tests are run and you get immediate feedback! That is awesome! The same happens when you edit a source file. See what happens when you remove that + symbol from the `subTotal` function. Your tests are run immediately and not only is your test for `subTotal` failing, but also that for `total` and `remove`, because they don't get string input data from `subTotal` instead of the number they were expecting.

By the way, if you wish to quit Karma in your console without actually closing your console, you can use *Ctrl + C* (on Windows) and it will ask you if you want to terminate the batch job, which you want.

Karma plugins

Karma alone does not do all that much. You need plugins to get anything done. In fact, if you check your dev dependencies, you will see Karma already has some plugins installed:

```
"devDependencies": {
    "angular-mocks": "^1.6.1",
    "jasmine": "^2.5.3",
    "karma": "^1.4.1",
    "karma-chrome-launcher": "^2.0.0",
    "karma-jasmine": "^1.1.0"
}
```

The Chrome launcher and Jasmine plugin come with Karma by default. At least the Chrome launcher makes sense, as Karma was developed for Angular.js, which was developed by Google, who also made Chrome. Google owns you now. In the next part, we are going to install and use some plugins.

Browser launchers

Maybe you do not have Chrome installed and you were trying to make this work with IE or Firefox. Unfortunately, when you configured *IE* or *Firefox* instead of *Chrome*, you were met with an error upon `karma start`. The error you see is `Cannot load browser "Firefox": it is not registered! Perhaps you are missing some plugin?`. Well, perhaps you are missing a plugin indeed, so let's install it:

```
npm install karma-firefox-launcher --save-dev
```

Now, you can change browsers in your Karma configuration to Firefox. If you run Karma now, you will see it uses Firefox instead of Chrome. You may need to restart your console before this works.

You can install launchers for IE, Edge, and other browsers as well:

```
npm install karma-ie-launcher --save-dev
npm install karma-edge-launcher --save-dev
npm install karma-safari-launcher --save-dev
npm install karma-opera-launcher --save-dev
```

Of course, you will never be able to run the Safari launcher on anything other than an Apple computer and the IE and Edge launchers on anything other than a Windows computer. I am pretty sure there are other browser launchers, but you get the idea.

When you configure Karma to run with IE, something funny happens. Your tests fail. Apparently, there is a syntax error in our `repository.js` file. We used the latest, greatest ES2015 arrow syntax and IE does not support that (C# has used it for almost 10 years, but ah well... also, IE). This is exactly the reason why you should test on multiple browsers: you never know which browsers support which functionality. You can easily test multiple browsers.

You may have noticed that the browser options take an array, so you can easily configure multiple browsers:

```
browsers: ['Chrome', 'Firefox', 'Edge'],
```

Back to IE for a moment. Personally, I think IE really needs to go. It is a horrible browser, impossible to work with, and it does everything just a little bit different than other browsers. Especially the old versions are a problem. We, developers, know we should not use IE for anything other than downloading another browser, but unfortunately, our customers just can not get enough of IE and, preferably, IE8 or even worse. Luckily for us, IE has a built-in time machine that lets you test against a specific version of IE (at least it does that right). In Karma, you can create a custom browser that lets you provide some flags for your installed browsers, allowing you to test against a specific version of IE.

Unfortunately, running against IE8 is a bit of a hassle with newer versions of Karma. Something to do with sockets not being supported by IE8 and lower. IE9 still works out of the box though, and IE8 would work the same if you got your IE settings right. In your Karma configuration, add `customLauncher` and add it to the browsers:

```
browsers: ['IE', 'IE9'],
customLaunchers: {
    IE9: {
        base: 'IE',
        'x-ua-compatible': 'IE=EmulateIE9'
    }
},
```

Our tests are still failing though, but that can be fixed by removing the ES2015 code and replacing it with some good old JavaScript. The only file that is affected is `repository.js`. You can change `getProduct` and `search` to look as follows:

```
getProduct: function (id) {
    return products.filter(function (p) {
        return p.id === id;
    })[0];
},
search: function (q) {
    if (q == null) {
        return [];
    } else {
        return products.filter(function (p) {
            return p.name.toLowerCase().indexOf(q.toLowerCase()) >= 0;
        });
    }
}
```

Once you save the file, your tests should be run automatically and you should see they are passing now.

Code coverage

Karma can also give you code coverage reports. Code coverage indicates how much of your code is tested. For example, if you have two functions, each 10 lines long, and you test one, you should have a code coverage of 50%. Code coverage is a little more sophisticated than that, as we will see in a moment.

Before we start, we will need to install the `karma-coverage` plugin:

```
npm install karma-coverage --save-dev
```

After that, we need to change our configuration, so Karma will run the coverage plugin. We will need to indicate the coverage preprocessor, the `coverageReporter`, and the type of reporter:

```
preprocessors: {
    '../scripts/*.js': ['coverage']
},
reporters: ['progress', 'coverage'],
coverageReporter: {
    reporters: [
        { type : 'html', subdir: 'html' }
    ],
```

```
    dir : 'coverage/',
},
```

So, all of our scripts in the `scripts` folder are checked for coverage. We already had the `progress` reporter, but we added the `coverage` reporter. We can then customize the `coverage` reporter. We want the `html` reporter, which should save its results to the `html` subdirectory. All coverage reports are written to the coverage directory (relative to the config file). Run Karma again and you will now find the HTML report in `test/coverage/html`. You can open `index.html` and it should show you the coverage of your files:

As you can see, the coverage of your statements, branches, functions, and lines are tracked separately. Our coverage is not all that good, but that makes sense, as we only really tested one file, which has **100%** coverage. Since we call the `angular.module` and `controller` functions in our tests, they are considered tested in all our files (that is why all files have at least some coverage). What is really nice is that you can click on a file and you can see everything that was not covered by your tests:

As you can see, the `return` statement was executed once during our tests. You can even see how often a particular line was executed. The line `return products.filter...` was executed six times and the callback thirty times. Executing a function more often does not increase your coverage rating. Your report is overwritten on each test run.

It is possible to enforce a minimum coverage. We can add this in our configuration. When the coverage falls below a certain percentage, your tests will fail. You can do this in your `coverageReporter`:

```
coverageReporter: {
    reporters: [
        { type : 'html', subdir: 'html' }
    ],
    dir : 'coverage/',
    check: {
        global: {
            statements: 50,
            branches: 50,
            functions: 50,
            lines: 50,
            excludes: ['../scripts/repository.js']
        }
    }
},
```

With the `check` object, you can set your global threshold. All files together should have at least 50% coverage. This will succeed if one file has 100% coverage while another has 0%. We are excluding `repository.js`, because including it would make our tests fail, as it sets our branch coverage to 0%.

Additionally, you can set thresholds on a per file basis. For example, we want at least 50% of our code tested, but at least 10% of each file should be tested as well. If we had a file with 100% coverage and a file with 0% coverage, our tests would now fail: even if the global threshold of 50% is met, the 10% per file minimum is not. You can even set thresholds for specific files. For example, our `shopping-cart.js` file is fully tested and we want to keep it that way:

```
check: {
    global: {
    statements: 50,
    branches: 50,
    functions: 50,
    lines: 50,
    excludes: ['../scripts/repository.js']
},
    each: {
        lines: 10,
        excludes: [],
        overrides: {
            '../scripts/shopping-cart.js': {
                statements: 100
            }
        }
    }
}
```

Ultimately, we want to be able to publish these coverage reports. The HTML report is awesome for people to read, but build systems, such as Jenkins, will have a hard time parsing it. Jenkins, specifically, uses a coverage report in the so-called Cobertura format (which is really just a specific XML file). What is so awesome about this coverage plugin is that the Cobertura report format is built-in. We can simply add it to our reporters:

```
reporters: [
    { type : 'html', subdir: 'html' },
    { type : 'cobertura', subdir: 'cobertura' }
],
```

It really is that simple. Other supported formats are `lcov` (Linux COVerage: also includes HTML), `lcov-only`, `text`, `text-summary`, `teamcity`, `json`, `json-summary`, `in-memory`, and `none`.

You can find this and more on the karma-coverage GitHub repository (`https://github.com/karma-runner/karma-coverage`) in the `docs` folder. It is really well documented, so I suggest you check it out.

By the way, since the coverage reports are generated every time you run your tests, you probably do not want to include them in your Git repository. Be sure to add a line in your `.gitignore` file and ignore the entire `coverage` folder:

```
**/coverage/**
```

A word of caution: code coverage tells you how much of your code is executed by tests. It does not tell you whether your tests are of high quality. In theory, you could have a code coverage of 100% that does not test anything! For example, I once worked on a web application that was thoroughly tested, or so I thought. Upon closer inspection of the code, I learned that an important part of the software could not be mocked and always returned null during tests. The result was that every test threw a null reference exception. The tests all succeeded, because all they did was test whether a null reference exception was thrown... I died a little inside that day. Even if your tests make sense, a single function should often have more than one test to test different scenarios and edge cases. Code coverage does not exceed 100%, but well-tested code should have at least 400%. Still, if your tests make sense, code coverage is a good indication of how well your code is tested.

JUnit reporter

A small but very useful plugin is `karma-junit-reporter`. When we are going to test our code using Jenkins, we want to know which tests failed and why. Our current `progress` reporter (which writes the results to the console) is not going to cut it. Jenkins makes use of the JUnit style XML to publish test results (not to be confused with coverage results). We can simply install the plugin and then add it to our reporters:

```
npm install karma-junit-reporter --save-dev
```

And in our configuration file, we can add it to `reporters`:

```
reporters: ['progress', 'junit', 'coverage'],
```

If you run your tests now, you should get a report for each browser and OS, for example, `TESTS-IE_11.0.0_(Windows_10_0.0.0).xml`. Of course, the JUnit reporter can be configured as well; simply add the following configuration somewhere in your Karma config file:

```
junitReporter: {
    outputDir: 'junit',
    suite: 'Web Shop',
    useBrowserName: true
},
```

Your JUnit reports are now saved in the subdirectory `junit` and somewhere in the file, it will say `package="Web Shop"`.

Again, the documentation is pretty spot on, so you should check it out (`https://github.com/karma-runner/karma-junit-reporter`).

Like the coverage reports, you do not want this report in Git. We can simply regenerate the report any time we want by running our tests. Add the following line to your `.gitignore` file:

```
**/junit/**
```

Running Mocha and Chai with Karma

As I said earlier, Karma is an abstraction, which makes it possible to run different tests from different test frameworks. While I do not want to dwell on this for too long, learning a single test framework is enough after all, I do wish to quickly show you how this is done.

So, let's install Mocha (`https://mochajs.org/`) and the popular Chai (`http://chaijs.com/`) assertion library:

```
npm install mocha --save-dev
npm install chai --save-dev
```

Now, create a file called `mocha-tests.js` inside your `test` folder. We are going to test `repository.search` in `mocha-tests.js`:

```
describe('web app tests', function() {
    describe('repository', function () {
        it('should search products with "fantas"', function() {
            var products = repository.search('fantas');
            products.should.have.lengthOf(3);
            // Alternatively, Chai supports the following syntax:
            //chai.expect(products).to.have.lengthOf(3);
```

```
        //chai.assert.lengthOf(products, 3);
    });
  });
});
```

Like Jasmine, Mocha can be set up to run on your browser. However, since we are focusing on Karma and not on Mocha, we are only going to run Mocha in Karma. You can read how to set up your Mocha for your browser on the Mocha home page. Now that we have Mocha and Chai, we can install the Karma plugins:

```
npm install karma-mocha --save-dev
npm install karma-chai --save-dev
```

The Karma configuration is so simple, I am not sure if I even need to show you:

```
frameworks: ['jasmine', 'mocha', 'chai'],
files: [
    'mocha-tests.js',
    '../node_modules/angular/angular.js',
    '../node_modules/angular-mocks/angular-mocks.js',
    'spec/*.js',
    '../scripts/*.js'
],
```

I have added mocha and chai to the frameworks and mocha-tests.js to the files. That is all you need to do and Karma will now also run your Mocha tests. You can verify by checking your code coverage report. You will see that repository.search is now tested.

You can download other frameworks, such as QUnit, and pretty much configure it like we have configured Jasmine and Mocha. Basically, if you have some test framework you want to use with Karma, simply Google for karma your-test-framework and you will probably find a plugin you can use. As this example also shows, you can use multiple frameworks side by side. That may come in handy when you decide to switch frameworks (maybe your current framework is not actively supported anymore) or when another framework can test some part of your code better than your current framework.

End-To-End testing with Selenium

The next thing we are going to do is **End-To-End** (**E2E**) testing using our browser-our actual browser, as if it was operated by a human, but fully automated. The popular web UI test framework Selenium (`http://www.seleniumhq.org/`) will do this for you. As you can imagine, this is no easy task. Selenium needs to interface with different browsers, different languages, and different frameworks and it is all set up so future browsers, languages, and frameworks can be implemented. As such, it can be a bit of a pain to set up. There are a few moving parts you need to install, either on your computer or in your project, and to make things more complicated, those parts have different versions with different names. Don't panic though: throughout the remainder of this chapter, all will be revealed.

Selenium has its own language, Selenese, in which you can write tests directly using the Selenium IDE, an add-on for Firefox. We, however, are not going to do that. You may download the IDE (`http://www.seleniumhq.org/projects/ide/`) and play around with it, but our focus will be on writing and automating Selenium tests in JavaScript. Selenium currently has client APIs for Java, C#, Ruby, Python, and JavaScipt. The client APIs communicate with the Selenium WebDriver, the central component in Selenium. The WebDriver can communicate with browsers directly. You may come across Selenium Remote Control, or Selenium RC, which is a deprecated technology that is replaced by Selenium WebDriver.

Let's start with the most basic Selenium example that is fairly easy to reproduce. First, we must install the Selenium WebDriver API for JavaScript. Of course, we can do this using npm:

```
npm install selenium-webdriver --save-dev
```

Next, we can write a file that will do some automated work for us. Let's keep it simple and do a Google search. Put your file in the `test` folder and name it `selenium-tests.js`. Put the following code inside it:

```
var webdriver = require('selenium-webdriver');
var by = webdriver.By;
var until = webdriver.until;

var driver = new webdriver.Builder()
    .forBrowser('firefox')
    .build();

driver.get('http://www.google.com/ncr');
driver.findElement(by.name('q')).sendKeys('selenium');
```

```
driver.findElement(by.name('btnG')).click();
driver.wait(until.titleIs('selenium - Google Search'), 5000);
driver.quit();
```

Here is where we use `require` ourselves. In this case, `require` checks the `node_modules` folder for a folder called `selenium-webdriver`. When it finds that folder, it will look for `index.js` by default. The `index.js` file should have `module.exports`, like our `karma.conf.js` file, or just `exports`, an object which is loaded by `require`. Other than that, the test reads as if you were reading regular English, so I suppose I do not have to explain what this does. I will get back to the syntax and API in a bit though. The `google.com/ncr`, link does not redirect to your own country page (**ncr** means **no country redirect**), so the title is fairly certain to be `selenium - Google Search`. Now, go to your console and run the file using Node.js. We have not used Node.js before, but we have it installed. Running a file in Node.js is as easy as `node yourfile.js`:

```
cd test
node selenium-tests.js
Error: The geckodriver.exe executable could not be found on the current
PATH. Please download the latest version from
https://github.com/mozilla/geckodriver/releases/WebDriver and ensure it can
be found on your PATH.
```

Unfortunately, we get an error message saying that we are missing the geckodriver. The geckodriver is the driver that runs Firefox. Selenium WebDriver needs a web driver to communicate with your browser. Firefox, Chrome, IE, Edge, and Safari all have their own drivers. You can find links to the pages with the driver downloads on the `selenium-webdriver` npm page, `https://www.npmjs.com/package/selenium-webdriver`. For your convenience, I have also included the web drivers in the `WebDrivers` folder in the root folder of the `ci-book` Git repository. Put the web drivers somewhere on your computer, for example, `C:\WebDrivers`, and add a reference to that folder in your PATH variable, so Selenium knows where it can find the drivers. On Windows, you can do this by going to **Control Panel**, then **System and Security**, if you have the **View by Category** option on, and then **System**. In **System**, go to **Advanced System Settings** and, from there, go to **Environment Variables...** You can now edit the PATH variable in your user or system variables. Add a new path and set it to `C:\WebDrivers` or wherever you put your drivers. You now have to restart your console and try `node selenium-tests.js` again.

You will now see your browser starting, searching for `selenium`, and then closing. One problem you will find with browser testing is that you will have to wait for pages to load and you will never know how long things are going to take. In the line `driver.wait(until.titleIs('selenium - Google Search'), 5000);`, we allow Google to take up to 5,000 milliseconds (5 seconds) to change the title. It usually loads the new page in a second, sometimes 2, so 5 seconds is quite generous (but 1 second is sometimes too slow). Now, watch what happens when you change the title in your script to something else, such as `something else`. After 5 seconds, you get an error:

```
TimeoutError: Waiting for title to be "something else"
Wait timed out after 5001ms
```

Apparently, our test failed. Selenium now leaves the browser open (which makes sense, since our code never hits `driver.quit();`). There are a few things to take into account when working with Selenium in JavaScript, but I will come back to that in a bit.

First, let's run our example on different browsers. To run the example on Chrome, simply get the Chrome web driver and change `'firefox'` to `'chrome'` in the `selenium-tests.js` file. IE, of course, is being difficult as always. In order to run IE, you need to set **Protected Mode** on or off for all zones. Go to **IE settings** and then the **Security** tab. There are the zones **Internet**, **Local Intranet**, **Trusted sites**, and **Restricted sites**. On each zone, there is a checkbox **Enable Protected Mode (requires restarting Internet Explorer)**. Either enable or disable them all (I recommend enabling them all) and close IE. Also, there seems to be a bug (or weird intended behavior?) with the x64 IE driver, so be sure to use the Win32 (x86) one. In your script, you can use `forBrowser('ie');`. To run Edge, you need to get the correct Edge web driver and then use `'MicrosoftEdge'` in `forBrowser`.

We are now able to run our little example on all major browsers (except Safari). The next step is to create actual tests. Here is where the trouble starts. Karma starts up a browser and runs your tests there. However, Selenium needs to be executed in Node.js. This should be possible, since Karma itself is also executed in Node.js. However, Karma is not the recommended tool for the job. The Angular.js team built Protractor (http://www.protractortest.org) specifically for E2E tests using Selenium.

Running Selenium tests with Protractor

So yes, we need yet another tool. It makes sense to use something else for E2E tests though. E2E tests are not unit tests. While unit tests must be executed fast to give you instant results on every change you make, E2E tests are usually a lot slower and more intrusive (starting browsers and all). So, we will be using Protractor in addition to Karma. The good news is that we can automate both, so we do not actually have to remember to run both to make a build, but we will get to that in the next chapter.

Protractor makes use of Selenium Server, also called Selenium Grid. You can download the server yourself (`http://www.seleniumhq.org/download/`), but Protractor can actually do this for us. Selenium Server makes it possible to call browsers on remote machines. It also has the added advantage that your Selenium tests can be configured in a central place, allowing you to run tests simultaneously and on different browsers. To install Protractor, we can use npm. This will also install a utility tool, `webdriver-manager`:

```
npm install protractor --save-dev
npm install protractor -g
webdriver-manager update
webdriver-manager start
[...]
21:13:08.723 INFO - Selenium Server is up and running
```

The `webdriver-manager update` command downloads Selenium Server along with the Firefox and Chrome web drivers using curl. You can read exactly what it does in your command window. The `webdriver-manager start` command actually starts the server. Of course, as soon as you terminate the batch or close this console window, your server is closed as well. So, for the remainder of the chapter, we will need a second console window and let this one be.

We can now change our `selenium-tests.js` script, so it contains an actual Jasmine test. Since Protractor is developed by the Angular.js team and the recommended testing framework for Angular.js is Jasmine, Protractor uses Jasmine by default. Protractor also has its own API, so our test is going to look a little different from the one we had before:

```
describe('Selenium tests', function () {
    var EC = protractor.ExpectedConditions;

    it('should google "selenium"', function (done) {
        browser.ignoreSynchronization = true;
        browser.get('http://www.google.com/ncr');
        element(by.name('q')).sendKeys('selenium');
        element(by.name('btnG')).click().then(function () {
            browser.wait(EC.titleIs('selenium - Google Search', 2500));
            expect(browser.getTitle()).toBe('selenium - Google Search');
```

```
                done();
          });
      });
  });
```

You should immediately notice a few things. First of all, you do not need to initialize the web driver yourself. We also do not specify a browser to use. Then, there is that weird `browser.ignoreSynchronization = true;` line. Protractor was built for Angular.js and, by default, it waits for a page to load Angular.js. Since `google.com`, the website we are requesting, does not use Angular.js, Protractor keeps waiting forever and eventually times out. By setting `ignoreSynchronization` to `true`, we tell Protractor not to wait for Angular.js. Last, the `click` function now takes a callback as argument. Because JavaScript executes your browser commands asynchronously, we either need to wait for a certain condition, like in the previous example with `driver.wait(until...)` (replaced with `EC.titleIs(...)`), or make use of callbacks or both, like in this example. Changing your code to click and then checking the title will probably be a few seconds too slow and make a difference between a failing and a passing test:

```
element(by.name('btnG')).click();
// This may fail as the click may not yet be performed.
expect(browser.getTitle()).toBe('selenium - Google Search');
```

Simply waiting for the title to change would have sufficed in this example. However, I wanted to show you a little trick when working with callbacks. Since the button click is performed asynchronously, the code simply continues while the browser is working. As such, your unit test would simply exit and the button click would not have any effect on your test as such. The `click` function returns `promise`, which has the `then` function. The `then` function takes a callback function that will be executed once the button is clicked. But we should also stop our test from exiting (and failing because no expect or assert was done). We can do this by passing the `done` argument to our `it` function and calling `done` whenever our test is really finished (in whatever asynchronous code):

```
it('should google "selenium"', function (done) {
    // Some code here.
    somethingAsync().then(function () {
        // More code here.
        done();
    });
    // Will not exit until done is called.
});
```

Here is the thing though: all of Protractor's functions return `promise`, which can be followed up by `then`. For the simpler scenarios, `expect` will resolve `promise` for us. So, `getTitle()` returns a promise and not a string, but `toBe('title')` will still evaluate to true or false.

There is one more thing we need to do before we can run our test. In your `test` folder, create a new file and name it `protractor.conf.js`. Put the following configuration in that file:

```
exports.config = {
    framework: 'jasmine',
    seleniumAddress: 'http://localhost:4444/wd/hub',
    specs: ['selenium-tests.js']
};
```

We can now finally run our test! Make sure you have Selenium Server running and then use the `protractor your-config-file.js` command:

```
cd test
protractor protractor.conf.js
```

You will now, again, see a browser opening and doing what you scripted in your test. Additionally, you can see the console window that is running your server logging exactly what it does. The command window running Protractor will give you your test results:

The default browser for Protractor is Chrome, but you can easily configure another browser in your Protractor configuration file. Simply add a `capabilities` object:

```
capabilities: {
    browserName: 'internet explorer'
},
```

You can also set up multiple browsers using the `multiCapabilities` object. You can set both `capabilities` and `multiCapabilities`, but one will overwrite the other:

```
multiCapabilities: [{
    browserName: 'chrome'
}, {
    browserName: 'MicrosoftEdge'
}],
```

Unfortunately, there is something strange going on with Firefox support at the moment (months before you are reading this). Selenium Server throws an error when trying to run it. There is a workaround, which is running with a direct connection, bypassing Selenium Server. Unfortunately, this option is only supported for Chrome and Firefox. If you use `directConnect`, you should remove `seleniumAddress`:

```
//seleniumAddress: 'http://localhost:4444/wd/hub',
multiCapabilities: [{
    browserName: 'chrome'
}, {
    browserName: 'firefox'
}],
directConnect: true,
```

Speaking of the `seleniumAddress` setting, I find it annoying that I have to start a Selenium server every time I want to run my tests. Running a separate server is great when something goes wrong and you need additional logging but, hopefully, you do not need that all that often. Protractor can run our own server, but you need a JAR file containing the server. You can download the JAR server file on the Selenium website (http://www.seleniumhq.org/download/). Now, you can simply put it anywhere on your computer and reference it in your configuration file. For this, you need the `seleniumServerJar` and the `seleniumServerPort` setting. Be sure to remove `seleniumAddress`:

```
seleniumServerJar: 'selenium-server-standalone-3.1.0.jar',
seleniumServerPort: 4444,
//seleniumAddress: 'http://localhost:4444/wd/hub',
```

In that example, I have put the Selenium server JAR file in the same folder as my tests, but we can place it anywhere, for example, on the desktop:

```
seleniumServerJar: 'C:\\Users\\sander.rossel\\Desktop\\selenium-server-
standalone-3.1.0.jar',
```

You can now simply start up Protractor and it will take care of the server for you.

Testing our website

Time to add some tests for our web shop. This also gives us the chance to see a bit more from the Protractor API. I can not explain it all in this chapter, but we will see a couple of functions on elements and lists of elements. Just keep in mind that every function in Protractor returns a `promise` and that Jasmine will resolve it for us automatically.

Personally, I am not a fan of HTML and CSS. It just does not work, so when it does, I would like to test that things stay as they are. How about we add a test that checks whether the titles of the *Other people bought...* products on our `homepage` are properly cut off to fit the thumbnails? It immediately becomes clear why I do not like HTML and CSS. There is no way to check this. Your text can overflow while the width of your `h3` element stays the same. There is also no way to get the actual width of your text, at least not an easy one. It would help if you could get the actual text, which would be *The Good, The Bad and The...*, but you can only get the complete text (with *Ugly* at the end). So, the only thing we can test is actually checking whether the CSS we defined is applied. Not a bad test, mind you, because CSS is easily overwritten or removed, especially when using some global CSS, if you or your coworkers are not careful:

```
describe('homepage', function () {
    it('should cut off long titles', function () {
        browser.get('file:///C:/Users/sander.rossel/Desktop/ci-
book/Chapter%205/Code/index.html');
        browser.wait(EC.presenceOf($('h3'), 1000));

        var elems = element.all(by.css('h3'));
        expect(elems.count()).toBe(3);

        var elem = elems.get(0);
        expect(elem.getCssValue('overflow')).toBe('hidden');
        expect(elem.getCssValue('text-overflow')).toBe('ellipsis');
        expect(elem.getCssValue('white-space')).toBe('nowrap');
    });
});
```

The first thing we do, of course, is browse to our website, which, in this case, is just a file on our local system. After that, we wait until the page is actually loaded and displays the h3 elements. Using `element.all(by.css('h3'))`, we can get all the elements that meet the CSS selector's criteria. We expect to get three h3 elements, since we show three *Other people bought...* products. Once we know we have three elements, we can check the CSS properties for either one of them. We could check all of them, but checking one of them will probably be enough.

Once you try to run this test, you will find that your browser navigates to `data:text/html,<html></html>`, after which your test fails. Protractor uses `data:text/html,<html></html>` as a reset URL, which is used when Protractor loads a page. Because we cannot navigate from the data URI scheme to the file protocol, we need to make this explicit. We can do this by adding the `onPrepare` function in our navigation and changing `resetUrl`:

```
onPrepare: function() {
    browser.resetUrl = 'file://';
},
```

When we run our tests now, we still get an error! Protractor waits for Angular.js to load, but cannot do this once we switch to the file protocol. We can do two things: either add `browser.ignoreSynchronization = true;` to our test (either in the test itself or using Jasmine's `beforeEach` function) or we can add it in the config, which sounds like a good plan because all our tests will either need it or not. Since `onPrepare` is called before any tests are run, but after Jasmine was loaded, we can simply add `ignoreSynchronization` in `onPrepare`:

```
onPrepare: function() {
    browser.resetUrl = 'file://';
    browser.ignoreSynchronization = true;
},
```

We could have added both to our test or in the `beforeEach,`, but having these sort of settings in the config file makes sense, as they are now easily turned on or off for all your tests at once. Internet Explorer will stop working now, but will start working again after we add a backend.

Up until this point, our Google test and our new test ran fine. However, we are now going to set a property in the config that will make our Google test fail, so be sure to remove it. Having that long path to your page is a bit of a pain. What is even more troublesome is that, later, we are going to run our web shop using an actual server and we want to be able to switch from one URL to another URL without having to change all our tests. The config file supports a `baseUrl` property that we can use. In this case, `baseUrl` is simply the path to our `index.html` file:

```
baseUrl: 'file://C:/Users/sander.rossel/Desktop/ci-book/Chapter 5/Code/',
```

Switching from file to HTTP will probably still require us to change all our tests, because we are going to add some routing on the server, but after that, we can easily change `baseUrl` from localhost to our test server. Of course, this also means that your test is now going to get a relative page, so we need to change the `browser.get();` line:

```
browser.get('index.html');
```

Let's add a few more tests to our homepage. The next test navigates to a product by clicking the *Other people bought...* product title:

```
it('should navigate to the clicked product', function () {
    browser.get('index.html');
    browser.wait(EC.presenceOf($('[ng-controller=homeController]'), 1000));

    var product = element.all(by.css('h3')).get(1);
    product.click();
    browser.wait(EC.presenceOf($('[ng-controller=productController]'),
2500));
    var title = element(by.css('h2'));
    expect(title.getText()).toBe('The Good, The Bad and The Ugly');
});
```

Nothing we have not seen already. Instead of waiting for the h3 to become visible we are waiting for `homeController` to become visible, which is a little safer, as it really is unique for the home page. The same goes for the `productController`:

And let's test the search functionality:

```
it('should search for all products containing "fanta"', function () {
    browser.get('index.html');
    browser.wait(EC.presenceOf($('[ng-controller=homeController]'), 1000));

    var input = element(by.css('[ng-model=query]'));
    input.sendKeys('fanta');
    var searchBtn = element.all(by.css('a.btn.btn-default')).get(0);
    searchBtn.click();
```

```
    browser.wait(EC.presenceOf($('[ng-controller=searchController]'),
2500)));
        var results = element.all(by.css('.thumbnail'));
        expect(results.count()).toBe(3);
});
```

Again, it is all pretty straightforward. As you can see, we are relying on the first
`a.btn.btn-default` element to be the element we need in order to find products
containing `fanta`. If someone added another anchor/button like that to the page, our test
might fail while nothing really broke. We could add a class or ID to the element, which
would make everything a little safer:

```
<a id="search-btn" href="views\search.html?q={{query}}" class="btn btn-
default">
    <span class="glyphicon glyphicon-search"></span>
</a>
```

The test would now select for `search-btn` of which only one exists on the page:

```
var searchBtn = element(by.css('#search-btn'));
```

The test expects three results to be found. We could be a little more specific. We could test
that one or more of the titles really are the titles we would expect, for example. We can
search for elements within elements by using the `element` function on another element:

```
var results = element.all(by.css('.thumbnail'));
expect(results.count()).toBe(3);

var firstElem = results.get(0);
var firstCaption = firstElem.element(by.css('h3')).getText();
expect(firstCaption).toBe('Final Fantasy XV');
```

Even better, we should loop through the results and check that each of the results has
`fanta` in the title. This is a little tricky, because we need to extract all values from all
promises and then do our assertions before returning. Protractor has a couple of array-like
functions, such as `map`, `filter`, and `each`. In this case, we will use `map`, then transform our
elements to a bunch of `getText()`, which will be resolved to strings in the `then` function.
We can then simply loop through our regular array of strings and expect each of them to
contain `fanta`:

```
var results = element.all(by.css('.thumbnail'));
expect(results.count()).toBeLessThan(20);

results.map(function (elem) {
    return elem.element(by.css('h3')).getText();
}).then(function (captions) {
```

```
        captions.forEach(function (caption) {
            expect(caption.toLowerCase().indexOf('fanta')).toBeGreaterThan(-1);
        });
        done();
    });
```

I have changed the count assertion to be less than 20. If we check all our elements individually, it does not matter how many results we get back, but let's pretend we have a page size of 20. Things get a little tricky with all these promises, especially since your test will not fail if no assertions were made. I recommend making your tests fail at least once, so you know it is actually executing your `expect()` functions. Also, please be aware that this function will fail 20 times if something broke the search functionality. Alternatively, you can simply keep track of whether every caption so far has `fanta` in it and then expect `hasFanta` to be `true`:

```
var hasFanta = true;
results.map(function (elem) {
    return elem.element(by.css('h3')).getText();
}).then(function (captions) {
    captions.forEach(function (caption) {
        hasFanta = hasFanta && caption.toLowerCase().indexOf('bla') > -1;
    });
    expect(hasFanta).toBeTruthy();
    done();
});
```

We can simplify this further using `reduce`, which allows you to create a value, or accumulator, based on all the elements on the list:

```
var allHaveFanta = results.reduce(function (acc, elem) {
    return elem.element(by.css('h3')).getText().then(function (caption) {
        return acc && caption.toLowerCase().indexOf('fanta') > -1;
    });
}, true);

expect(allHaveFanta).toBeTruthy();
```

The callback we pass to `reduce` returns `promise` (returned by `then`), which resolves to a boolean specifying whether `acc` (the accumulator) is true and the current caption contains `fanta`. If any caption does not contain `fanta`, the accumulator will be set to false and every subsequent call will also return false. The second parameter to `reduce` is the initial value of `acc`. Using this method, we can even get rid of the `done()` call!

You may think this test covers everything, but it only tests that the results we get back meet our search criteria; it does not check whether we actually get all the results from the server. Perhaps, we are actually receiving page 2, instead of page 1. That is not something we can test right now though, so all in all, this test is pretty solid.

 You may be confused about functions such as `map`, `reduce`, or `getText`. You may also be wondering what other functions you can use in Protractor. Luckily, the Protractor API is properly documented: `http://www.protractortest.org/#/api`.

As a last test, before we continue, I want to test whether a click on the **delete** button in the shopping cart really deletes the appropriate, and indeed any, item from the cart:

```
it('should remove an item from the shopping cart', function (done) {
    browser.get('views\\shopping-cart.html');
    browser.wait(EC.presenceOf($('[ng-controller=shoppingCartController]'),
1000));

    var items = element.all(by.css('.thumbnail'));
    var firstItem = items.get(0);
    var firstCaption = firstItem.element(by.css('h3')).getText();
    var deleteBtn = firstItem.element(by.css('button'));
    items.count().then(function (count) {
        deleteBtn.click().then(function () {
            var newItems = element.all(by.css('.thumbnail'));
            var newFirstCaption =
newItems.get(0).element(by.css('h3')).getText();
            expect(firstCaption).not.toBe(newFirstCaption);
            expect(newItems.count()).toBe(count - 1);
            done();
        });
    });
});
```

So, in this example, we get the items in the cart and then we get the caption of the first item and the delete button of the first item. After that, we need the current total count of items in the cart. We want the count as a number, and not as a promise, because we want to check that clicking the delete button removes exactly one item. After that, we click the delete button. Once the button is clicked, we get the items again. Now it is just a matter of checking whether the caption of the first item has changed, that is, the item we deleted, and whether the count of all the items is exactly one less than before.

We could write a dozen more tests, but at this point, that is really not all that exciting. We will leave it at this for now.

Customizing reporters

Running your tests from the console gives you a pretty crappy overview of what tests failed and succeeded. It works, but I prefer a less verbose overview. Later, we will also want to publish our test results in a different format, such as JUnit. Luckily, this is not very hard. First, we will need to install the `jasmine-reports` package:

```
npm install jasmine-reporters --save-dev
```

Now, we need to add a reporter to Jasmine in the Protractor configuration. Let's start with JUnit. We can use the `onPrepare` function for this task:

```
onPrepare: function() {
    var jasmineReporters = require('jasmine-reporters');
    var junitReporter = new jasmineReporters.JUnitXmlReporter({
        savePath: 'selenium-junit/',
        consolidateAll: false
    });
    jasmine.getEnv().addReporter(junitReporter);

    browser.resetUrl = 'file://';
    browser.ignoreSynchronization = true;
},
```

You can now simply run your tests and Protractor will create a report. There is still a tiny problem with this setup though. When you test using multiple browsers, only one file is generated, which contains the results of only one test run. Of course, there is a solution to this problem. We can set the reporter per browser config using `browser.getProcessedConfig()`:

```
onPrepare: function() {
    browser.resetUrl = 'file://';
    browser.ignoreSynchronization = true;
    var jasmineReporters = require('jasmine-reporters');
    return browser.getProcessedConfig().then(function(config) {
        var browserName = config.capabilities.browserName;

        var junitReporter = new jasmineReporters.JUnitXmlReporter({
            savePath: 'selenium-junit/',
            consolidateAll: false,
            filePrefix: browserName + '-',
            modifySuiteName: function(generatedSuiteName, suite) {
                return browserName + ' - ' + generatedSuiteName;
            }
        });
        jasmine.getEnv().addReporter(junitReporter);
    });
```

```
},
```

Please note that I have moved `resetUrl` and `ignoreSynchronization` up so that we can return `promise` that sets the browser configuration. You need `modifySuitName` so you can keep your Chrome results apart from your Firefox results. When you run your tests again, using different browsers, you get files such as `chrome-Seleniumtests.xml` and `firefox-Seleniumtests.xml`.

Now, adding the Terminal reporter is a piece of cake:

```
jasmine.getEnv().addReporter(junitReporter);

jasmine.getEnv().addReporter(new jasmineReporters.TerminalReporter({
    verbosity: 3,
    color: true,
    showStack: true
}));
```

This looks a whole lot better:

As usual, we do not want to include our generated reports in Git. So, add the following line in the `.gitignore` file:

```
**/selenium-junit/**
```

Testing with Mocha

Protractor allows you to use a different testing framework. Jasmine is the supported default, but Mocha has limited default support as well. You can set the `framework` property in the config file to `jasmine`, `mocha`, or `custom`. When you set it to custom, you need to specify the relative path to the framework, for example, Cucumber, using the `frameworkPath` property.

Unfortunately, we cannot run multiple frameworks in the same test run like with Karma. Copy your config file, name it `protractor.mocha.conf.js`, and change the following properties:

```
onPrepare: function() {
    browser.resetUrl = 'file://';
    browser.ignoreSynchronization = true;
},
framework: 'mocha',
specs: ['selenium-mocha-tests.js'],
```

We also need to install Mocha globally for this to work:

npm install mocha -g

Now we need to create the `selenium-mocha-tests.js` file too. Because the only thing that really changes is the assertion framework (most of it is just Protractor), our tests can stay pretty much the same. Chai is a little more explicit in that it is handling asynchronous code:

```
describe('Selenium Mocha tests', function () {
    var EC = protractor.ExpectedConditions;

    var chai = require('chai');
    var chaiAsPromised = require('chai-as-promised');
    chai.use(chaiAsPromised);
    var expect = chai.expect;

    describe('homepage', function () {
        it('should cut off long titles', function () {
            browser.get('index.html');
            browser.wait(EC.presenceOf($('h3'), 1000));
```

```
        var elems = element.all(by.css('h3'));
        expect(elems.count()).to.eventually.equal(3);

        var elem = elems.get(0);
expect(elem.getCssValue('overflow')).to.eventually.equal('hidden');
        expect(elem.getCssValue('text-
overflow')).to.eventually.equal('ellipsis');
        expect(elem.getCssValue('white-
space')).to.eventually.equal('nowrap');
      });
    });
});
```

We are almost there. As you can see, we are using Chai as Promised (because it deals with promises, get it?) instead of just plain Chai. So, we need to install that first:

```
npm install chai-as-promised --save-dev
protractor test\protractor.mocha.conf.js
```

We can customize the behavior of Mocha, for example, to get another reporter, although the default reporter already looks pretty good. We simply add the mochaOpts node in the config file. You can read about the various reporters on the Mocha website, https://mochajs.org/#reporters:

```
mochaOpts: {
    reporter: "spec",
},
```

Mocha is pretty crazy, it even has a NYAN cat reporter (code "nyan"):

Selenium, Protractor, and the various testing frameworks have lots of other features and plugins that you can use to further test your code. For example, it is possible to use two browsers in a single test in case two browser windows need to interact with each other, think chat applications or, more general, socket technology. However, we have seen some basics and it is enough to understand how browser testing works and how it can contribute to better-tested code that leads to fewer bugs.

 Protractor is not your only choice when you want to work with Selenium. Other popular options include Nightwatch.js (`http://nightwatchjs.org/`), which has a built-in testing framework, so it just works out of the box; and WebDriverIO (`http://webdriver.io/`), which requires you to install an external testing framework. Like everything, both have their pros and cons, but both are worth checking out.

Headless browser testing

There is just one problem we have not tackled yet. First, it is pretty annoying that you need to have all those browser windows open to test your code. Second, our server does not even have a user interface, so how is it going to open any browser? I will get back to the server issue later: even if we had a graphical interface, we would still have problems with IE, Edge, and Safari, so we need to tackle all of that. However, I am going to tackle that first issue right here.

While it is not necessarily a problem that we have multiple browser windows running, they come with a trade-off. First, of course, they take up space on your screen. You have to work around them, make sure you do not accidentally close any of them, and you should also not get too distracted by all the flashy test runs. Another issue with browsers is that it takes time to render your HTML and apply the CSS. Enter headless browsers.

A headless browser is really just a browser that has no interface. It runs silently in the background and pretends it is an actual browser. While it is not a replacement for an actual browser, it is a good first line of defense. You can test your website using a headless browser locally and then test on other browsers on your CI server. Because a headless browser does not render any graphics, it can be a lot faster than regular browsers. Especially when you get more E2E tests, headless browsers can be twice as fast. As an added bonus, you do not see them on your desktop, so they cannot annoy you and you cannot close them by accident.

PhantomJS

A popular headless browser is PhantomJS (http://phantomjs.org/). Since it is pretty popular and easy to set up, I want to discuss it here, but I should mention upfront that it does not work well with Protractor. The Protractor team actually recommends that you do not use PhantomJS with Protractor. I concur, I never got it to work together either. However, it works fine for Karma, so let's set that up.

Installation of PhantomJS is easy, it is just a regular npm installation. Of course, you will also need to install the appropriate Karma launcher:

```
npm install phantomjs --save-dev
npm install karma-phantomjs-launcher --save-dev
```

You can now use PhantomJS as a browser in your Karma configuration:

```
browsers: ['PhantomJS'],
```

If you now start Karma, you will notice not a single browser is started, but your tests are still executed. You can change a test to make it fail and you will see that Karma updates almost instantly in the command window. You might notice that PhantomJS gives you a big red error when it starts. Do not worry about it; it is some PhantomJS thing, but will not prevent it from starting and executing your tests. It is annoying at worst.

In theory, PhantomJS should work like any other browser, but unfortunately, this is not quite the case in practice. As said, for Karma, everything works as expected, but when it comes to Selenium and Protractor, PhantomJS just does not work that well. It may work for you on your exact system configuration, but you will likely run into a lot of issues. For example, personally, I could never get it to work on a global PhantomJS installation. I can make Selenium do some work on a local PhantomJS installation, but it will loop indefinitely on trying to select an element. The funny thing is that the Jasmine configuration works differently than the Mocha configuration, but neither work.

Just in case the terrible trio Selenium, Protractor, and PhantomJS ever get their stuff together, this is how your configuration is supposed to look:

```
seleniumAddress: 'http://localhost:4444/wd/hub',
multiCapabilities: [{
    browserName: 'phantomjs',
    'phantomjs.binary.path': require('phantomjs').path
}]
//directConnect: true
```

As with most browsers, directConnect is not supported at all.

PhantomJS can do more than just test your JavaScript code. It is a full-fledged browser that you can control. However, for the purpose of CI, it is not very interesting beyond headless testing.

Unfortunately, there is no good headless alternative for Selenium and PhantomJS on Windows. You can run browsers in headless state on Linux using **X virtual framebuffer** (**Xvfb**), but I have not tried it before, so you are on your own there.

Summary

In this chapter, we have tested various parts of our web shop. With Jasmine and Karma, it is possible to create unit tests that run whenever you change something. Depending on the quality and coverage of your tests, errors can be found as soon as they are introduced. Going a step further, we can test our application as though it was tested by an actual human using Selenium and Protractor. In the next chapter, we are going to automate our build, including testing, linting, and minifying, using Gulp, a JavaScript task runner.

6
Automation with Gulp

In the previous chapters, we have set up Git, a sample application, and some tests. However, while Git, or source control in general, and tests are very important for successful CI, perhaps the most important part is automation. You can write hundreds of tests, but if a programmer forgets to run them (or knowingly refuses to do so), those tests become pretty useless. The same goes for other tasks, such as linting and minifying your code. Later, when you need to release your application to a live environment, the human factor is your number one concern; one wrong move and the entire application goes down! For this reason, it is important to automate all the things.

When it comes to automating your HTML, CSS, and JavaScript tasks, there are two popular contenders for the job: Grunt (`https://gruntjs.com/`) and Gulp (`http://gulpjs.com/`). Both are labelled as JavaScript task runners. Grunt has been around a little while longer and is widely used. However, it has some issues that Gulp is supposed to address. Unfortunately, Gulp also introduces some new issues that Grunt does not have. Overall, the choice between Grunt or Gulp is pretty much a personal preference. However, in this chapter, we are going to work with Gulp.

Gulp basics

In abstract terms, a task runner takes some input, works with that, and produces an output. That output could then be used for further processing. For example, a JavaScript file could be the input, a minifying job could be the process (that is making your JavaScript unreadable, but very compact), and the minified JavaScript would be the output. Now, the minified JavaScript could be input to a new test process, which would have some report as its output. Gulp does exactly this. Gulp is a little different from other task runners in a way that it keeps intermediate results in memory instead of writing them to disk.

Installing Gulp is as easy as doing `npm install`. We also want the Gulp CLI for easy use:

```
npm install gulp --save-dev
npm install gulp-cli -g
```

The next thing we need is a so-called gulpfile. In the root of your project, Chapter06, in the book's GitHub repository, create a new file and name it `gulpfile.js`. Gulp simply starts a Node.js process, so we can do whatever Node.js can do in the gulpfile. We start by requiring Gulp and setting a default task:

```
var gulp = require('gulp');

gulp.task('default', function() {
    console.log("We're just running tasks...");
});
```

You can now run this from the command line by simply running the `gulp` command. Make sure your command line is in your project folder. You can, of course, also manually target your gulpfile:

```
gulp
[alternatively]
gulp --gulpfile path_to_your_gulpfile\gulpfile.js
```

The output should be **We're just running tasks...**. If it was, you know you did it right and Gulp is working.

The Gulp API

Gulp has four methods that you will be using a lot. Those are `src()`, `dest()`, `task()`, and `watch()`. Additionally, you will be using Node's `pipe()` method to pass the output from one function to the other. The following example takes the `css` folder and simply copies it to a new `css_copy` folder:

```
var gulp = require('gulp');

gulp.task('copycss', function () {
    gulp.src('css*.css')
        .pipe(gulp.dest('css_copy'));
});

gulp.task('default', ['copycss']);
```

As you can see, we defined two tasks, `'copycss'` and `'default'`. The `'default'` task is started by Gulp by, well, default. In this case, the default task simply starts the tasks defined in the array, so `copycss`. In the `copycss` task, we take all the CSS files from the `css` folder. As you can see, wildcards are allowed, which returns a Node.js `Stream` object, and pipes the contents of that `Stream` object to the `gulp.dest` function, which writes the contents to the `css_copy` folder. If you run this in Gulp, you will find your CSS files copied. You can also run the `copycss` task directly by passing the task name to the Gulp program on the command line:

```
C:\Windows\System32\cmd.exe                                    -    □    ✕

C:\Users\sander.rossel\Desktop\ci-book\Chapter 6\Code>gulp
[21:40:24] Using gulpfile ~\Desktop\ci-book\Chapter 6\Code\gulpfile.js
[21:40:24] Starting 'default'...
[21:40:24] Starting 'copycss'...
[21:40:24] Finished 'copycss' after 7.82 ms
[21:40:24] Finished 'default' after 12 ms

C:\Users\sander.rossel\Desktop\ci-book\Chapter 6\Code>gulp copycss
[21:40:29] Using gulpfile ~\Desktop\ci-book\Chapter 6\Code\gulpfile.js
[21:40:29] Starting 'copycss'...
[21:40:29] Finished 'copycss' after 7.06 ms

C:\Users\sander.rossel\Desktop\ci-book\Chapter 6\Code>
```

You can watch files and automatically run a series of tasks when a watched file changes. For example, let's say we want to copy all our CSS files if one changes:

```
gulp.watch('css*.css', ['copycss']);
```

We use `gulp.watch`, specify the files to watch, and then specify an array of tasks that need to be executed when a watched file changes. When you run the `gulp` command now, it will not end after it has executed the default task, but it will wait for changes. Try changing a CSS file and confirm that Gulp immediately copies it on save.

And there you have it, the entire Gulp API. Well alright, we may have missed some functions or overloads, but this is what it all boils down to.

Gulp plugins

You may have guessed it, but Gulp on its own does not do a lot (I am having deja vu here). You need plugins to get any serious work done. Luckily, Gulp has quite a lot of those. The initial idea was that any Gulp plugin takes some input and outputs the result as a Node.js `Stream` object. However, in practice, this is often not the case. Some plugins return nothing, some write their output to disk and return the original input, while some watch files and never return at all. That sounds bad, but it does not have to be. You have to take into account that a lot of plugins are simply wrappers around other programs that were not created to work with Gulp (or any task runner) at all. Just be sure you read the plugin's documentation and use it as it was intended. Luckily, Gulp can work around these issues quite well.

Minification

The first plugin we are going to look at is the minify plugin (`https://www.npmjs.com/package/gulp-minify`). This plugin lets you minify your JavaScript source. We can install it using `npm`:

```
npm install gulp-minify --save-dev
```

Now we can simply get some source, pipe it to the minify plugin, and output the results:

```
var gulp = require('gulp');
var minify = require('gulp-minify');

gulp.task('minify', function () {
    gulp.src('scripts/*.js')
        .pipe(minify({
            ext:{
                src:'.debug.js',
                min:'.js'
            }
        }))
        .pipe(gulp.dest('prod'));
});

gulp.task('default', ['minify']);
```

Now, when you run Gulp, you will see a `prod` folder containing all the scripts twice, a `.debug.js` and a `.js` variant. The `ext` object lets you specify the input and output suffixes. It is also possible to transform your filenames using regular expressions, but you can figure that out on your own. The minified `index.js` file should look something like the following:

```
angular.module("shopApp",[]).controller("homeController",function(o){o.topP
roducts=repository.getTopProducts(),o.searchTerm=""});
```

That is not very readable, but very compact. It is perfect for production systems where those precious bytes matter.

We can tweak the minify plugin even further. In our case, having the source files is not necessary at all, so we can exclude them:

```
.pipe(minify({
    ext:{
        min:'.js'
    },
    noSource: true
}))
```

Other than that, you can ignore files and folders, preserve comments (as they are removed by default), and keep the original variable names. Having all of those options in your gulpfile is fine, but sometimes it gets a little big for just one file. It is easy to move the options into a separate configuration file. Create a new file and name it `minify.conf.js`. Inside, it is just the options object you would like to pass to the minify plugin, but, like your Protractor script, exposed through the `module.exports` object:

```
module.exports = {
    ext:{
        min:'.js'
    },
    noSource: true
};
```

You can now simply require the configuration file in your gulpfile:

```
gulp.src('scripts/*.js')
    .pipe(minify(require('./minify.conf.js')))
    .pipe(gulp.dest('prod'));
```

That way, it becomes easy to share configurations between multiple gulpfiles or to change configurations, but not your gulpfile.

Cleaning your build

If you ran the previous sample, you might have noticed that when you ran it without the source files, your minified scripts were updated, but your copied source files were not removed from the `prod` folder. It is best practice to clean up any build folders before you create a new build. This assures that your build works from scratch and that you do not have any cached files. There used to be a plugin for this, but there is a Node.js module that already does what we need. As I said earlier, Gulp plugins should work on input and produce some output. Deleting files and folders does not fit that description though, so this is not really a Gulp plugin task anyway. So, we are going to use the Node.js `del` module (`https://www.npmjs.com/package/del`):

```
npm install del --save-dev
```

You can now just use `del` in a Gulp task:

```
var gulp = require('gulp');
var del = require('del');

gulp.task('clean', function () {
    del(['prod/*']);
});
```

Easy as that. Also, do not forget to configure your minify job, so it will run the new `clean` task before it does any minifying. You can pass in an array of task names that have to be executed (asynchronously) before the current task executes:

```
gulp.task('minify', ['clean'], function () {
```

If you now run `gulp` or `gulp minify`, you will find that it first deleted the `prod` folder and then put your newly minified scripts in it.

Checking file sizes

As you are deleting and minifying files, you may be interested in seeing exactly how many bytes you are saving. There is a plugin for that, called `gulp-size`:

```
npm install gulp-size --save-dev
```

Usage is simple:

```
var gulp = require('gulp');
var minify = require('gulp-minify');
var size = require('gulp-size');

gulp.task('minify', ['clean'], function () {
    gulp.src('scripts/*.js')
        .pipe(size())
        .pipe(minify(require('./minify.conf.js')))
        .pipe(size())
        .pipe(gulp.dest('prod'));
});
```

This outputs the size of all the files before and after minification to the command window. You can also pass in some additional options to `size`:

```
.pipe(size({
    title: 'Before minification',
    showFiles: true,
    showTotal: true,
    pretty: false
}))
```

The `title` can be used to keep a separate instance of size calls apart. The `showFiles` option indicates it should show the size of each file separately. Likewise, `showTotal` indicates whether the combined size should be displayed. Last, `pretty` indicates whether the file size should be displayed in a `pretty` format, such as KB, or in bytes.

Linting with JSHint

The next thing we want to do is lint our JavaScript files. Linting is the process of checking code for potential errors or *code smells*. You can try it manually at http://www.jslint.com/. Be careful though, that thing is merciless! I do not think I have ever had a perfect score on that thing. JSHint is based on the same linter, but a lot more forgiving. You can configure all kinds of rules to make it easier or harder on yourself. It also has a website, http://jshint.com/, where you can lint your JavaScript code on the fly. When you are going to use this linter, be sure to check out the documentation as well, as it has a lot of hints and use cases.

To use JSHint in Gulp, you need JSHint in addition to the Gulp plugin, `gulp-jshint`:

```
npm install jshint --save-dev
npm install gulp-jshint --save-dev
```

We can now create a separate lint task and have it execute before the minify task, but at the same time as the clean task:

```
var gulp = require('gulp');
var jshint = require('gulp-jshint');

gulp.task('lint', function () {
    gulp.src('scripts/*.js')
        .pipe(jshint())
        .pipe(jshint.reporter('default'));
});

gulp.task('minify', ['clean', 'lint'], function (done) {
```

As you can see, we lint the source and pipe the output to a reporter (that will print to the console). There is one caveat though. Gulp runs all of its tasks asynchronously, so the `jshint` function will execute during the `minify` function. If you run this now, your output will have file sizes and linting errors all mixed up. We can return the stream and Gulp will wait for it to finish though:

```
gulp.task('lint', function (done) {
    return gulp.src('scripts/*.js')
        .pipe(jshint())
        .pipe(jshint.reporter('default'));
});
```

You will now find the output to be sequential and pretty readable. Luckily, I have messed up our JavaScript pretty bad, so we actually have something to fix now:

As you can see, even when we have linting errors, Gulp still continues. Maybe we do not want that. After all, a missing semicolon can really mess up our minified code! So, we need to fail our build on linting errors. JSHint has some additional reporters and one of them is the fail reporter:

```
return gulp.src('scripts/*.js')
    .pipe(jshint())
    .pipe(jshint.reporter('default'))
    .pipe(jshint.reporter('fail'));
```

With this reporter, Gulp will throw an error, *Message: JSHint failed for: file1.js, file2.js*, and stop execution. After this, it does not make sense to clean our `prod` folder first, so we should change that so it lints first and cleans on success:

```
gulp.task('clean', ['lint'], function () {
[...]

gulp.task('minify', ['clean'], function () {
[...]
```

Beware with these kind of tools though, whether you are using JavaScript or any other language. Sometimes, your linter is just wrong. Take, for example, the warning in `repository.js`: Use `===` to compare with `null` (in the `search` function). The line `if (q == null)` will evaluate to `true` if q is `null` or `undefined`, changing `==` to `===` has the effect that the expression will now evaluate to `false` for `undefined`, possibly breaking your code! So whatever you do, keep using your head!

Luckily, you can tell JSHint to shut up and ignore various issues:

```
search: function (q) {
    /* jshint ignore: start */
    if (q == null) {
        return [];
    } else {
        return products.filter(function (p) {
            return p.name.toLowerCase().indexOf(q.toLowerCase()) >= 0;
        });
    }
    /* jshint ignore: end */
}
```

This will make the error go away, but now the entire function is not linted. We cannot put `ignore: end` on the following line, because then JSHint will think the line `if (q == null)` does not exist at all and it will start complaining about `else` without `if (...)` and `return [];` that makes other code unreachable. However, what we can do is specify exactly what issues to ignore:

```
/* jshint eqnull: true */
[...]
/* jshint ignore: end */
```

And if you do it like that, you can even end the ignore on the next line. So, if you put another `something == null` in that function, JSHint will pick it up again:

```
/* jshint eqnull: true */
if (q == null) {
    /* jshint ignore: end */
    return [];
} else {
[...]
```

If you need to globally ignore certain issues, you can pass in an options object to the `jshint` function:

```
.pipe(jshint({
    eqnull: true
}))
```

Alternatively, you can create a JSON file and define your settings there. Create a file called `jshint.conf.json` in your project folder and put the following JSON in it:

```
{
    "eqnull": true
}
```

Now you can pass the file into the `jshint` function:

```
.pipe(jshint('jshint.conf.json'))
```

There are quite a lot of options; you can find them in the documentation, `http://jshint.com/docs/options/`.

You can fix all of the JavaScript errors; JSHint gives you the exact cause and line of the error. In one instance, we have a comma instead of a semicolon at the end of the line. Also, instead of `getQueryParams()['id']`, we can simply use `getQueryParams().id`. The only issue that is a little bit harder to fix is the one in `utils.js`. The JSHint approved code should not do an assignment in a `while` loop:

```
tokens = regex.exec(qs);
while (tokens) {
    params[decodeURIComponent(tokens[1])] = decodeURIComponent(tokens[2]);
    tokens = regex.exec(qs);
}
```

Personally, I am a big fan of linting. Not only does it scan your code for possible errors, it also makes you think about your code in a way that you may learn from it. By the way, we have seen linting before in Chapter 2, *Setting Up a CI Environment*, but with SonarQube. We will get back to SonarQube later and use it with JavaScript and C#.

By the way, because we made linting a separate job, we can now also run it without having to clean or minify; simply run the `gulp lint` command (that is, `gulp [task name]`).

Next to the built-in default and fail reporters, you can get some external reporters as well. I can recommend the stylish reporter (`https://github.com/sindresorhus/jshint-stylish`). Install it using `npm install jshint-stylish --save-dev` and replace the default reporter with `'jshint-stylish'`.

Running your Karma tests

Next, we want to run our tests. Of course, we already created some tests and ran them with Karma. No worries, we are not going to undo all that. Instead, we are going to run Karma automatically using Gulp. That way, we lint, test, and minify our code with a single `gulp` command. There used to be a Karma plugin for Gulp, but now it is recommended to just run Karma directly from Gulp. This is actually surprisingly easy:

```
var gulp = require('gulp');
var karma = require('karma').Server;

gulp.task('test', function () {
    new karma({
        configFile: __dirname + '/test/karma.conf.js'
    }).start();
});
```

The `__dirname` variable is a global Node.js variable and contains the current file path. So, we set up a new Karma server from code, pass it our config file, and start it up. The config file still has PhantomJS set up and watches files as they change. This is a bit of a problem, as our Gulp file can watch files as well, but currently does not. So, Gulp never returns because of our tests, but whenever a file changes, it is only tested, but not linted or anything else. So, let's tweak the Karma configuration a bit so it plays nicely with Gulp. We are going to set `singleRun` to `true`. Now we can put any file watchers in our gulpfile. Luckily, we do not need to change our configuration file; we can override our configuration from Gulp directly:

```
new karma({
    configFile: __dirname + '/test/karma.conf.js',
    singleRun: true
}).start();
```

Also, we want to test our code after linting, but before minification:

```
gulp.task('lint', function () {
[...]

gulp.task('test', ['lint'], function () {
[...]

gulp.task('clean', ['test'], function () {
[...]

gulp.task('minify', ['clean'], function () {
[...]
```

I realize that the dependencies are becoming a bit confusing, but for now, this is the only way to guarantee tasks are run in series without using a plugin. Starting in Gulp 4, we get `gulp.series('firstTask', 'secondTask')`, but, unfortunately, it has not yet been officially released at the time of writing.

To make things worse, the test task is run asynchronously and we do not have any stream to return. Luckily, Gulp has one more trick up its sleeve. We can pass in a callback to signal when our task is completed, much like we did with Protractor and Jasmine in the previous chapter:

```
gulp.task('test', ['lint'], function (done) {
    new karma({
        configFile: __dirname + '/test/karma.conf.js',
        singleRun: true
    }, done).start();
});
```

When we run Gulp now, we can see that our code is linted and then tested. On success, our `prod` folder is cleaned and finally our source is minified, in that order.

There is just one more issue though. It is more of an annoyance than an actual issue, but I would like to fix it nonetheless. Whenever a test fails, Gulp gives us this huge error message with some Gulp stack trace that is of no importance to us. Other Gulp plugins, such as JSHint, have this covered, but Karma is not a Gulp plugin and does not even use streams. So, as you may have guessed, we will need another plugin, `gulp-util` (https://www.npmjs.com/package/gulp-util):

```
npm install gulp-util --save-dev
```

We now have to write our own function for the Karma server callback. We get an error number in the callback; when it is greater than 0, we can pass in an error to the `done` callback. Not any error though, this would give us the useless stack trace we got earlier. Instead, we will use the `PluginError` function from `gulp-utils` and pass it to the `done` callback:

```
var gutil = require('gulp-util');
[...]

new karma({
    configFile: __dirname + '/test/karma.conf.js',
    singleRun: true
}, function (err) {
    if (err > 0) {
        return done(new gutil.PluginError('karma', 'Karma tests
        failed.'));
    }
    return done();
}).start();
```

Gulp will give us a neat little error message instead of the garbage it throws at us now:

We can now clearly read that the Karma plugin failed and we can also still see exactly where it has gone wrong.

Next, we are going to run our Karma tests. Again. It is great that we can lint and test and minify, but we should definitely test our minified code as well. We want to test our original code on at least one browser. PhantomJS will do, so when something goes wrong, we immediately see the error, file, and line number. We also need this for our code coverage. However, our code gets pretty messed up during minification, so it cannot hurt to test again. At least most errors that may occur have been eliminated by our linting process; we do not have missing semicolons or anything like that. For testing the minified files, we can use a completely different Karma configuration. Of course, you can specify it completely in Gulp or overwrite some options from our original configuration file, but I like to keep a completely separate Karma configuration for my minified tests. So, create a new file in your test folder and name it `karma.min.conf.js`. Make sure you remove the coverage reporter and settings completely, we do not need them for these tests. Also, make sure you reference your minified scripts and test on as many browsers as you wish to support:

```
module.exports = function(config) {
    config.set({
        files: [
            [...]
            '../prod/*.js'
        ],
        reporters: ['progress', 'junit'],
        browsers: ['IE', 'IE9', 'Edge', 'Chrome', 'Firefox'],
        singleRun: true,
        [...]
    })
};
```

We can now create another task in Gulp, which is almost an exact copy of our regular test task:

```
gulp.task('test-min', ['minify'], function (done) {
    new karma({
        configFile: __dirname + '/test/karma.min.conf.js'
    }, function (err) {
        if (err > 0) {
            return done(new gutil.PluginError('karma', 'Karma tests
failed.'));
        }
        return done();
    }).start();
});
```

Do not forget to change your default task as well:

```
gulp.task('default', ['test-min']);
```

You will immediately see why testing your minified code is so important. Run Gulp and you will see that a couple of tests fail on all your browsers! They worked fine before minification, but they are totally broken after. Your console window will give you a lot of garbage (a complete stack trace for every failing test for every browser), but after some digging, we find the following error: *[$injector:unpr] Unknown provider: tProvider <- t <- shoppingCartController*. Angular.js uses dependency injection and does so based on variable names. The same variables that get completely messed up by our minification process. Luckily, the fix is simple. Angular.js lets you annotate your variables:

```
angular.module('shopApp', [])
    .controller('shoppingCartController', ['$scope', function ($scope) {
        [...]
    }]);
```

After this, fix your tests and they will run again. Remember that we only unit tested the shopping cart page though, so all your other pages will still break at this point.

You have another option though. We can change the settings of our minification process, so it will keep variable names intact. Not ideal, but better than code that does not run at all. In your `minify.conf.js` file, add the following property:

```
mangle: false,
```

You can now keep your shopping cart file as it was and the tests will still run as expected. I am all for mangling our variable names (to save some extra bits), so I am going to annotate our Angular.js variables in every file. You can do whatever suits you best though.

> Speaking of tests and linting, you can lint your test files to make sure your tests are up to par. You do not want a test to succeed (or fail) because you used == instead of ===. It might make a difference, for example, when we expect `1.23`, but we get `"1.23"` (notice the double quotes), like in the shopping cart tests. Of course, using Jasmine (or Chai) assertions such as `toBe` and `toEqual` minimizes the risks, but you may still want to lint your tests anyway. Minifying your tests is rather useless though.

Getting our site production ready

Now that we have minified and tested our JavaScript and got some work done using Gulp, we are going to do a fast forward and minify our HTML and CSS and bundle our scripts and replace the ones in our HTML files with the minified ones.

Minifying HTML

First, let's start with minifying our HTML. There are various plugins you can use, but we will use HTML Minifier (`https://www.npmjs.com/package/html-minifier`). We will need the Gulp plugin, which will also install HTML Minifier (`https://github.com/jonschlinkert/gulp-htmlmin`):

```
npm install gulp-htmlmin --save-dev
```

The usage is quite simple:

```
var htmlmin = require('gulp-htmlmin');

gulp.task('minify-html', function() {
    return gulp.src(['index.html', 'views/*.html'])
        .pipe(htmlmin({
            collapseWhitespace: true
        }))
        .pipe(gulp.dest('prod'));
});
```

The possible options can be found in the HTML Minifier documentation. Beware some options: they may break your page. For example, some libraries, such as `Knockout.js`, can depend on comments, but HTML Minifier has an option to remove comments. Again, (automated) testing may help you find such issues. Our folder structure is messed up now: we have `index.html` together with all the other HTML files and JavaScript files. This is only a problem now, since we are using the file protocol and will depend upon relative path files. It may be a good idea to output the views and scripts to their own folders though. And since we are now minifying multiple resources, we can rename our `'minify'` task to something like `'minify-js'`:

```
gulp.task('minify-js', ['clean'], function () {
    [...]
        .pipe(gulp.dest('prod/scripts'));
});

gulp.task('minify-html', function() {
    [...]
```

```
        .pipe(gulp.dest('prod/views'));
});
```

We will worry about the dependencies later. First, let's just make sure we have all the tasks we want to run. You can run a single task using the `gulp [task-name]` command, or in this case, `gulp minify-html`.

The result should look something like the following:

```
<!DOCTYPE html><html><head><meta charset="UTF-8"><title>CI Web
Shop</title><link...
```

All your HTML is now on a single line, attributes with default values are removed, comments may have been removed depending on your options, and more optimizations have been applied.

Minifying CSS

Next, we are going to give our CSS the same kind of treatment. I think you pretty much get the point by now, so I will be short about this. First, install the `gulp-clean-css` package (`https://github.com/scniro/gulp-clean-css`):

npm install gulp-clean-css --save-dev

The Gulp clean CSS plugin makes use of clean CSS, so for any options, check their documentation, `https://github.com/jakubpawlowicz/clean-css`. There are a lot of options. I will not go over them, but I am sure you can figure them out if you need them.

And then simply create a task that does the work:

```
gulp.task('minify-css', function() {
    return gulp.src('css/*.css')
        .pipe(cleancss({
            compatibility: 'ie9'
        }))
        .pipe(gulp.dest('prod/css'));
});
```

Run the `gulp minify-css` command and behold the fruits of our labor:

```
.wrap{overflow:hidden;text-overflow:ellipsis;white-space:nowrap}
```

That is the entire `utils.css` file on a single line (although it was not very big to begin with). Also, notice that all the spaces and the semicolon after `white-space:nowrap` have been removed.

Bundling JavaScript with Browserify

Now that we have minified all of our code, we want our HTML files to reference the newly created files. The easiest solution is to keep the complete folder structure and filenames the same as before minification. If you move `index.js` to the `views` folder and fix all the references to other files, you are pretty much done. However, if you did not do that, for whatever reason you have, or you suffixed your minified files with `.min.ext`, you will need to do some additional work. You probably want to do some additional work anyway, as we have not yet bundled our JavaScript and CSS yet.

Bundling JavaScript is difficult. The pain is in managing your dependencies. Let's say we have scripts A, B, and C. C depends on B and B depends on A. This is easy when you have three scripts, but when you get to thirty, things start to get messy. One method to keep track of dependencies is doing this by hand, which is what we currently do and which is difficult and error prone. The next developer will pull out his hair trying to figure out all the dependencies.

Another method is by using the `require` function we have been using in Node.js. Node.js uses CommonJS for module loading through `require`. The `require` function loads a script on the fly, so when you need script C, you can just reference script C using `require('C')`. Once script C loads, it will load script B and script B will load script A, all through `require`. This method, however, depends on some `module.exports` variable in your script. We do not have that. Adding it to our scripts now is not much of a problem, but it is something to think about before you start writing those thirty or more scripts. If we used CommonJS, our scripts would look as follows:

```
// a.js
var b = require('./b.js');
console.log('a');
b.log();

// b.js
module.exports = {
   log: function () {
      console.log('b');
   }
};
```

Unfortunately, browsers do not support the `require` function like Node.js does. Another method, designed for the browser, is by using **Asynchronous Module Definition** (**AMD**). Using AMD on the browser still requires the use of third-party libraries, such as `require.js`. Since we currently have to make a choice between CommonJS and AMD (although we can support both), we are going for CommonJS. Using CommonJS, we get Node.js support out of the box and there are tools that can convert CommonJS to something we can use on the browser, most notably Browserify (`http://browserify.org/`).

So first of all, we must change our scripts. The only scripts that need to export anything are `repository.js` and `utils.js`, because those are the scripts that we reuse in other scripts. Because of the way we set up our scripts in the first place, changing them is as easy as replacing the first line of the scripts to the following:

```
//var repository = (function () {
//var utils = (function () {
module.exports = (function () {
```

Next, we need to use `require` in our other scripts. Depending on the script, we need to require repository and/or `utils`. Simply add the following lines to your scripts (at the top or inside your controller; it does not really matter):

```
var repository = require('./repository.js');
var utils = require('./utils.js');
```

So far, we have made our scripts Browserify-ready and we have broken our entire website. After all, the browser does not understand `require`. So, the next thing we need to do is install Browserify and run it on our scripts:

```
npm install browserify -g
npm install browserify --save-dev
```

We can now bundle up our scripts using the command line. For example, let's make a bundle of our `product.js` script. The bundle will contain `repository.js`, `utils.js`, `product.js`, and a bit of overhead from Browserify. Please note that the overhead is relatively big, but that is only because our files are rather small. We do get the added benefit that the browser now only has to download one file instead of three. The advantages in loading speed becomes bigger once you get more files:

```
browserify scripts/product.js -o scripts/bundles/product.bundle.js
```

We now have to edit our `product.html` file, so it references our new `product.bundle.js` file rather than `repository.js`, `utils.js`, and `product.js` (in the right order):

```
<!--script src="..scripts\utils.js"></script>
<script src="..scripts\repository.js"></script>
<script src="..scripts\product.js"></script-->
<script src="..scripts\bundles\product.bundle.js"></script>
```

If you now browse to `file://filelocation/product.html?id=3`, you will see everything works as expected. However, all your scripts are now one script and it has some Browserify gibberish, making debugging more difficult. Luckily, Browserify has a switch that let's you specify this is a debug build and adds the so-called source maps to your file, making it appear as the three original files on your browser:

`browserify scripts/product.js -o scripts/bundles/product.bundle.js --debug`

You can generate all your bundled scripts this way and never have to worry about dependencies. The only thing left for us to do is automate this process. Unfortunately, Browserify does not have an actively maintained Gulp plugin. Instead, we can directly call Browserify from Gulp.

Using Browserify is a bit of a hassle, so I am going to take you through it step by step. Browserify can create one bundle at a time. Creating a single bundle is a pretty straightforward task. Unfortunately, the return value of Browserify is not compatible with other Gulp stream functions. Luckily, we can use `vinyl-source-stream` (https://www. npmjs.com/package/vinyl-source-stream) to handle this for us:

`npm install vinyl-source-stream --save-dev`

Once we have `vinyl-source-stream`, we can run Browserify on a file, convert the result, and save it like we normally would:

```
var browserify = require('browserify');
var source = require('vinyl-source-stream');

gulp.task('browserify', function () {
    browserify({
        entries: ['scripts/product.js'],
        debug: true
    })
    .bundle()
    .pipe(source('product.bundle.js'))
    .pipe(gulp.dest('prod/scripts'));
});
```

Doing this for all our scripts seems rather cumbersome. Browserify can take multiple entries, but that will still just create a single script. So, we need a mechanism to get the files we need, loop through them, and Browserify them one by one. The glob module (https://www.npmjs.com/package/glob) can take care of the first step. It fetches the names of the files as an array using wildcards. With an array of the filenames, we can loop and create an event stream for each filename. Once all the files have been processed, we can signal Gulp that the task has completed. In psuedo-code, it would look as follows:

```
gulp.task('browserify', function (done) {
    glob('./scripts/*.js', function (err, files) {

        var streams = files.map(function (file) {
            // Create Browserify stream.
        });
        streams.execute().on('end', done);
    });
});
```

The glob functions gets all of our scripts asynchronously, hence the callback. In the callback, we map the filenames to Browserify streams, that is to say that for each filename, a function like the one we had before this is executed. Once we have executed all the streams, we signal done to Gulp. This pseudo-code is actually pretty close to what we need to do already. We can use the event-stream module (https://www.npmjs.com/package/event-stream) to wait for all the streams to complete:

```
npm install glob --save-dev
npm install event-stream --save-dev
```

We can use the modules as follows:

```
var glob = require('glob');
var browserify = require('browserify');
var source = require('vinyl-source-stream');
var es = require('event-stream');

gulp.task('browserify', function (done) {
    glob('./scripts/*.js', function (err, files) {
        if (err) {
            done(err);
        }

        var streams = files.map(function (file) {
            return browserify({
                    entries: [file],
                    debug: true
                })
```

```
            .bundle()
            .pipe(source(file))
            .pipe(gulp.dest('prod'));
        });
    es.merge(streams).on('end', done);
    });
});
```

This introduces just one more tiny problem. In the previous sample, we Browserified just one file, so in the source function we could rename it. We now get a variable number of files with different names, so we do not know what name to pass to the source function except for the original. We could keep the original name, but I would like to rename it to .bundle.js anyway. We can use the gulp-rename module (https://www.npmjs.com/package/gulp-rename) for this task. As an added bonus, we can remove the folder structure, so instead of writing to 'prod', we must now write to 'prod/scripts', which gives us a little more flexibility:

```
npm install gulp-rename --save-dev
```

And now we just need to add an additional piped function to our pipe chain:

```
var rename = require('gulp-rename');
[...]

.bundle()
.pipe(source(file))
.pipe(rename({
    extname: '.bundle.js',
    dirname: ''
}))
.pipe(gulp.dest('prod/scripts'));
```

And there you have it, all your JavaScript files nicely bundled! Do notice that we now also bundle utils.js and repository.js even though we never use them. You still want to write your bundles to your scripts bundles directory for debugging as well. You can simply add another gulp.dest:

```
.pipe(gulp.dest('prod/scripts'))
.pipe(gulp.dest('scripts/bundles'));
```

Unfortunately, I do not dare say it, this pretty much messed up our Karma tests.

Karma and Browserify

And so, we are drawn deeper and deeper into the web of JavaScript frameworks and modules. Our Karma tests still use the regular JavaScript files that now use the `require` function, which is not found. And so, we need to install another plugin:

```
npm install watchify --save-dev
npm install karma-browserify --save-dev
npm install brfs --save-dev
```

We can now change our Karma configuration(s):

```
frameworks: ['browserify', 'jasmine', 'mocha', 'chai'],
preprocessors: {
    '../scripts/*.js': ['browserify', 'coverage'],
    'mocha-tests.js': ['browserify']
},
browserify: {
    debug: true,
    transform: ['brfs']
},
```

We must add the `'browserify'` framework and preprocess some files. The `'scripts/*.js'` files use `require`, so they must be browserified. `mocha-tests.js` does not use `require` yet, but it tests the repository directly, which is now browserified. So, we do need to change the `mocha-tests.js` file as well. Simply add the following line:

```
var repository = require('../scripts/repository.js');
```

All of our Angular.js tests make use of the Angular.js apps and controllers, which do `require`, but do not expose it. So, with these few changes, our Karma tests should run again. Do not forget to change the configuration for our minified files as well.

Our Protractor tests are unaffected, because they use the original source files that already make use of the browserified scripts.

Unfortunately, Browserify breaks our coverage. The coverage plugin works on the original source files, but Browserify creates new sources. What we need to do is take the Browserify scripts and run coverage on those files. For this, we can use yet another plugin, Istanbul. Istanbul (`https://istanbul.js.org/`) is a popular JavaScript code coverage tool. And then, we need a plugin for our plugin, `browserify-istanbul` (`https://www.npmjs.com/package/browserify-istanbul`):

```
npm install istanbul --save-dev
npm install browserify-istanbul --save-dev
```

Luckily, the implementation is very simple:

```
module.exports = function(config) {
    var istanbul = require('browserify-istanbul');

    config.set({
        [...]
        preprocessors: {
            '../scripts/*.js': ['browserify'],
            'mocha-tests.js': ['browserify']
        },
        browserify: {
            debug: true,
            configure: function(bundle){
                bundle.on('prebundle', function(){
                    bundle
                        .transform('brfs')
                        .transform(istanbul({
                            defaultIgnore: true
                        }));
                });
            }
        },
        [...]
    });
};
```

First, make sure you remove the `'coverage'` preprocessor. It is not going to work. Second, in the Browserify options, we now specify a `configure` function, which gets a `bundle` object. On `bundle`, we call the `transform` function and use it to transform our scripts to the Istanbul coverage reports. Other than that, nothing changes. We still need the coverage reporter and its settings do not need to change.

Concatenating CSS

The next step is a simple one. Since we only have two CSS files, let's bundle them. It is not as complicated as our JavaScript bundles. Just concatenate the two files and save them in a single file:

```
npm install gulp-concat --save-dev
```

The `concat` step is just a single step and does exactly what you expect it to do:

```
var concat = require('gulp-concat');
gulp.task('css-concat', function () {
    return gulp.src('css/*.css')
        .pipe(concat('all.css'))
        .pipe(gulp.dest('prod/css'));
});
```

The result is a file called `all.css` and contains the contents of all the CSS files in the `css` folder.

Replacing HTML references

We now have only one problem left: our debug HTML is referencing `scripts`**`/bundles`**`/some-bundle.js` while our production build is referencing `scripts/some-bundle.js`. Additionally, we would like to replace some CSS files with the `all.css` file we created. We can replace patterns in our HTML using the `gulp-html-replace` module (`https://www.npmjs.com/package/gulp-html-replace`). For more generic string replacement, check out `gulp-replace` (`https://www.npmjs.com/package/gulp-replace`):

```
npm install gulp-replace --save-dev
npm install gulp-html-replace --save-dev
```

All we have to do now is edit our views and indicate the parts we want to replace. This is from the `index.html` file:

```
<head>
    <meta charset="UTF-8">
    <title>CI Web Shop</title>

    <!-- build:css -->
    <link rel="stylesheet" type="text/css"
href="node_modules\bootstrap\dist\css\bootstrap.css">
    <link rel="stylesheet" type="text/css" href="css\layout.css">
    <link rel="stylesheet" type="text/css" href="css\utils.css">
    <!-- endbuild -->
    <!-- build:js -->
    <script src="node_modules\angular\angular.js"></script>
    <script src="node_modules\jquery\dist\jquery.js"></script>
    <script src="node_modules\bootstrap\dist\js\bootstrap.js"></script>
    <script src="scripts\bundles\index.bundle.js"></script>
    <!-- endbuild -->
</head>
```

Now that we have a `css` build step and a `js` build step, we can create a task that replaces its contents. Lucky for us, whenever we replace a CSS or JavaScript file, the plugin will take care of the HTML element, so we only need to specify filenames:

```
var htmlreplace = require('gulp-html-replace');

gulp.task('html-replace', function () {
    return gulp.src('index.html')
        .pipe(htmlreplace({
            css: [
                'node_modules/bootstrap/dist/css/bootstrap.min.css',
                'css/all.css'
            ],
            js: [
                'node_modules/angular/angular.min.js',
                'node_modules/jquery/dist/jquery.min.js',
                'node_modules/bootstrap/dist/js/bootstrap.min.js',
                'scripts/index.bundle.js'
            ]
        }))
        .pipe(gulp.dest('prod/views'));
});
```

As you see, we can now replace all `node_modules` to give them the correct minified sources. Note that this all scripts have the same path as our current files, because when we are releasing, we are just going to replace our source files with the minified production files. We can replace our scripts and CSS files with the production versions as well. This is a bit of a hassle though, doing this for all our HTML files. We can make this easier by using patterns:

```
.pipe(htmlreplace({
    [...]
    node_modules: [
        'node_modules/angular/angular.min.js',
        'node_modules/jquery/dist/jquery.min.js',
        'node_modules/bootstrap/dist/js/bootstrap.min.js'
    ],
    js: {
        src: 'scripts',
        tpl: '<script src="%s/%f.bundle.js"></script>'
    }
}))
```

As you can see, I have added an extra `node_modules` build step. We could require them in our scripts, and we probably should, but I also wanted to show you how to simply replace some files with their minified versions. In the `js` build step, I am replacing `%s`, which returns the current folder name, with `scripts`. The `%f` variable returns the name of the current (HTML) file being processed without extension (use `%e` to include extensions). We are not overwriting it, so it returns `'index'`. Since we name our JavaScript files the same as our HTML files, we can just append `.bundle.js` to it and we will have `scripts/index.bundle.js`. This will work for all our HTML pages.

One last thing: our anchor tags in index reference other views in the `views` folder and the views in the `view` folder reference the index page by going a page up. Once we have minified everything, they are all in the same folder, so your links will break. There is a simple solution using `gulp-concat`:

```
var replace = require('gulp-replace');
[...]

return gulp.src(['index.html', 'views/*.html'])
    .pipe(replace('href="views', 'href="'))
    .pipe(replace('href=".."', 'href="'))
    .pipe(htmlreplace({
[...]
```

This will replace all instances of `'href="views'` (second to escape the backslash) and `'href=".."'` with `'href="'`. This, effectively, fixes all of our links.

Putting it all together

By now, you are probably wondering if it is all worth it. There is just so much to do, with so many plugins and so many tasks and dependencies. Well, fear not. We can combine a lot of tasks in one task to make it easier.

We are going to do all of our JavaScript-related tasks in a single task. We now have the tasks `lint`, `browserify`, `minify-js`, `test`, and `test-min`. Unfortunately, the `lint` and `test` steps need to remain separate, but we can Browserify and minify in the same step. To run additional plugins after Browserify, we need to buffer the vinyl streams using the `vinyl-buffer` module:

```
npm install vinyl-buffer --save-dev
```

After that, we can just pipe `browserify`, `source`, `buffer`, `size`, `minify`, and `dest` in a single task:

```
return browserify({
    entries: [file],
        debug: true
    })
    .bundle()
    .pipe(source(file))
    .pipe(buffer())
    .pipe(rename({
        extname: '.bundle.js',
        dirname: ''
    }))
    .pipe(gulp.dest('scripts/bundles'))
    .pipe(size({
        title: 'Before minification',
        showFiles: true
    }))
    .pipe(minify(minifyOpts))
    .pipe(size({
        title: 'After minification',
        showFiles: true
    }))
    .pipe(gulp.dest('prod/scripts'));
```

It is quite a bit of code, but handles most of your JavaScript issues in one go!

We can give our CSS and HTML tasks the same treatment:

```
gulp.task('css', ['clean'], function () {
    return gulp.src('css/*.css')
        .pipe(concat('all.css'))
        .pipe(cleancss({
            compatibility: 'ie9'
        }))
        .pipe(gulp.dest('prod/css'));
})
.task('html', ['clean'], function () {
        return gulp.src(['index.html', 'views/*.html'])
            .pipe(replace('href="views', 'href="'))
            .pipe(replace('href=".."', 'href="'))
            .pipe(htmlreplace({
                [...]
            }))
            .pipe(htmlmin({
                collapseWhitespace: true
            }))
```

```
        .pipe(gulp.dest('prod/views'));
});
```

They can all run simultaneously, but all depend on clean. The clean task should be changed as well. Clean needs no dependencies and should clean the `scripts/bundles` folder as well:

```
gulp.task('clean', function () {
    del(['prod/*', 'scripts/bundles/*']);
});

gulp.task('build', ['js', 'css', 'html']);
```

We can now run `gulp clean` to clean everything and then `gulp js`, `gulp css`, or `gulp html` to build a specific part of the application. Running `gulp build` will simply clean our build files and minify and replace everything again. You could create separate clean tasks for `js`, `css`, and `html` as well, but I do not really see a need for it.

That leaves only the linting and testing. Our tests are, obviously, dependent on our build, because we need our bundled and minified scripts. The linting, however, is not depending on anything. Other than that, those tasks can stay as they are:

```
gulp.task('lint', function () {
[...]

gulp.task('test', ['build'], function (done) {
[...]

gulp.task('test-min', ['test'], function (done) {
[...]
```

Now, we can change our default task to fire up the `lint`, `test`, and `test-min` tasks. Notice that the `test-min` task is depending on the test task. Since both the tasks clean and build, one clean might undo the other's build, so let's just not go there and run them one after the other:

```
gulp.task('default', ['lint', 'test-min']);
```

By the way, in the source file, you will see that I have chained the `task` function calls for a slightly less bloated gulpfile:

```
gulp.task([...]
})
.task([...]
})
.task('build', ['js', 'css', 'html'])
.task('default', ['lint', 'test', 'test-min']);
```

The linting now runs during the build and, when it fails, the tests will not be fired (unless they are already running). Due to the asynchronous nature of Gulp, the linting can be a bit weird. Of course, you can tweak it if you want.

As icing on the cake, we are going to automate everything we just created. As soon as you change a CSS, JavaScript, or HTML file, we want a new build, and when we change a JavaScript file, we also want our linter and tests to run:

```
gulp.watch(['css/*.css', 'views/*.html', 'index.html'], ['build']);
gulp.watch('scripts/*.js', ['default']);
```

And that is it. Everything is now automated! On your local machine, that is.

Check whether everything still works by (manually) running your Protractor tests.

Also, since your entire bundles and prod folder are generated from your build, you may want to add it to your `.gitignore` file. Running a single build will probably mark all your generated files as changed even when you only edited a single source file:

```
**/prod/**
**/bundles/**
```

I have shown you quite a few tasks you can do when working with frontend technologies. It seems like a lot (although some of it is because we are still using the file protocol), but it is really good practice to minify, lint, and test your frontend files as soon as possible. Optionally, you can leave the minified tests and run them manually when you are done fixing some code. The Browserify part is just a bit of a pain, but it is a one-time setup. After that, you have all the goodness of `require` on your browser, so I think it is definitely worth it. By the way, we have not yet linted our CSS and HTML files, so you can add those yourself if you like.

Summary

In this chapter, we came to the core of CI, automation. Using Gulp, we automated our build, linting, and testing. That is all very nice, but for now, it only works locally. You can still forget to run Gulp, or ignore it, and commit a broken build. In the next chapter, we are going to take a closer look at Jenkins. Jenkins, like Gulp, is all about automation. While Gulp and Jenkins are nothing alike, besides the fact that they both assist in automation, the most important difference is that Jenkins runs on a server and will check your commit even if you did not.

7
Automation with Jenkins

So far, we have pretty much automated our entire build, including testing, on our local computer. Unfortunately, we still need to manually start the automation process and that is not something we can enforce before a commit. Luckily, we can kick off the build process on a commit from our server. This is where Jenkins comes in to play. With Jenkins, we can poll for changes on our Git repository and run the build process automatically. When a build fails, Jenkins can send an email to the entire team to let them know someone broke the build and that it should be fixed. In this chapter, we are going to explore Jenkins in more depth to automate our build upon every commit.

Jenkins has a ton of settings, options, and plugins and some plugins have another ton of settings and options. Not to mention that Jenkins and plugins keep changing with each new update. It is impossible for me (or anyone) to cover them all. However, Jenkins and its plugins are pretty well documented. A lot of fields have an icon with a question mark next to them that show additional information of the field when clicked. Additionally, you should check the wiki page for each plugin; they can help you in getting started with a plugin. In this chapter, I am going to guide you through some common use cases. You should get familiar with Jenkins, so you can figure out what applies to you personally in your daily job yourself.

In case you forgot, you can access Jenkins by starting up your VM and browsing to `ciserver:8080`.

Installing Node.js and npm

First things first, for our build, we need Node.js and npm (again) at the very least. Like on Windows, we can install Node.js and get npm as a bonus. We must install them on our CI server. Unlike Jenkins, Node.js has an install package in `apt-get`. Unfortunately, this is an old version and we want to use the latest LTS version. So again, we are going to run some arcane Linux commands:

```
curl -sL https://deb.nodesource.com/setup_6.x | sudo -E bash -
sudo apt-get install -y nodejs
```

The `L` switch (from `-L`) in curl tells it to redo the request if the response returns that the requested page has moved. We know the pipe character; it gives the output of the left side of the pipe's input to the right side of the pipe. `sudo -E bash -` will run the bash command as the root user (super user). `-E` means that any environment variables will be kept. The last `-` means that the standard output is given as a command to bash. Simply said, we are using curl to download some script that we pass as a parameter to the bash program. In case you were wondering how I got so smart, I did not. This is simply pasted from the Node.js documentation (`https://nodejs.org/en/download/package-manager/#debian-and-ubuntu-based-linux-distributions`).

Last, but not least, we can install `nodejs`. The `-y` switch in `sudo apt-get install -y nodejs` is optional and tells `apt-get` to assume `y` as any input to prompts (such as `Are you sure you wish to install this package (Y/n)`.

To check whether everything was successfully installed, you can check the versions of Node.js and npm:

```
nodejs -v
v6.9.4
npm -v
v3.10.10
```

Creating a Jenkins project

Our next step will be to create a Jenkins project. Make sure the web shop project is completely pushed to Git (your local GitLab installation). For clarity, everything inside the Chapter06 code folder of the code samples (in the GitHub repository for this book) should be in your GitLab repository. Personally, I have put it in the web-shop repository. We have created this repository in Chapter 4, *Creating A Simple JavaScript App*. We have already created a Jenkins project in Chapter 2, *Setting Up a CI Environment* in the *Configuring Jenkins* section, but I will take you through some of the steps again (you should also really follow the steps in Chapter 2, *Setting Up a CI Environment*, as they take you through the installation of some plugins and credentials). Speaking of plugins, be mindful that a lot of plugins are created and maintained by people like you and me, people who have taken up programming as a hobby. These people are not paid to create or maintain these plugins. These people are busy and may not find the time, need, or drive to update their plugin, leaving you with an outdated plugin that does not support Jenkins or your language's latest features. It is always good to check whether a plugin is still actively maintained before you install it (that is not to say every plugin that is not maintained is bad; some just do what they must and do it well).

So log in to Jenkins and click **New Item** on the left-hand side menu. Enter an item name, either Web Shop, Chapter 7, or My Little Pony, whatever you fancy, although I recommend a name that says something about the project you are working on. I have named it Chapter 7. You will now be taken to the configuration screen of your new project.

In our new project, we will want to check out the Git repository. So, under **Source Code Management**, select **Git** and enter the repository URL. This is the URL that is also displayed on the GitLab project page. You should still have your credentials from Chapter 2, *Setting up a CI Environment*, so select those as well. If your credentials changed (because we have been playing around with Git and GitLab a bit), you can add new credentials or change your existing one, which you can find under the left-hand side menu option **Credentials** on the main page. As with a project, you can select a credential and then update or delete it from the left-hand side menu.

Once you have selected your credentials, save the project and build it from the project page:

You should see a blue ball for success. Whether you have a blue ball or a red ball, you can click the ball next to your build number and you will see exactly what commands Jenkins has executed. For example, when you enter incorrect credentials, the output will be something as follows:

```
Started by user admin
[...]
 > git fetch --tags --progress http://ciserver/sander/web-shop.git
+refs/heads/*:refs/remotes/origin/*
ERROR: Error cloning remote repo 'origin'
hudson.plugins.git.GitException: Command "git fetch --tags --progress
http://ciserver/sander/web-shop.git +refs/heads/*:refs/remotes/origin/*"
returned status code 128:
stdout:
stderr: remote: HTTP Basic: Access denied
fatal: Authentication failed for 'http://ciserver/sander/web-shop.git/'
   [...]
ERROR: null
Finished: FAILURE
```

You can also view this information by clicking on the build number and then clicking **Console Output** from the left-hand side menu. Fun fact, you can view it as it is executing. You will have to be really quick for this two second build to see some action, but once you get bigger projects, builds can take up to minutes (hours really, depending on how crazy you get).

I am assuming everything went well. The next thing we want to do is assure that Jenkins has really pulled your code from Git. On the project page, there is a menu item labeled **Workspace**. You can click it to browse the files inside the Jenkins project. This is also where you can clear out your workspace, which means Jenkins will simply delete all the files inside the project. This is sometimes useful when you are dealing with some bad caching issues. Of course, clearing your workspace is no problem at all, since you can simply run the project again and Jenkins will pull your code from Git once more.

You will notice that Jenkins has pulled all your source files from Git. The next thing we want to do is restore our npm packages. Once you realize Jenkins is just running a series of console commands, things get pretty easy. Go to your project configuration and add a build step **Execute Shell**. Put npm install in the command input:

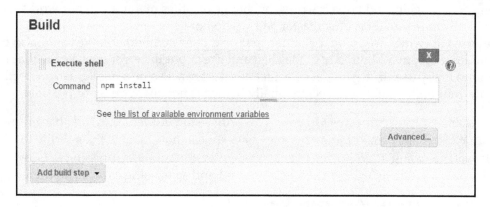

Now build the project again and you will notice that it downloads all of your npm modules. If you check out the workspace, you will see the node_modules folder with all of the modules.

Executing Gulp in Jenkins

Running your build should now be easy, because it is just another shell command. The only problem is that we do not have Gulp, Karma, or any other tool installed globally on our VM, so a `gulp` or `karma start` command will fail. Any command-line tool installed through Node.js will have their executables in the `node_modules.bin` folder (which is why we installed all those tools in our project in addition to globally on our development machine). So we can now simply run `node_modules/.bin/gulp`. The shell still operates from the root of our project and so will also use our local gulpfile.

Unfortunately, a lot will go wrong. Your tests will fail, the browsers will not start, and your job will never finish. You may have already guessed why. First, we do not have any browsers installed on our Ubuntu machine. We do not even have a user interface! So, of course, Jenkins cannot start IE, Edge, Chrome, and Firefox. Second, we have a file watch in our gulpfile, which prevents Gulp from exiting and so it prevents our build from ever finishing.

For now, let's just get it to work. We have two options, change our files, push them to Git, run our project again, and hope it works, or change our files manually in our workspace. Changing them manually is much faster and we do not get a ton of *try to fix Jenkins build* commits in Git (which we could, of course, put on a persisted branch). We could also try to run our build on our VM directly in the shell and check out the error logs. While that is sometimes really useful, as you get direct feedback, it can also be a hassle, as you need to replicate your entire Jenkins project manually, which is not always easy or possible.

So let's change our files directly. On your VM, browse to your Jenkins workspace using `cd "var/lib/jenkins/workspace/Chapter 7"`. We can now change the gulpfile to disable the file watcher using `sudo vi gulpfile.js`. Enter edit mode by pressing `i`. Now, simply comment out the two `gulp.watch` lines at the end and save using escape and then `:wq`:

```
cd "var/lib/jenkins/workspace/Chapter 7"
sudo vi gulpfile.js
i

[..]
//gulp.watch(...);
//gulp.watch(...);

esc
:wq
```

Likewise, change your `test/karma.conf.js` and `test/karma.min.conf.js` files and set the `browsers` property to `['PhantomJS']`. Remember, PhantomJS is a headless browser, is easily installed using npm, and does not require a user interface. Unlike, IE, Edge, Firefox, and Chrome, it will run just fine on our current system.

Now, go back to your Jenkins project and change **Source Code Management** to **None** (so we do not overwrite our local changes). Run the project again and it should succeed this time. Unfortunately, there is not an easy way to troubleshoot issues in Jenkins. Sometimes, it is just a bit of trial and error (but sometimes, that is what programming is all about).

Now that we know the problem, we can change our files on our development machine and push them to Git. However, if we change our gulpfile, it will break our development usage of Gulp, and we do want that. We could copy our gulpfile, remove the watch, and use the new one in Jenkins, but that would mean we have two gulpfiles to maintain. What we really need is a way to specify our environment to Gulp. Luckily, this is easy enough using the `gulp-util` plugin, which we already have. Of course, we still need to change our gulpfile. You can pass any variable to Gulp using `--something=value` from the command line:

```
gulp --env=prod
```

In our gulpfile, we can read any environment variable using `gutil.env.something`:

```
var gulp = require('gulp'),
    [...]

gutil.log(gutil.colors.cyan('Environment: '),
gutil.colors.blue(gutil.env.env));

gulp.task('clean', function () {
    [...]

if (gutil.env.env !== 'prod') {
    gulp.watch(['css/*.css', 'views/*.html', 'index.html'], ['build']);
    gulp.watch('scripts/*.js', ['default']);
}
```

At the top of our gulpfile, we can log the value of env, using colors for clarity. At the bottom of the file, we can then skip `gulp.watch` if we are running a `prod` build. You may use any variable and value you like. I have called the variable env and given it the value of prod, but if you want to call it `monkey` with the value `astronaut`, you can.

We have the same issue with our browsers. For now, we want to use different browsers for a Jenkins build than a local build. Our development machine has all the browsers installed, while Ubuntu only has PhantomJS installed through npm. With the new env variable, we can easily fix this in the test and test-min tasks:

```
new karma({
    configFile: __dirname + '/test/karma.min.conf.js',
    browsers: gutil.env.env === 'prod'
        ? ['PhantomJS']
        : undefined
}, [...]
```

If we are not building in 'prod', we use the browsers as defined in the configuration file, or else we overwrite it with PhantomJS. Commit these changes to your Git repository, so we can pull it in Jenkins.

Now, in the Jenkins project, we must change the job to run Gulp with the prod environment:

```
npm install
node node_modules/.bin/gulp --env=prod
```

If you have removed the Git settings under **Source Code Management**, be sure to set your Git repository so you can get the latest version of the gulpfile. If you save your configuration and run the built, you should see that it will now finish within a minute.

There is one thing we are not doing yet, which is cleaning our workspace for every new build. That means that we do not have to pull our entire project from Git every time we start a build and that we do not have to install every node_module on every build. npm install alone costs about two minutes for our small project; add to that the time it costs to check out large projects and skipping these steps may save you about five precious minutes. However, it is good practice to always start a clean build. For example, npm packages may be removed from npm (it happens) or you may remove files from the Git repository yourself. When you clean the workspace before each build, these files would be missing on your next build. If you do not remove them, however, Jenkins will use the cached files and you will not know some files are missing until it is too late.

Under the Git settings, you can add additional behaviors; be sure to add *Clean before checkout*. If you save and run your job again, it will take considerably longer than the last time you built it, but Jenkins will clear the entire workspace before building.

If you are running Jenkins on Windows, you can use the *Execute Windows batch command* step instead of the *Execute Shell* step. Other than that, everything looks the same. Of course, especially when your Jenkins machine is the same as your development machine, Jenkins should be able to run IE, Edge, Firefox, and Chrome. This is true for Firefox and Chrome, but IE and Edge cannot run under the default Local System account under which Jenkins is running. We will look into these problems later; for now, follow with the PhantomJS browser instead.

Publishing test results

Now that we have run some tests using Karma we will also get our test reports. We had three; the JUnit report, which shows us the test results; the Cobertura reports, showing us how much of our code is covered by tests; and the HTML coverage report, showing exactly what lines are tested and not tested.

JUnit report

The easiest one to implement is the JUnit report as it comes straight out of the box. Simply configure the **Publish JUnit test result report** post-build action. The report can, of course, be found in the `test/junit/` folder (after building). We need any XML files, so the complete pattern for the reports field is `test/junit/*.xml`:

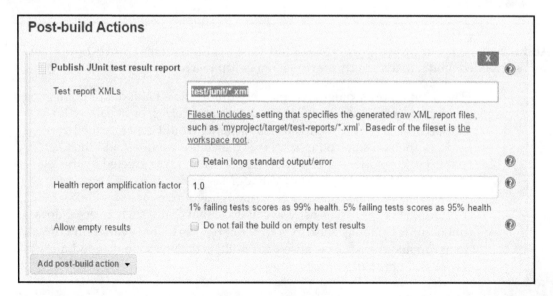

After that, you can make another build and the test results will be published to Jenkins. You can find the results in your build on the left-hand side menu under **Test Result**. Alternatively, there is a drop-down menu in the build overview on the left-hand side (the one with the red and blue balls). The dropdown has a **Test Result** menu item, which takes you to the test results page of the build. Now, when you mess up your code, or a test, and a test fails, Jenkins will fail the build and you will know something is not as it should be. The test report should give you a pretty detailed overview of what went wrong:

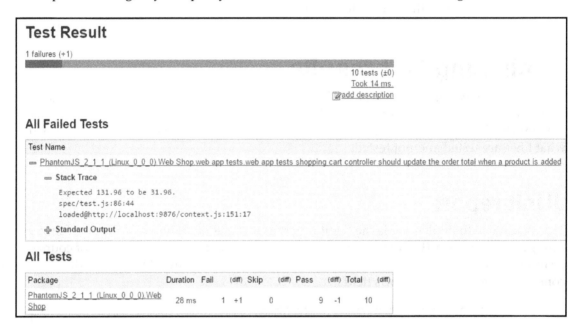

Additionally, on your project page, you should see a trend graph that shows how many tests succeeded (and failed) in your previous builds (up to a few builds back).

> The JUnit reporter plugin has the very unfortunate habit of not publishing *old* reports. I am not sure what the definition of *old* is, but I believe it is a few seconds. I once ran into an issue where I would generate the JUnit reports, then do some other stuff that took a few minutes, and then publish the reports. Imagine my surprise when I was greeted by the message `ERROR: Step 'Publish JUnit test result report' failed: Test reports were found but none of them are new. Did tests run?`. The least you can do to make sure such an error does not occur too often is to clean your JUnit reports before every build. If you ever run into the issue because your build is taking too long, good luck. I never got it properly fixed.

Cobertura report

Next up is the Cobertura report. We will need an additional Jenkins plugin for this one. So go to the Jenkins manager and, from there, to the plugin manager. Search for `Cobertura plugin` (`https://wiki.jenkins-ci.org/display/JENKINS/Cobertura+Plugin`) and install it without restarting (this will also install the Maven Integration plugin). Go back to your project configuration and add a new post-build action, **Publish Cobertura Coverage Report**, which was not there before. Use `test/coverage/cobertura/*.xml` as the report pattern. Now, if you save and run the project, you will see that your build fails even when all your tests succeed. That is because the Cobertura makes your build fail if you do not have a minimum coverage percentage. We have seen this in Karma as well.

In your post-build action, click on the **Advanced** button in the lower-right corner. You now get a couple of additional options, but the most interesting are **Coverage Metric Targets**. You can set a minimum threshold for a stable, failing, or unstable build. Unfortunately, the options are not as advanced as those in Karma. We can only set overall thresholds and we cannot exclude files. Since our coverage is not all that great, you can either set the targets very low or remove the metrics completely. Your Karma run will still fail your build if your threshold does not meet your Karma settings. Speaking of failing builds, the Cobertura reporter has an advanced option **Consider only stable builds**, which makes sense to enable. When your build or a test fails, there is a good chance that it affects your coverage. If an exception is raised, for example, further code will not be executed and so your coverage is lower than when your build would have passed. However, in this case, it also means that when Karma fails your build because your coverage is too low, your coverage is not published. For that reason, I am keeping the option disabled, but I thought you should still know about it.

When you run your build and it succeeds, you can see some nice trend graphs on your code coverage. Ideally, the graph should go up over time. The graph should at least have a straight line as time passes. If the line goes down, you know your coverage is going in the wrong direction. There is also a **Cobertura Coverage Report** option on the left-hand side menu now. When you click it, you will be taken to a report that is not unlike the HTML report Karma generates.

In this report, you can see which files and lines were tested and which were not:

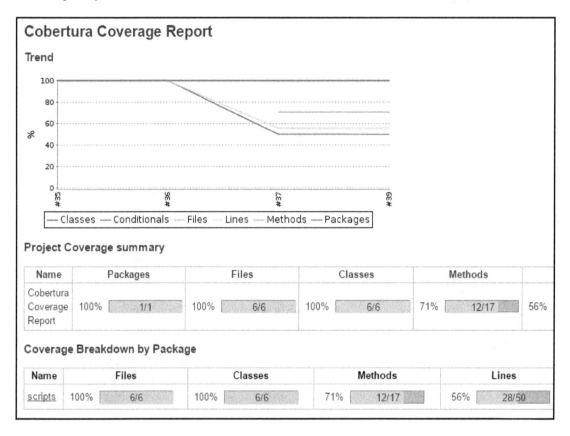

HTML report

Karma also generates an HTML report that shows exactly what lines were tested. The Jenkins report already shows pretty much the same, but I prefer the Karma report. Besides, I want to show you how to publish HTML reports. You can publish pretty much any HTML page. First, we need to install an additional plugin. Go to the plugin manager, find the HTML Publisher plugin (https://wiki.jenkins-ci.org/display/JENKINS/ HTML+Publisher+Plugin), and install it. After that, go back to your project configuration. You can now add another post-build action, **Publish HTML Reports**. You will get a box where you can add reports, so you can only add the action once, but then add as many reports as you like. So, add one and specify test/coverage/html as the HTML directory to archive.

The default index page, `index.html`, is already set and we can keep the default. You can give your report a title, such as `Coverage HTML`. Make another build of your project and you should see a link to your report on the left-hand side menu, right underneath **Coverage Report** from the Cobertura plugin. You will find your report published there.

The HTML Publisher plugin has some additional settings, which can be set through the **Publishing options...** button on the right-hand side under your **HTML report** settings. They are well documented under the question mark icon, so I will leave it to you to try them all out.

Build triggers

Whenever we push code changes to Git, we want our Jenkins project to start as soon as possible. After all, the sooner we know something is broke, the easier it is for us to fix it. You have probably already seen the *Build Triggers* section in the configuration of your Jenkins project. There are four build triggers currently available to us.

First, we can build the project remotely, which we will not do. Second, we can build after other projects, which is handy when you have multiple projects that depend on each other. Next is the periodic build, which should speak for itself. And last, we have the poll SCM option, which polls your SCM-in our case Git-for changes and triggers a build when something changed.

For now, we will look at the periodic build and the poll SCM triggers. Both use cron syntax (cron comes from the Greek word for time, chronos), which I find rather difficult to grasp. Luckily, each of the trigger options has a question mark behind it, which gives pretty detailed information about the specific trigger. Cron is also explained in those help texts, so I suggest you read them. If you are stuck on cron, do not worry. Many people are and Google will help you in giving you the (almost) exact cron expression you need.

Build periodically

The first build trigger we are going to use is the periodic built trigger. This trigger is pretty handy when you have some tasks that can be executed every few hours, once a day, and so on. For our build, it has a downside. Cron is flexible enough to express a schedule like - *every hour between 9 AM and 5 PM (or 9:00 and 17:00)*, so you can do periodic builds during office hours. Of course, you can also still trigger a build manually in case you are working overtime. The downside to this trigger, for us, is that we may have no commits for a few hours, but we will have builds. Or worse, we have multiple commits in one hours and they will all be tested at the same time.

When our build fails, we will not know what commit made it fail and finding the problem will be harder. Anyway, let's just build every minute, so we can see the trigger in action. Simply check **Build periodically** and put in the cron schedule for every minute, which is `* * * * *` (every possible value for minute, hour, day of month, month, and day of week). Jenkins is pretty smart and even gives a warning `Do you really mean "every minute"`.... Yes! We do. Save your configuration and simply wait a few minutes. You will see a build being triggered every minute:

☑ Build periodically

Schedule: `* * * * *`

⚠ Do you really mean "every minute" when you say "`* * * * *`"? Perhaps you meant "`H * * * *`" to poll once per hour
Would last have run at Saturday, May 13, 2017 11:32:37 PM CEST; would next run at Saturday, May 13, 2017 11:32:37 PM CEST.

Poll SCM

The next trigger we are going to try is the SCM polling. This is a good option when you want to periodically check for new commits to your repository. The downside to this option is that your commits are not being build instantly and that all commits since the last build will be build all at once. However, when you have lots of commits in short periods of time this option may also save you time and resources. Notice that this trigger is not mutually exclusive with the periodic build (you can poll your SCM and build every few hours regardless of commits). To check out the SCM polling, uncheck the periodic build, and check the **SCM polling** option. Put in the schedule for every minute again. This time, you will not see any builds being triggered; at least, not every minute. You may have guessed, but we need to make some change to our code and commit it to Git. Your change can be anything, just add a space or new line somewhere and commit it to your repository. Once you have committed your change, you will have to wait another minute (at most) and you should see a build being started. Wait for a few more minutes and you should not see any additional builds being started until you make another commit (maybe to reverse your change). Now, if you commit any code that breaks your build, you should get an automatic build that fails. This, in turn, should trigger you to fix that build! Personally, I find that a period of about 15 minutes is good enough if you have to poll your SCM. Speaking of changes in your code, Jenkins tells you what commits are new in any specific build. Just go to the specific build page and it will show you the changes from the previous build at the top. Again, there is also a button on the menu that takes you to the same page.

You have probably got quite a few builds by now. If you have not found it already, at the top of your project configuration is a **Discard old builds** checkbox. You probably want to check it and keep around five to ten builds at a time. You may also specify to keep builds for a number of days. You can also do both of course, clear your builds after a week, but keep no more than 10 builds at a time.

On commit

Getting a Jenkins build to start on commit is a little tricky, but well worth it. Unlike a poll, this option can build any commit instantly so you get direct feedback on every single commit. We need the GitLab plugin, so install it and, this time, restart after success (check **Restart Jenkins when installation is complete and no jobs are running**). After you have installed the plugin and Jenkins has restarted, head over to GitLab. In GitLab, go to the profile settings of your account. Now, go to **Access Tokens**. Create an access token by entering a name and select the API scope. Make sure you copy the token, as this will be the only time you get to see it. If you lose it, it is really gone. Don't worry, you can create as many access tokens as you like. Now, with the freshly created access token, go to **Jenkins Management** and **Configure System**. There will be a new section in **Configure System** that was not there before, GitLab. Fill out the fields as you see fit. Disable the **Enable authentication for '/project' end-point** checkbox. Give the connection a name, such as Local GitLab. The host URL is not http://ciserver, but http://localhost or http://127.0.0.1 (since Jenkins and GitLab are running on the same machine and ciserver is just an alias, if you followed my examples). You will need to create a new credential. Choose the GitLab API token kind and use your access token. Give it an ID such as GitLabToken, so you know what this is for.

Test your connection and if it succeeds, Jenkins should now be able to receive messages from GitLab:

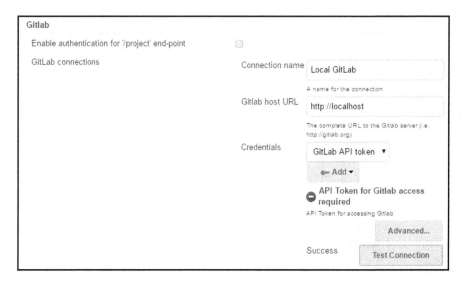

Now that this is done, we can configure our project to trigger on GitLab hooks. Simply go to your project configuration, disable all the current triggers, and select the new trigger, **Build when a change is pushed to GitLab**. GitLab CI Service URL: `http://ciserver:8080/project/Chapter%207` (where `Chapter%207` is your project name). Here comes the tricky part that cost me a good hour while configuring this. Your browser will show that your current page is `http://ciserver:8080/`**job**`/name`, but the GitLab plugin listens at `http://ciserver:8080/`**project**`/name` (and again, replace `ciserver` with `localhost` or `127.0.0.1`). This is important in the next step. Configuring a GitLab webhook. For now, we do not have to change any configuration on this trigger. An optional, but very nice addition, is the post-build action **Publish build status to GitLab commit (GitLab 8.1+ required)**. Add this post-build action and watch the magic happen in the final step.

Next, we need to tell GitLab to give Jenkins a little push when a commit is pushed. So, go to your GitLab project and find the **Webhooks** settings. In the URL field, you need to put the URL of your Jenkins project (project, not job), `http://127.0.0.1:8080/project/Chapter%207`. However, this will not work in our case. Jenkins will need to log in, but we have not specified any username and password. In a later chapter, we will enable SSH, but for now, we need to add the username and password to the URL. The new URL is then `http://username:password@127.0.0.1:8080/project/Chapter%207`. Make sure you uncheck **Enable SSL verification**.

Other than that, the only hook we need is `Push events`. Now, create the webhook. You can test it and if all goes well, you will get a message **Hook executed successfully: HTTP 200**. To verify that everything really works, go back to Jenkins and verify that a build was triggered (if you replace `project` with `job` in the URL, you will get the same message, but no build is actually triggered):

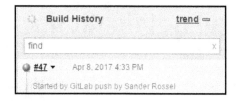

Make a change to the same file, add some whitespace, commit it, and push it to your Git repository. And now, the moment we have all been waiting for, check whether your Jenkins triggers a build automatically. If it does, congratulations! This is actually a pretty cool milestone in our CI process.

There is just one more thing, if you have added the post-build action, head over to your GitLab project page. If you check out your commits, you will find that they have a little icon next to them indicating the status of your commit. It now becomes pretty easy to recognize which commits broke your build:

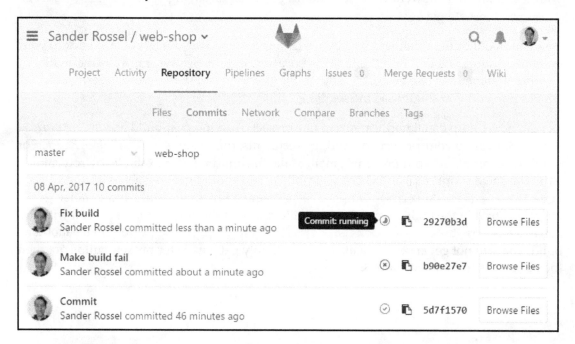

Another surprise, if you have configured your actual email address, there is a good chance you have got an email from GitLab telling you that your build passed. If you do not have it, make sure to also check your spam folder. You can change your email settings in GitLab under your account's notification settings.

Setting up email notifications

Now that we have configured a project and know it can fail when we mess up our code, we need to set up some sort of notification so we know when our build breaks or gets fixed. You could have your Jenkins project open all day and check it after every commit, but we need to make sure everyone is notified when a build fails. So we are going to set up email notifications. I am going to show you this example using a Gmail account (Google mail), but this will work with any email provider as long as you have an SMTP server and login credentials. Go to the Jenkins system configuration and find the email notification (near the bottom). Google's SMTP server is `smtp.gmail.com`, so be sure to put that in **SMTP server** under **Advanced**. Check **Use SMTP Authentication** and use your Gmail username and password (that is, the credentials you use to log in to GMail). Also, check **Use SSL** and set the port to `465`, which is the default for SMTPS (SMTP with SSL). Check the **Test configuration by sending test e-mail** box and enter the email address you want to send your test email to. If all went well, you should get an email saying `This is test email #1 sent from Jenkins`.

You will find that the email was sent by `address not configured yet`. Go back to your system configuration and find the **Jenkins Location** section. Set **System Admin e-mail address** to something like `Jenkins admin <you.email@hostname.com>`. Send a test email again and you should see the sender is `Jenkins admin`.

We can now set up email notifications in our project. Add the post-build action `E-mail Notification` to your project and add the recipients, for example, `my.team@work.com` or in this case, probably, your personal email. Make the build fail (for example, by returning `-1` in the batch script step) and check your inbox. You should get an email with the subject `Build failed in Jenkins: Chapter 7 #69` and a link to the build and detailed console output in the body. Now, fix your build and you should get another email with the subject `Jenkins build is back to normal : Chapter 7 #70`. If you make another build, you will not get another email, as you will only get emails for broken builds or when the build goes from failed status to success.

Setting up SonarQube

Now that we can run our Gulp tasks and trigger a build automatically on commit, it is time to add the next step towards quality code, SonarQube. We have already installed, configured, and used SonarQube in Chapter 2, *Setting Up a CI Environment*, so I assume you have it ready for use. If things do not work, be sure to review Chapter 2, *Setting Up a CI Environment*, and the part on SonarQube in particular. Here is a little reminder: SonarQube is accessible on ciserver:9000. So, go to your project configuration and add the Execute SonarQube Scanner build step. Put the following configuration in the **Analysis Properties** field:

```
sonar.projectKey=chapter7
sonar.projectName=Chapter 7
sonar.projectVersion=1.0

sonar.sources=.

sonar.exclusions=node_modules/**, prod/**, scripts/bundles/**, test/**
```

I strongly suggest you exclude node_modules (because these are not your files) and prod and bundles (because they are generated). I have excluded tests as well, although you could add them to make sure your tests are properly written. Now, run the project in Jenkins and check the project in SonarQube. Because the SonarQube default quality profiles are quite forgiving and we already took care of our issues using JSHint in Gulp, our project is doing pretty good! Not a single issue in fact. However, we should not use the default SonarQube quality profile. Creating your own is a hell of a job; SonarQube has hundreds of rules that you can activate at different levels of severity. Luckily, you can copy the default quality profiles and go from there. In SonarQube, go to **Quality Profiles** and copy the JavaScript **Sonar way** profile (from the drop-down menu). Call it whatever you like, I called mine Sander way. You can now activate more rules. For example, enable **Source files should have a sufficient density of comment lines** (at the default 25%). Because we have not written a single comment, this will be sure to add some technical debt to your project. You can set the new quality profile as your default profile or you can assign it to your project. Go to your quality profile page and **Change Projects**. Now, run your project again in Jenkins. You should see some technical debt being added.

Next, we are going to change the quality gate. The quality gate defines whether your project's code fails or succeeds to meet certain quality criteria. The criteria for quality is defined in the quality profile. For example, our criteria for quality is that all the files should have a minimum amount of comments. Failing to do so results in a code smell. Our quality gate defines how many code smells our code may have before we fail our project. Let's make our quality gate fail.

We have eight files that are not properly commented according to our new quality profile. So, go to the quality gates, copy the **SonarQube way** (again, I have named the new one `Sander way`), and add a new condition. Add the `Code Smells` condition and make it error at greater than five. Assign the new quality gate to our project. Now, run the build again in Jenkins. You should now see that SonarQube reports that our project fails to meet its quality gate's criteria. You can also see this on the Jenkins project page. Unfortunately, our Jenkins build still succeeds. We have a few options, install the Quality Gates plugin or send an email from SonarQube (or both).

Go to the Plugin Manager and install the Quality Gates plugin (`https://wiki.jenkins-ci.org/display/JENKINS/Quality+Gates+Plugin`). The plugin is a bit buggy if you do not configure it correctly, but it is not very hard to configure. Now, go to the Jenkins System Configuration and find the configuration for the Quality Gates plugin. Unfortunately, we need to add our SonarQube instance again. The plugin does not support token authentication, so we are stuck with a username and password authentication. So, give the instance a name, specify the URL (you can leave it empty for the default, which it is if you followed my examples) and your username and password. Now, go to your project and add the quality gates post-build step. Specify `Chapter 7` as project key. Run your build again and you should see the build fail because the SonarQube analysis fails. Now, if you remove the quality gate from the SonarQube project and run another build, you will see that both SonarQube and Jenkins succeed again:

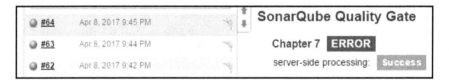

So far, we have put the SonarQube configuration in our Jenkins job. It is possible to put it inside a text file and have it in Git. This has the benefit that your SonarQube configuration is also in source control. Create a file in the root folder of your project and name it `sonar-project.properties`. Put the Sonar analysis properties that you have in your Jenkins project configuration in the file and clear the analysis properties in Jenkins. Push the file to Git and see how Jenkins executes a SonarQube analysis as if nothing changed. You have now moved the configuration to your Git repository. If you decide to put your `sonar-project.properties` anywhere else, you can configure this in the SonarQube step in Jenkins.

Setting up email

Because the Quality Gate plugin is a little quirky and requires you to use a username and password instead of a token, you may not want to use it. Also, if you are dealing with legacy projects or projects that only just use SonarQube, you may not find it a problem for now that the SonarQube quality gate fails. While you do not want to fail your Jenkins build, you do want to keep an eye on SonarQube. No worries, you can configure emails from SonarQube. First, you need to set the email address of your user. If you are still logged in as admin, go to **Administration**, then **Users** (under **Security**), and edit the admin user to set the email address. Next, go to **My Account** (upper right corner) and change your notification settings to receive an email on a new quality gate status (and any other email you want to receive). You can set some global email settings or specify email settings per project.

Then, you need to set your SMTP settings. Go to **Administration** and then find the email settings under **General Settings**. Again, I am going to show you an example using Gmail, but this would work with any other email provider as well, as long as you have an SMTP server. To follow along, you either need a Gmail account or figure out your own (provider's) SMTP settings. Set the SMTP Host to `smtp.gmail.com` and the secure connection to `starttls`. The SMTP password and username are your email address and the password you use to login. Now, try to send a test email and you should receive an email that says `This is a test message from SonarQube.`

Change the quality gate of your project (either set or unset the quality gate we just created) and run your build in Jenkins. You should get an email like the following:

```
Project: Chapter 7
Quality gate status: Green (was Red)

See it in SonarQube: http://localhost:9000/dashboard/index/chapter7
```

HTML and CSS analysis

You may have noticed that when we run a SonarQube analysis only, our JavaScript files are being analyzed. We would surely like to analyze our HTML and CSS files as well. Noncompliant HTML or CSS may break your page just as much as noncompliant JavaScript. In SonarQube, go to **Administration** and then **Update Center** under the **System** submenu. This is where you can update and install SonarQube plugins. The most important plugins are the analyzers and we need two of them, one for HTML and one for CSS. Other than that, you can find analyzers for pretty much anything.

Java, C#, and JavaScript come preinstalled, but there are analyzers for PHP, Python, Visual Basic(.NET), XML, and even COBOL. Go to available plugins and search for HTML. You should find the Web plugin, the Code analyzer for Web (HTML, JSP, JSF, ...). Install it and you should get a message **SonarQube needs to be restarted in order to install 1 plugins**. Before we restart, search the available plugins for CSS. You should now find the CSS/SCSS/LESS analyzer that Enables analysis of CSS and Less files. SCSS and LESS are both CSS pre-processors, in case you were wondering. Install it and the restart message now updates to two plugins. You can now restart SonarQube from the message box.

Once SonarQube is restarted, run another build in Jenkins. Unfortunately, this will fail the quality gate, since we have four bugs in our HTML. The bugs are a bit silly though; we need to add favicon declarations in the header tags. We also get a good deal of code duplication (because we duplicated the header in each HTML file) and some extra code smells and technical debt. You can now decide whether these issues are legitimate issues that need to be addressed or whether these rules should be deactivated in the quality profile. At least, all our files are being analyzed. I have chosen to fix the bugs though, simply add a favicon link, right under the title element, in each HTML file. Yeah, I have used the Packt icon:

```
<link rel="shortcut icon" href="https://www.packtpub.com/favicon.ico">
```

Including code coverage

We can also include our code coverage results in SonarQube and set rules in our quality gates. For example, we can set the minimum amount of coverage or the minimum amount of coverage for new code.

According to the documentation, SonarQube supports the Cobertura format for code coverage out of the box. Unfortunately, I was never able to get that to work. Luckily, we can get it to work with the LCOV format. Getting an LCOV report is as easy as adding it to the coverage reporters in your Karma configuration:

```
[...]
   coverageReporter: {
      reporters: [
         { type : 'html', subdir: 'html' },
         { type : 'cobertura', subdir: 'cobertura' },
         { type : 'lcov', subdir: 'lcov' }
      ],
[...]
```

Now, adding code coverage to SonarQube is as easy as adding the path to your report file to the analysis properties in the Jenkins configuration:

```
sonar.javascript.lcov.reportPaths=test/coverage/lcov/lcov.info
```

If you run a build, you should see a coverage block being added to your SonarQube project page:

It should be possible to get your JUnit test results in SonarQube, but this functionality changed a couple of times in the last few years. It currently needs some specific JUnit format that is slightly different from the JUnit format that Karma uses. To get it to work, we must change our tests and the way Karma outputs the file. Personally, I have never bothered. We have unit test reporting in Jenkins and the only metric we need is 100% success. Both SonarQube and the Karma JUnit Reporter plugin have some documentation on the subject should you be willing to try: `https://docs.sonarqube.org/display/PLUG/Code+Coverage+by+Unit+Tests+for+Java+Project` and `https://github.com/karma-runner/karma-junit-reporter#produce-test-result-with-schema-acceptable-in-sonar`.

Leak periods

The last thing I wish to discuss relating to SonarQube is the so-called leak period. The leak period is basically a time frame in which you monitor new code. Let's say the leak period is a week. Within that week, the code smells, bugs, and technical debt are measured and accumulated. After a week, you start fresh, but keep track of how much smells, bugs, and debt was added since the last leak period. Your issues do not go away, but there were no issues added since the last leak period. This strategy is especially useful for legacy projects; projects that did not use SonarQube before and projects that just have been ignored in SonarQube. For such projects, especially if they are big, you may have a year worth of technical debt. You are not interested in a yearly technical debt. However, if you push to Git and get an email that you have just added 10 minutes of technical debt, you are inclined to look and fix it:

By default, your leak period is a new project version. So, SonarQube will keep track of new debt since the previous version of your project. You can change the version in your `sonar-project.properties` file. I have changed the version to 2.0 and removed the favicon from a file (we know that causes a bug). As you can see, there are two bugs in my code, but only one was introduced since version 1.0. You can be notified by email by going to your account and changing the notifications. You will want to check **My new issues** specifically. Also, **Changes in issues assigned to me** is pretty nice in case you, or someone else, accidentally fixes an issue for you.

You can change the leak period for your projects. You can set a global leak period for all your projects and overwrite it at a project level. Either go to **Administration** and then **General Settings** or go to your project and, from there, to **Administration** (not the one at the top, but below it), and then **General Settings**. Find the **Differential Views** settings. As you can see, on the page there are a few options for setting leak periods. Your options are a number of days, a specific date, the previous analysis, the previous version, or a specific version. You will also see periods 2 and 3 on global level and levels 4 and 5 on project level. These periods are deprecated and will be removed from SonarQube, so do not pay attention to them.

Artifacts

Now that we have a complete build and we know our code is pretty well tested and probably works as it should, we probably want to deliver our files. We are not yet ready for automated deployment, but at the very least, we want only those files we need to manually copy and paste somewhere. Go to your job configuration and add the post-build action `Archive the artifacts`. You can now specify the files you want to archive. At the very least, we want to archive the `prod` folder, but we also need to archive some node modules. The node modules could have been better; we could have copied them to the `prod` folder so that was all we needed to worry about, but we did not. If you want to do it, you know how. For now, we are going to specify the files one by one. So, you want to include the following files, seperated by a comma: `prod/`,
`node_modules/bootstrap/dist/css/bootstrap.min.css`,
`node_modules/angular/angular.min.js`,
`node_modules/bootstrap/dist/js/bootstrap.min.js`,
`node_modules/jquery/dist/jquery.min.js`. You may also want to take a look at the advanced settings. Personally, I only need artifacts when the build succeeds and I like to uncheck the case sensitivity setting. Now, build your project and you should see your artifacts on the project page:

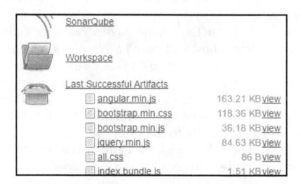

It looks like Jenkins messed up your folder structure, but it did not. When you click on **Last Successful Artifacts**, you can browse your artifact files in their original folder structure. It also lets you download all your artifacts in a ZIP file, so all you need to do is unpack the zip in your production environment and you are pretty much done.

We will need our artifacts later as there are multiple things we can do with them.

Running on Windows with Jenkins Slaves

We have come pretty far in what we can do using Jenkins, all automated. However, there is still the issue that we are running on Ubuntu. We still need to test our code on Internet Explorer and Edge and, in the real world, probably Safari. Unfortunately, we are stuck on Ubuntu, or so it seems. Luckily, Jenkins has a neat feature that enables us to run Jenkins remotely on different computers, slaves, or nodes.

Go to your Jenkins management and find **Manage Nodes**. On the menu, click **New Node**. Pick a node name, for example, `Windows Slave`, and make it **Permanent Agent** (at this point you probably have no other choice). In the next form, choose a remote root directory, something like `C:\Jenkins` (this is going to run on Windows!). Also, give this node the `windows` label and choose **Only build jobs with label expression matching this node** for usage. Optionally, you can set the `# of executors` to something other than 1. This value specified how many builds may run on this machine at the same time. If you have a very fast machine with lots of memory, you may be able to build five projects at a time, but if your server is a little slower, one or two might be a good option. If you have more builds than available executors, some builds will be queued until an executor becomes available again. Now comes the part where things get a little tricky. Jenkins needs to launch the Jenkins slave service. If this service is not available on the remote machine, Jenkins cannot communicate with the machine (assuming the Jenkins and remote machines can properly communicate otherwise). Jenkins can launch the slave service via a command on the master or it can take control of the remote host and install a Windows service. That last option sounds tempting, but unfortunately, Jenkins uses DCOM and it already warns you for the subtle problems you might encounter. Luckily, Jenkins also proposes an alternative, Java Web Start. However, Java Web Start is not an option right now. Just save this node and we will enable Java Web Start. Go to Jenkins management and then to **Global Security**. Set **TCP port for JNLP agents** from **Disable** to **Random** and save. Now, go back to your node configuration and you should be able to pick the **Launch agent via Java Web Start** launch method. Once you save your node, you should get a download. If you are not getting a download, go to the node page and click the Java **Launch** button:

Once you have downloaded the Jenkins slave agent, it should run automatically. If it does not run, you can start it manually. Once it is running, Jenkins should report the slave as connected. However, running some frontend program all the time is not really a viable solution. **Jenkins slave agent** can install itself as a service though. Just a single click and it is done. You may get an error when you try to install the slave as a service. If that is the case, try running it as an administrator and try again:

We can now change our project so that it uses our new slave. Go to the project and find **Restrict where this project can be run** in the **General** section of your configuration. You can restrict your projects to only run on certain slaves and slaves can be identified by labels. We gave our slave the `windows` label, so use that as the label expression. You should see the message `Label windows is serviced by 1 node` underneath the input field. While you are at it, give your master node the `linux` label.

A good way to label your slave is by the tools it provides. For example, we could have given our slave the labels ie and edge. By doing this, you can create multiple slaves with these labels and Jenkins can pick either one of those slaves to build your project. When you have 10 builds running consecutively, it may come in handy to have multiple slaves to handle them all. You can combine labels using logical and or symbols, for example, edge && ie or windows || linux. Jenkins will give you a warning when you have selected multiple labels that are not configured on a single machine, such as edge && safari.

Next we need to specify where to find SonarQube. Our Ubuntu server uses localhost:9000 for SonarQube; Windows is not going to find that SonarQube installation. Go to the Jenkins management and then to **Global Tool Configuration**. Find the **SonarQube Scanner** section and click the button to show your SonarQube Scanner installations. You should have one SonarQube Scanner, the Local one. The SONAR_RUNNER_HOME variable is set to /opt/sonar-scanner-2.8 or something like that. Let the Local installation be, but add a new installation. Give it a name, such as Slave Scanner, and check **Install automatically** (should be on by default). You can now add one or more installers, but one should be added automatically, **Install from Maven Central**. Leave the Maven Central installation and, from the drop-down menu, pick **SonarQube Scanner [your/latest version]**. This will download your scanner automatically using Maven (a Java *software project management and comprehension tool*). So, this installation should work just like that. We still need to tell our project to use it though. Go back to your project configuration and find **Execute SonarQube Scanner build step**. This should now have a new field, SonarQube Scanner. From the dropdown, you can now pick **Local** and **Slave Scanner**. Pick **Slave Scanner** and save the configuration.

Running our tests

If we were to run our project now, it would fail miserably. We still need to change our project so it runs on Windows. Remove the shell step and add the **Execute windows batch command** step. You would think the batch command itself would be the same, but that is slightly different too:

```
npm install && node_modules\.bin\gulp.cmd --env=prod
```

Unfortunately, the batch script does not execute multiple lines, so we need to use && to execute multiple statements. Other than that, we still run npm install and the Gulp script. Notice that I have changed the gulp script to gulp.**cmd**.

Now that we are running on Windows, we probably want some real browsers to test with. We can make that as an options just like the `env` variable. We cannot pass arrays from the command line though, but we can easily parse it. Put the following code at the top of your gulpfile (underneath all the `require` statements):

```
var browsers = gutil.env.browsers ? gutil.env.browsers.split(',') :
undefined;

gutil.log(gutil.colors.cyan('Environment: '),
gutil.colors.blue(gutil.env.env));
gutil.log(gutil.colors.cyan('Environment: '), gutil.colors.blue(browsers));
```

If we have browsers defined, we use those and, otherwise, we use undefined (meaning we use the ones from the configuration file). Now, in the `test-min` Karma task, replace the `browsers` option with the `browsers` variable (only in the `test-min` task, just pretesting in PhantomJS is fine):

```
[...]
new karma({
    configFile: __dirname + '/test/karma.min.conf.js',
    browsers: browsers
}, function (err) {
[...]
```

We can now change the Jenkins command, so it also runs the specified browsers (case-sensitive):

```
npm install && node_modules\.bin\gulp.cmd --env=prod --
browsers=Chrome,IE,IE9,Firefox
```

This will work for all your browsers except (can you guess it?) `IE` and Edge. The problem with `IE` is that it cannot run under your **Local System** account, but that is exactly what your Jenkins slave is running on. The easiest way to get this to work is to download a small utility program called PsExec from `https://technet.microsoft.com/en-us/sysinternals/bb897553`. Download the PsTools package and unzip PsTools. Open up a Command Prompt (as Administrator) and run `path_to_psexec\PsExec -s -i "%programfiles%\Internet Explorer\iexplore"`. This will open IE under the Local System account (the `-s` switch). I do not know why, but in this session, go to your IE options and then to the **Security** tab.

Click the **Reset all zones to default level** button and then uncheck the **Enable Protected Mode** option for all four security zones. Then restart IE. Now that your Local System IE is completely vulnerable, it will work in Jenkins. Weird IE stuff. Even now, it is still kind of sketchy, changing the order of browsers may break IE again. Unfortunately, I have not been able to find anything on Edge; it just does not work. Probably some security issue like IE, but I was not able to find it. However, if everything works on IE, IE9, Chrome, and Firefox, it is a pretty safe bet to assume everything works on Edge as well. In any case, Edge is maturing as a browser and a fix or workaround may be available by the time you are reading this.

The next step, now that we are running on Windows with all of our browsers, is to also run Protractor. Unfortunately, there are a load of issues with Jenkins and Protractor. And Protractor and Node.js and Protractor and npm and even Protractor and your browsers... The short story is that when npm installs packages globally, it only does so for the current user. Your Jenkins slave is running under the Local User account and not the account you used for installing all those packages globally. That is why we use the cmd files in the `node_modules\.bin` folder rather than calling `gulp` or `protractor` directly. However, it seems the `protractor.cmd` file is not quite the same as executing `protractor` directly. Even when you run the Jenkins slave under your own account, it seems Protractor hangs when running in Jenkins. Long story short, just use Chrome. You have tested your frontend on all the browsers (except Edge) using Karma; it is usually not necessary to run your E2E tests on all the browsers as well. So, make sure your Protractor configuration uses Chrome only. Hopefully, these issues get fixed in the future. It is a good idea to also run the `webdriver-manager update` command before running Protractor. This makes sure you always have the latest Chrome driver. This makes the final batch command as follows:

```
npm install && node_modules\.bin\gulp.cmd --env=prod --
browsers=Chrome,IE,IE9,Firefox && node_modules\.bin\webdriver-manager.cmd
update && node_modules\.bin\protractor.cmd test\protractor.conf.js
```

You are welcome to put it in multiple batch command build steps. And just to make sure, here is the part of the Protractor configuration that matters to get this to work:

```
[...]
    seleniumServerJar: 'selenium-server-standalone-3.1.0.jar',
    seleniumServerPort: 4444,
    //seleniumAddress: 'http://localhost:4444/wd/hub',
    multiCapabilities: [{
        browserName: 'chrome'
    }]
    //directConnect: true
};
```

Now that our Protractor tests work, we should also publish the JUnit reports it outputs. So, make sure to add it to the JUnit post-action, `test/junit/*.xml, selenium-junit/*.xml`. Selenium puts the output in the current folder, not the folder of the config file.

Try to build your project and if everything went well, the build should succeed!

When things go awry in Gulp, Karma, or Protractor, your Jenkins job may hang indefinitely. This prevents other projects from building and hogs up resources. We do not want hanging builds. You can install the Build-timeout plugin (`https://wiki.jenkins-ci.org/display/JENKINS/Build-timeout +Plugin`). It cannot stop all the hanging builds, but it is better than nothing.

Triggering a project pipeline

At this point, we can run our build on the Ubuntu master node or on the Windows slave node. Now, we want to build our code on Ubuntu and then, when the build succeeds, test it on Windows. We face a few problems though: we do not feel like repeating the entire build just to run some additional tests. Passing all the necessary files to the next job is quite a lot, but we do need pretty much all of our node modules. You may not like it, but to test our code using different browsers, we may as well just run the entire build again.

Let's create two new projects, one project to build our source on the master and another project to (build and) test on the slave. On the Jenkins home page, create a new item. Enter a name for the item, for example, `Build Chapter 7` or `Build Web Shop`, and then choose to copy from another project. You can enter the name of the project to copy (this is case-sensitive, so be sure to match the casing). We are going to copy the project we have created in this chapter; I named it `Chapter 7`, but you should enter whatever you called it. You will now be taken to the configuration for your new project. Give it the `linux` label expression, so we are sure it only runs on our Linux VM. Remove the Protractor JUnit report, as we are not going to run Protractor in this project. We also need to switch the Windows batch command with the Ubuntu shell script and change the commands accordingly:

```
npm install
node_module/.bin/gulp --env=prod --browsers=PhantomJS
```

Other than that, we can leave this project as it is.

Create another new item and name it `Test Chapter 7` or `Test Web Shop` and, again, copy it from the project we have created in this chapter. Configure it to run on Windows only. Also, remove the SonarQube Runner build action and the quality gates post-build action.

At this point, we have a bit of a problem. Our project is triggered on a push to our Git repository, just like the build project. However, we would like to run the build job first and only test further when it succeeds. Select the **Build after other projects are built** trigger and set **Build Chapter 7** (or **Build Web Shop**) as **Projects to watch**. Now, we have another problem; when this project is triggered, it will check out our entire Git repository. However, it is possible that a new commit was made while the previous project was running. This project would also test that new commit while the previous job is still building that commit. Our commit states would be a mess. What we need is to copy the entire workspace from the previous build to this one so we are sure we are working on the same files and the same commit. Sharing a workspace between two projects is easy when you are working on the same machine. In the advanced settings of the general section of your job configuration, there is an option to **Use custom workspace**. Simply enter a custom workspace and make sure both projects target the same workspace. However, since we are working on different machines, we are in a bit of a bind. Jenkins does not support sharing workspaces between slaves out of the box and I have yet to find a good plugin that enables this completely. For now, there is nothing we can do but to check out the entire Git repository and hope for the best.

That leaves us with another problem, we could publish the status to the GitLab commits, but it may be overwritten. Imagine the following scenario: commit 1 is pushed and our build project builds it. While it is building, commit 2 is pushed. When the build project finishes, the test project is started and pulls commit 1 and 2 and tests them both. Meanwhile, the build project is going to build commit 2. Commit 2 does not pass the tests and both commits get a failed status (while commit 1 was actually fine!). After that, the build project finishes and gives commit 2 a passed status. You now have two commits that have a wrong status. So I am going to leave the status updating to the build project and remove the updating from the test project. We may be able to fix this in a later chapter.

Last, but not least, we need to create a new webhook in GitLab, so it notifies the Build Web Shop project that it should run whenever a change is pushed to the repository. You may also disable the first project we created, so it will not run at the same time as our new project.

Now, the moment of truth, push a change to your Git repository and watch Jenkins work its magic. When all goes well, you have automated the entire build and test flow of our project.

Summary

In this chapter, we have taken a better look at Jenkins. We have learned how to configure Jenkins, how to install and use plugins, how to create a project and expand on it as our needs for quality grow, and how to install Jenkins slaves and run multiple projects consecutively. In addition, we have played around with SonarQube and its quality gates and profiles. All in all, it is a lot of work to set up everything, but it is worth it in the long run. Your code is automatically reviewed and tested on multiple browsers, which ensures some baseline quality for your software. In the next chapters, we are going to expand on backend technologies, starting with Node.js and MongoDB, and learn how to fit those into Jenkins.

8
A NodeJS and MongoDB Web App

So far, we have tested and automated all of our HTML, CSS, and JavaScript jobs. However, all of it was frontend code. In this chapter, we are going to add some backend. We will use Node.js and MongoDB, so it will still be JavaScript. However, it will still be quite an undertaking. In our current HTML code, we have copied and pasted the entire header and search bar, but when we have a backend, we can generate HTML using a template engine. Since we are using Node.js, we can reuse our `shopping-cart.js` file with some slight modifications. Also, we are currently minimizing all of our code using Gulp, and hence, in using a backend, we may be able to minimize our code `on the fly` and have it cached.

After we have hauled over our website, so it uses a proper backend, we can run our tests to see if everything still works. However, we may have to change our tests a bit as well. Protractor is currently running on the file protocol, but with a backend, we will have to change that to the HTML protocol.

We will also use a complete new piece of technology, the database. Once we have a database in place, we may want to test if it all works as it should. Like programming languages, databases have testing options.

Once everything is in place, we will change our Jenkins projects accordingly.

I want to emphasize that this book is not about many of the technologies discussed in this chapter, but Continuous Integration, Delivery, and Deployment. Continuously Delivering databases, including NoSQL, and other server-side software are just a part of that. I am not assuming any knowledge on MongoDB or Node.js, so if you follow my lead, I am pretty sure you will get it all working just fine. I am not going to give detailed explanations on the code samples though, but they should not be too complex. For the sake of simplicity, I am ignoring best practices and security issues. What you see here is not production-ready code, but the process to getting there and how CI helps in putting the pieces together.

Installing MongoDB

In this chapter, we are going to use MongoDB, one of the most popular NoSQL databases at the time of writing. It is even pretty popular when compared to SQL databases. According to DB-Engines Ranking (`https://db-engines.com/en/ranking`), MongoDB is the fifth most popular database right after all the major SQL databases. In case you have no experience with NoSQL, it means Not-only-SQL (and not No-SQL-whatsoever). MongoDB is a document-oriented database, meaning it stores *document-oriented* or semi-structured data. It is not very different from SQL and so is a perfect introduction to the world of NoSQL. Additionally, it is quite easy to get started with. And so I chose to use it for this chapter.

I just want to quickly mention the biggest differences with SQL databases, such as SQL Server, MySQL, and Oracle. First of all, MongoDB stores its data as **Binary JSON** (**BSON**). In practice, this means everything can be queried using JavaScript. We can put JavaScript objects in it and we get JavaScript objects back (but you can use MongoDB in any major programming language). Like JavaScript, and completely unlike SQL, JavaScript objects have no set structure. Properties and even functions are added on the fly. As such, it is possible to have a `SalesOrder` object in your `Person` table (or collection, as tables are called in MongoDB). Even collections are created on the fly. Because collections and objects do not have a set structure, MongoDB is called a **schemaless** database. Perhaps the biggest difference, and the one that a lot of programmers and DBAs shun, is that there is no such thing as a foreign key constraint. That means that you are probably going to store redundant data and that data is not necessarily consistent.

Installing MongoDB on Ubuntu

Let's start with installing MongoDB, so we can be done with that. Luckily, the documentation on installing MongoDB on Ubuntu is pretty spot on (`https://docs.mongodb.com/manual/tutorial/install-mongodb-on-ubuntu/`):

```
sudo apt-key adv --keyserver hkp://keyserver.ubuntu.com:80 --recv
0C49F3730359A14518585931BC711F9BA15703C6
echo "deb http://repo.mongodb.org/apt/ubuntu xenial/mongodb-org/3.4
multiverse" | sudo tee /etc/apt/sources.list.d/mongodb-org-3.4.list
sudo apt-get update
sudo apt-get install -y mongodb-org
```

The first command, `sudo apt-key`, is used to manage package keys. Keys authenticate packages and packages that are authenticated with a key are considered trusted. The `adv` switch allows for advanced options. With `--recv`, we can download keys from a server and put them directly into a trusted list of keys. We know the `deb` command; it gets a Debian package file from the specified URL. The `multiverse` switch indicates the package is restricted by copyright or legal issues. Our use case is training, so we are good to go. The `sudo tee` command really just saves the file to the specified directory. Next, we update our `sudo-apt` repository and install `MongoDB`.

Next, we need to set up our first database and user and make the MongoDB instance visible from outside the VM. First we are going to create the database and user. This is possible because authorization is off by default in MongoDB. Type `mongo` to enter the MongoDB shell. MongoDB uses JavaScript, so the commands should look pretty familiar. We need to create a database and then insert a user and give it read and write access to our database. To insert a user, we simply pass an object to the `db.createUser` function. Writing everything on a single line can be messy (I failed to properly close an object/array/object/function twice that way), but you can enter a new line using *Shift + Enter*:

```
mongo
use webshop
db.createUser({
user: 'your_user',
pwd: 'your_password',
roles: [{ role: 'readWrite', db: 'webshop' }]
})
exit
```

The `use` `webshop` command automatically creates a new database if it does not yet exist. The `db` variable now points to the webshop database and `createUser` adds the user to that database:

```
> use webshop
switched to db webshop
> db.createUser({
... user: 'sander',
... pwd: 'sander',
... roles: [{ role: 'readWrite', db: 'webshop' }]
... })
Successfully added user: {
        "user" : "sander",
        "roles" : [
                {
                        "role" : "readWrite",
                        "db" : "webshop"
                }
        ]
}
> exit
bye
sander@ciserver:~$
```

To make our MongoDB database visible to our client, we must edit the `/etc/mongod.conf` file. Use `vi` (or any other editor) to edit the file. Comment out the `bindIp: 127.0.0.1` line (by putting # in front of it) and uncommit the `#security:` line and put `authorization: 'enabled'` under it. When you are done editing, the configuration file should look as follows:

```
sudo vi /etc/mongod.conf
i

[...]

# network interfaces
net:
  port: 27017
#  bindIp: 127.0.0.1


#processManagement:

security:
  authorization: 'enabled'
```

```
[...]

esc
:wq
sudo service mongod restart
```

Please note that we cannot create new users anymore after this point because we are now required to log in with a user that has sufficient privileges and we don't have such a user.

MongoDB should automatically start as a service on startup, so we do not need to worry about that. Be sure to restart the service after having made the configuration changes.

Installing MongoDB on Windows

Head over to the MongoDB website and download the installer from the download center (https://www.mongodb.com/download-center). The version you want is probably the most recent Community Server Edition for Windows Server 2008 R2 64-bit and later, with SSL Support x64. Simply download it and run the installer. Choose a complete installation and leave the defaults. The following information is all in the MongoDB documentation, but I have summarized it for you.

Now, head over to your C:\ drive and create a folder and name it data. Inside your new folder, create two new folders and name them log and db. Of course, you can name them whatever you want and place them wherever you want, but I have put it in C:\, so that is the path I will use in the upcoming examples. This is also the default path MongoDB will use (on the drive where you installed it). You can now run MongoDB from your Command Prompt. Simply run mongod.exe, which is located in the install folder. Your default install folder is C:\Program Files\MongoDB\Server\3.4:

```
cd C:\Program Files\MongoDB\Server\3.4\bin
mongod.exe
```

You can specify a different data folder by passing the --dbpath parameter to the mongod program:

```
mongod.exe --dbpath c:\something\db
```

Be sure the folder exists or MongoDB will not run. When it runs successfully, it will create a number of files in the specified folder.

You can also put `dbpath`, along with other configuration, in a custom configuration file. For example, put a file called `mongod.cfg` in `C:\data` and put the following configuration in it:

```
systemLog:
    destination: file
    path: c:\data\log\mongod.log
storage:
    dbPath: c:\data\db
```

You can now run MongoDB using this configuration:

```
mongod.exe --config c:\data\mongod.cfg
```

Last, we want to install MongoDB as a service. You can simply use the extra `--install` parameter to `mongod.exe` and it will install MongoDB as a service. We also need the configuration because we need to configure a log file. Be sure to execute the installation command from an elevated Command Prompt:

```
mongod.exe --config "c:\Program Files\MongoDB\Server\3.4\mongod.cfg" --
install
net start mongodb
```

If nothing happens and you cannot find MongoDB in your services, see the configured log file for details. If everything is alright, you should be able to find the MongoDB service in your services. You can now add a user in the exact same way as on Ubuntu. In your Command Prompt, type `mongo` to open the MongoDB shell and use *Shift + Enter* to go to a new line without executing your command:

```
mongo
use webshop
db.createUser({
[...]
```

You can enable authorization in your configuration file like we did on Ubuntu:

```
security:
    authorization: 'enabled'
```

Next, we need to connect with MongoDB. There are a few clients available. We are going to use Robomongo (`https://robomongo.org/`). Simply head over to their website and download the installer or the portable version. Once you start Robomongo, you will be taken to the connection manager. Create a new connection and name it `CI Server` (or whatever you like). The address is `ciserver` (or your VMs IP address or localhost if you installed it on the same machine) and the port is `27017` (unless you changed it in the configuration). Go to the **authentication** tab and check **Perform authentication**. Put `webshop` for **Database** and your username and password in their respective fields. Test your connection to validate that everything works. You can now connect to the database and create collections (the SQL table variant) and functions and read, insert, update, and delete data:

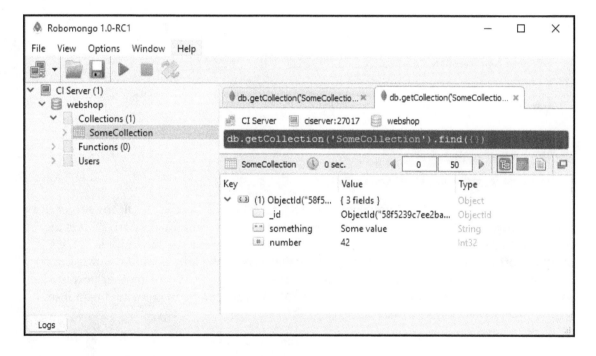

Creating the Node.js Back-end

Now that the database is in place and we know how to browse collections and data in the database, we can start creating a backend powered by Node.js. To get your website to run on Node.js, all you need to do is create a JavaScript file and load it using Node. Node provides some packages that are at your disposal by using `require` as we have done before. The Node.js website had some `Hello, Node.js!` script on their website, but it was removed when the platform got more mature and the user base grew. Luckily, I still have it laying around somewhere and so we will create our first Node.js website. Put the following JavaScript code in a new file and name it `index.js`:

```
var http = require('http');
var server = http.createServer(function (req, res) {
    res.writeHead(200, {'Content-Type': 'text/plain'});
    res.end('Hello, Node.js!');
});
server.listen(80, '127.0.0.1');
console.log('Server running at http://127.0.0.1:80/');
```

You can run the file in Node by opening up a Command Prompt and passing `file` as a parameter to `node`:

node path_to_your_file\index.js

Now, browse to localhost and you should see the text `Hello, Node.js!`. If the server did not start correctly, there is a big chance something is already running on port 80. It is the default HTTP port and many services make use of it. Simply change the script so it uses another port instead of 80. You can use any available port, the only advantage of using port 80 is that we do not have to specify that port in the browser. If you use another port, such as 1337, you need to browse to `localhost:1337`.We can change the returned response so that it returns HTML rather than plain text:

```
var server = http.createServer(function (req, res) {
    res.writeHead(200, {'Content-Type': 'text/html'});
    res.end('<h1>Header</h1><p>Hello, Node.js!</p>');
});
```

Restart your Node server from the command (*Ctrl* + *C* to close the current server) and refresh your localhost page. You should now get some pre-styled header and paragraph.

Closing and re-opening the Node server is a bit distracting and tedious, especially when you are still developing and need to refresh a lot. There are some tools that open a server for you and restart it whenever your JavaScript file changes. The easiest I have found is nodemon (`https://nodemon.io/`). Nodemon is just an npm package, so you can install it using npm. Now, instead of opening a Node server using the `node` command you can use `nodemon` and make changes without restarting:

```
npm install nodemon -g
nodemon path_to_your_file\index.js
```

Browse to localhost to see if it worked. Now, change your `index.js` file (just make it return some different text) and refresh your browser. You should see the new text without having restarted your Node server:

Express

To make things easier for ourselves in the long run, we are going to use a framework for Node.js. Node is pretty bare bones, which means it can do everything, but it probably needs some work. That work is done for us in different frameworks that all work a little differently. Express (`https://expressjs.com/`) is one of the more popular frameworks (among `Hapi.js` and `Sails.js`), so let's go with that. Simply install Express using npm. Please note that we need Express to run the software, so we use `--save` instead of `--save-dev`:

```
npm install express --save
```

We can now change our file so it uses Express. We do not need to `require` the `http` module because Express has that all wrapped for us. Other than that, the code looks pretty much the same. With Express, we can map multiple paths to the same route handler though, so `localhost` and `localhost/index.html` will now return the same page. The `*` wildcard handles all other requests and, in our case, returns a 404:

```
var express = require('express'),
    app = express();

app.get(['/', '/index.html'], function (req, res) {
    res.writeHead(200, {'Content-Type': 'text/html'});
    res.end('<h1>Header</h1><p>Hello, Node.js!</p>');
});
app.get('*', function (req, res) {
    res.writeHead(404, {'Content-Type': 'text/html'});
    res.end('<h1>404 - Page not found!</h1><p>What were you even trying to
do...?</p>');
});

var server = app.listen(80, '127.0.0.1');
console.log('Server running at http://127.0.0.1:80/');
```

Next, we want to serve our HTML files instead of the HTML string we send now. That is easy enough, but there is a catch:

```
app.get(['/', '/index.html'], function (req, res) {
    res.sendFile(path.join(__dirname, 'index.html'));
});
```

As you can see, we can simply return an HTML file using `res.sendFile`. Express will sort out our response headers based on the file format. However, if you refresh your website (using *Ctrl* + *F5* to clear the cache), it looks crazy. In your browser's console, you can find plenty of 404s. What happens is that your browser received the HTML file and then requests all the CSS and JavaScript files. The browser tries to GET files such as: `http://localhost/css/layout.css` and `http://localhost/scripts/bundles/index.bundle.js`.

Unfortunately, we have a GET router for / and `.index.html` and all the other GET requests end up in the wildcard (*) route, which returns a 404.

Express has a method for returning static files. It is really quite easy, enter a folder or filename, and Express will serve the files in the folder or the specified file. The files are available on the path relative to the specified path. The easiest method of just making everything available is by specifying __dirname:

```
var express = require('express'),
    path = require('path'),
    app = express();

app.use(express.static(__dirname));

[...]
```

By adding the `app.use(express.static(...))` statement to your Node file, you make all the files in your web folder available. For more fine-grained control, which is recommended from a security point of view, specify only the files and folders you want to make public. We can add the debug files and minified files. If you want, you can add a Boolean switch and only get the debug files for a debug run and only the minified files for a production run:

```
app.use('/node_modules/bootstrap/dist/fonts',
express.static('node_modules/bootstrap/dist/fonts'));
app.use('/node_modules/bootstrap/dist/css/bootstrap.css',
express.static('node_modules/bootstrap/dist/css/bootstrap.css'));
app.use('/node_modules/bootstrap/dist/css/bootstrap.min.css',
express.static('node_modules/bootstrap/dist/css/bootstrap.min.css'));
app.use('/css', express.static('css'));

app.use('/node_modules/angular/angular.js',
express.static('node_modules/angular/angular.js'));
app.use('/node_modules/angular/angular.min.js',
express.static('node_modules/angular/angular.min.js'));
app.use('/node_modules/jquery/dist/jquery.js',
express.static('node_modules/jquery/dist/jquery.js'));
app.use('/node_modules/jquery/dist/jquery.min.js',
express.static('node_modules/jquery/dist/jquery.min.js'));
app.use('/node_modules/bootstrap/dist/js/bootstrap.min.js',
express.static('node_modules/bootstrap/dist/js/bootstrap.js'));
app.use('/scripts', express.static('scripts'));
app.use('/scripts/bundles', express.static('scripts/bundles'));
```

Because Express finds the files relative to the static directory, we need to explicitly specify the path for the given resource. To illustrate this, `app.use(express.static('css'));` serves `localhost/layout.css` and `localhost/utils.css`, while `app.use('/css', express.static('css'));` serves `localhost/css/layout.css` and `localhost/css/utils.css`.

Now that we have taken care of that, we can add the rest of the routes:

```
app.get(['/', '/index.html'], function (req, res) {
    res.sendFile(path.join(__dirname, 'index.html'));
});
app.get('/views/product.html', function (req, res) {
    res.sendFile(path.join(__dirname, 'views/product.html'));
});
app.get('/views/search.html', function (req, res) {
    res.sendFile(path.join(__dirname, 'views/search.html'));
});
app.get('/views/shopping-cart.html', function (req, res) {
    res.sendFile(path.join(__dirname, 'views/shopping-cart.html'));
});
```

The website does the same as it did before. Lo and behold, we can verify this with relative ease! Go to your Protractor configuration file and set `baseUrl` to `http://localhost` and remove `browser.resetUrl`. We now work with the HTTP protocol instead of the file protocol:

```
exports.config = {
    baseUrl: 'http://localhost',
    onPrepare: function() {
        //browser.resetUrl = 'file://';
        browser.ignoreSynchronization = true;

        [...]
    },
    [...]
};
```

Now that we use HTTP, we can also run Firefox without a direct connection, meaning we can run all the browsers in a single configuration. Anyway, run your Protractor tests and verify that all tests succeed.

EJS

Now that we can serve files and HTML from our backend, we can use some sort of HTML template engine. Basically, I am pretty satisfied with the HTML files we have so far, except for the fact that the navigation bar at the top is duplicated in each file. We can do better than that. Express has built-in support for several templating engines, most notably Jade. On top of that, it is fairly easy to create your own templating engine. While Jade is pretty awesome, it has very clean and concise syntax, we are going to use EJS, or Embedded JavaScript (http://www.embeddedjs.com/). All we want to do is create some sort of partial view (the navigation bar) and insert that into our pages. EJS supports just that (and more):

```
npm install ejs --save
```

Now, in your `views` folder, create a new file and name it `navbar.ejs`. Simply put the entire `nav` element from any of your views into the file. We can start with the product page because it is a very simple page:

```
<nav class="navbar navbar-default navbar-fixed-top">
    <div class="container">
        <div class="navbar-header">
            [...]
        </div>
    </div>
</nav>
```

Rename the `product.html` file to `product.ejs` and replace the `nav` element with an EJS directive:

```
<!DOCTYPE html>
<html>
    <head>
        [...]
    </head>
    <body ng-app="shopApp">
<%- include navbar.ejs %>
        <div class="container" ng-controller="productController">
            [...]
        </div>
    </body>
</html>
```

In the Node file, we have to make two changes. First, we must set EJS as the view engine for Express. Second, we need to use it to render the product page rather than serve some static HTML:

```
var express = require('express'),
    path = require('path'),
    app = express();

app.set('view engine', 'ejs');

[...]

app.get('/views/product.html', function (req, res) {
   res.render('product');
});

[...]
```

EJS will look for the `product.ejs` file in the `views` folder by default. You can now make this change for all your HTML files and place `index.html` to the `views` folder (after all, we already have `index.js` in the root). You should also change the source in your `html` task in the gulpfile:

```
.task('html', ['clean'], function () {
    return gulp.src(['views/*.ejs'])
       .pipe(replace('href="views\\', 'href="'))
       [...]
```

Also, change your gulpfile, so it watches `views/*.ejs` instead of `views/*.html`. There is just one more issue we need to fix. Currently, all our pages, except index, are routing to `/views/page.html`. Note that this is completely random. It does not necessarily serve HTML pages and the pages do not have to be in the `views` folder. We could route to `monkey` and return the product page. So, let's make that routing a bit more friendly on the eye and remove the `/views` bit from the URL. We can keep the `.html` part because it is pretty standard and we do still return HTML (although it is completely optional):

```
app.get('/product.html', function (req, res) {
[...]
app.get('/search.html', function (req, res) {
[...]
app.get('/shopping-cart.html', function (req, res) {
```

You should now fix your `nav.ejs` and `index.ejs` files so the anchors do not link to `../index.html` and `views/...html`, but directly to the correct page.

Try running your Protractor tests. One test fails because the test is trying to open `'views\\shopping-cart.html'`, which obviously is not going to work. So, just change that to `'shopping-cart.html'` and try again. Your tests might still fail if you have not copied the `nav` element in `navbar.ejs` from the `index.html` page. We gave the a element for the search button an `id`, so our tests can easily locate that element, but we only did that on the `index.html` page. That is what you get for duplicating code. Add `id="search-btn"` to the anchor and run your tests again. They should succeed now.

At this point, I would like to point out how even these minimal tests give us the confidence to completely rebuild some frontend-only pages to backend Node with EJS.

However, I would also like to point out that two tests failed because the tests themselves were not quite correct. The search functionality would have worked even without `id`, which was only there for the test to begin with. Having tests is great, but they come at the cost of some debugging and maintenance once in a while.

The Login Page

Our next step is to create some method of logging in together with saving what is in our shopping cart. We are not going to create a full fledged web shop, so for the sake of learning, we will manually insert two users into the database, so we can log in and remember what is in each of their shopping carts. Before we can save anything to MongoDB, we must first create a login page for our website. Create a view and name it `login.ejs`. The contents are pretty much the same as that on other pages. Same stylesheets, scripts, and footer. The part that is different goes in `container div`. I am using a `form` element so Angular does the `required` validation for us. Other than that, it is not much different from doing a regular AJAX POST later on:

```
[...]
    <script src="..\scripts\bundles\login.bundle.js"></script>
    <!-- endbuild -->
</head>
<body ng-app="shopApp">
    <%- include navbar.ejs %>
    <div class="container" ng-controller="loginController">
        <div class="row">
            <form ng-submit="login()">
                <div class="col-lg-3 center text-center">
                    <h2>Login</h2>
                    <p class="bg-danger" ng-show="notFound">User or password
were incorrect.</p>
                    <div class="input-group center">
```

```
                    <p class="clearfix">
                        <input class="form-control"
placeholder="Username..." ng-model="username" required />
                    </p>
                    <p class="clearfix">
                        <input type="password" class="form-control"
placeholder="Password..." ng-model="password" required />
                    </p>
                </div>
                <p class="clearfix">
                    <input type="submit" class="btn btn-success"
value="Login" />
                </p>
            </div>
        </form>
    </div>
    <footer class="footer">
        [...]
```

To make this work, we need to add some CSS to the `utils.css` file:

```
.center {
    float: none;
    margin: 0 auto;
}
```

And you need a `login.js` file that does not do anything yet:

```
angular.module('shopApp', [])
    .controller('loginController', ['$scope', function ($scope) {
        $scope.username = null;
        $scope.password = null;
        $scope.notFound = false;
        $scope.login = function () {
            console.log($scope.username + ' - ' + $scope.password);
        };
    }]);
```

And, of course, we need to route it in our Node file:

```
app.get('/login.html', function (req, res) {
    res.render('login');
});
```

Last, but not least, we must change the `navbar.ejs` file so the login button actually brings us to the login page:

```
<li><a href="login.html"><span class="glyphicon glyphicon-user"></span>
Login</a></li>
```

Be sure to run Gulp, so our new scripts are bundled. Your Karma tests will fail because our code coverage just went below the 50% threshold, but do not worry about that for now.

Connecting with AJAX

Now that we have the login page in place, we can actually connect to our backend, something we have not done yet! Basically, what we want is to log in and redirect to the shopping cart (which kind of serves as our personal page for this project). In the frontend, this is easy enough. We need to inject the `$http` module to our Angular controller that we can use to make an AJAX call. After that, we can call our backend and redirect on success or show an error when the user was not found:

```
$scope.login = function () {
    $scope.notFound = false;
    $http.post('/login', {
        username: $scope.username,
        password: $scope.password
    }).then(function (response) {
        if (response.data.success) {
            window.location.replace("/shopping-cart.html");
        } else {
            $scope.notFound = true;
        }
    }, function () {
        alert('An error has occurred.');
    });
};
```

So, I am making a distinction between a 500 error code (which should not occur, ideally) and a nonsuccessful user lookup. When the user is found, we continue to the shopping cart page.

On the backend, things are a little different. First, we need the Express body parser to parse JSON to regular JavaScript. This used to be included in Express, but they made it a separate plugin. So, we need to install it using npm:

```
npm install body-parser --save
```

Using it is simple enough. Attach the middleware to Express and that is that:

```
var bodyParser = require('body-parser');
app.use(bodyParser.json());
```

We can now inspect the `body` property on our `request` variable on our login POST call:

```
app.post('/login', function (req, res) {
    if (req.body.username === 'username' && req.body.password ===
'password') {
        res.json({success: true});
    } else {
        res.json({success: false});
    }
});
```

We will also need a session, so we can *remember* the logged in user. Like the body parser, Express has some middleware plugin for session management, `express-session` (https://www.npmjs.com/package/express-session):

```
npm install express-session --save
```

The default session store is in-memory. However, there are various plugins for other session stores, such as MongoDB, Redis, Oracle, MySQL, and many more. Usage is not particularly difficult, however, it is not production-ready (you will need another session store for that). The session makes use of a cookie, so when you log in and then clear your cookies, you will be logged out again:

```
var session = require('express-session');
app.use(session({
    secret: 'some secret',
    resave: false,
    saveUninitialized: true,
    cookie: {}
}));

[...]

app.post('/login', function (req, res) {
    if (req.body.username === 'username' && req.body.password ===
'password') {
```

```
      req.session.authenticated = true;
      req.session.username = req.body.username;
      res.json({success: true});
   } else {
      res.json({success: false});
   }
});
```

And, of course, we will need a `logout` method as well:

```
app.get('/logout.html', function (req, res) {
   if (req.session) {
      req.session.destroy();
   }
   res.redirect('/');
});
```

We can now show a login or a logout button depending on whether you are logged in or not. With EJS, we can easily add this. However, it would be cumbersome to add some `authenticated` variable to each view:

```
res.render('some-view', {authenticated: req.session.authenticated});
```

Instead, we can add some middleware to Express. It is important that this is added after you add the session middleware:

```
app.use(session([...]));
app.use(function(req, res, next) {
   res.locals.authenticated = req.session.authenticated;
   next();
});
```

`res.locals` is available in your templates, so adding this to your Node script will make `authenticated` available to all your views. And we will need it in all views. Luckily, we only have to change this in one file, being `navbar.ejs`:

```
[...]
<ul class="nav navbar-nav navbar-right">
   <% if (authenticated) {%>
      <li><a href="logout.html"><span class="glyphicon glyphicon-
off"></span> Logout <%= username %></a></li>
   <% } else { %>
      <li><a href="login.html"><span class="glyphicon glyphicon-
user"></span> Login</a></li>
   <% } %>
   <li><a href="shopping-cart.html"><span class="glyphicon glyphicon-
shopping-cart"></span> Order</a></li>
</ul>
```

```
[...]
```

You can now log in with the username `username` and the password `password` and you should see the logout icon appear on every page until you log out or restart Node.js or your browser.

Saving to MongoDB

The next step is getting our users from the database. As we said, we are not going to create a registration method, so we will need to insert at least one user manually. You can log in to the webshop database using Robomongo. Right-click on **Collections** and choose **Create collection...** Name your new collection `user`. Now, you can right-click on the user collection and pick **Insert Document...** The document you are going to insert is just a JavaScript object, so enter some object with the `username` and `password` properties:

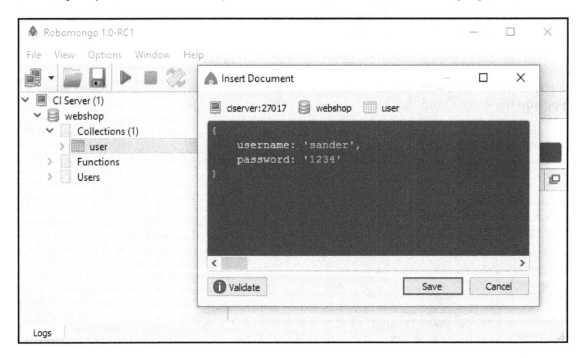

You can now browse the newly inserted document(s):

We can now query the database from Node and check for a user with the given username and password. To connect with MongoDB, we are going to use the Node.js MongoDB API Mongoose (http://mongoosejs.com/). As always, we can install Mongoose with npm:

```
npm install mongoose --save
```

After that, using Mongoose is surprisingly easy. No wonder we are using JavaScript to insert JavaScript in a database that uses JavaScript. The only thing that makes working with Mongoose a little messy is the asynchronous API. It kind of works like we know from Protractor:

```
var MongoClient = require('mongodb').MongoClient,
    mongoUrl = 'mongodb://your_user:your_password@ciserver:27017/webshop';

[...]

app.post('/login', function (req, res) {
    if (req.body.username && req.body.password) {
        MongoClient.connect(mongoUrl, function (err, db) {
            if (err) {
                console.log(err);
                res.status(500).send(err);
            } else {
                db.collection('user').findOne({
                    username: req.body.username,
```

```
                password: req.body.password
        }, function (err, user) {
            if (err) {
                console.log(err);
                res.status(500).send(err);
            }
            if (user) {
                req.session.authenticated = true;
                req.session.username = req.body.username;
                res.json({success: true});
            } else {
                req.session.destroy();
                res.json({success: false});
            }
        });
    }
    });
} else {
    res.json({success: false});
}
});
```

That is quite a bit of code, but I think it is not that hard to follow. We use
`MongoClient.connect(mongoUrl)` to get a connection to the database. The `callback`
function gets an error object and a reference to the database. When an error is returned, we
log the error and return an internal server error. If we do not get an error, we use the
database to find the `user` collection and find a document with the specified `username` and
`password`. `callback` gives us an error and a found document. The error handling is the
same as before. Now, if we find a user, we create the session variables `authenticated` and
`username` and return `success true`. If no user was found, we destroy the session (in case
you were already logged in as someone else) and return `success false`. This should do
the trick. So, try logging in as the user you entered in MongoDB. Also, try inserting a
second user and logging in as both of them in separate browsers (or in private windows of
the same browser).

Moving our Products to MongoDB

We still have that weird `repository.js` file that has some hardcoded products in it.
Having products like that in a JavaScript file is not going to work, so let's move them to the
database as well. Again, we are going to insert them manually, but this time, we can create
a little script that inserts all of the products at once. In Robomongo, right-click on the
database and pick **Open Shell....** This opens a new tab with a single line for you to type in.
Do not worry, you can enter as many new lines as you want.

Your command will simply be some JavaScript and, since we already have all our products written down in JavaScript, this is basically a copy and paste action:

```
db.getCollection("product").insert([{
    id: 1,
    name: 'Final Fantasy XV',
    price: 55.99,
    description: 'Final Fantasy finally makes a come back!',
    category: 'Gaming'
}, {
    [...]
}]);
```

You can run the query using *F5* or the play button (the green triangle) in the menu. **Robomongo** tells you it **Inserted 1 record(s) in 13ms**, but it actually inserted the entire array:

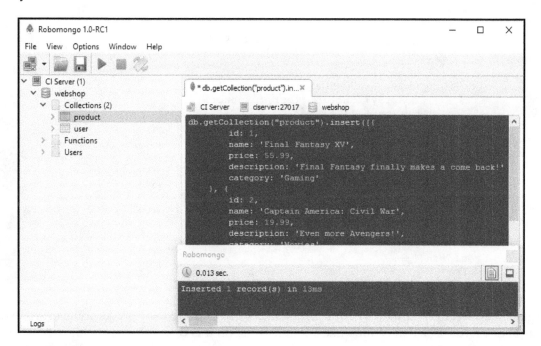

Next, we need to rewrite the other functions in the repository file so that they make AJAX calls to the server and return the products from the database. The first function we are going to rewrite is `search`. We are going to create a `searchProducts` POST method in our Node file and search for the products there based on a `q` parameter. The functionality should remain the same as the frontend function though:

```
function handleErr (err, res) {
    if (err) {
        console.log(err);
        res.status(500).send(err);
    }
}

app.post('/searchProducts', function (req, res) {
    req.body.q = 'fanta';
    if (req.body.q) {
        MongoClient.connect(mongoUrl, function (err, db) {
            if (err) {
                handleErr(err, res);
            } else {
                db.collection('product').find({
                    name: new RegExp(req.body.q, 'i')
                }).toArray(function (err, products) {
                    if (err) {
                        handleErr(err, res);
                    } else {
                        console.log(products);
                        res.json(products);
                    }
                });
            }
        });
    } else {
        res.json([]);
    }
});
```

Again, it is a bit of code with a couple of callbacks, but nothing too bad. As you can see, we can find records with some value like another value (in this case, [Name] LIKE '%' + q + '%' in SQL) using regular expressions. I am not a fan of regex, but they do the job and this one is not particularly complicated. The `i` option is just there to make the lookup case-insensitive. We now need to call this function from the repository file in the frontend and process the results:

```
search: function (q, $http, callback) {
    var $http = angular.injector(["ng"]).get("$http");
```

```
$http.post('/searchProducts', {
    q: q
}).then(function (response) {
    callback(response.data);
}, function () {
    alert('An error has occurred.');
});
}
```

In this example, we are getting the Angular `$http` variable using dependency injection. After that, we simply execute an AJAX POST and pass the result to `callback`:

```
var q = utils.getQueryParams().q;
repository.search(q, function (results) {
    $scope.$apply(function () {
        $scope.results = results;
    });
});
```

The `search.js` file simply calls the `repository.search` function. In the callback, we need to use `$scope.$apply` because we are working on another thread. Doing things this way has the least impact on our existing functionality. Indeed, when you run the Protractor tests, you will see everything worked as before. Note that using `$scope.$apply` is not the best practice (it is one of a few dodgy workarounds), but we will fix that in a bit. However, when you run your unit tests, you will notice one of them fails. We wrote a unit test for the `repository.search` function using the Mocha framework. Since this function cannot be properly unit tested anymore, it is a data retrieval action on the server, we can remove this test completely (and with that I am removing Mocha completely). However, the Protractor tests still cover this page so we are good.

This is really the important thing here. No matter how you would have solved this (we get the page and then the data, but it would have been perfectly valid to get the page and the data in one go as well), your tests ensure that everything keeps working as it should. When your tests fail you should start thinking whether you introduced a bug or if the specs changed and you should fix your tests.

I have fixed the other two repository functions, `getTopProducts` and `getProduct`, in the same way. It is not very interesting to repeat it here.

Putting the Shopping Cart in MongoDB

The only thing left to do before we are completely *backend driven* is to add functionality for adding and removing products from the shopping cart and remembering them. First, some rules. When you are trying to buy something while you are not logged in, you will be taken to the login page. When you go to the shopping cart page, you will also be taken to the login page and, when you log in, you will be taken to the shopping cart page. When you buy something, it will be added to your shopping cart and it will be remembered across sessions. That is really how easy it is.

First, let's create a function that gets us the logged in the user's shopping cart from the database. I am going to show the relevant backend code. On the frontend, we are just going to create another repository method and use it like we use any of the other methods:

```
db.collection('user').findOne({
    username: req.session.username
}, { shoppingCart: [] }, function (err, user) {
    if (err) {
        handleErr(err, res);
    } else {
        res.json({
            authenticated: true,
            shoppingCart: user.shoppingCart || []
        });
    }
});
```

The second parameter to `findOne` is a projector, which tells MongoDB to only get the `shoppingCart` field of the found user. In the response, we just return `shoppingCart`. Since MongoDB, like JavaScript, is schemaless, the `shoppingCart` field is not guaranteed to exist. It is not even guaranteed to be an array, but we are going to assume that anyway. We are setting authenticated to `true` (as opposed to false) just to let the frontend know everything went well.

The `addProductToCart` function uses the MongoDB `findOneAndUpdate` method. The `$addToSet` update operator tells MongoDB to insert the item only if the item is not yet present in the array (as opposed to `$push`, which just adds the item). We are not updating the `number` field (ever) for multiple items. It would mess up `$addToSet`, but maybe, we will add this feature in the future:

```
db.collection('user').findOneAndUpdate({
    username: req.session.username
}, {
    $addToSet: {
        shoppingCart: {
```

```
        product: req.body.product,
        number: 1
      }
    }
}, function (err) {
    if (err) {
        handleErr(err, res);
    } else {
        res.json({authenticated: true});
    }
});
```

Of course, we need to change all of our buy buttons for this one. The following example is from the `index.ejs` file. Other buy buttons are on the product and search pages:

```
<button ng-click="addToCart(product)" class="btn btn-primary pull-
right">Buy</button>
```

Last, we need some method of removing a product from the shopping cart:

```
db.collection('user').findOneAndUpdate({
    username: req.session.username
}, {
    $pull: {
        shoppingCart: {
            product: req.body.product
        }
    }
}, function (err) {
    if (err) {
        handleErr(err, res);
    } else {
        res.json({authenticated: true});
    }
});
```

The `$pull` update operator will remove any objects that meet the query from an array. In our case, it will remove any objects that have the specified product.

Moving the Shopping Cart Module

I want to do one last thing. The shopping cart controller is mighty handy. No doubt we want to reuse this functionality in Node.js to create invoices. Luckily, we have kind of future proofed our frontend scripts with Browserify already, so we can simply create a module and use it on both the frontend and backend.

Create a new file in your `scripts` folder and name it `order.js`. In it goes most of the code from the `shopping-cart.js` file:

```
module.exports = (function () {
    var Order = function () {
        this.lines = [];
    };

    Order.prototype.removeLine = function (line) {
        this.lines.splice(this.lines.indexOf(line), 1);
    };

    [...]

    return {
        Order: Order,
        Line: Line
    };
})();
```

Since we are not working on the `$scope` object anymore, we need some new object to contain the `Line` objects. So, we create an `Order` constructor that has a `lines` array. The `total` function and the `removeLine` function are put on `Order prototype`. Please note that `removeLine` no longer makes an AJAX call to the backend. That kind of functionality would not make it usable in Node.js. The `Line` object is exactly the same as it was.

Now, in the `shopping-cart.js` file, we need to change a thing or two as well:

```
var order = require('./order.js');

$scope.order = new order.Order();

repository.getCart(function (data) {
    if (data.authenticated) {
        $scope.$apply(function () {
$scope.order.lines = data.shoppingCart.map(function (l) {
                return new order.Line({
                    [...]

$scope.removeLine = function (line) {
    repository.removeFromCart(line.product, function () {
        $scope.$apply(function () {
$scope.order.removeLine(line);
[...]
```

First, we need to `require` the `order.js` file and create a new `Order` object. After that, we need to assign the `order.Line` objects to `$scope.order.lines`. The `removeLine` function stays, but only because we still need to remove the line in the backend. We still need to call `$scope.order.removeLine(line)` to actually remove the product on screen.

In the shopping cart view, the `ejs` file, we also need a few changes. Basically, we need to replace any reference to `lines` to `order.lines` and we need to replace `total` to `order.total`. Only the `removeLine` reference stays put:

```
[...]
<div class="row" ng-hide="order.lines.length">
[...]
<div ng-repeat="line in order.lines">
[...]
      <p class="pull-right">{{'&euro;' + order.total()}}</p>
[...]
```

That wraps up our coding so far. We have now successfully added a MongoDB database and a Node.js backend to our website. It is probably not the best web shop you have ever seen, but it has all the functionality we need to continue with our Gulp, Karma, Protractor, and Jenkins examples.

Speaking of Karma and Protractor, our tests broke somewhere along the way. That makes perfect sense as we added the login functionality. However, we are now unable to test if our website works as it should, which is unfortunate. Time to fix our tests.

Our Karma tests have been failing for a while now. Unit tests should not depend upon external systems. They should ideally test small and isolated pieces of code. When revisiting our Karma tests, we see that we test `shoppingCartController`. However, we changed the repository so that it gets our data from the backend making our unit tests fail. Our unit tests should not depend upon external systems, such as Node.js and MongoDB. So, this change pretty much makes `shoppingCartController` impossible to test.

After that, we removed the `Line` object completely, created a new `Order` object instead, and put them in a separate file. This is good news because we have now abstracted the calculations away from the controller and the AJAX calls. That means we can test it again. However, because we used the `module.exports` object, we need to be able to load the script using `require`. If we do not, we have to directly use `module.exports`, which will be overwritten once we start to load more packages like this. We already know about Browserify and CommonJS. So, one option we have is to just Browserify our spec file too. We can edit the Karma configuration.

Keep in mind that I have removed Mocha and Chai from the configuration as well. So, what changes are the `frameworks`, `files`, and `preprocessors`:

```
[...]
frameworks: ['browserify', 'jasmine'],
files: [
    '../node_modules/angular/angular.js',
    '../node_modules/angular-mocks/angular-mocks.js',
    'spec/*.js',
    '../scripts/*.js'
],
preprocessors: {
    '../scripts/*.js': ['browserify'],
    'spec/*.js': ['browserify']
},
[...]
```

And now we have to fix the tests. Of course, loading some controller is not going to cut it anymore. That, unfortunately, means that we have to rewrite our tests pretty much completely. We can use the Jasmine `beforeEach` function to set up some initial order and then use our tests to update the order and check the totals:

```
describe('web app tests', function () {
    describe('order object', function () {
        var o = require('../../scripts/order.js');
        var order;

        beforeEach(function () {
            order = new o.Order();
            order.lines.push(new o.Line({
                product: {
                    price: 1.23
                },
                number: 1
            }));
            order.lines.push(new o.Line({
                product: {
                    price: 5
                },
                number: 1
            }));
        });

        it('should correctly calculate the total', function() {
            expect(order.total()).toBe(6.23);
        });
    });
});
```

```
});
```

And we should add some tests to check whether adding and removing products also correctly updates the totals:

```
it('should update the line sub total when the number of products is
changes', function() {
    var line = order.lines[0];
    line.number = 2;
    expect(line.subTotal()).toBe(2.46);
});

it('should update the total when a product is added', function() {
    order.lines.push(new o.Line({
        product: {
            price: 2
        },
        number: 1
    }));
    expect(order.total()).toBe(8.23);
});

it('should update the total when a product is removed', function() {
    order.removeLine(order.lines[0]);
    expect(order.total()).toBe(5);
});
```

And that is pretty much it. We have now fixed our Karma tests. However, we still have somewhat of a problem. We can now run our tests from the Command Prompt, but we also had a handy page that showed us all our tests in HTML and enabled us to run and debug tests. Unfortunately, that page broke. In order to fix it, we should bundle the spec file just like we bundle all our other JavaScript files or we should remove the `require` from our test somehow. We will get back to the test page shortly.

We have now come at a point that we really want to be able to test our controllers as well. After all, they may contain page-specific logic that we want to test without all the hassle of creating a new file that we have to Browserify and all that. The controllers, however, are calling our backend and we really do not want that. Luckily, we are using Angular, which has built-in dependency injection. So, let's make use of that feature.

Adding dependency injection to Angular is not all that difficult, which is probably one of the reasons it is so popular. You simply have to change your `repository.js` file so that it adds the repository as a service to the shop app:

```
angular.module('shopApp', [])
    .service('repositoryService', ['$http', function ($http) {
        'use strict';

        return {
            [...]
        };
    }]);
```

Because we are now creating an Angular service, we can use dependency injection to inject the `$http` module as well. Let's fix the index page first. `homeController` in the `index.js` file can now inject `repositoryService` rather than `require` it:

```
angular.module('shopApp')
    .controller('homeController', ['$scope', 'repositoryService', function
($scope, repository) {
        repository.getTopProducts(function (results) {
            $scope.topProducts = results;
        });
        $scope.searchTerm = '';
        $scope.addToCart = function (product) {
            repository.addToCart(product);
        };
    }]);
```

Notice the few effects this has. First, we retrieve the module rather than instantiate it. The second parameter to `angular.module` was removed. Next, since we are now *all Angular*, the need for `$scope.$apply` is gone! This is really Angular's recommended way of working.

Last, we will need to fix our HTML because the bundled JavaScript is not going to work anymore. Simply replace the `<!-- build:js -->` block in your `index.ejs` file with the original scripts for now. This will break the pages that still use `require`, but we will fix that in a bit:

```
<script src="scripts\repository.js"></script>
<script src="scripts\index.js"></script>
```

And, of course, for this to work, we need to tell Node.js that it may serve files from this folder:

```
app.use('/scripts', express.static('scripts'));
```

We can do this for every page. Remove the second parameter to `angular.module`, inject the `repositoryService`, remove `$scope.$apply`, and fix the EJS files. We should do the same for `utils.js` and make it Angular `utilsService`. Unfortunately, we are now getting stuck again with dependencies and who should create the Angular module. So, here is a different approach. We are still going to require all of our files, including the repository, but we are also going to inject them as a service. This gives us the best of both worlds and it will make our services interchangeable for testing purposes. So, once again, change the `repository.js` file, so it exports a function that will serve as a service for Angular:

```
module.exports = function($http) {
    'use strict';

    return {
        [...]
    };
};
```

We can now create the `shopApp` module, create `repositoryService`, and inject it into the controller:

```
angular.module('shopApp', [])
    .service('repositoryService', ['$http', require('./repository.js')])
    .controller('homeController', ['$scope', 'repositoryService', function
($scope, repository) {
        [...]
```

Also, change `index.ejs`, so it looks like it did before. And now we can change `utils.js` just a bit, so it returns a function instead of an object and we can use it as a service:

```
module.exports = function () {
    'use strict';

    return {
        [...]
    };
};
```

`productController`, for example, should now look as follows:

```
angular.module('shopApp', [])
    .service('utilsService', require('./utils.js'))
    .service('repositoryService', ['$http', require('./repository.js')])
    .controller('productController', ['$scope', 'utilsService',
'repositoryService', function ($scope, utils, repository) {
        [...]
```

Now that we have dependency injection in place, we can change our tests and inject an alternative repository:

```javascript
describe('web app tests', function () {
    describe('shopping cart controller', function () {
        // module has a name collision with Browserify,
        // so use the full angular.mock.module.
        beforeEach(angular.mock.module('shopApp'));

        var controller;
        var $scope = {};
        var repositoryService = {
            getCart: function (callback) {
                callback({
                    authenticated: true,
                    shoppingCart: [{
                        product: {
                            price: 1.23
                        },
                        number: 1
                    }, {
                        product: {
                            price: 5
                        },
                        number: 1
                    }]
                });
            },
            removeLine: function () {
                // Do nothing.
            }
        };

        beforeEach(inject(function ($controller) {
            controller = $controller;
            controller('shoppingCartController', {
                $scope: $scope,
                repositoryService: repositoryService
            });
        }));

        it('should load the cart', function () {
            expect($scope.order.total()).toBe(6.23);
        });
    });
});
```

Keep in mind that you only have to mock the functions that are going to be called in your tests. In this case, we know `getCart` is going to be executed in the controller so that is the function we mock. Services that you do not need to mock, such as the `utilsService`, can simply be omitted from the controller options object. We are now testing the `order.js` file using `require` and the `shoppingCartController` using Angular dependency injection, all in one spec file!

The next thing we want to do is unit test our `order.js` file in Node.js. We are already testing it in our browsers, but testing it on the backend is equally important, as JavaScript in your backend can behave differently from your JavaScript in the frontend. In our case, we are not using `order.js` in the backend, but for the sake of learning, we are going to test it anyway.

Again, we can use Jasmine, Mocha, or others. Since we are using Jasmine, let's stick with that. We need to install a separate package though, `jasmine-node` (`https://github.com/mhevery/jasmine-node`):

```
npm install jasmine-node -g
npm install jasmine-node --save-dev
```

Create a new file in your `spec` folder and name it `node-spec.js`. Jasmine-node needs your specs to be in the `spec` folder and your files to have a name such as `*spec.js`, `*spec.coffee`, or `*spec.litcoffee` (for CoffeeScript). So, create a new file in the `spec` folder and name it `node-spec.js`. Just make sure your Node tests do not mix with your browser tests. For now, we are safe as our browser tests are in a file named `test.js` and so they are not picked up by jasmine-node.

Now, because this is still just Jasmine and we want to test our `order.js` file, again, we can just copy and paste our browser tests to this file:

```
(function () {
    'use strict';
    var o = require('../../scripts/order.js');

    describe('web app tests', function () {
        describe('order object', function () {
            var order;

            beforeEach(function () {
                [...]
            });

            it('should correctly calculate the total', function() {
                expect(order.total()).toBe(6.23);
            });
```

```
        [...]
    });
  });
})();
```

Now, remove the `describe('order object', ...);` section from the `test.js` file. Our Karma config includes all the JavaScript files in the `spec` folder so the `node-spec.js` file is already included. Try running Karma once to see if the tests are indeed executed and pass. As for the `node-spec.js` file, that title does not cover it anymore, rename it to `order-spec.js`.

Now, to run the tests in jasmine-node, open up a Command Prompt in the `test` folder and simply run `jasmine-node spec`:

jasmine-node spec

Like with Karma, it is possible to watch files and automatically run the tests when any files changes. To watch the test files (all files in spec), simply add the `--autotest` flag. To also watch for changes in the application JavaScript files, add the `--watch` option with the folders you want to watch for changes:

jasmine-node spec --autotest --watch ..\scripts

Now that we have removed the `require` call from the test script, our `index.html` test page works again, but only for the controller tests. Just make sure you add the `order.js` and the `shopping-cart.bundle.js` file to your page:

```
<script src="../scripts/order.js"></script>
<script src="../scripts/bundles/shopping-cart.bundle.js"></script>
```

We still cannot add the order tests to our test HTML page, but at least we have got something.

And, of course, we want some reporting. The `jasmine-node` command can output JUnit style reports by specifying an output folder and adding the `--junitreport` flag:

jasmine-node spec --autotest --watch ..\scripts --junitreport --output node-junit

Of course, we also want code coverage for our Node tests. For this, we can use Istanbul (`https://github.com/gotwarlost/istanbul`). We already have it installed in `node_modules`, because we also use it to generate coverage in our Karma tests. Usage with `jasmine-node` is a bit different and sometimes unexpected. For example, we need to run the command from the root of our project (where our `node_modules` folder and `package.json` are). We must also use the locally installed `jasmine-node`, but not in the `.bin` folder, but the `jasmine-node` installation folder:

```
node_modules\.bin\istanbul.cmd cover node_modules\jasmine-node\bin\jasmine-
node test\spec
```

That is quite a lot of typing! Luckily, we have a shortcut. Up until now, we have been using npm as a package manager only, but it can run scripts as well. In `package.json`, add (or replace) the following node:

```
"scripts": {
    "test": "node_modules/.bin/istanbul.cmd cover node_modules/jasmine-
node/bin/jasmine-node -- --junitreport --output node-junit test/spec"
},
```

The double dash (`--`) separates the Istanbul flags from the Jasmine-node flags (otherwise, the `--output` flag causes trouble). And now, we can simply run npm test from the command. You can add more scripts like that to your `package.json` file, such as `prepublish`, `preinstall`, `install`, `version`, and `postversion`. I suggest you read the documentation (`https://docs.npmjs.com/misc/scripts`).

So, we can now test our scripts in Node.js and generate coverage. The only thing we need is a report in the Cobertura format for Jenkins to process. The default report is LCOV, which we also want for SonarQube. Istanbul allows us to add various reports to the command:

```
"scripts": {
    "test": "node_modules/.bin/istanbul.cmd cover --report cobertura --
report lcov node_modules/jasmine-node/bin/jasmine-node -- --junitreport --
output node-junit test/spec"
},
```

And that adds all reports to our Node.js tests.

Next, we are going to fix our Protractor tests. When you run your tests, you will see that two tests still succeed and two tests fail. We can easily fix one of the failing tests. We used to return products 1, 2, and 3 as top products, but with MongoDB in place, we return 0, 1, and 2. So the products shifted a bit and we now get a product in a place where we did not expect it. If we had some actual logic in place to select the top three products, this could have been a problem, but now, we can choose to return 1, 2, and 3 or we can choose to fix the test so it expects product 1 instead of 2. Let's go with the latter:

```
it('should navigate to the clicked product', function () {
    [...]
    //expect(title.getText()).toBe('The Good, The Bad and The Ugly');
    expect(title.getText()).toBe('Captain America: Civil War');
});
```

The second failing test is a little more difficult to fix. The test checks whether removing an item from the shopping cart succeeds. However, it times out after about 30 seconds. That is because we are not taken to the shopping cart page until we log in. So, we will need to change the test so that it logs in first. It is also nice to request the shopping cart page, but expect the login page to come up:

```
it('should remove an item from the shopping cart', function (done) {
    browser.get('shopping-cart.html');
    // redirect
    browser.wait(EC.presenceOf($('[ng-controller=loginController]'), 2000));

    var username = $('input[ng-model=username]');
    var password = $('input[type=password]');

    username.sendKeys('some_user');
    password.sendKeys('some_password');

    var submit = $('input[type=submit]');
    submit.click()
    // another redirect
    browser.wait(EC.presenceOf($('[ng-controller=shoppingCartController]'),
2000));

    [...]
});
```

When we add this to the test, we first log in and proceed to the shopping cart page. However, there is still a problem. The contents of our shopping cart are remembered from our last session. Earlier, when we did not have a backend yet, we always had the same items in our cart upon opening the page. Now, we may or may not have items in the cart. So here is what we will do. We will load the index page, add two out of three top products to our cart, go back to the cart, and proceed to test whether we can remove an item from the cart. If we succeed, we will refresh the page, check whether the product is still gone, and log out. That is quite a test, but it will test the entire shopping cart mechanism. As you can imagine, it will be pretty annoying to have your tests mess up your own test user, so be sure to create a user specifically for your tests. So, the next step is to add two products to our cart:

```
browser.get('index.html');
browser.wait(EC.presenceOf($('.btn.btn-primary'), 2000));

var alert;
var buttons = $$('.btn.btn-primary');

buttons.get(0).click();
browser.wait(EC.alertIsPresent(), 2000);
alert = browser.switchTo().alert();
alert.accept();

buttons.get(1).click();
browser.wait(EC.alertIsPresent(), 2000);
var alert = browser.switchTo().alert();
alert.accept();
```

As you can see, we click the first button, wait for the alert to pop up, accept it, and do the same with the second button. That should have added two products to our shopping cart. Next, we can request the shopping cart page, get the products (thumbnails), delete the first product, and check that the number of thumbnails changed as well as the caption of the first product. The code that was already there does that, so we do not need to change it much. Of course, we do need to add some code to refresh the page and check whether the product is still gone:

```
browser.get('shopping-cart.html');
browser.wait(EC.presenceOf($('[ng-controller=shoppingCartController]'),
2000));

browser.wait(EC.presenceOf($('.thumbnail'), 2000));

var items = $$('.thumbnail');
items.count().then(function (count) {
    var first = items.get(0);
    first.$('h3').getText().then(function (caption) {
```

```
        first.$('button').click().then(function () {
            // we don't really have anything to wait on...
            // waiting for the element not to be there may cause
            // an infinite loop, so just sleep for a second and continue.
            browser.sleep(1000);
            var newItems = $$('.thumbnail');
            expect(newItems.count()).toBe(count - 1);
            expect(newItems.get(0).$('h3').getText()).not.toBe(caption);

            // Refresh and check if the deleted item is still gone.
            browser.refresh();
            browser.wait(EC.presenceOf($('.thumbnail'), 2000));

            var afterRefresh = $$('.thumbnail');
            expect(afterRefresh.count()).toBe(count - 1);
            done();
        });
    });
});
```

It is quite a bit of code, some even duplicated, but I will leave the refactoring up to you. For now, we just have a test that counts over 50 lines of code. So, this last test almost does what it did before, except it logs in first, adds some products to the cart, and then refreshes the page to check again. That means it does not really matter how many items were in the shopping cart to begin with; there will always be at least two items in the shopping cart (unless the test fails for whatever reason). It is probably a good idea to create a separate function that handles the login, so you can reuse it for other tests that require you to be logged in.

You see I also made a remark about an infinite loop. This one cost me hours to debug, so I will give you this tip here and now. Waiting for elements that are not on the page (anymore) to be removed from the page is not a good idea. You would hope Selenium (or Protractor) would not find the element on the page and continue right away, but unfortunately that is not how it works. So beware! When you find your tests failing, it is a good idea to start up the Selenium server in a separate command window and check the logs (start the server using `webdriver-manager start`).

Gulp

You may have noticed, but our Gulp file fails to run. Basically, everything is well up to the tests of the minified JavaScript files. Luckily, we can fix this really easy! In the `karma.min.conf.js` file, simply make sure you browserify everything in the `spec` folder:

```
[...]
  preprocessors: {
      '../prod/scripts/*.js': ['browserify'],
      'spec/*.js': ['browserify']
  },
[...]
```

That should fix your Gulp run. Everything should work now, testing, linting, minifying, and so on. Another thing though, we have added the Node.js tests, which are not yet included in our gulpfile. We can simply create an extra task and run `jasmine-node` `tests`. Of course, we need an extra Karma plugin, the `karma-jasmine-node` plugin (`https://www.npmjs.com/package/gulp-jasmine-node`):

```
npm install karma-jasmine-node --save-dev
```

We can now add it to our gulpfile. It is a very small task, the only thing worth mentioning is that we have to specify our file explicitly, because we cannot just take every JavaScript file because `test.js` does not run in Node.js:

```
var jasmineNode = require('gulp-jasmine-node');

gulp.task('test-node', ['build'], function () {
    return gulp.src('test/spec/order-spec.js')
        .pipe(jasmineNode());
});
```

Unfortunately, we now miss our JUnit result report and the Istanbul code coverage. Adding the JUnit report is easy enough:

```
.pipe(jasmineNode({
  reporter: [
      new jasmine.JUnitXmlReporter(__dirname + '/node-junit', true, true),
      new jasmine.TerminalVerboseReporter({
          color: true,
          includeStackTrace: true
      })
  ]
}));
```

However, for our Istanbul code coverage, we need an additional plugin:

```
npm install gulp-istanbul --save-dev
```

We can now call Istanbul before running our tests and then generate our reports after the test. Istanbul needs a little setup as well. It needs to intercept required files in order to track coverage:

```
var istanbul = require('gulp-istanbul');
var jasmineNode = require('gulp-jasmine-node');

gulp.task('istanbul-setup', ['build'], function () {
    return gulp.src('scripts/order.js')
        .pipe(istanbul())
        .pipe(istanbul.hookRequire());
})
.task('test-node', ['istanbul-setup'], function () {
    return gulp.src('test/spec/order-spec.js')
        .pipe(jasmineNode({...}))
        .pipe(istanbul.writeReports({
            reporters: ['cobertura', 'lcov']
        }));
});
```

The `istanbul-setup` task picks up all the files that should be covered; in our case that is only the `order.js` file. It then calls `hookRequire()`, which overwrites `require()` so it can track coverage. We can then call `writeReports` and specify the reports to generate. Let's add an HTML report. By default, all the HTML files are written to the `coverage` folder, which makes it kind of a mess. It is possible to add report specific options:

```
.pipe(istanbul.writeReports({
    reporters: ['cobertura', 'lcov', 'html'],
    reportOpts: {
        html: { dir: 'coverage/html' }
    }
}));
```

We have now added Istanbul code coverage to our `jasmine-node` testing through Gulp. We can now simply execute `gulp test-node` instead of `npm test`. We now only need to add the test-node task to our default task so it runs every time we execute gulp:

```
.task('default', ['lint', 'test-min', 'test-node']);
```

We should also add the new report files to our SonarQube exclusions, so be sure to add the two folders to the `sonar.exclusions` property in the `sonar-project.properties` files, `coverage/**`, `node-junit/**`. The same goes for your `.gitignore` file.

One last thing, we want to Browserify our spec file so we can use it in the test HTML page. We already have a task that Browserifies all our JavaScript files; we only need to add the spec file(s) to it. We use `glob` to find the files and, with glob, we can indicate multiple patterns like this, `{pattern1,pattern2,...}`:

```
glob('{./scripts/*.js,./test/spec/order-spec.js}', function (err, files) {
```

That fetches the `order-spec.js` file, but it places it in `scripts/bundles`. Personally, I would rather have it in `test/spec/bundles`, where it belongs. This is a little more complex, but still not difficult. We are processing our files one by one, which means we have the name of the file while we are processing it. We simply need to get the directory of the file and append the bundles folder to it. To get the directory, we can use the path module. No need for extra plugins, we already have it:

```
var path = require('path');
[...]
.task('js', ['clean'], function (done) {
    [...]
glob('{./scripts/*.js,./test/spec/order-spec.js}', function (err, files) {
        [...]
        var tasks = files.map(function (file) {
            return browserify({
                [...]
.pipe(gulp.dest(path.dirname(file) + '/bundles'))
                [...]
```

That is really all we need to change to select files from different directories and output those files to `[original directory]/bundles`. So, you should now find your bundles file in `test/spec/bundles`. That means we can change our test page:

```
<!-- include spec files here... -->
<script src="spec/test.js"></script>
<script src="spec/bundles/order-spec.bundle.js"></script>
```

And you will now have all the tests in your test page overview, including source mapping for easy debugging.

Jenkins

If you committed your work to Jenkins, you may have noticed the Jenkins build broke somewhere. We fixed most of it; we fixed our Gulp build after all. However, some issues remain. The build project fails because of some SonarQube issues. You can do three things, fix your code (you would have to remove some `alert()` and `console.log()` statements), disable the rules in SonarQube, or configure your Jenkins project, so it will not fail because of SonarQube. That last option is the quickest; simply remove the `Quality Gates` post-build action. In production code, we would not use `alert()` and `console.log()`, but for now, I do not find that a problem.

With the build project running again, we should publish the extra reports we are generating for our Node.js tests. We have an extra Cobertura report, so the XML report pattern should now be `test/coverage/cobertura/*.xml,coverage/*.xml`. We should also add an extra HTML report. The HTML directory is `coverage/html` and the title is something like `NodeJS Coverage HTML`. Last, there is the extra JUnit test result; the report XMLs are now `test/junit/*.xml,node-junit/*.xml` or `test/junit/*.xml, selenium-junit/*.xml, node-junit/*.xml` for your test project. Make sure you add the new reports to both your build and test projects.

Other than that, the test project fails (after quite a long time). Reading the output, we can find that everything goes well, right up to the Protractor tests. All the Protractor tests timeout, which makes sense, since we added a backend that is not currently running. Before this chapter, we only had frontend files, so we did not need to start up anything. You may think fixing this issue is as easy as adding a `node index.js` command to the build, but that will only make your build hang indefinitely. Instead, we need something to get our Node.js server up and running without blocking the console. We could, of course, permanently host our website, but that would be quite a hassle. In fact, getting your scripts deployed and running fully automated is the topic of a later chapter. For now, we just need to start it, run our tests, and stop it. Enter pm2.

PM2

To run and manage Node.js applications, you will need something more sophisticated than nodemon. The tool we are going to use is PM2, an *advanced, production process manager for Node.js* (`http://pm2.keymetrics.io/`). We are going to install it locally for Jenkins and globally for our convenience:

```
npm install pm2 --save-dev
npm install pm2 -g
```

With PM2, we can start and stop Node.js scripts:

```
pm2 start index.js
pm2 list
pm2 stop index.js
pm2 delete index.js
pm2 kill
```

In the command user interface we can see that our website is actually running.

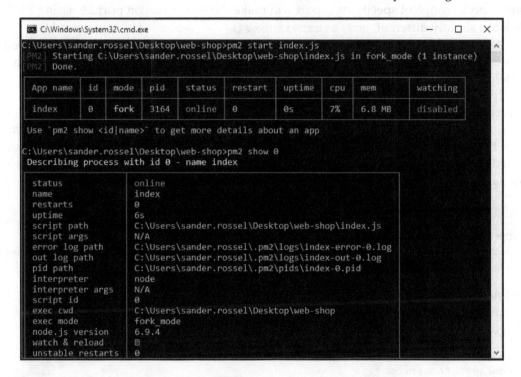

In Jenkins, we have a bit of a problem though, we can start up PM2 and run our tests, but when our tests fail the next statement, which would be stopping PM2, is never executed. Any next build steps will be ignored as well. We could just let the script run, so it will be available on localhost, but that would prevent us from starting it locally as our Jenkins slave and our development machine are the same (which is not really an ideal situation anyway). So, basically we need to be able to run the server twice on the same machine. Time to introduce some command-line arguments to our Node.js script, so we can use different ports. We can do this using command-line-args (`https://www.npmjs.com/package/command-line-args`):

```
npm install command-line-args --save
```

The package itself works pretty easy:

```
var commandLineArgs = require('command-line-args');

var options = commandLineArgs({ name: 'port', defaultValue: 80 });
var server = app.listen(options.port, '127.0.0.1');
console.log('Server running at http://127.0.0.1:' + options.port);
```

We can now start the server using `node index.js --port=1234`. This works exactly the same in nodemon. Not specifying a port will make the server run on port 80. Using PM2, this looks slightly different, `pm2 start index.js -- --port=1234`; you need the double dash. We can now run our script on a different port in Jenkins. We would do well to name our process as well, so we can reference it by name rather than script name or random ID. Before we start a script, we must make sure it is not already running. If the script is already running, then PM2 will return an error, stopping the execution of our tests. Unfortunately, when Protractor fails, any subsequent commands will not be executed either, so we cannot delete the website after our tests. So, we really only have one option: delete the website before we try to start it. However, PM2 also returns an error when you try to delete a website that does not exist. We should add the −s, or silent, flag to the delete command, so any errors are not returned and the script continues execution:

```
npm install && node_modules\.bin\gulp.cmd --env=prod --
browsers=Chrome,IE,IE9,Firefox && node_modules\.bin\webdriver-manager.cmd
update && node_modules\.bin\pm2.cmd delete -s jenkins &&
node_modules\.bin\pm2.cmd start --name=jenkins -f index.js -- --port=1234
&& node_modules\.bin\protractor.cmd test\protractor.conf.js
```

The final piece of the puzzle is to have Protractor test the website running at port 1234, not the one we may or may not have running on port 80. We can easily overwrite any configuration setting by adding an extra command-line argument:

```
node_modules\.bin\protractor.cmd --baseUrl='http://localhost:1234'
test\protractor.conf.js
```

At this point, we have pretty much everything ready, backend, tests, and Jenkins, everything except deployment. We will get to deployment in a later chapter and, as you might have guessed, we will need PM2 again.

Summary

In this chapter, we have added a Node.js and MongoDB backend for our website. As a result, we had to add some additional Node.js tests, change our Protractor tests, and spawn a Node.js server in Jenkins. In the next chapter, we are going to do the same, but using C# and PostgreSQL. In the next chapter, we will see some different technologies and the techniques that come with them.

9

A C# .NET Core and
PostgreSQL Web App

In the previous chapter, we completed our web shop example. After the frontend we created, built, and tested in the previous chapters, we added the backend and adjusted our tests. All we used so far was JavaScript. However, languages, such as Java and C#, require other methods of testing and building. Some of the major differences here are that these are typed and compiled languages. In this chapter, we are going to set up the website again but this time, using C#. As a backend, we will use PostgreSQL, a popular SQL database. Along the way we will see how building and testing differs from that of JavaScript and how the Visual Studio environment tooling helps us to do the things we need.

To build our C# website, we are going to use Visual Studio Code, the little brother of Microsoft's flagship IDE Visual Studio. Unlike Visual Studio, Visual Studio Code is a multiplatform editor that runs on Windows, Linux, and Mac. All examples in this chapter are tested on Windows only, but should work on Linux. Other than that, we are using .NET Core, the relatively new multiplatform version of .NET.

Installing .NET Core and Visual Studio Code

The first thing we need to do before we get to work is install the .NET Core SDK. Head over to `https://www.microsoft.com/net/download/core` to download the latest version. I have used version 2.0, but I am assuming Microsoft is keeping things backward compatible. As said, I am using this on Windows so I am assuming you are also using Windows, but it should work on Linux just as well. Installation of the .NET Core SDK is straightforward.

Once you have followed the installation wizard and installed .NET Core, it is time to install Visual Studio Code (**VS Code**). Head over to `https://code.visualstudio.com/` to install the latest version of VS Code for your platform. Again, installation is straightforward. By the way, you are free to use the full Visual Studio (Community Edition) if you like. The main point of this chapter is the code, not the editor. However, since we will need to compile our C# code, I really recommend using either one of these as they come with a built-in compiler that compiles your code on a single key press. In this chapter, I will not be covering how to manually compile your C# code (well, we will have to in Jenkins, but for now, I will not).

After installation, start VS Code. It may surprise you, but VS Code is so lightweight it does not come with standard C# tooling. To install these head over to Extensions, which is the button at the bottom of the left-hand side menu. You should see the C# extension along with other extensions, such as Python, C/C++, PowerShell, and Go. Simply install the C# extension, which should only take a few seconds:

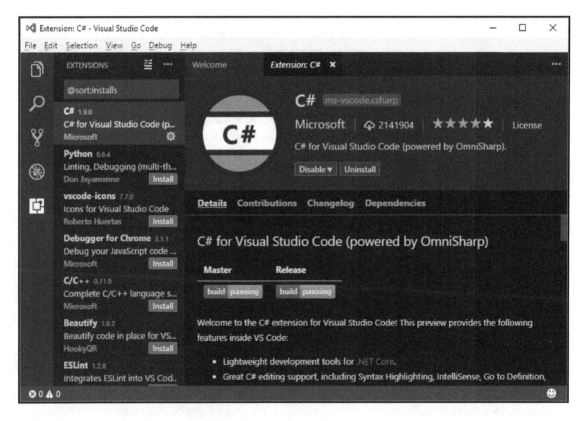

Next, go to the Explorer, which is the top button on the left-hand side menu. It will say there are no folders selected, but instead of selecting our `web-shop` folder, we will create a new folder. Since C# is so very different from Node.js, we will probably not be reusing a lot of code, save for the HTML, CSS, and JavaScript, but it is easier to copy those later. Since I have two folders, one for `web-shop` and one for the book as a whole, I have deleted the `web-shop` folder and recreated it as an empty folder. So, for this example, I will still use the `web-shop` folder. Once your new folder is created, open up the VS Code command window or a separate command window. You can open the command in VS Code using `Ctrl +` ` (that is the back-quote character) or from the **View** menu at the top, which lists it as **Integrated Terminal**. Inside the terminal window, enter `dotnet new mvc`. This will scaffold a new ASP.NET Core MVC project, the multiplatform Microsoft web platform:

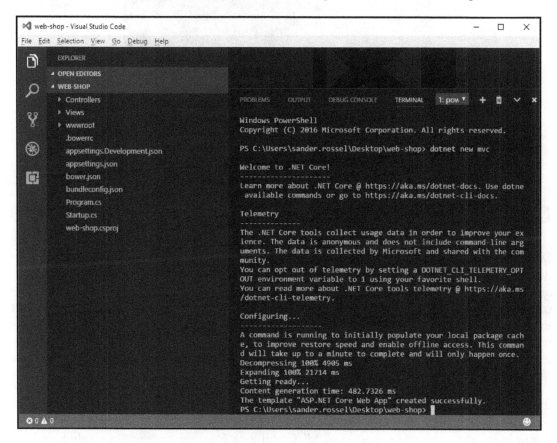

Before we continue, I can recommend creating another new project and initializing it using just `dotnet new console`. This will create a Hello World program that you can use to play around with. VS Code will warn you that required assets to build and debug code are missing and will ask if you want to add them. I guess you know the answer to that one: yes, we want to add them. And, there are also unresolved dependencies, so you can either restore right away or execute the `dotnet restore` command from the terminal. You can run and debug the code using *F5* or from the **Debug** menu. You can add breakpoints to your code by clicking on the column before the row numbers. VS Code will break on these breakpoints during debugging so you can inspect variables:

```
0 references
class Program
{
    0 references
    static void Main(string[] args)            {string[0]}
    {
        Console.WriteLine("Hello World!");
    }
}
```

So that was a really quick tour of VS Code. Now, let's return to our web-shop project.

Creating the views

Let's return to the `web-shop` project. If you have not yet added the required assets for debugging and resolved your dependencies, you should do this. Now, a little information on ASP.NET MVC. MVC is short for Model-View-Controller. Basically, we have a controller, which is sitting on our backend waiting for requests. Whenever a request is sent to the controller, it will serve up an HTML page, a so-called view. The controller typically passes a model, some C# class with properties and methods, to the view which the view can use to render information on the page. MVC is a common pattern used in many languages (it is certainly not C#- or .NET-specific).

In your file explorer, you can see that .NET already created a `HomeController` and Home view. MVC is convention-based, meaning that when you browse for a Home page, in this example `http://mywebsite.com/Home`, MVC will look for `HomeController`, which will look for a Home view to serve. The following code is the `Index()` method on `HomeController`. The `Index()` method is called by default when you browse to a page. Notice how it simply returns `View()`, but still knows what view to return:

```
public IActionResult Index()
{
    return View();
}
```

This code will look for the `Index.cshtml` (C# HTML) file in the `Views\Home folder`. The same goes for the `About()` and `Contact()` methods on `HomeController`; they will look for `Views\Home\About.cshtml` and `Views\Home\Contract.cshtml`, respectively. You can change these rules, as they are simply configured in code. You can find this in `Startup.cs`:

```
app.UseMvc(routes =>
{
    routes.MapRoute(
        name: "default",
        template: "{controller=Home}/{action=Index}/{id?}");
});
```

As for the `cshtml` files, they are transformed by .NET to proper HTML pages, like EJS transformed our HTML in Node.js. This is called the Razor engine. By default, MVC creates a _Layout page in the `Shared` folder. This _Layout page is used as a base layout for all your scripts. If you look at it you will find a `@RenderBody()` method call in the _Layout page which renders the HTML in the page that is currently being requested. So, put differently, the `View()` function looks for the appropriate view and wraps it in the `_Layout.cshtml` view. At the bottom of the layout page is also `@RenderSection("Scripts", required: false)`, which means any page can import additional scripts, which are placed at the bottom of the page. The last important detail is in the title of the page, `<title>@ViewData["Title"] - web_shop</title>`. The `ViewData` is a dictionary-like object that is shared between controllers and views and can contain any value you like. You can see the titles being set in the separate views, `ViewData["Title"] = "Home Page";`. Furthermore, it is important to know that the `cshtml` files are rendered in the backend and so it is possible to run any C# code within by prefixing with `@`, like `@RenderBody()` does. For a block of C# code, like when setting the titles, you can use curly braces `@{ ... }`. You can find the JavaScript and CSS files in the `wwwroot` folder. Simply hit *F5* and your website will be hosted locally and you can browse to `localhost:5000`, `localhost:5000/Home/About`, and all other controllers and methods you have. The prebuilt standard website is actually some information on ASP.NET Core, Visual Studio, Azure, and other Microsoft products.

So, let's start by changing the the `_Layout.cshtml` file. We are basically going to invert our previous views. With EJS, we had a piece of common HTML that we injected into each view. But with Razor, we are going to inject the view into the common HTML:

```
<!DOCTYPE html>
<html>
    <head>
        <meta charset="UTF-8">
        <title>CI Web Shop</title>
        <link rel="shortcut icon"
href="https://www.packtpub.com/favicon.ico">

        <link rel="stylesheet" type="text/css"
href="~/lib/bootstrap/dist/css/bootstrap.css" />
        <link rel="stylesheet" type="text/css" href="~/css/layout.css">
        <link rel="stylesheet" type="text/css" href="~/css/utils.css">

        <script src="~/lib/jquery/dist/jquery.js"></script>
        <script src="~/lib/bootstrap/dist/js/bootstrap.js"></script>
        <script src="~/lib/angular/angular.js"></script>
        @RenderSection("Scripts", required: false)
    </head>
    <body ng-app="shopApp">
        <nav class="navbar navbar-default navbar-fixed-top">
            <div class="container">
                <div class="navbar-header">
                    [...]
                    <a class="navbar-brand" href="@Url.Action("Index",
"Home")">CI Web Shop</a>
                </div>
                [...]
            </div>
        </nav>
        <div class="container" ng-controller="@ViewData["ngController"]">
            @RenderBody()
            <footer class="footer">
                <p>Copyright &copy; 2017</p>
            </footer>
        </div>
    </body>
</html>
```

So, that is a lot of code and I even left the biggest part out. It should look familiar though. In the head element, you can see how we reference the stylesheets and scripts. ~ (tilde symbol) denotes the `wwwroot` folder. That way, no matter where your view is located, you always start from the same root folder. You can simply put the `layout.css` and `utils.css` files in the `wwwroot/css` folder--just copy them from a previous chapter. You can also delete the CSS files generated by .NET. While you are at it, you can delete the complete `wwwroot\images` folder. Next are the JavaScript scripts. They are added in pretty much the same way, except that we have not yet added any of these libraries. We will do that in a minute. Next is the `@RenderSection` function, which can be used to render any other scripts required for the page that we are requesting. After that simply comes the entire `navbar`; again, you can copy it from a previous chapter (before the backend changes, so without `<% if (authenticated) {%>...`). Then, notice the `@ViewData["ngController"]` bit. ng-app is the same for our entire application (although it does not have to be), but `ng-controller` is different on each page. Because the footer is the same everywhere and it is contained in the `ng-controller` element, we are going to inject the controller through `ViewData`. After that comes `RenderBody` and the footer.

One change we are going to make is that our URLs are not going to end with `.html`. It is simply not the default in MVC, so we are going to remove them from our URLs as well (which we could have done with Node.js, but never did). And, instead of `index`, our main page is called `home` (as it calls `HomeController`). One safe and easy way to create URLs in Razor is by using the `UrlHelper.Action` function, shortened as `@Url.Action`. The first parameter is the name of the action you want to call, so that is `Index`, and the second parameter is the name of the controller without the `"Controller"` suffix, so `Home`. Personally, I am not a fan of Razor, but this is one of those utilities that you just have to have. Other than that, we are not actually using any Razor.

Now we need to install the scripts. The ASP.NET Core MVC template uses Bower (`https:/ /bower.io/`) as the default package manager for frontend libraries (it uses NuGet for backend packages--more on that later). However, we need to install Bower before we can actually make use of it. Open up the terminal inside VS Code or just a command window in Windows and install Bower using *pause for dramatic effect* npm. Yes, we need a package manager to install a package manager:

```
npm install bower -g
```

Like npm, Bower uses a JSON file to keep track of what packages and versions are installed. You can find it in your `web-shop` folder already. It looks a little like the `packages.json` npm uses. Anyway, you can see that MVC Core comes preinstalled with bootstrap, jquery, jquery-validation, and jquery-validation-unobtrusive. Unfortunately, the libraries installed by MVC are not up to date and we do not need half of them. So, we are going to delete them all and then install the ones we need again:

```
bower uninstall jquery-validation-unobtrusive --save
bower uninstall jquery-validation --save
bower uninstall jquery --save
bower uninstall bootstrap --save
bower install bootstrap --save
bower install angular --save
```

Installing Bootstrap will automatically install jQuery, which is the only reason we need it. Finally, we can install Angular. That takes care of `_Layout`. We can now change the `Views/Home/Index.cshtml` file, so we get the actual index page of our web shop:

```
@{
    ViewData["ngController"] = "homeController";
}
@section Scripts {
    <script src="~/js/repository.js"></script>
    <script src="~/js/index.js"></script>
}
<div class="jumbotron">
    <h1>CI Web Shop</h1>
    <p class="lead">Welcome to the CI Web Shop!<br />
    Browse our wares, but remember: if you break it you buy it!</p>
</div>
<div class="row">
    [...]
</div>
```

I have left most of it out, but it is exactly the same as in the previous chapters. It is good to notice that the HTML starts at the Bootstrap Jumbotron component, because that is pretty much where the `navbar` ends and the index page begins. This is also where we specify `ngController` in `ViewData` and specify the `Scripts` section. I do not think there is any rocket science going on here. We do still need to create some index and repository scripts though. For now, copy the scripts from `Chapter 4`, *Creating A Simple JavaScript App*, and put them in `wwwroot/js`.

Now, hit *F5* and you should see the index page as it once was.

We can now add the other pages and scripts. Just remember that each page, ideally, gets its own controller and, thus, its own folder in views. This helps to separate concerns. Where we had one huge JavaScript file in Node.js, we are getting a lot of small files in C#. You can also remove the `About` and `Contact` functions from the `HomeController` and the `cshtml` files that go with it and the `site.js` and `site.min.js` files. Leave the `Error` function. So, let's continue with the Product page:

```
using Microsoft.AspNetCore.Mvc;

namespace web_shop.Controllers
{
    public class ProductController : Controller
    {
        public IActionResult Index()
        {
            return View();
        }
    }
}
```

That is how all your controllers are going to look for now. The `Product/Index.cshtml` page looks like it did in Chapter 4, *Creating A Simple JavaScript App*:

```
@{
    ViewData["ngController"] = "productController";
}
@section Scripts {
    <script src="~/js/repository.js"></script>
    <script src="~/js/utils.js"></script>
    <script src="~/js/product.js"></script>
}
<div class="col-lg-12 text-center">
    <h2>{{name}}</h2>
    <p>
        <img src="http://placehold.it/300x300" alt="..." />
    </p>
    <p>{{description}}</p>
    <p>{{'&euro; ' + price}}</p>
    <p>
        <button class="btn btn-primary">Buy</button>
    </p>
</div>
```

When you continue on like this, you will end up with pretty much what we had in Chapter 4, *Creating A Simple JavaScript App*, but with a backend. The controller for the shopping cart is named `ShoppingCartController` because `shopping-cart` is not a valid name for a class in C#. The JavaScript file can still be named `shopping-cart`, of course.

Running tasks

Just because we are now working in C# it does not mean we do not have any frontend worries anymore. We still need to minify, bundle, Browserify, and many more. We can handle minification and bundling in .NET. For Browserify, we will need Gulp again. First, take a look at the `bundleconfig.json` file. It contains some bundling and minification information that is handled by .NET:

```
// Configure bundling and minification for the project.
// More info at https://go.microsoft.com/fwlink/?LinkId=808241
[
    {
        "outputFileName": "wwwroot/css/site.min.css",
        // An array of relative input file paths. Globbing patterns supported
        "inputFiles": [
            "wwwroot/css/site.css"
        ]
    },
    [...]
]
```

To get this to work, we first need to install the `BundlerMinifier.Core` tool. You can do this by manually editing your `csproj` file and adding a reference to the `BundlerMinifier.Core` tool:

```
<ItemGroup>
    <PackageReference Include="BundlerMinifier.Core" Version="2.4.337" />
    [...]
    <PackageReference Include="Npgsql.EntityFrameworkCore.PostgreSQL"
Version="1.1.0" />
    <DotNetCliToolReference Include="BundlerMinifier.Core" Version="2.2.281"
/>
</ItemGroup>
```

Do not forget to restore it too; VS Code will prompt you for it or you can run the command `dotnet restore` manually. After that, you can simply execute `dotnet bundle` and your scripts are bundled according to `bundleconfig.json`:

```
dotnet restore
dotnet bundle
```

Of course, the bundle tool will give some warnings that it cannot find your files (if you have deleted them). For now, we can just minify and bundle our CSS files, as we are going to bundle our JavaScript using Browserify anyway. `bundleconfig` should look as follows:

```
[
    {
        "outputFileName": "wwwroot/css/site.min.css",
        "inputFiles": [
            "wwwroot/css/layout.css",
            "wwwroot/css/utils.css"
        ]
    }
]
```

You can now simply replace all the CSS files with this one file in your views.

The next step is to create a task. In the `.vscode` folder is a `task.json` file. It defines some tasks that can be executed using VS Code. You will find the `build` task already defined. We are going to add a `bundle` task:

```
{
    "version": "0.1.0",
    "command": "dotnet",
    "isShellCommand": true,
    "args": [],
    "showOutput": "always",
    "tasks": [
        {
            "taskName": "build",
            [...]
        },
        {
            "taskName": "bundle",
            "isBuildCommand": true
        }
    ]
}
```

`taskName` is used as command to `dotnet`, so we do not have to specify any `args`. You can run any task from the Command Palette (found under the View menu item or the shortcut *Ctrl + Shift + P*). Simply type `Task` and choose `Tasks: Run Task`. You can then choose from your defined tasks:

As you can see from the screenshot, there is also a **Tasks: Run Build Task** (*Ctrl + Shift + B*) command. Running this runs your default task, which is the first task that has `isBuildCommand` set to true.

Next, we need to set up Browserify. We can do this using Gulp. This is basically a copy and paste from our previous chapter with a few edits. So, create `gulpfile.js` and put in the `js` task from the previous chapter, but rename it to `browserify`:

```
var gulp = require('gulp'),
    glob = require('glob'),
    browserify = require('browserify'),
    source = require('vinyl-source-stream'),
    path = require('path'),
    rename = require('gulp-rename'),
    es = require('event-stream'),
    buffer = require('vinyl-buffer');

gulp.task('browserify', function (done) {
    glob('wwwroot/js/*.js', function (err, files) {
        if (err) {
            done(err);
        }

    var tasks = files.map(function (file) {
        return browserify({
                entries: [file],
                debug: true
            })
```

```
        .bundle()
        .pipe(source(file))
        .pipe(buffer())
        .pipe(rename({
            extname: '.bundle.js',
            dirname: ''
        }))
        .pipe(gulp.dest(path.dirname(file) + '/bundles'));
    });
    es.merge(tasks).on('end', done);
  });
})
.task('default', ['browserify']);
```

Of course, we also need to install the necessary npm packages, such as `gulp`, `glob`, `browserify`, and many more. Basically, everything that is required in the gulpfile. You know how to do it, but do not forget to create a `package.json` file either manually or using `npm init`. Of course, it is easiest to just copy and paste `package.json` from the previous chapter. Whatever you do, `dependencies` and `devDependencies` should look as follows:

```
"dependencies": {
},
"devDependencies": {
    "browserify": "^14.1.0",
    "event-stream": "^3.3.4",
    "glob": "^7.1.1",
    "gulp": "^3.9.1",
    "gulp-rename": "^1.2.2",
    "vinyl-buffer": "^1.0.0",
    "vinyl-source-stream": "^1.1.0"
}
```

You can now simply run `npm install` so all packages will be installed and then you can run `gulp` and your files will be Browserified. We can now set up a task so you can run Gulp tasks from VS Code. You can set up Gulp as your default task runner and VS Code will pick up any tasks you define automatically, but since you can only have one task runner, that would prevent us from running our current command-line tasks. Of course, we can still set up a task that just runs Gulp from the command line. We need to do a bit of reworking in our `task.json` file though:

```
{
    "version": "0.1.0",
    "tasks": [
        {
            "taskName": "build",
            "command": "dotnet",
```

```
            "args": ["build"],
            "isBuildCommand": true,
            "problemMatcher": "$msCompile"
        },
        {
            "taskName": "bundle",
            "command": "dotnet",
            "args": ["bundle"]
        },
        {
            "taskName": "gulp",
            "command": "gulp",
            "isShellCommand": true
        }
    ]
}
```

Because each task now has a local `command`, the `suppressTaskName` option is `true` by default and so the task name is not added to the command anymore, hence the `args` parameters. You can now run the `gulp` task from VS Code. Optionally, you can add a task specifically for Browserify--just add `"args": ["browserify"]` to the `gulp` task (or to a new task that is copied from `gulp`).

So, you are now probably thinking this is awesome and you want to make all tasks build commands, so they all get executed when you build your software. Unfortunately, and I personally think this makes the entire task system pretty useless, you can only run one task at a time. In your `.vscode` folder, there is a `launch.json` file. It has a `preLaunchTask` property. It can only handle one task from the `tasks.json` file:

```
{
    "version": "0.2.0",
    "configurations": [
        {
            "name": ".NET Core Launch (web)",
            "type": "coreclr",
            "request": "launch",
            "preLaunchTask": "build",
            [...]
        }
}
```

So, you see how defining everything in Gulp still makes sense even with this brand new shiny VS Code task system. However, we are still going to use this task system just for fun. After all, we have seen plenty of Gulp in the previous chapter. We simply define a new task, descriptively name it doItAll, and make it do everything:

```
{
    "taskName": "doItAll",
    "command": "cmd",
    "isShellCommand": true,
    "args": [
        "/C \"dotnet build && dotnet bundle && gulp\""
    ],
    "isBuildCommand": true
}
```

Make sure to remove "isBuildCommand": true from the build task. Now, set preLaunchTask to "doItAll" in launch.json. Of course, we can see this becomes a mess when our project gets bigger, but it will not. By the way, it may be a good idea to throw npm install in there somewhere.

Now that we have Browserify in place and running on a build, we need to actually use it in our views. And we might as well implement minification while we are at it. First, the bad news: this is no job for bundleconfig.json because Browserify is already a bundler. So, we are going to use Gulp. Then the good news: it is not as difficult as you would think. First, we need two more npm packages, gulp-size (optional) and gulp-minify. After that, it is just a matter of putting it in the browserify task:

```
return browserify({
        entries: [file],
        debug: true
    })
    .bundle()
    .pipe(source(file))
    .pipe(buffer())
    .pipe(rename({
        extname: '.bundle.debug.js',
        dirname: ''
    }))
    .pipe(gulp.dest(path.dirname(file) + '/bundles'))
    .pipe(size({
        title: 'Before minification',
        showFiles: true
    }))
    .pipe(minify({
        ext:{
            min:'.js'
```

```
    },
    noSource: true
  }))
  .pipe(size({
    title: 'After minification',
    showFiles: true
  }))
  .pipe(rename(function (file) {
    file.basename = file.basename.replace('.debug', '');
  }))
  .pipe(gulp.dest(path.dirname(file) + '/bundles'));
```

First of all, notice that I am naming the original bundled files .bundle.**debug**.js. After that, we are minifying our bundles and renaming the files to get .debug out again. Both the original bundles and the minified bundles are written to wwwroot/js/bundles. We can now easily reference one or more specific scripts based on our build configuration:

```
@section Scripts {
<environment names="Development">
  <script src="~/js/bundles/index.bundle.debug.js"></script>
</environment>
<environment names="Staging,Production">
  <script src="~/js/bundles/index.bundle.js"></script>
</environment>
}
```

You can find the configuration in the launch.json file:

```
[...]
"env": {
  "ASPNETCORE_ENVIRONMENT": "Production"
},
[...]
```

We can now change all of our scripts so that they use Angular.js dependency injection again:

```
// repository.js
module.exports = function($http) {
  [...]
};

// index.js
angular.module('shopApp', [])
  .service('repositoryService', ['$http', require('./repository.js')])
  .controller('homeController', ['$scope', 'repositoryService', function
($scope, repository) {
    [...]
```

```
    }]);

// etc.
```

That sets up our tasks and frontend work for now. We are set to get our data from the database. After that, we can add testing and linting and build our website in Jenkins.

Adding the database

Now that we have what we pretty much started with in the previous chapters, this time, in C#, we can continue by adding a database connection. You can find all SQL scripts in this chapter in the GitHub repository in the sql folder in the chapter folder. We installed PostgreSQL and pgAdmin in Chapter 2, *Setting Up A CI Environment*, because we also needed it to run SonarQube. So, open up pgAdmin and find the connection you made in Chapter 2, *Setting Up A CI Environment*. If you do not have it anymore, you can read how to get it in Chapter 2, *Setting Up A CI Environment*, so I will not repeat that here. Now that you are connected to the server in pgAdmin, we can create the webshop database. Either right-click on the **Databases** node and select **Create** and then **Database;** just give the database the name webshop and save. Or you can connect to the default postgres database, right-click on it, and then open **Query Tool**. Put the following SQL script inside the query tool and execute it (using the button with the thunder icon or by pressing *F5*). You may need to change the owner if your username is not sa, like mine. Before you can see your new database, you have to refresh the list by right-clicking on the **Databases** node and then clicking **Refresh**:

```
CREATE DATABASE webshop
    WITH
    OWNER = sa
    ENCODING = 'UTF8'
    CONNECTION LIMIT = -1;
```

The output is as follows:

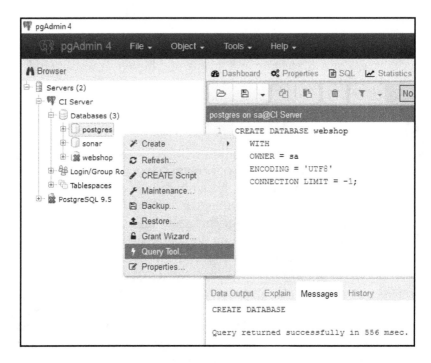

It is a good idea to keep a script of everything. In fact, it is absolutely necessary if you want to continuously deliver your database (or at least do a somewhat smooth manual deployment).

The next thing we need is a couple of tables. Unlike MongoDB, PostgreSQL is a SQL database and has a fixed schema. All of our tables (collections in MongoDB) are known up front and have a known set of columns. Our first table is the product table. Following the previous chapter, a product has an ID, name, price, description, and category. They are all pretty straightforward, except maybe category. We have two options here: make it a regular text column or specify a set of categories and create a foreign key relation. Let's go with the easy option and just make it a text column. Right-click on the **webshop** database and open **Query Tool**. You can now execute the following SQL statement to create the product table:

```
CREATE TABLE public.product
(
    id serial NOT NULL,
    name text NOT NULL,
    price money NOT NULL,
    description text,
```

```
    category text,
    PRIMARY KEY (id)
)
WITH (
    OIDS = FALSE
)
TABLESPACE pg_default;

ALTER TABLE public.product
    OWNER to sa;
```

The next table is the user table. The user table is pretty easy--just `username` and `password`:

```
CREATE TABLE public."user"
(
    id serial NOT NULL,
    username text NOT NULL,
    password text,
    PRIMARY KEY (id)
)
WITH (
    OIDS = FALSE
)
TABLESPACE pg_default;

ALTER TABLE public."user"
    OWNER to sa;
```

In MongoDB, this was pretty much it. Any products were stored in an array in the user table. However, that is not how SQL works. We will need a third table that serves as a shopping cart and connects our user to one or more products:

```
CREATE TABLE public.shopping_cart
(
    id bigserial NOT NULL,
    user_id integer NOT NULL,
    product_id integer NOT NULL,
    "number" integer NOT NULL DEFAULT 1,
    PRIMARY KEY (id),
    CONSTRAINT fk_shopping_cart_user FOREIGN KEY (user_id)
        REFERENCES public."user" (id) MATCH SIMPLE
        ON UPDATE NO ACTION
        ON DELETE NO ACTION,
    CONSTRAINT fk_shopping_cart_product FOREIGN KEY (product_id)
        REFERENCES public.product (id) MATCH SIMPLE
        ON UPDATE NO ACTION
        ON DELETE NO ACTION
```

```
)
WITH (
    OIDS = FALSE
)
TABLESPACE pg_default;

ALTER TABLE public.shopping_cart
    OWNER to sa;
```

The following database diagram was created using SchemaSpy (http://schemaspy. sourceforge.net/). It visualizes your PostgreSQL database quite well for free. Pretty awesome. Anyway, your database should now look as follows:

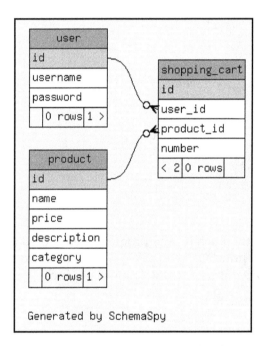

Our database is still pretty empty, so let's insert some data. First the products, then our user:

```
INSERT INTO public.product(
    name, price, description, category)
    VALUES
    ('Final Fantasy XV', 55.99, 'Final Fantasy finally makes a come back!',
'Gaming'),
    ('Captain America: Civil War', 19.99, 'Even more Avengers!', 'Movies'),
    ('The Good, The Bad and The Ugly', 9.99, 'This timeless classic needs no
description.', 'Movies'),
    ('J.K. Rowling - Fantastic Beasts and Where to Find Them', 19.99, 'Not
```

```
Harry Potter.', 'Books'),
   ('Fantastic Four', 11.99, 'Supposedly, a very bad movie.', 'Movies');

INSERT INTO public.user(
   username, password)
   VALUES
   ('user', 'password');
```

You can check the contents of your tables using a SELECT statement (one by one):

```
SELECT * FROM public.product;
SELECT * FROM public.user;
```

We have now set up the database and we are ready to use it from C#.

Entity Framework Core

For our database operations we are going to use the Entity Framework, Microsoft's **Object Relational Mapper (ORM)**. The **Entity Framework (EF)** has a .NET Core version and PostgreSQL has an EF Core Provider. I could write a book on EF alone, but for now, it suffices to know there are basically three ways of working with EF: database first, code first, or a mix of the two. The database first approach assumes you have a database already in place and generates, or lets you manually write, classes based on that. In code, first you basically describe your database in code, after which EF generates the scripts necessary to (automatically) update your database to the latest schema. The third approach assumes you already have a database, but also allows you to work code first from there on. Code first is ideal from a continuous integration perspective as all your database scripts are already automatically generated and executed. Unfortunately, this is not really an option for most mature projects, as huge (legacy) databases are sometimes hard to script like that. An even greater limiting factor is a DBA or project manager, who strictly forbids all automatic schema alteration on a database because it is *unreliable* or *poses a risk* (like people and manual scripts are not). Anyway, code first is not always an option. For this project, we will be using database first, as it introduces some nice challenges later on when we are going to continuously deliver our software.

First, we need to install the PostgreSQL EF Core driver, which can be done using the VS Code terminal. You may need to restart VS Code because the intellisense does not always reload automatically and VS Code may not recognize the package in the editor.

Usually, we would use `dotnet add package`
`Npgsql.EntityFrameworkCore.PostgreSQL` from the terminal, but somehow, there is a bug that prevents us from installing packages after we have installed a tool and have installed the BundlerMinifier. So, we can do two things: remove BundlerMinifier from the `csproj` file and add the latest session package through `dotnet add package` or we can manually paste the package into `csproj`. By the time you are reading this, chances are that this bug has been resolved and you can just use `dotnet add package`:

```
[Disable the BundlerMinifier tool]
<!--DotNetCliToolReference Include="BundlerMinifier.Core" Version="2.2.281"
/-->
[Install the PostgreSQL package using the terminal]
dotnet add package Npgsql.EntityFrameworkCore.PostgreSQL
[Re-enable BundlerMinifier tool]
<DotNetCliToolReference Include="BundlerMinifier.Core" Version="2.2.281" />

[Add to csproj manually]
<PackageReference Include="Npgsql.EntityFrameworkCore.PostgreSQL"
Version="2.0.0" />

[In any case]
dotnet restore
```

After that, we must write our database context class and our **Plain Old CLR Object (POCO)** classes (a big word for *just* a class). Create a new folder and name it `Database` or some such. In it, create a new file named `WebShopContext.cs`. The `WebShopContext` class should look as follows:

```
using Microsoft.EntityFrameworkCore;

namespace web_shop.Database
{
    public class WebShopContext : DbContext
    {
        public DbSet<Product> Products { get; set; }
        public DbSet<User> Users { get; set; }

        protected override void OnConfiguring(DbContextOptionsBuilder
optionsBuilder)
        {
optionsBuilder.UseNpgsql("Host=ciserver;Database=webshop;Username=sa;Passwo
rd=sa");
        }
    }
}
```

`WebShopContext` is inheriting from `DbContext`, an EF base class. In it, we find our `DbSet<T>`; basically, a collection object that represents a query to the database. In the configuration, we can specify our connection string to PostgreSQL. Be sure to change `Username` and `Password` if you need to.

Normally, you would not create your database context and classes in the same project as your controllers, views, and scripts. In any serious project, there should be a clear separation of concerns, and a frontend layer should not be handling database requests. However, VS Code cannot handle multiple projects at once (use regular Visual Studio for that) and so we are stuck with writing everything in the same project (there is no real project notion in VS Code--it is really just a single folder). Further down the road, we are going to place SQL queries in controllers--such practices would be the stuff of nightmares! For our example it is fine though.

Now, create two new files, also in the `database` folder, named `Product.cs` and `User.cs`. The `Product` class looks as follows:

```
using System.ComponentModel.DataAnnotations.Schema;

namespace web_shop.Database
{
    [Table("product")]
    public class Product
    {
        [Column("id")]
        public int Id { get; set; }
        [Column("name")]
        public string Name { get; set; }
        [Column("price")]
        public decimal Price { get; set; }
        [Column("description")]
        public string Description { get; set; }
        [Column("category")]
        public string Category { get; set; }
    }
}
```

Unfortunately, both the table and column names are case-sensitive. I like sticking to a certain technology's preferred naming style, `camelCase` in JavaScript, `PascalCase` in .NET, and `all_lower_case` in PostgreSQL. That means we have to make some sort of mapping between naming in PostgreSQL and .NET. As you can see, this can be done using the `Table` and `Column` attributes. If you do not find naming conventions worth the trouble, I cannot blame you and you may just want to use `PascalCasing` in your database or `all_lower_case` in .NET (although I recommend the former). The `User` class looks pretty much the same.

We will also need to add a `ShoppingCart` class. Usually, it would make sense to have some header-detail relationship, as in `ShoppingCart` and `ShoppingCartDetails`. However, in our example, the `user` serves as the master record and `shopping_cart` is already a detail table. A user can only have one shopping cart ever. It can be changed or emptied, but never can a user have more than one shopping cart (but it can have more than one `shopping_cart` row in it, as they are really just details). In EF, we can indicate that a property is a foreign key property, so-called navigation properties, so EF can load these entities for us automatically. For `ShoppingCart`, we want to create foreign key properties for `User` and `Product` so we can easily query for them later:

```
using System.ComponentModel.DataAnnotations.Schema;

namespace web_shop.Database
{
    [Table("shopping_cart")]
    public class ShoppingCart
    {
        [Column("id")]
        public int Id { get; set; }
        [Column("user_id")]
        public int UserId { get; set; }
        [Column("product_id")]
        public int ProductId { get; set; }
        [Column("number")]
        public int Number { get; set; }

        [ForeignKey("UserId")]
        public User User { get; set; }
        [ForeignKey("ProductId")]
        public Product Product { get; set; }
    }
}
```

With the `WebShopContext`, `User`, `Product`, and `ShoppingCart` classes, we have modeled out our database in C#.

Selecting the data

We are now ready to get to work to replace our repository methods to use AJAX requests to fetch the data from the backend. Let's start with the top three products on the home page. First, we must decide where to put our `GetTopProducts` function. Since the products are being shown on the home page, `HomeController` seems like a good spot. The function itself is pretty easy, especially compared to the JavaScript MongoDB callbacks:

```
public IActionResult GetTopProducts()
{
    using (var context = new WebShopContext())
    {
        var products = context.Products.Take(3).ToList();
        return Json(products);
    }
}
```

That is really all there is to it. These three lines of code open up a connection to the database, generate a SQL query that is roughly equivalent to `SELECT TOP 3 [all fields] FROM product`, map them to your class, and return them as a JSON result to your browser. Not only that, the browser receives all this `camelCased` like we are used to in JavaScript! You can see the result when you browse to `localhost:5000/Home/GetTopProducts`. However, we were kind of expecting `GetTopProducts` to be a POST call, not a GET call. We can easily change this behavior by decorating the function with `HttpPostAttribute`:

```
[HttpPost]
public IActionResult GetTopProducts()
[...]
```

One last thing--EF supports navigation properties, like we saw in the `ShoppingCart` class. This can lead to infinite references: a `ShoppingCart` entity has a `Product` entity, is contained in `ShoppingCart` entities, has a `Product` entity, and many more. For this reason, it is never a good idea to send an entity directly to your frontend; chances are that, one day, you'll end up with an endless loop in your object graph and you will need to do some additional work to properly serialize your objects (which you will not find out at design time!). So, to eliminate the chances of serialization exceptions, we are going to map the entities to a custom (anonymous) model that has the added benefit of only sending the fields we need to the frontend:

```
var products = context.Products
    .Select(p => new
    {
        Id = p.Id,
```

```
            Name = p.Name,
            Price = p.Price
        }).Take(3)
        .ToList();
    return Json(products);
```

We can now fix the frontend like we did before. In `repository.js`, we just quickly inject the `$http` module and change `getTopProducts`:

```javascript
return {
    getTopProducts: function (callback) {
        $http.post('/Home/GetTopProducts')
        .then(function (response) {
            callback(response.data);
        }, function () {
            alert('An error has occurred.');
        });
    },
    [...]
};
```

And, in the `index.js` file, we can change the controller:

```javascript
repository.getTopProducts(function (results) {
    $scope.topProducts = results;
});
```

Next, we can implement `GetProduct` in `ProductController`:

```csharp
[HttpPost]
public IActionResult GetProduct([FromBody]ValueModel<int> model)
{
    using (var context = new WebShopContext())
    {
        var product = context.Products
            .Select(p => new
            {
                Id = p.Id,
                Name = p.Name,
                Price = p.Price,
                Description = p.Description,
                Category = p.Category
            })
            .SingleOrDefault(p => p.Id == model.Value);
        return Json(product);
    }
}
```

Because this function takes POST requests, we need to get the data from the body of the request (instead of the URL parameters). `FromBodyAttribute` on the input parameter makes that happen. The body will map to some object. I have created a small generic class for single-value functions. We could simply put the value in the body, but that will cause some problems when putting strings in your body (is it a string or invalid JSON?). I have put the model in a new folder named `Models`:

```
public class ValueModel<T>
{
    public T Value { get; set; }
}
```

Other than that, it pretty much looks like `GetTopProducts`, except we are using `SingleOrDefault` instead of `Take(1)`. On the frontend, we can implement this pretty much like before with just a minor difference--the POST data which now has `value` instead of `id`:

```
getProduct: function (id, callback) {
    $http.post('/Product/GetProduct', {
        value: id
    })
    .then(function (response) {
        callback(response.data);
    }, function () {
        alert('An error has occurred.');
    });
},
```

And, of course, do not forget to edit both the `Product/Index.cshtml` file and the `product.js` file. I do not think I need to explain `SearchController.SearchProducts` and `ShoppingCartController.GetCart`. They work pretty much the same as `GetTopProducts` and `GetProduct`. You can also remove `products` from the `repository.js` file now.

Fixing the login

Next, we are going to fix the login. After that, our website is pretty much complete again and we can get to testing. First things first, our login method makes use of sessions. Getting session state in .NET Core is pretty well documented at `https://docs.microsoft.com/en-us/aspnet/core/fundamentals/app-state`. To enable sessions in .NET Core, we must install a package.

Again, you may need to disable the `BundlerMinifier` tool first and you may need to restart VS Code to get it to recognize the added tool in the intellisense:

```
[Install using the terminal]
dotnet add package Microsoft.AspNetCore.Session

[Add to csproj manually]
<PackageReference Include="Microsoft.AspNetCore.Session" Version="2.0.0" />

[In any case]
dotnet restore
```

To get the session working, we need to add some initialization in `Startup.cs`. The `ConfigureServices` method needs to add the session first:

```
public void ConfigureServices(IServiceCollection services)
{
    services.AddMvc();

    // Adds a default in-memory implementation of IDistributedCache.
    services.AddDistributedMemoryCache();

    services.AddSession(options =>
    {
        options.Cookie.HttpOnly = true;
    });
}
```

And, in the same Startup file, we need to explicitly call `app.UseSession()` in the `Configure` method:

```
public void Configure(IApplicationBuilder app, IHostingEnvironment env,
ILoggerFactory loggerFactory)
{
    loggerFactory.AddConsole(Configuration.GetSection("Logging"));
    loggerFactory.AddDebug();
    app.UseSession();
    [...]
```

And that is all that we need to do to enable sessions. In the controllers, we can access our session pretty easily as well. In `LoginController`, we can create a `Login` method:

```
using Microsoft.AspNetCore.Http;

[...]

[HttpPost]
public IActionResult Login([FromBody]LoginModel model)
```

```
{
    using (var context = new WebShopContext())
    {
        bool success = false;
        if (context.Users.Any(u => u.Username == model.Username && u.Password
== model.Password))
        {
            HttpContext.Session.SetString("Username", model.Username);
            HttpContext.Session.SetString("IsAuthenticated", bool.TrueString);
            success = true;
        }
        return Json(new
        {
            Success = success
        });
    }
}
```

The `Session` object can be accessed through the `HttpContext` property (inherited from `Controller`). For the `SetString` (extension) method, we need to add a reference to `Microsoft.AspNetCore.Http`. So, we can simply check whether the user exists in the database and, if it does, we set the session variables.

We can now change `_Layout.cshtml` so it shows the login or the logout button depending on your session:

```
@using Microsoft.AspNetCore.Http;

[...]

@if (Context.Session.GetString("IsAuthenticated") == bool.TrueString)
{
    <li><a href="@Url.Action("Logout", "Login")"><span class="glyphicon
glyphicon-off"></span> Logout
@(Context.Session.GetString("Username"))</a></li>
}
else
{
    <li><a href="@Url.Action("Index", "Login")"><span class="glyphicon
glyphicon-user"></span> Login</a></li>
}
```

The Session object can be accessed through the `Context` property, which is accessible in all your views. We use the `GetString` function to check whether the user is authenticated. If the user is authenticated, we show the logout button. The logout button links to the `Logout` action on `LoginController`:

```
public IActionResult Logout()
{
    HttpContext.Session.Remove("Username");
    HttpContext.Session.Remove("IsAuthenticated");
    return RedirectToActionPermanent(nameof(Index));
}
```

In our JavaScript, everything stays pretty much as it was in Chapter 8, *A NodeJS And MongoDB Web App*. There are just some minor details.

Adding to the cart

For the inserting of products into the database, I want to do things a little different. Basically, when it comes to SQL, I have known two types of people. The people who think databases are a necessary evil and should be used for data storage only and the people who love databases and who think all logic should be in the database's stored procedures and functions. Personally, I am somewhere in the middle. The database certainly has its place when it comes to business logic, but I prefer to keep it to a minimum. Anyway, for the insertion of products, I do want to use a stored procedure. We are going to send a user ID and a product ID to the database and let the database figure out whether to insert the product for the user or to update the number field. So, open up the query tool and execute the following SQL script:

```
CREATE OR REPLACE FUNCTION add_product_to_cart
(
    p_username TEXT,
    p_product_id INT
)
RETURNS void AS $$
    DECLARE v_user_id INT;
BEGIN
    v_user_id := (SELECT id FROM public.user WHERE username = p_username);
    IF EXISTS(SELECT * FROM shopping_cart
                WHERE user_id = v_user_id
                    AND product_id = p_product_id) THEN
        UPDATE shopping_cart
            SET number = number + 1
        WHERE user_id = v_user_id
            AND product_id = p_product_id;
```

```
    ELSE
        INSERT INTO shopping_cart
        (
            user_id,
            product_id,
            number
        )
        VALUES
        (
            v_user_id,
            p_product_id,
            1
        );
    END IF;
END;
$$ LANGUAGE plpgsql;
```

You can try it out by running the stored procedure in the query tool and checking the shopping_card table:

```
SELECT add_product_to_cart('username', 1); -- Make sure the IDs are valid!
SELECT * FROM shopping_cart;
```

We can add the function call in WebShopContext by simply executing a query and passing the username and product IDs as parameters:

```
public virtual void AddProductToCart(string username, int productId)
{
    this.Database.ExecuteSqlCommand("SELECT add_product_to_cart(@username,
@product_id);",
        new NpgsqlParameter("@username", username),
        new NpgsqlParameter("@product_id", productId));
}
```

In ShoppingCartController, we can simply call this method. It is really not all that interesting so I am leaving that part out. The only part that may be interesting to mention is the RemoveProductFromCart method, that makes use of the User navigation property for querying and deletes a record before calling SaveChanges() which saves any edits, adds, and removals in the context. The GetCart method seems a bit bloated (and it kind of is), but most of it is the mapping of the shopping cart, using the Product navigation property, to a custom object.

Testing the database

Now that we have this procedure we probably want to test it, just like we test our other code. Next to testing whether your SQL is in order, you can also test whether your schema is in order (does table `product` exist and does it have a `price` column, for example). This is something that is completely different from MongoDB as it did not have a schema. Testing databases can be a bit difficult. You need test data, maybe, inserted with some seed function, maybe, already present. You do not want to mess up your test data by making changes in your application. You probably need to set up database connections and transactions. It can be a hassle. However, there are some tools that make it a bit easier. pgTap is one of those tools. Using pgTap, you can write a test script in SQL, run it in a console, and output your data in TAP format (Test Anything Protocol, `https://testanything.org/`).

Installing pgTap

The installation guide for Linux is on `http://pgtap.org/`, but I will take you through it here as well as I had some issues with the documentation. The bad news about pgTap is that it works best on Linux. It can work on Windows, but it is a bit of a hassle and you need Perl, so I am not going to guide you through it. So, we are going to install pgTap on the server that runs PostgreSQL, which is our Linux server. First, we need to download the latest version (0.97.0 at the time of writing). After that, we need to unzip the downloaded file and build it using make (as described in the docs). After that, we can run the installation script so PostgreSQL installs all the necessary scripts for testing our code:

```
sudo apt-get update
sudo apt-get install make
wget http://api.pgxn.org/dist/pgtap/0.97.0/pgtap-0.97.0.zip
unzip pgtap-0.97.0.zip
cd pgtap-0.97.0
sudo make
sudo make checkinstall
sudo make install
sudo cpan TAP::Parser::SourceHandler::pgTAP
cd sql
psql [username] -h 127.0.0.1 -d webshop < pgtap.sql
[enter password]
```

This will install a dazzling 916 functions in your database's `public` schema. For any serious applications, you would do well to create custom schema's for your own functions. The `cpan` command is for downloading and building Perl modules. In this case, it installs pg_prove (http://pgtap.org/pg_prove.html) which we will use later. Anyway, we can now create a test script. Basically, we need a test user and for him to add a product to his cart, check whether it was added, add the same product again, check whether the number went up, and then add a different product and check whether that was also added correctly. So, create a test user and two test products. Then, put the following script in a file named `test.sql` **under** `test/sql`:

```
\set QUIET 1
-- Turn off echo and keep things quiet.

-- Format the output for nice TAP.
\pset format unaligned
\pset tuples_only true
\pset pager

-- Revert all changes on failure.
\set ON_ERROR_ROLLBACK 1
\set ON_ERROR_STOP true
\set QUIET 1

BEGIN;
    SELECT plan(1);

    DO $$
    BEGIN
        PERFORM add_product_to_cart('test_username', 1);
        PERFORM add_product_to_cart('test_username', 1);
        PERFORM add_product_to_cart('test_username', 2);
    END $$;

    SELECT results_eq(
        'SELECT user_id, product_id, number FROM shopping_cart WHERE user_id
= 1',
        $$VALUES ( 1, 1, 2 ), ( 1, 2, 1 )$$,
        'The products should be inserted into the shopping cart.'
    );

    SELECT * FROM finish();
    ROLLBACK;
END
```

The stuff at the top is some standard pgTap stuff, taken right from the tutorial. It is commented, so you can read what it does. After that comes the real pgTap test. Using the `plan` function, you can specify how many tests you want to run. The only test we have is that we are going to select some data and check whether it is the data we expected, so we have one test. After that, we simply insert the products into the user's shopping cart. We do this in a PL/pgSQL block, because we do not need the result (using `SELECT` will output an empty line in our test results). With `results_eq`, we can confirm that the correct number of products was indeed inserted into the `shopping_cart` table. This is also our test, so `1` in `plan(1)` if you will. With `finish()`, we tell pgTap we are done and it can output the results. Finally, we rollback the transaction so our shopping cart is emptied again and we can run the test again.

You can run your tests in Windows using the command prompt. Simply use the psql tool (in your PostgreSQL installation folder) and run the script:

```
cd "C:\Program Files\PostgreSQL\9.5\bin"
psql -U sa -h ciserver -d webshop -f C:\Users\sander.rossel\Desktop\web-shop\test\sql\test.sql
Password for user sa: [enter password]
```

The result should look as follows:

We know it works because, if we change the function so that it inserts two products instead of one, we get an error message:

```
Command Prompt                                          —    □    ×
C:\Program Files\PostgreSQL\9.5\bin>psql -U sa -h ciserver -d webshop -f C:\Users\sander.
rossel\Desktop\web-shop\test\sql\test.sql
Password for user sa:
1..1
not ok 1 - The products should be inserted into the shopping cart.
# Failed test 1: "The products should be inserted into the shopping cart."
#     Results differ beginning at row 1:
#          have: (1,1,3)
#          want: (1,1,2)
# Looks like you failed 1 test of 1
psql:C:/Users/sander.rossel/Desktop/web-shop/test/sql/test.sql:35: WARNING:  there is no
transaction in progress

C:\Program Files\PostgreSQL\9.5\bin>
```

Let's quickly add three other tests to ensure (part of) our schema is correct:

```
SELECT plan(4);

SELECT has_table('shopping_cart');
SELECT has_column('shopping_cart', 'number');
SELECT col_type_is('shopping_cart', 'number', 'integer');

[...]
```

The `has_table`, `has_column`, and `col_type_is` functions do not really need additional explanation--their names say it all. You can, optionally, add a schema as the first parameter, `SELECT has_table('my_schema', 'my_table');`, but we are using the default `public` schema so there is no need for that. Notice that we now plan for four tests (`plan(4)`) instead of one. Each function is an additional test. You can find functions, such as `plan`, `results_eq`, and `has_table` in the documentation (`http://pgtap.org/documentation.html`).

Testing our C# code

Now that we have our SQL covered, let's go back to our C# code for a bit. There is not really anything to unit test, as we have little to no business logic. It is all just selecting data and returning it to the frontend. Great for E2E tests; not so great for unit testing. So, just as in Node.js, let's create an `Order.cs` file and pretend we need it for invoicing later. I have created a new folder in the project root and named it `Invoicing`. In it, I have placed two files, `Order.cs` and `OrderLine.cs`. Both are pretty straightforward.

The `OrderLine` class is pretty much the same as in JavaScript, except we can work with the decimal data type which does not have rounding errors and so we do not need to round. The methods `GetSubTotal` and `GetTotal` could be implanted as properties with just a getter, but for some reason, our code coverage will not cover them later on. I am guessing this is some .NET Core incompatibility (I know this works in full .NET and this issue actually cost me hours to find!):

```csharp
public class OrderLine
{
    public Product Product { get; set; }
    public int Number { get; set; }
    public decimal GetSubTotal()
    {
        return Product.Price * Number;
    }
}
```

And the same goes for the `Order` class:

```csharp
public class Order
{
    public List<OrderLine> Lines { get; set; }
    public decimal GetTotal()
    {
        return Lines.Sum(l => l.GetSubTotal());
    }
}
```

And now we want to test them. We can use the same tests as we had in JavaScript, but written in C#.

Unfortunately, your C# tests cannot be in the same project as your code (well, they probably can, but just because you could, does not mean you should). The reason for this is that when you try to start a project that has both executable code and unit tests, VS Code will find two program entry points and will not know which one to start (your program or your tests). So, at this point, we have to create a new project. In the same folder as your `web-shop` folder, create a new folder and name it `web-shop-tests`. Open the folder in VS Code. We can now initialize a new project using the console. For the `web-shop` project, we used the `mvc` template but for this project, we need the `xunit` template:

```
dotnet new xunit
dotnet restore
```

You now get a `csproj` file and `UnitTest1.cs`. We are going to use the `cs` file. First, rename it to `OrderTests.cs`. Also, rename the class in the file to `OrderTests`. .NET Core generated one empty test, which you can run now. It does not do much, but try running `dotnet test` in the terminal. If all goes well, you should see the test passing. Next, we need to make a reference from our `web-shop` project to our tests project:

```
dotnet add reference ../web-store/web-store.csproj
dotnet restore
```

Alternatively, you can add it to your `csproj` file manually:

```
<ItemGroup>
    <ProjectReference Include="..\web-shop\web-shop.csproj" />
</ItemGroup>
```

We can now use code from the `web_shop` project in the tests project. Let's change the `OrderTests` class and add a test:

```
using System;
using System.Collections.Generic;
using web_shop.Database;
using web_shop.Invoicing;
using Xunit;

namespace web_shop_tests
{
    public class OrderTests
    {
        private Order CreateOrder()
        {
            return new Order
            {
                [...]
            };
        }

        [Fact]
        public void CalculateTotal_Test()
        {
            var order = CreateOrder();
            Assert.Equal(6.23M, order.GetTotal());
        }
    }
}
```

To test it, run the `dotnet test` in the terminal:

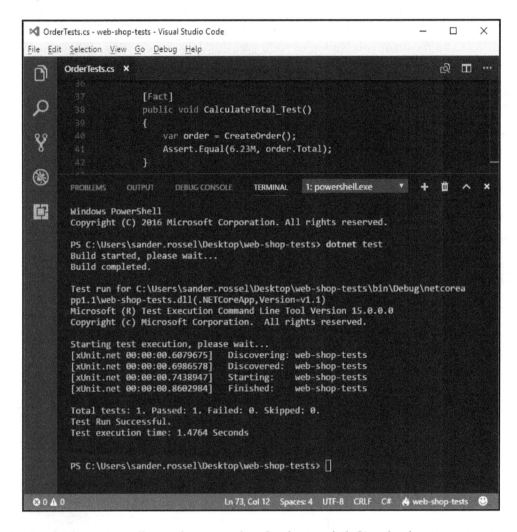

To check whether it actually works, try and make the test fail. Simply change 6.23M to something else and run the test again. This time, the test should fail:

```
Starting test execution, please wait...
[xUnit.net 00:00:00.6045309]   Discovering: web-shop-tests
[xUnit.net 00:00:00.6971649]   Discovered:  web-shop-tests
[xUnit.net 00:00:00.7490012]   Starting:    web-shop-tests
[xUnit.net 00:00:00.8773519]     web_shop_tests.OrderTests.CalculateTotal_Test [FAIL]
[xUnit.net 00:00:00.8784274]       Assert.Equal() Failure
[xUnit.net 00:00:00.8785371]       Expected: 7.23
[xUnit.net 00:00:00.8784274]       Assert.Equal() Failure
[xUnit.net 00:00:00.8785371]       Expected: 7.23
[xUnit.net 00:00:00.8785834]       Actual:   6.23
[xUnit.net 00:00:00.8795181]       Stack Trace:
[xUnit.net 00:00:00.8805833]           C:\Users\sander.rossel\Desktop\web-shop-tests\Ord
erTests.cs(41,0): at web_shop_tests.OrderTests.CalculateTotal_Test()
[xUnit.net 00:00:00.8942034]   Finished:    web-shop-tests
Failed   web_shop_tests.OrderTests.CalculateTotal_Test
Error Message:
 Assert.Equal() Failure
Expected: 7.23
Actual:   6.23
Stack Trace:
   at web_shop_tests.OrderTests.CalculateTotal_Test() in C:\Users\sander.rossel\Deskto
p\web-shop-tests\OrderTests.cs:line 41

Total tests: 1. Passed: 0. Failed: 1. Skipped: 0.
Test execution time: 1.5109 Seconds
Test Run Failed.
```

Change the expected result back again. We can now add the other three tests we used to have in JavaScript:

```csharp
[Fact]
public void UpdateLineTotalOnNumberChange_Test()
{
    var order = CreateOrder();
    order.Lines[0].Number = 2;
    Assert.Equal(2.46M, order.Lines[0].GetSubTotal());
}

[Fact]
public void UpdateTotalOnLineInsert_Test()
{
    var order = CreateOrder();
    order.Lines.Add(new OrderLine
    {
        Product = new Product
        {
            Price = 2
        },
        Number = 1
    });
    Assert.Equal(8.23M, order.GetTotal());
}
```

```
[Fact]
public void UpdateTotalOnLineRemoval_Test()
{
    var order = CreateOrder();
    order.Lines.RemoveAt(0);
    Assert.Equal(5, order.GetTotal());
}
```

Run your tests again and validate that they succeed. Now, go back to your web-shop project. You probably want an easy way to test your code from here as well. Open up the tasks.json file and add a new task:

```
{
    "taskName": "test",
    "command": "dotnet",
    "isShellCommand": true,
    "args": ["test", "../web-shop-tests/web-shop-tests.csproj"]
},
```

You can add it to your doItAll task as well, if you want:

```
"args": [
    "/C \"dotnet build && dotnet bundle && gulp && dotnet test ../web-shop-tests/web-shop-tests.csproj\""
]
```

Now, if a test fails, you will not be notified when you try to debug the application and you can fix the test first. Personally, I think it is a bit overkill to run all your tests at every build, especially when you have hundreds and it takes a few seconds to run them, but it's your choice.

Reporting

Of course, we will need some test reports that we can publish to Jenkins later on. Unfortunately, and it pains me to say this, Microsoft is doing a really bad job at this. You can forget about an out-of-the-box code coverage option unless you are running Visual Studio Enterprise Edition (which costs you an arm and a leg and only runs on Windows). Even a simple JUnit style report is too much to ask for at this point; Microsoft only outputs TRX files (Test Result X...?), which is just another XML file.

First, let's just output the TRX file. It is quite easy actually--just append `--logger trx`, or `-l trx` for short, to your `dotnet test` command:

```
dotnet test -l trx
```

The file will be generated in a `TestResults` folder. We can also specify a custom filename:

```
dotnet test -l "trx;LogFileName=result.trx"
```

So, now we have a TRX file that we can publish to Jenkins later.

Back to the code coverage. This is rather tricky as there is no built-in support for this. Our best bet is to use OpenCover (`https://github.com/OpenCover/opencover`), but this (otherwise great tool) does not officially support .NET Core yet. The problem is that it depends on some library that is not yet fully ported to .NET Core, so we are going to run into some issues. The good news is that there is quite a lot of demand for official .NET Core support for OpenCover and people are working on it. Meanwhile, people have figured out how to get the current version working with .NET Core. Of course, without .NET Core support, it only works on Windows.

The first issue is with actually getting OpenCover to work. Normally, you would install OpenCover as a NuGet package, which would install OpenCover in your solution packages folder. However, this is not the case with .NET Core and VS Code. So, get the latest `msi` file from GitHub, `https://github.com/opencover/opencover/releases`, and install it. You probably want to go into the advanced options and install OpenCover for all the users on this machine (so Jenkins will be able to run it too).

Now that OpenCover is installed, we can, theoretically, simply run it from the console and target our test project:

```
"C:\Program Files (x86)\OpenCover\OpenCover.Console.exe" -
target:"C:\Program Files\dotnet\dotnet.exe" -targetargs:"test" -
register:user -filter:"+[web-shop]* -[web-shop-tests]*" -
output:"TestResults/OpenCover Coverage.xml"
```

That is quite a command-line program. We are running `OpenCover.Console.exe` (in the folder where you have installed it, `Program Files (x86)\OpenCover` is the default) and specify `dotnet.exe` (in `C:\Program Files\dotnet`) as the target to run. The argument given to `dotnet.exe` is simply `test`; this is equivalent to running `dotnet test` from the terminal in VS Code. The `-filter` switch tells OpenCover which files to include or exclude. The default include filter is `+[*]*`, or everything. There are also some default exclude filters, such as `[System]*`, `[System.]*`, and `[mscorlib]*`.

We want to include `web-shop*`, but exclude `web-shop-tests*`. The `-output` switch just tells OpenCover in what file to put the result. We are putting the result with the rest of our test results generated by xUnit. Last but not least, we just want to add the `-register:user` switch which is necessary to get it all working. It registers the profiler OpenCover uses for tracking your covered code. Without it, you will get an error message:

```
No results, this could be for a number of reasons. The most common reasons
are:
    1) missing PDBs for the assemblies that match the filter please review
the
    output file and refer to the Usage guide (Usage.rtf) about filters.
    2) the profiler may not be registered correctly, please refer to the
Usage
    guide and the -register switch.
```

So, run the command and you still get that error message! We can open the generated file and look for the cause:

```
<Module skippedDueTo="MissingPdb" hash="B5-C4-7A-
E0-72-26-30-32-27-17-25-28-B2-D0-1A-95-DD-94-E2-57">
    <ModulePath>C:\Users\sander.rossel\Desktop\web-shop-
tests\bin\Debug\netcoreapp2.0\web-shop.dll</ModulePath>
    <ModuleTime>2017-06-03T12:34:39.9752551Z</ModuleTime>
    <ModuleName>web-shop</ModuleName>
    <Classes />
</Module>
```

The `MissingPdb` reason is a bit misleading. When you look in your `bin` folder, you will find a **Program Database** (**PDB**) file, but it is not in the correct format. A PDB file is used for matching runtime code to the lines of code, allowing you to debug your code. However, .NET Core apparently uses a different format than full .NET. We can easily fix this though. Head over to your `web-shop` project file and add the following `PropertyGroup` to it:

```
<PropertyGroup Condition="'$(Configuration)|$(Platform)'=='Debug|AnyCPU'">
    <DebugType>full</DebugType>
    <DebugSymbols>True</DebugSymbols>
</PropertyGroup>
```

This tells .NET to use a full PDB file. The default for .NET Core is `portable`. Now run OpenCover again and find that it works, except that you get zero coverage on everything:

```
Committing...
Visited Classes 0 of 17 (0)
Visited Methods 0 of 72 (0)
Visited Points 0 of 193 (0)
Visited Branches 0 of 84 (0)
```

```
==== Alternative Results (includes all methods including those without
corresponding source) ====
Alternative Visited Classes 0 of 28 (0)
Alternative Visited Methods 0 of 133 (0)
```

There is one more trick to getting this right. OpenCover does not support .NET Core because the Profiler API is not yet converted to .NET Core. We need to add the -oldStyle switch, which is pretty hacky and not really intended for this purpose, but it does the trick:

```
"C:\Program Files (x86)\OpenCover\OpenCover.Console.exe" -
target:"C:\Program Files\dotnet\dotnet.exe" -targetargs:"test" -
register:user -filter:"+[web-shop]* -[web-shop-tests]*" -
output:"TestResults/OpenCover Coverage.xml" -oldStyle
```

You should now get an output that looks like the following:

Keep in mind that OpenCover only covers .NET code. Any JavaScript code (or other non .NET code) is ignored. So, when you have a thousand lines of JavaScript and one line of C# and you test that one line, you will have a 100% coverage (according to OpenCover). Keep in mind that properties are not covered (probably because of some .NET Core incompatibility). You may also want to work with the `-skipautoprops` switch, which does not take auto properties (properties with empty getters and setters, such as `public int SomeProperty { get; set; }`) into account for code coverage.

Unfortunately, we still have a problem. We have this OpenCover coverage report and there is nothing we can do with it. Jenkins cannot publish it, we cannot read it, and VS Code is at a loss as well. We need two additional packages to get useful reports. The first, a rather long and descriptive name, is the `OpenCoverToCoberturaConverter` (`https://github.com/danielpalme/OpenCoverToCoberturaConverter`) and the second is the `ReportGenerator` (`https://github.com/danielpalme/ReportGenerator`). The first package does what its name implies--it converts the report created by `OpenCover` to a Cobertura-styled XML. The `ReportGenerator` can generate various reports, such as HTML and text, from various inputs among which are OpenCover and Cobertura. As with OpenCover, we cannot really install these tools using VS Code and run them. Instead, we need NuGet to download them. Go to `https://www.nuget.org/` and install the latest `nuget.exe` (not the vsix). Now, you can simply run it from the command and install `OpenCoverToCoberturaConverter`:

```
nuget.exe install OpenCoverToCoberturaConverter
```

This will put the package in your current folder. Put it somewhere where you can easily access it. Putting it in your `web-shop-test` folder is actually a pretty good idea, so you will always have the converter with your package. You really only need the `Tools\OpenCoverToCoberturaConverter.exe` file so you can just keep that and discard the other files. You can download `ReportGenerator` the same way or you can get it from GitHub at `https://github.com/danielpalme/ReportGenerator/releases`. If you downloaded from GitHub, make sure you unpack the zip file. You do not need all the files, but we are going to create a separate folder for this tool anyway, so you might as well keep them all.

Usage of both tools is pretty straightforward now and gives us the results we need. The following commands are executed from the `web-shop-tests` folder and assume that `OpenCoverToCoberturaConverter.exe` is in the same folder and that `ReportGenerator` is in a folder named `ReportGenerator`:

```
OpenCoverToCoberturaConverter.exe -input:"TestResults\OpenCover
Coverage.xml" -output:TestResults\Cobertura.xml
```

```
ReportGenerator\ReportGenerator.exe -reports:"TestResults\OpenCover
Coverage.xml" -targetDir:TestResults\CoverageHTML
```

`OpenCoverToCoberturaConverter` will output a warning, but we can ignore it as we are not going to merge files. We now get a nice Cobertura file and a detailed HTML page showing us what lines are and are not covered. The overview page shows us coverage per assembly, class, or namespace (you can slide the grouping slider at the top) and total coverage statistics:

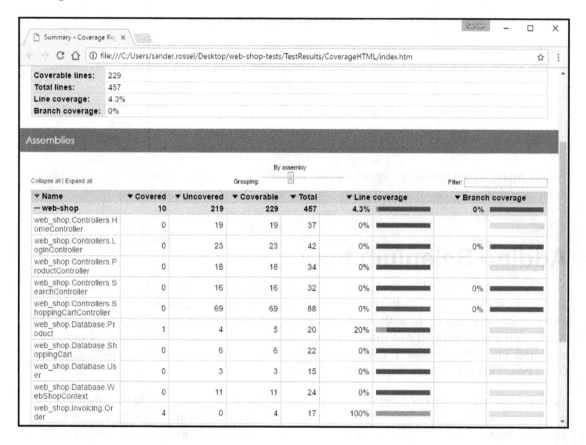

Clicking on a class shows the coverage per line:

```
        4   namespace web_shop.Database
        5   {
        6       [Table("product")]
        7       public class Product
        8       {
        9           [Column("id")]
  0    10           public int Id { get; set; }
       11           [Column("name")]
  0    12           public string Name { get; set; }
       13           [Column("price")]
 16    14           public decimal Price { get; set; }
       15           [Column("description")]
  0    16           public string Description { get; set; }
       17           [Column("category")]
  0    18           public string Category { get; set; }
       19       }
       20   }
```

This is pretty much the same report we had earlier and it is a report we can actually use in Jenkins and that we can read ourselves. So that sets up our test reporting for now.

Adding Selenium tests

Next, we are going to add Selenium tests to our application. You could, of course, use the JavaScript tests we wrote in the previous chapters. After all, Selenium tests your frontend and that has nothing to do with our C# backend. Our routing changed a bit so they will not work until we fix the URLs in the tests, but apart from the routing, everything should be as expected. However, Selenium has a C# implementation, so let's keep this project as much C# as possible and explore the Selenium C# API.

To make this work, we need yet another project. Strictly speaking, we do not need a new project and we could simply put our Selenium tests in our regular test project. However, your test project depends on your `web-shop` project and needs to access it in order to build. Your Selenium tests are going to need your `web-shop` project to run. And here is the problem: your unit test project cannot build when your `web-shop` project is running because the files will be locked. In any case, it is best to create a new project anyway, as you probably do not want your unit tests and Selenium tests to always run at the same time. So create a new folder, name it `web-shop-selenium` (or something like that) and initialize it with `dotnet new xunit`.

I should warn you, the .NET Core Selenium implementation is still in beta phase at the time of writing. Not all the features are supported, but we will manage. As luck has it, with the latest release of .NET Core, which was released while writing this book, we can simply add the Selenium packages to our csproj. You will get an error that the packages were restored using .NET Framework v4.6.1 and that the package may not be fully compatible with your project. As always, you can use `dotnet add package` or add the reference to the project file manually. You will eventually get an error that `System.Security.Permission` is missing, so be sure to install that one too. You may need to restart VS Code:

```
<PackageReference Include="Selenium.Support" Version="3.5.2" />
<PackageReference Include="Selenium.WebDriver" Version="3.5.2" />
<PackageReference Include="System.Security.Permissions" Version="4.4.0" />

dotnet add package Selenium.Support
dotnet add package Selenium.WebDriver
dotnet add package System.Security.Permissions

dotnet restore
```

Rename the test file to `SeleniumTests.cs`. In it, we are going to place our tests. This one is going to be a bit different. We need a web driver, for example, the Chrome driver, to work with. We can use the same driver across all tests so we do not need to open up a new browser window for every test. So, the driver is created as a field that will need to be properly disposed. Since the very beginning, .NET has the **IDisposable** interface, which must be implemented in a specific manner for it to work properly. Luckily, VS Code helps you with the exact code (including comments) to implement this. Here is the bare bones version of our test class, including dispose, but excluding the comments:

```csharp
using Xunit;
using OpenQA.Selenium;
using OpenQA.Selenium.Chrome;
using System;

namespace web_shop_selenium
{
    public class SeleniumTests : IDisposable
    {
        private IWebDriver driver = new ChromeDriver();

        #region IDisposable Support
        private bool disposedValue = false;

        protected virtual void Dispose(bool disposing)
        {
            if (!disposedValue)
            {
```

```
            if (disposing)
            {
                driver.Dispose();
            }
            disposedValue = true;
        }
    }

    void IDisposable.Dispose()
    {
        Dispose(true);
    }
    #endregion
    }
}
```

`ChromeDriver` is hardcoded for now, but it can be exchanged with other drivers such as `FirefoxDriver` and `EdgeDriver`. This works because we have the driver for Chrome, and other web drivers, in our PATH variable, as explained in `Chapter 5`, *Testing your JavaScript*. Alternatively, you can specify the path to your web driver in the `ChromeDriver` constructor:

```
private IWebDriver driver = new ChromeDriver("C:\\WebDrivers");
```

This is the part where we need our web-shop project. In your csproj file, add a project reference:

```
<ItemGroup>
    <ProjectReference Include="..\web-shop\web-shop.csproj" />
</ItemGroup>
```

Because the web-shop needs an `appsettings.json` file, it needs to be copied to any output folder that is going to use this project. Now, in your `web-shop.csproj` (not the Selenium project!), add the following code to always copy the `appsettings.json` file:

```
<ItemGroup>
    <Content Update="appsettings.json">
        <CopyToOutputDirectory>PreserveNewest</CopyToOutputDirectory>
    </Content>
</ItemGroup>
```

We can now implement the constructor of our `SeleniumTests` class. This is where we create a reference to our server and construct a client using the `StartUp` class of our web-shop project:

```
private readonly TestServer server;
private readonly HttpClient client;
public SeleniumTests()
{
    server = new TestServer(new WebHostBuilder()
        .UseStartup<Startup>());
    client = server.CreateClient();
    client.BaseAddress = new Uri("http://ciserver:5000");
}
```

We can now write our first test. Let's start with the test that checks whether the product titles on the home page are properly wrapped:

```
[Fact]
public void ShouldCutOffLongTitles_Test()
{
    driver.Navigate().GoToUrl("http://localhost:5000");
    driver.Manage().Timeouts().ImplicitWait = TimeSpan.FromSeconds(2);
    var elems = driver.FindElements(By.CssSelector("h3"));
    Assert.Equal(3, elems.Count);

    var elem = elems[0];
    Assert.Equal("hidden", elem.GetCssValue("overflow"));
    Assert.Equal("ellipsis", elem.GetCssValue("text-overflow"));
    Assert.Equal("nowrap", elem.GetCssValue("white-space"));
}
```

The only weird thing going on in this sample is the `driver.Manage().Timeouts().ImplicitWait` thing. This sets the wait period to find elements. We are explicitly setting it to 2 seconds, because we want the top three products to load within two seconds (and actually that is pretty long already). If it takes longer, we will get a timeout exception. In the regular version of .NET, we could use the `Selenium.Support` package, which adds a `WebDriverWait` class that lets us wait for certain conditions, such as the `ExpectedConditions` utility in JavaScript. Unfortunately, we are stuck with the `ImplicitWait` property, which sets the wait time for all the operations the driver executes. I do expect `Selenium.Support` to come to .NET Core as well though.

The next two tests are still pretty straightforward:

```
[Fact]
public void ShouldNavigateToTheClickedProduct_Test()
{
    driver.Navigate().GoToUrl("http://localhost:5000");
    driver.Manage().Timeouts().ImplicitWait = TimeSpan.FromSeconds(2);

    var product = driver.FindElements(By.CssSelector("h3"))[1];
    product.Click();

    var title = driver.FindElement(By.CssSelector("h2"));
    Assert.Equal("Captain America: Civil War", title.Text);
}

[Fact]
public void ShouldSearchForAllProductsContainingFanta_Test()
{
    driver.Navigate().GoToUrl("http://localhost:5000");
    driver.Manage().Timeouts().ImplicitWait = TimeSpan.FromSeconds(2);

    var input = driver.FindElement(By.CssSelector("[ng-model=query]"));
    input.SendKeys("fanta");
    var searchBtn = driver.FindElement(By.CssSelector("#search-btn"));
    searchBtn.Click();
    var results = driver.FindElements(By.CssSelector(".thumbnail"));
    Assert.True(results.Count < 20);

    var allHaveFanta = results.All(elem =>
    {
        var caption = elem.FindElement(By.CssSelector("h3")).Text;
        return caption.ToLowerInvariant().Contains("fanta");
    });

    Assert.True(allHaveFanta, "Not all found results contain the text
'fanta'.");
}
```

As you can see, we still use the `SendKeys` and `Click` methods and the found elements (of the type `IWebElement`) can still be searched for nested elements. One major difference, however, is that the text of an element is simply a property. No difficult asynchronous calls and callbacks.

The last test is less difficult than the JavaScript equivalent, but it is still quite tricky:

```
[Fact]
public void ShouldRemoveAnItemFromTheShoppingCart_Test()
{
    driver.Navigate().GoToUrl("http://localhost:5000/ShoppingCart");
    driver.Manage().Timeouts().ImplicitWait = TimeSpan.FromSeconds(2);

    // redirect
    var username = driver.FindElement(By.CssSelector("input[ng-
model=username]"));
    var password =
driver.FindElement(By.CssSelector("input[type=password]"));

    username.SendKeys("user");
    password.SendKeys("password");

    var submit = driver.FindElement(By.CssSelector("input[type=submit]"));
    submit.Click();
    // another redirect
    driver.Navigate().GoToUrl("http://localhost:5000");

    var buttons = driver.FindElements(By.CssSelector(".btn.btn-primary"));

    buttons[0].Click();
    driver.SwitchTo().Alert().Accept();

    buttons[1].Click();
    driver.SwitchTo().Alert().Accept();

    driver.Navigate().GoToUrl("http://localhost:5000/ShoppingCart");
    var items = driver.FindElements(By.CssSelector(".thumbnail"));
    var count = items.Count;
    var caption = items[0].FindElement(By.CssSelector("h3")).Text;
    items[0].FindElement(By.CssSelector("button")).Click();

    // Like with the JavaScript tests, just wait for a second...
    Thread.Sleep(1000);
    var newItems = driver.FindElements(By.CssSelector(".thumbnail"));
    Assert.Equal(count - 1, newItems.Count);
    Assert.NotEqual(caption,
newItems[0].FindElement(By.CssSelector("h3")).Text);

    driver.Navigate().Refresh();
    var afterRefresh = driver.FindElements(By.CssSelector(".thumbnail"));
    Assert.Equal(count - 1, afterRefresh.Count);
}
```

Here, we see that the Selenium API is quite different from the JavaScript one. Again, no callback nesting. Also, we see the `SwitchTo().Alert()` functions to catch an alert window, and `Accept()` to accept the alert. Using `Navigate()`, we can refresh the browser with the `Refresh()` method. Other than that, this method does the same as the JavaScript one. We go to the shopping cart page, get redirected to the login page, log in, get redirected to the shopping cart page, go to the home page, add two products to the cart, go to the shopping cart page, remove an item, and, finally, refresh the page and check whether the item is still removed. Quite a test, but it is worth it.

Jenkins

We now have our code, our unit tests with code coverage, our E2E tests, and our database test. Time to get it to work in Jenkins. First, we must commit everything to Git. We need the three folders in the same Git repository though (strictly, we do not, but it makes everything so much easier). It is a good idea to create a new Git repository using GitLab. I have named it `web-shop-csharp`. Clone the `web-shop-csharp` repository to your machine and put `web-shop`, `web-shop-tests`, and `web-shop-selenium` in the repository. You will now have over 4,000 files to commit. Create (or copy) a `.gitignore` file so we exclude some generated files. Those include Bower and npm files, generated JavaScript, CSS files, and test results. You will be left with less than 100 files (69 if you followed my exact directions):

```
**/bin/**
**/obj/**
**/TestResults/**
**/node_modules/**
**/bundles/**
**/wwwroot/lib/**
**/site.min.css
```

This is also a good moment to test if our software builds at all if we remove these files (you can commit and push these changes and then do another clean repository checkout). Spoiler--it does not. When you try to run, .NET Core will complain that it is missing some files in the `obj` folder. To fix this, we need to do `dotnet restore`. After that, Gulp is not able to run, so we need `npm install`. Last but not least, everything goes as planned, except the website is not working properly. We are missing jQuery, Bootstrap, and Angular, so we must do `bower install` as well. Of course, we want all that to automatically happen when we build the software. All we have to do is change the `doItAll` task in the `tasks.json` file:

```
"args": [
    "/C \"dotnet restore && dotnet build && dotnet bundle && bower install
&& npm install && gulp\""
```

```
],
```

So fix the build and push that to Git as well.

Building the project

Time to start up Jenkins again. Jenkins does not support .NET out of the box. If you are really serious about .NET and CI, you may want to look at **Team Foundation Server (TFS)**, the CI platform from Microsoft (`https://www.visualstudio.com/tfs/`). TFS is not free (unless you are using the limited Express version) and works on Windows only. So we are going to use Jenkins again.

So, create a new project, name it something such as `CSharp Web Shop - Build`, and pick the Freestyle Project template. The configuration should be obvious by now, but I will walk you through it just in case. I have ticked the **Discard old builds** checkbox and set it to keep 5 builds. We are going to build this on Linux, just because we want to make use of the multiplatform capabilities of .NET Core. So, it goes without saying that we should **Restrict where this project can be run** to **Linux**. Set the correct Git URL and credentials in the Source Code Management. You may want to set a build trigger, but at this point, we just want to get it to run manually first.

Building our project just for the sake of building it is quite important. Unlike JavaScript, C# is a compiled language. There are many reasons for a project not to compile. A programmer could have committed invalid syntax by mistake or files can be missing. Anyway, if a program does not compile, even if it is only because of a missing semicolon, it cannot be executed as a whole. So build.

For the build step, we are going to execute a shell command:

```
cd web-shop
dotnet restore
dotnet build
dotnet bundle
npm install
bower install
gulp
```

That is pretty much what our `doItAll` task does as well. When you run this, it will fail right away. Our Linux server does not have .NET Core installed yet. So let's install it on our VM. You can find how to install .NET Core on the Microsoft .NET Core website as well (`https://www.microsoft.com/net/core#linuxubuntu`):

```
sudo sh -c 'echo "deb
https://apt-mo.trafficmanager.net/repos/dotnet-release/ xenial main" >
/etc/apt/sources.list.d/dotnetdev.list'
sudo apt-key adv --keyserver hkp://keyserver.ubuntu.com:80 --recv-keys
417A0893
sudo apt-get update
sudo apt-get install dotnet-sdk-2.0.0
[agree with installation] y
```

When you run the Jenkins job again, .NET Core is going to set up some telemetry stuff (one time only) and then build your project. And then, the next step will fail because Bower is not found. So far, we have used Bower as a global package, which is fine, but we also know it is difficult to install global packages as they are installed per user. So, the easiest solution is to install Bower locally, so it can always be run anywhere without having to install it for that specific user. We are doing the same with Gulp:

```
npm install bower --save-dev
```

That also means we have to slightly change our Jenkins configuration:

```
npm install
node_modules/.bin/bower install
node_modules/.bin/gulp
```

Your Jenkins build should succeed now, on Linux! The next thing we want to do is to add SonarQube to the build. Create a `sonar-project.properties` file in the root of your Git repository. We can now set the `sources` property to `web-shop`, since we do not really want to include our test files in the SonarQube analysis. `exclusions` are, unfortunately, not relative to the `sources` property:

```
sonar.projectKey=CSharpWebShop
sonar.projectName=C# Web Shop
sonar.projectVersion=1.0

sonar.sources=web-shop

sonar.exclusions=**/node_modules/**, **/wwwroot/lib/**, **/bundles/**,
**/obj/**, **/bin/**, **/.vscode/**
```

Now the fun part: SonarQube will not analyze C# files when the analyzer does not run on Windows. So, we need to make our project run on Windows after all (change the label from `linux` to `windows`). We will need to replace our shell script with a `cmd` command. The `cmd` command is the same as the shell command, except we need to replace the new lines with `&&`:

```
cd web-shop && dotnet restore && dotnet build && dotnet bundle && npm
install && node_modules\.bin\bower.cmd install &&
node_modules\.bin\gulp.cmd
```

Also, make sure the SonarQube runner uses the Windows Slave instead of Local. When you run the project and check out SonarQube, you will see a couple of issues. Again, the usage of `alert` in JavaScript causes eight vulnerabilities. What we really want to know is how well our C# code does. It does really very well (after all, I have been coding C# for a couple of years). Actually, the only C# issue we have is in some code that .NET generated for us, the `Program.cs` file. The fix is easy enough--add the `static` keyword to the class declaration:

```
namespace web_shop
{
    public static class Program
    {
        public static void Main(string[] args)
        {
            [...]
```

When you push this to Git and run the Jenkins project again, you will find that our project is pretty clean. We already knew about the `alert` issues and the experimental `text-overflow`. We can resolve them as *Won't fix* to get rid of them.

Testing the project

Next, we are going to test our project. We have various tests in place, but we will start with the unit tests. We will need to install a new Jenkins plugin before we can publish our TRX results to Jenkins. So, go to the Jenkins plugin manager and search for `mstest`. You should see two plugins, the MSTest plugin and the MSTestRunner plugin. The MSTestRunner is for running tests using MSTest. We are using xUnit though and we are running it through OpenCover using the command line anyway. So, we need the MSTest plugin, which can transform TRX files to the JUnit format and publish them to Jenkins.

We have two choices now. We can create a new project, like we did with the Node.js website, or we can just add a new build step to the current project. Let's go with the former, so we can create a pipeline of projects. Copy the current project (the name of the project to copy from is case-sensitive) and name the new one `CSharp Web Shop - Test` (by putting `CSharp Web Shop` in front of the task, your projects are nicely sorted together). The only thing you really need to do is change the batch command build step. Also, set the build trigger to **Build after other projects are built** and watch the previous project (only when stable). Also, remove the SonarQube analysis. You could possibly keep the SonarQube runner in this project and remove it from the build project, so you can build that one on Linux again.

To test our project, we need to do a few things: run the tests using OpenCover and transform the reports. After that, we can publish the reports. There is a little problem with `dotnet`, as it does not have rights to create the `TestResults` directory, so we need to do that manually as well. Because of these same rights issues, OpenCover also cannot register the Profiler `dll` with the user account, so we can omit `user`:

```
cd web-shop-tests && dotnet restore && (if not exist TestResults mkdir
TestResults) && "C:\Program Files (x86)\OpenCover\OpenCover.Console.exe" -
target:"C:\Program Files\dotnet\dotnet.exe" -targetargs:"test -l
"trx;LogFileName=result.trx"" -register -filter:"+[web-shop]* -[web-shop-
tests]*" -output:"TestResults\OpenCover Coverage.xml" -oldStyle &&
OpenCoverToCoberturaConverter.exe -input:"TestResults\OpenCover
Coverage.xml" -output:TestResults\Cobertura.xml &&
ReportGenerator\ReportGenerator.exe -reports:"TestResults\OpenCover
Coverage.xml" -targetDir:TestResults\CoverageHTML
```

That is a pretty big command, so you may want to split it up into multiple commands:

```
[Create the TestResults folder]
cd web-shop-tests && (if not exist TestResults mkdir TestResults)

[Run OpenCover]
cd web-shop-tests && dotnet restore && "C:\Program Files
(x86)\OpenCover\OpenCover.Console.exe" -target:"C:\Program
Files\dotnet\dotnet.exe" -targetargs:"test -l "trx;LogFileName=result.trx""
-register -filter:"+[web-shop]* -[web-shop-tests]*" -
output:"TestResults\OpenCover Coverage.xml" -oldStyle

[Convert to Cobertura]
cd web-shop-tests && OpenCoverToCoberturaConverter.exe -
input:"TestResults\OpenCover Coverage.xml" -
output:TestResults\Cobertura.xml

[Convert to HTML]
cd web-shop-tests && ReportGenerator\ReportGenerator.exe -
```

```
reports:"TestResults\OpenCover Coverage.xml" -
targetDir:TestResults\CoverageHTML
```

Nothing we have not seen before, but it is a lot in one command. Do not forget to publish the generated reports. The Cobertura report can be found in `web-shop-tests/TestResults/Cobertura.xml`. The HTML report is in `web-shop-tests/TestResults/CoverageHTML` and the index page is `index.html`. In the Cobertura Coverage Report, it will seem like your classes with only properties have no code and your other classes have less code. For example, it seems like `Order.cs` only has three lines of code. Anyway, you know why you are getting these results:

Database/Product.cs		N/A		N/A		N/A	N/A
Database/ShoppingCart.cs		N/A		N/A		N/A	N/A
Database/User.cs		N/A		N/A		N/A	N/A
Database/WebShopContext.cs	0%	0/1	0%	0/2	0%	0/6	N/A
Invoicing/Order.cs	100%	1/1	100%	1/1	100%	3/3	N/A
Invoicing/OrderLine.cs	100%	1/1	100%	1/1	100%	3/3	N/A

You may be surprised to find that while the Cobertura report does not properly cover properties, the HTML report does.

The TRX report is new. With the MSTest plugin, you got a new post-build action named **Publish MSTest test result report**:

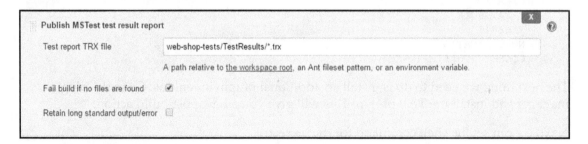

It is not very difficult, but you have to know it is there. Another side effect of the MSTest plugin is that the Emma plugin was also installed. Emma is another code coverage format that is used by Microsoft. Even though we are not using it, there is a new report on the menu named Coverage Trend. Clicking it just shows a broken image. We are not going to use it either, so it just sits there being useless. You can ignore it.

Testing the database

So, we now have the build, SonarQube, unit tests, and code coverage in place and it is time to test the database. We are going to run this one on Linux again. So, copy the build project and name this one `CSharp Web Shop - Database`. Make sure your label expression is `linux`, so it runs on the VM.

For this one, we are going to use `pg_Prove`, a command-line utility we installed earlier with the `cpan TAP` command in Linux (`http://pgtap.org/pg_prove.html`). With `pg_Prove`, we can omit the top part of our SQL test script because `pg_prove` does that for us:

```
-- This can be removed.
\set QUIET 1
[...]

-- From here is what we need.
BEGIN;
```

First of all, `pg_Prove` will try to log in to PostgreSQL using a Jenkins user. For simplicity, we are going to create that user without a password and make it a superuser so nothing will keep Jenkins from doing its job:

```
CREATE USER jenkins WITH
    LOGIN
    SUPERUSER
    CREATEDB
    CREATEROLE
    INHERIT
    NOREPLICATION
    CONNECTION LIMIT -1;
```

The next thing we need to do is install an additional plugin in Jenkins. Go to the plugin manager and install the TAP plugin. This will give you a new post-build action.

Next, we can set the shell command for the project:

```
pg_prove -d webshop -v web-shop/test/sql/*.sql | tee tap.txt
```

The -v switch outputs all the tests to the console. The files that will be tested are
web_shop/test/sql/*.sql. The | tee outputs any output to the console and to a file
called tap.txt. Only the stderr output is not written to the file. We can now publish our
tap.txt file to Jenkins. Add the Publish TAP Results post-build action and publish
tap.txt. Also, go into the advanced options and make sure **Fail the build if no test results
(files) are found** and **Failed tests mark build as a failure** are checked. Not checking them
will make the build unstable, but we want it to fail explicitly. There are now two new
reports. The TAP Extended Test Results and the pre-build TAP Test Results:

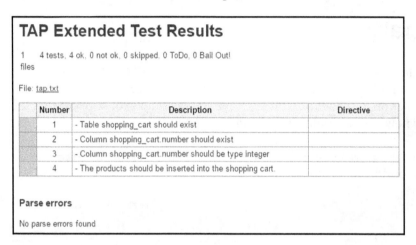

The per-build TAP Test Results shows you the results per build, like it says:

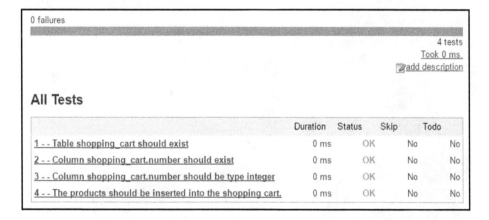

In the TAP Test Results, there is also a link to a History report, but it seems to be broken. To check whether it works, try breaking our database function and trigger the build. You will see it fails and you can see the results in the reports as expected.

The only thing left for us to do now is to run our Selenium tests. Since we need our software to run for that and it is a bit harder to run it in a way that is non-blocking for our console, we are going to have a look at that in later chapters.

Summary

In this chapter, we have repeated the entire process of building and testing an application and then automating it. We have seen some differences between JavaScript and C#. C# needs compilation and does not always have the same level of support that JavaScript has. Completely new was the database testing with TAP.

In the next chapter, we are going to have a more in-depth look at Jenkins so we can further enhance our builds.

10
Additional Jenkins Plugins

We have come pretty far. We have built a JavaScript application with Node.js and automated it with Gulp. We then did the same in C# and did all the work during the build. After that, we automated everything in Jenkins, so not a single commit is not tested and build. However, as far as Jenkins is concerned, we did the bare minimum to get our software to be tested and built.

Unfortunately, in a limited testing environment, such as ours, we do not run into the problems you are going to face in the real world. For example, we currently have two projects, JavaScript and C#, which together make up for six projects. In my daily job, we have, maybe, two hundred projects. Personally, I probably need about fifty of those because those are from the projects I am working on. Jenkins has all kinds of options and plugins to make sense of it all. In this chapter, we are going to dive deeper in to Jenkins and explore some of the plugins and options you have to further enhance your builds and overall Jenkins experience.

Views

When you get a lot of projects for multiple projects for multiple customers, you may lose overview, which makes it difficult to properly maintain your projects. Jenkins has views to manage your projects. A view is basically a collection of projects that you think should be grouped together. These can be all the projects you have access to, all the projects for a certain customer, or all the projects for a certain application. In our case, we have two projects, the JavaScript web shop and the C# web shop (I have some additional test projects, but you may ignore them).

At the top of your projects list, you find the global views. Currently, there is only one view, **All**:

Click on the plus tab to create a new view. Pick the **List View** type of view and name it JS Web Shop or something similar. On the next page, you can pick the projects to list in your view:

Here, you can manually select projects or select them based on a regular expression. You can also pick columns to show in your view. Hit the **OK** button and your new view will be created. You now have a list with the Build Web Shop and Test Web Shop projects. For the next view, **CSharp Web Shop**, I am going to use a regular expression. Using regular expressions is pretty difficult, but when your naming convention is right, it should not be a problem. As you can see, my CSharp Web Shop projects are all named **CSharp Web Shop - (some build step)**. That makes the regular expression pretty simple, (CSharp Web Shop)(.*). The view that is created looks like you would expect:

The pro to using a regular expression is that new projects are automatically added to the view. For example, if you create a new project and name it CSharp Web Shop - Deployment, it is automatically added to the CSharp Web Shop view. Good naming conventions would be Customer - Project - Build step (configuration), for example, ACME - Web site - Build (debug). But it is all up to you of course. Worst case scenario, you have to hand pick all your projects for a view. It is possible to use a regular expression and hand pick some projects that do not fit the regular expression.

Another view type is the **My View** type. This view shows all the projects that the currently logged in user has access to. All users currently have access to all the projects by default, so this view type is not very useful to us now. You can restrict access to projects on a per user basis, but you may lock yourself out while enabling it. We are going to look at security later though, so just take my word for it now.

Next to global views, you can have your own personal views. From the main page, you can pick the **My Views** menu item from the left-hand side menu. Any views created here will not be visible to other users. When creating a personal view, you get an extra view type, **Include a global view**. This does nothing more than link to a global view (unfortunately, viewing this view also takes you to the global views). It may be handy when you want to filter out some global views and add them to your personal views. For example, we have customer-specific global views at work, but I am not involved with all of those customers. So, I added the global customer views that are relevant to me to my personal views. Using views this way can really save you a lot of time, effort, and frustration when looking for a project.

Cleanup workspaces

When we first worked with Jenkins, I recommended you to always clean your workspace before building your software. That way, you can always be sure all the necessary packages can be downloaded from npm or NuGet and you do not accidentally use cached files for your build. However, doing all of that comes at a cost. Cleaning, checking your entire Git repository, and downloading your npm or NuGet packages make take a few minutes every time you start a build. An alternative approach is to only clean a part of your workspace. To enable this feature, go to the plugin manager and install the Workspace Cleanup plugin (`https://wiki.jenkins-ci.org/display/JENKINS/Workspace+Cleanup+Plugin`). This plugin adds an additional check in the build environment as well as an additional postbuild action.

We can see this plugin in action really easy. Create a new project and name it `Cleanup Test` or something similar. Make it run on Linux and add a shell build step. In the shell, we are going to create two files, `src/.src` and `bin/.exec`; two files that do absolutely nothing except sit there for us to see:

```
mkdir -p bin
touch bin/.exec
mkdir -p src
touch src/.src
```

Run the project and verify that the files were created as expected. We are now going to clean the `bin` folder after the build. Add the new **Delete workspace when build is done** postbuild action. Click on the **Advanced...** button. Everything is pretty self-explanatory and there are help question marks, but let's go through it real quick. We want to keep our `src` folder, but clean out the `bin` folder:

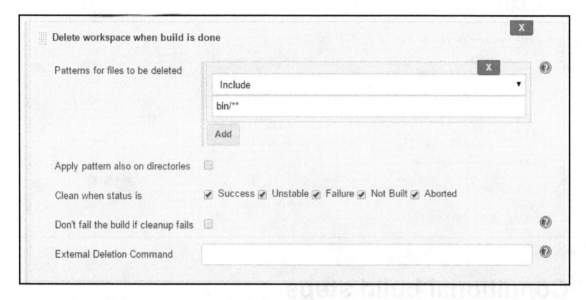

We want to include all the files in the `bin` folder in our deletion. Alternatively, we could exclude everything inside the `src` folder from deletion. We can also check the **Apply pattern also on directories** checkbox and simply use the `bin` pattern to simply delete the entire `bin` folder. We always want to clean the workspace, no matter the result. But if a cleanup fails, we do not fail the build. The **External Deletion Command** uses some external program to clean your workspace. It's best you read the help text in case you want to ever use this.

Now, run the build again and check whether your `bin` folder is indeed empty (or deleted, based on your setup).

You can also clean up your workspace before the build starts. This option is a little different because you do not know the status of your build yet. Whether to clean or not is based on a parameter passed to the build. At this point, we cannot pass parameters to build yet, but we will check that out later in this chapter:

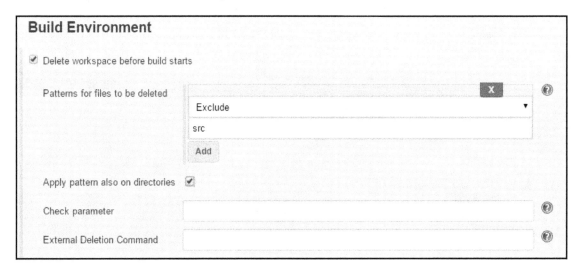

Conditional build steps

Another useful Jenkins plugin is the Conditional BuildStep plugin (`https://wiki.jenkins-ci.org/display/JENKINS/Conditional+BuildStep+Plugin`). This plugin lets you skip or include build steps based on some condition. For example, you can build and unit test your source on every commit, but only run Selenium tests every three hours using a periodic build trigger (so your build is being tested even though there are no commits).

Install the Conditional BuildStep plugin in the plugin manager. After installation, you get two new build steps: `Conditional step (single)` and `Conditional steps (multiple)`:

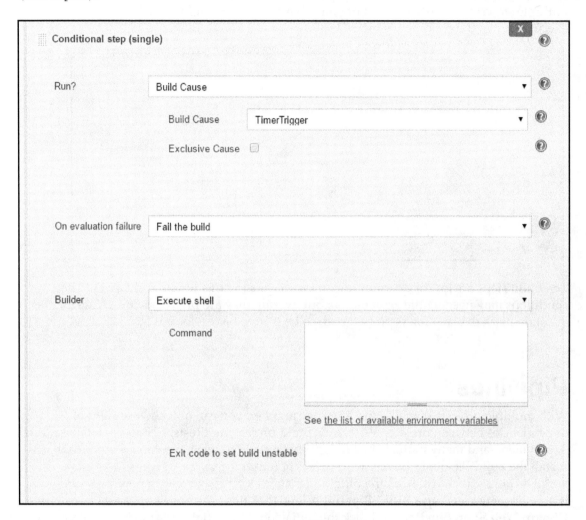

There are quite a few conditions to choose from. The **Build Cause** determines how the build was triggered (manual, SCM, or timer...), but you can also specify a day of the week, a time of the day, combine conditions with logical AND and OR clauses, and much more. The multiple steps work the same, except you can add multiple build steps that will all be executed when the condition is met:

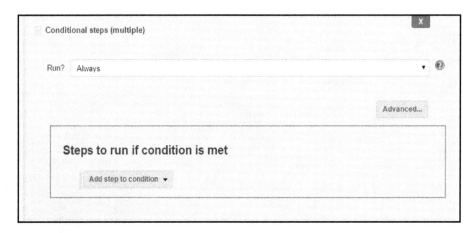

The build steps are just like before, so you can start using this plugin right away. The conditions may need a little explanation, but overall, they are pretty obvious. Luckily, the question mark explanation is pretty good, so be sure to have a look at it.

Pipelines

With multiple projects that all build after one another, you can quickly lose sight of dependencies between projects. We have a build project, unit tests, E2E tests, database tests, deployment, and many more. Who knows what else. Well, we have got a plugin for that. Install the Build Pipeline plugin (`https://wiki.jenkins-ci.org/display/JENKINS/Build+Pipeline+Plugin`) from the plugin manager. After that, create a new view and you will find a new view type, **Build Pipeline View**. Pick this type, give it a name, for example, **CSharp Web Shop Pipeline**, and pick the initial job. The initial job is the first project that is started and which will trigger other builds.

For example, I have set up my builds so that deployment (which is just an empty project) is triggered after the E2E tests (which we will fix shortly), which is triggered after database testing, which is triggered after unit testing, which is triggered after the build. Quite a pipeline. By setting up the build as my initial job in the pipeline view, we get a view that is not quite what you are used to from Jenkins:

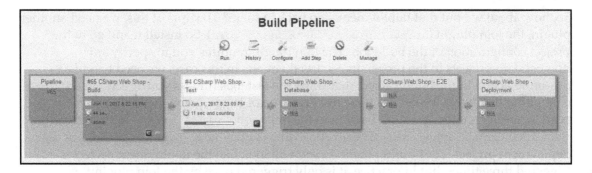

As you can see, the view shows what projects ran, are running, and still need to run. It is also possible to run multiple projects in parallel, for example, the unit tests, the database tests, and the E2E tests. The problem, of course, lies in when we will deploy the web shop. We cannot deploy on all three, but all three must pass before deployment can be done. So, forget about the deployment job for now and let's trigger all the test projects after the build project:

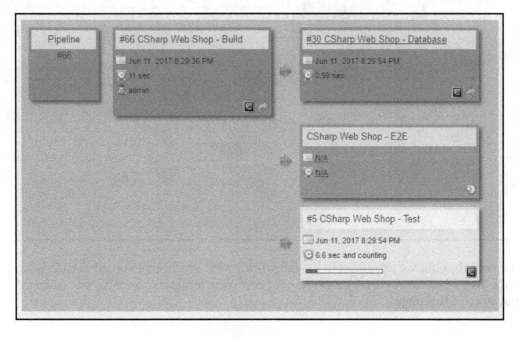

The best part is that you only need to change your project configurations (either the **Build other projects** postbuild action or the **Build after other projects are built** build trigger) and the view is updated automatically.

So, how about we put that deployment step back in there? To support this, we need another plugin, the Join plugin (`https://plugins.jenkins.io/join`). So install it and go to the project configuration of the build job. The Join plugin requires you to specify any downstream projects in the project that starts them. So, in this case, we need to add a postbuild action in the build project that starts the test jobs (unless you already had it configured that way). Make sure your test jobs are not triggered by the build job. Now, you need to specify another postbuild action in the build job, `Join Trigger`. In the `Projects to build once, after all downstream projects have finished` field, put the deployment project. Your build pipeline view will look like the deployment project is triggered three times, but in practice, it is only triggered once by the Join plugin:

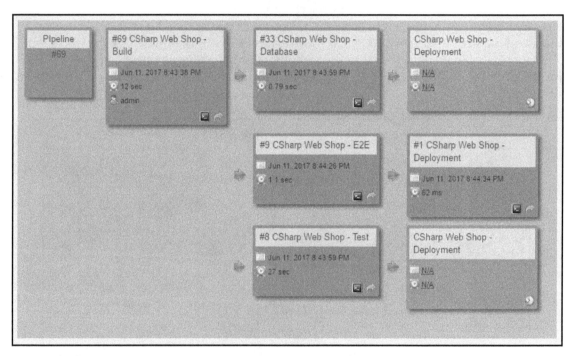

In the next chapter, we are going to look at workflows, which give you an even greater control over what runs when by having your complete Jenkins project in code (using the Groovy script language).

Promoted builds

Another very cool plugin is the Promoted Builds plugin (`https://wiki.jenkins.io/display/JENKINS/Promoted+Builds+Plugin`). This plugin solves some of the problems we had earlier. It also makes the Join plugin obsolete. The idea behind promoted builds is that a build can be *promoted* based on various criteria (including promotion of other projects). Upon promotion, one or more additional build steps can be executed (including triggered another project). Whenever a build is promoted, it gets a promotion symbol on the build list. So, install the Promoted Builds plugin from the plugin manager.

We just used the Join plugin to wait for our database tests, browser tests, and E2E tests before triggering the deployment project. Instead, we can now use a promotion. Go to the **CSharp Web Shop - Build** project configuration and find the **Promote builds when...** checkbox in the **General** section. You must now enter a name for your promotion, for example, **Tests Completed Successfully**. Do not forget this or you will get an error on saving your configuration and you will have to start over. You can pick an icon or go with the default.

Then, we need to pick a criteria that must be met for the build to be promoted. Pick **When the following downstream projects build successfully** and then enter the projects you want to wait for, `CSharp Web Shop - Database`, `CSharp Web Shop - Test`, `CSharp Web Shop - E2E`.

After that, we can specify actions that we want to execute when the criteria are met and the build gets promoted. Pick **Build other projects** and choose **CSharp Web Shop - Deployment** as the project to build. Unfortunately, this does not show in the pipeline view, so you will lose that.

Remove the Join postbuild action at the bottom of your configuration and save it. That is really all there is to it. You can now manually trigger the build and see it in action. When everything goes well, your build should get promoted and you should see a promotion star in the build history of the project:

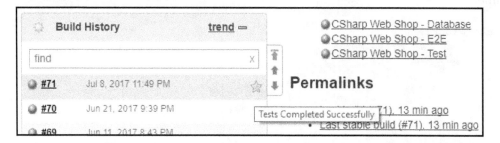

As you have already seen, there are other criteria you can pick, such as waiting for upstream builds to get promoted, having to be manually approved, a custom Groovy script, and more. And you can also pick a whole lot of actions to trigger when the build gets promoted.

Parameterized builds

It is possible to parameterize your builds in Jenkins. Create a new job and name it `Parameterized Project` or whatever. Now, almost at the top of the configuration is an option **This project is parameterized**. Check it and add a parameter. There are a couple of parameters and some plugins will add additional parameters. Most of them are pretty straightforward and all of them are explained in the help text. Let's go with a string parameter for simplicity. Pick a single word name, such as `YourText`, an optional default value, and an optional description:

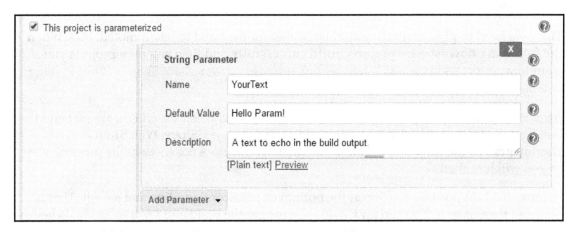

Let your build run on Linux and add a shell script build step. That is where we can use any parameters:

```
echo $YourText
```

If you go back to the project page, you will notice that the **Build** button changed to **Build with Parameters**. If you try to run the build, you will be prompted with the parameters that you have to select first:

Project Parameterized Project

This build requires parameters:

YourText

```
Hello Param!
```

A text to echo in the build output.

Build

And if you build, you will, of course, see your text in the build output.

Another plugin, which you should already have installed through some other plugin, makes it possible to trigger parameterized projects from other projects. Check whether you have the Parameterized Trigger plugin (`https://wiki.jenkins.io/display/JENKINS/Parameterized+Trigger+Plugin`) installed and if you have not installed it. Create yet another project and the only thing you need to do is add a postbuild action and trigger parameterized build on other projects.

Specify the parameterized project we just created as a project to build. You can pick to use the current parameters as input to the next project, but we do not have any parameters for this project. So instead pick **Predefined parameters**. You can now specify parameters as `Key=Value`, where each line is a key-value pair. So, for our project, you can specify `YourText=I'm triggered from another project!`. Now, build this project and you will see it triggers the parameterized project, which will output `I'm triggered from another project!`.

It is also possible to use environment variables that we can also use in a shell or command build step. For example, `YourText=I'm build from project $JOB_BASE_NAME!`, which will print `I'm build from project [your project name]!`.

Triggering builds remotely

In the previous chapters, we have looked at the various build triggers that are available to us. We even added the GitLab trigger with the GitLab plugin. There is one trigger we have not tried yet, which is the remote trigger. So, create a new project; I am simply naming it `Remote Test`, and check the **Trigger builds remotely** (for example, from scripts) trigger. You are now presented with an authentication token. This is your secret token that allows anyone who has it to remotely trigger the build. So, you best pick something that is not easy to guess (something like `47d6753c6f307c13edf010a2730f03a6`). However, for our test, we are going to pick something that is a bit more readable and easy to type, so just put `my_token` in the field.

Normally, you can browse to a URL to trigger a regular build, for example, `http://ciserver:8080/job/Remote%20Test/build` (`%20` is a URL encoded space). You will get a message that you should do a POST request instead of a GET request, but you can continue and the build will still trigger. However, if you try to do the same from an incognito window, you will be taken to the login screen. Instead, you need anonymous access, which is exactly what the authorization token gives you (for this one specific project only). So, open an anonymous window and browse to `http://ciserver:8080/job/Remote%20Test/build?token=my_token` instead. If you keep the project page and the anonymous window next to each other, you can see the build being triggered.

Now, try adding a parameter to your project. I have added a string parameter named `MyString`. Also, add a build step to echo the parameter's value. If you trigger the project remotely, you will be prompted for the parameter values. However, once you have entered a value, you will be taken to the login screen again and the build will not be triggered. Instead, you need to browse to `buildWithParameters`, such as `http://ciserver:8080/job/Remote%20Test/buildWithParameters?token=my_token`. Any parameters come at the end of the URL, `buildWithParameters?token=my_token&MyString=Value`. If you omit parameters, they will simply take their default value.

Blue ocean

Perhaps the single most awesome plugin for Jenkins comes from the Jenkins team itself and changes your Jenkins into something completely different. Jenkins is not the most beautiful and also not always the most intuitive tool you will work with. It is nonetheless a great tool, but it could be even greater. That is where Blue Ocean comes in! Blue Ocean is very new. It went into alpha release last year and went into production while writing this book. So, let that be a warning up front; it probably still has some issues. The good news is that you can run Blue Ocean and the classic Jenkins side by side. So, go to the plugin manager and install Blue Ocean. This will install lots of stuff, such as the GitHub plugin (why though?), Common API For Blue Ocean, REST API For Blue Ocean, Metrics Plugin... About thirty of which most are `... For Blue Ocean`.

In this section, we are going to generate a script using a tool; you can find the final script in the GitHub repository for this book under `Chapter 10/Code/Jenkinsfile` (open with any other text editor).

Once everything is installed, go back to your main page and click the new **Open Blue Ocean** button on the left-hand side menu. The new page looks nothing like Jenkins:

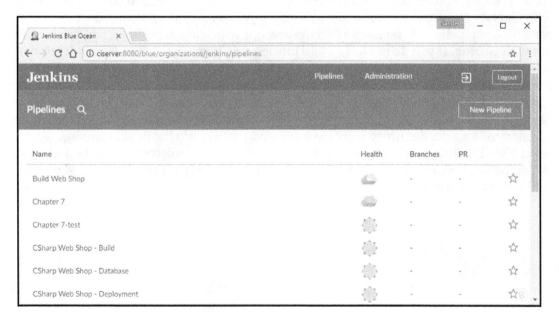

For some things, such as administration and (classic) job configuration, Blue Ocean reverts to the classic Jenkins layout. This new look and feel is all about pipelines, a feature that we are going to have an extensive look at in the next chapter.

What you need to know about pipelines right now is that they let you code your build rather than add steps through a user interface. The upside to this is that your build is **just code** that is checked into source control. The downside, of course, is that it requires additional knowledge on the syntax and functions of your pipeline file. We will look at the syntax of these files in the next chapter.

So, here is the great new thing about Blue Ocean; it lets you edit these pipeline files directly into a more intuitive user interface, giving you the best of both worlds. The bad news is that this so-called *pipeline editor* is still very much a work in progress. The GitHub page for this project (`https://github.com/jenkinsci/blueocean-pipeline-editor-plugin`) is quite clear about it, **Important!** This software is a work in progress and is not complete (and here be dragons, this may not be up to date, and many more). However, because this feature is so awesome, I really want to give you a little sneak peak right here. We will get back to pipelines and the Blue Ocean plugin in the next chapter as well.

So, this newest feature, unfortunately, is largely undocumented and, so far, it only works with GitHub. However, we can create a *dummy* pipeline that still generates the code we need for our pipeline. If you have a GitHub account with some repository, you can try this out with GitHub. If you do not have a GitHub account, you can skip the remainder of this paragraph. You can even fork the `ci-book` repository to try it out on the chapters in this book. In the new dashboard, you should see a **New Pipeline** button in the upper-right corner. Click it and choose GitHub as your store. You then need to create a token on GitHub; simply follow the link in the editor and you will be taken to GitHub where a token is generated for you. Be sure to copy the token and paste it into the field in Jenkins. Next, select **New Pipeline** to create your pipeline file. You can then select a repository and create your pipeline. Jenkins will say **There are no Jenkinsfiles in [your repository]** and you can go ahead and create one by clicking the button:

If you do not have a GitHub repository, you can still create a pipeline. You will have to copy and paste the generated code from the editor into your own file. To get to the pipeline editor, simply browse to the following URL `http://ciserver:8080/blue/organizations/jenkins/pipeline-editor/` (of course, you should replace `ciserver:8080` with your own Jenkins instance). You do not need a Jenkins project or anything; you will just be taken to the editor.

No matter what approach you followed, you will be taken to a new screen with a start node and a plus node and **Pipeline Settings** on the right-hand side:

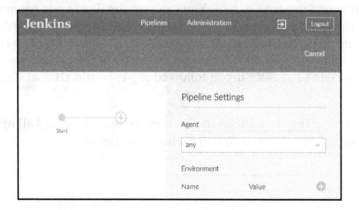

A pipeline consists of *stages*. Each stage has one or more *build steps*, like the *classic* Jenkins project configuration has build steps. Adding a node by clicking on a *plus node* adds a new stage. Each stage has its own pipeline settings. That means *each* of your build steps can have their own settings as opposed to settings that apply to *all* your build steps. That adds a lot of flexibility to your builds! For example, stage one can run on Linux, while stage two can run on Windows, all in a single project! With the new pipelines, it is also now possible to run stages in parallel and have a next stage wait until all parallel stages have finished. Basically, what the Join plugin does, but much more transparent. Just click some plus nodes and you will see what I mean.

Unfortunately, the pipelines added a whole new set of problems as well: backward compatibility. A lot of plugins do not work with this new feature. The reason is that the Jenkins pipeline is a Groovy script, so steps are triggered from a script instead of from the Jenkins Java environment (Jenkins was built in Java). Not all plugins have a command-line interface that can be called from a (Groovy) script. However, plugin support is increasing and you can always use the good old Linux shell or Windows command line. So, this may not be much of an issue in the future.

Now, let's create our first stage. Add the first stage and give it a name in the Pipeline settings. I am not actually working in a project right now, so I am assuming we are going to build the JavaScript web shop (with no way of testing our script, for now). In our first stage, we are simply going to check out our code from Git and install our npm packages, so let's name the first stage **Checkout**. Next, we are going to add a step. Simply click the **+ Add step** button in the settings. First, we want to specify a node on which to build, so add the `Allocate node` step and put Linux in the label. We can now create child steps, which are the steps that will be executed on this node. First, we need to check out our code from Git, so add a Git step. In the settings for the Git step, we need to specify a URL, which can be found in your GitLab repository. We also need a branch, for which we can pick `master`. Finally, you need your `CredentialsId`. You can find the ID of your credentials on the classic Jenkins left-hand side menu (in a new tab, because we cannot save our current pipeline). In the menu, go to **Credentials** and you should see your GitLab credentials (name/password) and your GitLab API token. Get the ID of the GitLab username and password; it will be `GitLabCreds` if you followed my example. `GitLabCreds` go into the **CredentialsId** field.

Next, add a `Shell Script` step. In the shell script, we want to install all npm packages. We will want a Gulp build as well, but we will do that at a later stage:

```
npm install
```

The pipeline settings window still feels a bit clunky. It is impossible to switch steps around and the delete button is hidden in the upper-right menu on each step. Hopefully, this window will get a bit more intuitive in the near future. Anyway, when you have found all the settings, you can click *Ctrl + S* and you should see the generated script. If something went wrong, all you see is *There were validation errors, please check the editor to correct them.* You can click that text and an additional error might be shown (it is really trial and error). Anything could be wrong. Your stages need a name and at least one build step, but this may not be immediately clear. If everything went well, you should see the following script being generated:

```
pipeline {
  agent any
  stages {
    stage('Checkout') {
      steps {
        node(label: 'linux') {
          git(branch: 'master', url: 'http://ciserver/sander/web-shop.git',
credentialsId: 'GitLabCreds')
          sh 'npm install'
        }
      }
    }
  }
}
```

It looks a little bit like JavaScript, but it is Groovy (`http://groovy-lang.org/`). The window you are seeing when you press *Ctrl + S* can be edited. You can, for example, change your current shell command or add a complete new shell step (or whatever step if you know the syntax). When you click the **Update** button, the changes will be reflected in the editor. When your script has errors, you may get an error (such as `illegal colon after argument...`) or nothing may happen, in which case, you can go on a little bug hunt. The latter happens when, for example, you add a step that does not exist; you can change `sh` to `shhh`. The window has no close or cancel button, but *Esc* does the trick.

Next, let's add a test stage. We want to make a Gulp build and test it in PhantomJS on Linux, which should not be a problem. Unfortunately though, it actually is a bit of a problem. A new stage basically means a new project and so Jenkins creates a new workspace and starts from scratch. That means we have to check out our code from Git again and do an npm install to get all necessary packages. That is rather cumbersome and kind of defeats the purpose of this whole exercise. Luckily, there is an alternative. We can allocate a custom workspace and use that workspace again in a next stage. The workspace will still have all of its files, so we do not need to pull from Git and do `npm install`. We first need to change our Build stage so that it allocates a custom workspace.

Unfortunately, the *Allocate workspace* step must be a child of the *Allocate node* step and all other steps must be children of *Allocate workspace* and the editor as it currently is does not allow reordering steps. So, we need to remove the `Git` and `Shell script` steps to insert the `Allocate workspace` step and then readd the two steps as children of *Allocate workspace*. A bit of a hassle. The `Allocate workspace` step only needs one value, which is `Dir` (or directory). This is the name of your workspace. Make sure it does not overlap with the workspaces of other Jenkins projects. I am naming mine `web-shop-pipeline`:

Now that we have the custom workspace in place, we can use it in our next stage, the *Build* stage. In the build stage, we are first going to allocate our Linux node, then we allocate the web-shop-pipeline workspace, and last we add a shell script to build our project using Gulp:

```
node_modules/.bin/gulp --env=prod --browsers=PhantomJS
```

If all went well, your pipeline script should now look something like this:

```
pipeline {
  agent any
  stages {
    stage('Checkout') {
      steps {
        node(label: 'linux') {
          ws(dir: 'web-shop-pipeline') {
            git(url: 'http://ciserver/sander/web-shop.git', branch:
'master', credentialsId: 'GitLabCreds')
            sh 'npm install'
          }
        }
```

```
      }
    }
    stage('Build') {
      steps {
        node(label: 'linux') {
          ws(dir: 'web-shop-pipeline') {
            sh 'node_modules/.bin/gulp --env=prod --browsers=PhantomJS'
          }
        }
      }
    }
  }
}
```

Sharing workspaces like that was already possible in the classic Jenkins by the way. In the **General** section of the configuration page are the **Advanced** options. One of these advanced options is **Use custom workspace**. When two projects on the same node have the same custom workspace, they will effectively be sharing workspaces.

The next step for our pipeline is to test in IE, Chrome, and Firefox on Windows. As you can imagine, we pretty much have the same problems as before. We need to check out our Git repository again; we lose our current Git commit and, at the end of the build, we will not be able to push our status back to GitHub. Luckily, this is where the pipeline approach has some tricks up its sleeve that were not previously (easily) available. We can stash files and share them between stages, nodes, and workspaces (we could have used this instead of sharing workspaces too).

Of course, we first need to stash our files before we can retrieve them. We can stash the files after we have pulled them from Git, installed all npm modules, and ran the build. So, add an additional step in the Build stage, *Stash some files to be used later in the build*. You have to name your stash; I have named it `Everything` and you must specify which files to include and exclude. We are going to exclude the `node_modules` folder, because we need to install them again on Windows (for the Windows cmd scripts), so put `node_modules/**` in the exclude field. We want everything else, so put `**/**` in the include field (that is all the files and folders from all folders). You could, optionally, exclude some report files. You can also exclude the `node_modules` folder and simply do an npm install again on Windows, but that is your choice.

Next, we can create a new `Test Chrome` stage. Allocate the windows node and, as a child step, add `Restore files previously stashed` and put in the `Everything` stash. The next step is a Windows Batch Script and this is heavily bugged. This is the thing, you get a really small field to put in your script. Our script can get pretty big, but that will cause the `Allocate node` side window to become as wide as your script, meaning your back buttons and everything will probably be so far left you cannot see them on your screen anymore.

However, the `Test` stage side window will simply wrap your script and show as you expect. So, when you create the script step as a child step of your allocate node step, just put in a single character, then go back to the stage side window, open the script step from there, and put in the entire script. You will have to do this every time you want to open the allocate node step. What is worse, we need to escape certain characters in a pipeline batch step. One of the characters is the backslash that Windows uses in its filesystem. So, instead of `C:\Program Files`, we get `C:\\Program Files`. However, when you open and save the script (using *Ctrl + S*), the editor will un-escape the backslash and turn `C:\\P...` into `C:\P...` again, which will cause an error when you try to open your script again. Hopefully, all these issues will be solved by the time you get to use the editor, but I am giving you a heads up just in case. Anyway, the scripts we want to execute is the just Chrome tests:

```
npm install && node_modules\\.bin\\gulp.cmd test-min --browsers=Chrome
```

If you have done everything right, the pipeline script should now look as follows:

```
pipeline {
  agent any
  stages {
    [...]
    }
    stage('Build') {
      steps {
        node(label: 'linux') {
          ws(dir: 'web-shop-pipeline') {
            sh 'node_modules/.bin/gulp --env=prod --browsers=PhantomJS'
            stash(name: 'Everything', includes: '**/**', excludes:
'node_modules')
          }
        }
      }
    }
    stage('Test Chrome') {
      steps {
        node(label: 'windows') {
          unstash 'Everything'
          bat 'npm install && node_modules\\.bin\\gulp.cmd test-min --
env=prod --browsers=Chrome'
        }
      }
    }
  }
}
```

Remember, when you paste this into the script window and save it, you need to manually change the Windows batch script step to escape the backspaces.

Here is another cool feature of the pipeline we want to test in IE and Firefox as well and we can do so in parallel. Simply add two more stages and name them `Test IE` and `Test Firefox`. They are completely identical to `Test Chrome`, except for the `--browsers=Chrome` part, of course. At this point, your pipeline should have a **Checkout** stage, then a **Build** stage, and then three test stages:

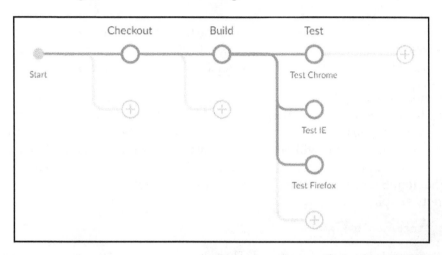

The script now has a parallel node in the Test stage. Under the parallel node are three steps, `Test Chrome`, `Test IE`, and `Test Firefox`:

```
[...]
    stage('Test') {
        steps {
            parallel(
                "Test Chrome": {
                    node(label: 'windows') {
                        unstash 'Everything'
                        bat 'npm install && node_modules\\.bin\\gulp.cmd test-min --
env=prod --browsers=Chrome'
                    }
                },
                "Test IE": {
                    node(label: 'windows') {
                        unstash 'Everything'
                        bat 'npm install && node_modules\\.bin\\gulp.cmd test-min --
env=prod --browsers=IE'
                    }
                },
```

```
            "Test Firefox": {
              node(label: 'windows') {
                unstash 'Everything'
                bat 'npm install && node_modules\\.bin\\gulp.cmd test-min --
env=prod --browsers=Firefox'
              }
            }
        )
      }
  [...]
```

For some reason, it seems that the editor gives the first step the same name as your stage. Our stage was initially named Test Chrome, so I edited that in the script manually so that the stage is called Test and the individual steps include the browser name.

Testing without reporting is of little use, so we will need to publish our reports like we did before. The JUnit report is pretty straightforward; just add a Publish JUnit test result report step to each of the testing stages. The TestResults* field should be test/junit/*.xml. Jenkins will now publish five reports, the Chrome, IE, and Firefox results, obviously, and the PhantomJS results from Windows (executed on each Gulp build) and the PhantomJS results from Linux, which was copied from the stash. The generated code is pretty simple:

```
junit 'test/junit/*.xml'
```

The HTML report is less straightforward. There is a Publish HTML reports build step, but it only has a very small input field. It is not clear what should go in the field. Once you know what should be in there, you wonder whether this is just a bug. Also, it seems that the editor cannot generate your code for you no matter what you put in there. So, anyway, you can add it to the script manually (and saving it will mess up the editor for both the backslashes and the HTML step). The script for the HTML editor contains pretty much what is also in the classic configuration:

```
publishHTML target: [
  allowMissing: false,
  alwaysLinkToLastBuild: false,
  keepAll: false,
  reportDir: 'test/coverage/html',
  reportFiles: 'index.html',
  reportName: 'Coverage Report'
]
```

We do not have to publish the coverage of all three browsers, so just pick one and place it there. The HTML report is published to your project page and not your specific build page.

I do have some bad news for you now. We have two more reports, the cobertura report and, in the C# project, the TRX report. We cannot publish them using the pipeline, editor, or otherwise. There is a workaround for the TRX report, but so far, I have not found a workaround for the cobertura report. We could use the lcov report and use SonarQube for our coverage reporting instead. For the TRX file, you can run an **XML Transformation** (**XSLT**) to convert TRX format to JUnit format and publish that instead. Anyway, we are not doing either of those now.

With the HTML publisher not working and the editor messing up our batch scripts, this is becoming a drag. However, there is one more feature I would like to discuss, the GitLab commit trigger and updating the commit status. There is a `Update the commit status in GitLab depending on the build status` build step. All it needs is a name. You can add this to every stage and put the stage name as the name for the update step. Your build steps go inside it as child steps:

```
[...]
stage('Build') {
  steps {
    node(label: 'linux') {
      ws(dir: 'web-shop-pipeline') {
        gitlabCommitStatus(name: 'Build') {
          sh 'node_modules/.bin/gulp --env=prod --browsers=PhantomJS'
          stash(name: 'Everything', excludes: 'node_modules/**', includes:
'**/**')
        }
      }
    }
  }
}
```

This will report the status of each stage to GitLab and GitLab will mark the commit as succeeded or failed. You can find the status of each stage in GitLab by going to the commit and selecting the **Builds** tab:

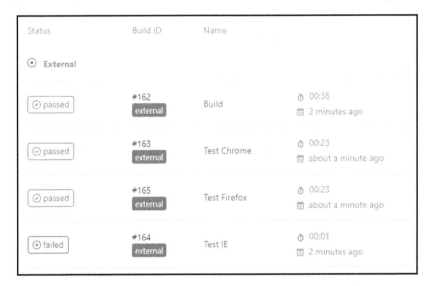

There is just one more thing though. For this to work, you need to set something in your script manually. The editor will not remove these values, but for now, they cannot be edited using the editor either:

```
options {
  gitLabConnection('Local GitLab')
}
triggers {
  gitlab(triggerOnPush: true, branchFilterType: 'All')
}
```

The name that goes in the `gitLabConnection` option is the name of a GitLab connection in the global Jenkins system configuration. The `gitlab` trigger triggers the build on a commit, like we had before in the classic configuration. Of course, we will need to create a webhook in GitHub once we are going to run this script in the next chapter. You can now also remove the Git build step from the **Checkout** stage.

Blue Ocean is obviously a work in progress. Not everything works as it should and some things do not work at all. However, pipelines are becoming more popular and so is configuration in code (and not just in Jenkins). In the next chapter, we will look at pipelines in more detail. For now, I think, we have seen enough of Blue Ocean and the pipeline editor.

Security

Security is often an afterthought, but it is quite important. When you are running Jenkins in your local network, you are probably good to go. However, when you need either your Jenkins server to be accessible outside of your network, you will need to do some additional work to make sure no uninvited guests come snooping at your data. Also, especially when lots of people are using the same Jenkins instance, you may want to limit who sees what by managing users and groups.

Jenkins on HTTPS

Your first concern is getting Jenkins to run on HTTPS instead of HTTP. A lot of this information is already in the Jenkins documentation (`https://wiki.jenkins.io/display/JENKINS/Starting+and+Accessing+Jenkins`), but as always I am going to walk you through it because the documentation is a bit hard to follow. Getting things to run on HTTPS is a bit difficult because we need a certificate for our VM and local Windows installation. Anyway, the focus here is not on obtaining a certificate, but in getting Jenkins to use it.

HTTPS on Linux

Starting with HTTPS in Linux, we can create a self-signed certificate using the `openssl` tool. Once you generate the certificate, you need to answer a couple of questions about you and/or your organization. Answer the questions (or pick the default or enter a dot, `.`, to leave it blank):

```
sudo openssl req -x509 -nodes -days 365 -newkey rsa:2048 -keyout
ciserver.key -out ciserver.crt
Country Name (2 letter code)[AU]:NL
State or Province Name (full name) [Some-State]:.
Locality Name (eg, city) []:
Organization Name (eg, company) [Internet Widgits Pty Ltd]:Private
Organizational Unit Name (eg, section) []:
Common Name (e.g. server FQDN or YOUR name) []:Sander Rossel
Email Address []:
```

So, we are requesting an `-x509` structure instead of a certificate request; `-nodes` prevents the output key from being decrypted. It is valid for a year (`-days 365`) with a new 2048 bits RSA key and we are outputting the key to `ciserver.key` and x509 to `ciserver.crt`. We now have our private key and SSL certificate. They are not signed by an authority, but that is not important here.

The next thing we need to do is convert our certificate to an intermediate format named **Public-Key Cryptography Standards #12 (PKCS 12)**. Again, we can use the `openssl` tool:

```
sudo openssl pkcs12 -inkey ciserver.key -in ciserver.crt -export -out
keys.pkcs12
Enter Export Password: your_password
Verifying - Enter Export Password: your_password
```

In go the `ciserver.key` and `ciserver.crt` files we just created; out comes a `keys.pkcs12` file. Make sure you remember the password you entered.

The next step is creating a file Jenkins can use. We need a **Java Keystore (JKS)**, which can be generated from the PKCS using the Java Keytool:

```
keytool -importkeystore -srckeystore keys.pkcs12 -srcstoretype pkcs12 -
destkeystore /var/lib/jenkins/jenkins.jks
Enter destination keystore password: your_password
Enter source keystore password: your_password
```

When prompted for the password, use the same password as before. Notice that we are saving the output JKS file as `jenkins.jks` in the `/var/lib/jenkins` folder.

The last thing we need to do is change our Jenkins configuration so that it uses HTTPS instead of HTTP. For this, we must change the startup Jenkins configuration, which can be found at `/etc/default/jenkins`. So, you can edit it using `vi` or your own favorite text editor. We need to change `JENKINS_ARGS` at the bottom of the file. `--webroot` should be there and you can add all the rest:

```
sudo vi /etc/default/jenkins
i
[...]
JENKINS_ARGS="--webroot=/var/cache/$NAME/war --httpPort=-1 --
httpsPort=$HTTP_PORT --httpsKeyStore=../../var/lib/jenkins/jenkins.jks --
httpsKeyStorePassword=your_password"
Esc
:wq
```

Setting `--httpPort` to `-1` disables HTTP entirely. For `--httpsPort`, we use the default port, `8080`. `--httpsKeyStore` has the path to your `jenkins.jks` file, so we go two folders up and then into `var/lib/jenkins` where the file is located. Last, `-httpsKeyStorePassword` should have the password you entered when generating the JKS file.

After that, you can restart Jenkins and check whether everything went alright by checking the service status:

```
sudo service jenkins restart
sudo service jenkins status
```

After that, you can open your browser and go to http://ciserver:8080 and https://ciserver:8080 and verify that http does not work and https does. You will get an error when browsing to https, but you can ignore it. Chrome, for example, gives the error code NET::ERR_CERT_AUTHORITY_INVALID, which is right, because our certificate is not backed by a certificate authority. Firefox gives us the same error, Error code: SEC_ERROR_UNKNOWN_ISSUER, and IE gives us the error too (and, for some reason, I still cannot connect to ciserver on Edge).

Unfortunately, because we only switched to HTTPS now, our GitLab webhooks just became invalid because they connect to http://... Any other link you may have to Jenkins (maybe, some remote build triggers) must be changed to target https. However, since our certificate is not backed by a certificate authority, it is a lot easier (and practical) to just turn it off again.

HTTPS on Windows

On Windows, in our case, things are a bit more easy. The Jenkins documentation is pretty spot on for Windows (https://wiki.jenkins.io/display/JENKINS/Starting+and+Accessing+Jenkins). Open a Command Prompt as an administrator and run the following commands:

```
cd C:\Program Files (x86)\Jenkins\jre\bin
keytool -genkeypair -keysize 2048 -keyalg RSA -alias jenkins -keystore
keystore
Enter Keystore Password: your_password
Re-enter New Password: your_password
[Answer questions]
Is CN=... correct?
  [no]: yes

Enter key password for <jenkins>
        (RETURN if same as keystore password): [Enter]
```

This will pretty much do all of the steps necessary in Linux at once. Although, admittedly, we may skip a few steps because we are now working localhost. Again, remember your password.

You can verify that the keystore was successfully created by running the following command:

```
keytool -list -keystore keystore
Enter keystore password: your_password
```

You now need to move your keystore file to the Jenkins secrets directory. The keystore file was created at `C:\Program Files (x86)\Jenkins\jre\bin` and needs to be copied to `C:\Program Files (x86)\Jenkins\secrets`. You can do this manually or use the Command Prompt, whatever you like. We can now change the startup configuration, which is in `C:\Program Files (x86)\Jenkins\jenkins.xml`. You only need to change the line starting with `<arguments>`:

```
<arguments>-Xrs -Xmx256m -
Dhudson.lifecycle=hudson.lifecycle.WindowsServiceLifecycle -jar
"%BASE%\jenkins.war" --httpPort=-1 --httpsPort=8080 --
httpsKeyStore="%BASE%\secrets\keystore" --
httpsKeyStorePassword=your_password</arguments>
```

This looks pretty much the same as the Linux arguments. So again, `--httpPort=-1` disables log in through HTTP. We will use our current port for `--httpsPort`. `--httpsKeyStore` points to the keystore file in the `secrets` folder, and the `--httpsKeyStorePassword` is the password you chose.

You can now restart the Jenkins service through the Windows Services window or in the Command Prompt:

```
net stop jenkins
net start jenkins
```

Again, when trying to connect to `https://localhost:8080`, you will get an error saying the certificate is invalid because the certificate authority is unknown. We know. Also, all your URLs pointing to Jenkins, such as GitLab webhooks, are now invalid and you will have to fix the URLs or regenerate the webhooks. You can change the configuration back to HTTP if you want.

Jenkins security

Now that your network communication is encrypted, we can worry about the next layer of security. Go to Jenkins management and then to **Configure Global Security**. The help (question marks) on this page is pretty helpful, so be sure to read it when you want to know something. Before doing anything here is a warning, you can shut yourself out. At the top is an **Enable security** setting, which is on. When you lock yourself out, you can disable this setting in the Jenkins `config.xml` (in `var/lib/jenkins` on Linux or in `C:\Program Files (x86)\Jenkins` on Windows) by changing the value of the `useSecurity` element. After restarting Jenkins, you (and everyone else) can undo whatever you did and enable security again in Jenkins. Alternatively, you can manually change the `authorizationStrategy` element in the config.xml (if you know what `class` attribute it should have).

So, anyway, we are currently interested in access control. There are a few security realms you can pick, for example, LDAP or Unix user/group database. We are not going to change the security realm though because that is a little difficult without a properly functioning network with users and groups. So the Jenkins' own user database is fine. Plugins may add other realms.

So, what we are going to look at here is the authorization. The first option is that anyone can do anything. That is really what it says, only useful in fully trusted environments. Legacy mode is not really interesting to us since we are not running a legacy version of Jenkins. The next authorization mode is the one we are currently using; logged-in users can do anything. People need accounts or they cannot perform any actions. Optionally, anonymous users can still read Jenkins, but not perform any actions. This mode is fine when you are in a trusted environment, but you do not want everybody to have full access to Jenkins. This mode also keeps track of who does what, so if someone messes up, you know who did it. Additionally, you can set a checkbox that determines whether people can sign up to your Jenkins.

The next two options are more interesting and dangerous, because you can lock yourself out with these. With matrix-based security, you can specify specific privileges for users and groups. With project-based matrix authorization strategy, you can do the same, but on a per-project basis, allowing for very fine-grained control. Selecting any of these two, not doing anything and saving, locks you out. There are no default settings for admin users or anything. As I recall, there is even a bug in one of these modes that if you do not configure any permissions for, at least, one user Jenkins just fails to load any page and shows an error message instead.

Let's take a look at the matrix-based security. Enable it and immediately add your admin user to the matrix. Make sure your admin user gets all the privileges (scroll to the right for a **(un)check all** button). Likewise, you can add other users and give them specific permissions. Certain plugins may add new permissions:

You can also add (LDAP/Unix) groups to the matrix, but since we are not using that, we cannot add roles. You can add non-existing roles and users, but Jenkins will indicate that this user or role does not exist. In order for a user to be able to log in, the user should at least have the Overall Administer or the **Overall Read** permission. If neither of these permissions are set, you will get an error when trying to log in saying [user] is missing the Overall/Read permission.

The project-based matrix authorization works pretty much in the same way as the matrix-based security, but when you open a project configuration, you get an additional checkbox, **Enable project-based security**. Here, you can give users permissions for this specific project. Not enabling this will simply take the user's global permission set, but enabling it allows you to give stricter global permissions and then set these permissions on projects. For example, give some user only the **Overall Read** permission on a global level and then pick any project and check all permissions (or a couple of permissions) in the project for that user. Now, if you log in as that user, the user will only see that one project:

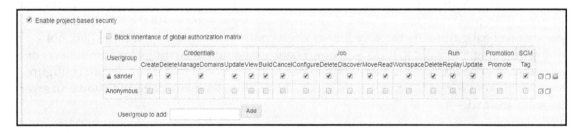

Optionally, you can block the inheritance of the global authorization matrix. That means the global authorization is ignored. Watch out though, because that means users do not have any permissions for this project, even when they do have permissions in the global authorization, so you can lock yourself out. If you enable the inheritance block and do not set permissions for any user, your project is gone (well, it is still there, but no one may view or change it). Plugins can add additional permissions, as you can already see from the **Promote** permission.

Role-based authorization strategy

Having to enable all these permissions for individual users can be a bit tedious and gets pretty annoying after a while. Luckily, there is a plugin to solve this, the Role-based Authorization Strategy plugin (`https://wiki.jenkins.io/display/JENKINS/Role+Strategy+Plugin`). This plugin does quite a lot. First, it adds a new option for global security, **Role-based Strategy**. Once you have chosen this type of authorization, a new item is added to the Jenkins management menu named **Manage and Assign Roles**. This opens up a new menu with three items of which we will discuss two, **Manage Roles** and **Assign Roles**.

On the **Manage Roles** screen, you can add roles and assign permissions just like in the matrix-based security. There are three kinds of roles: global roles, project roles, and slave roles. The global admin role is created by default. Here is what I want to do, I have a project team that is working on the C# Web Shop and I want every new member of the team to have only (full) access to those projects. Using the previous project-based matrix security, this would have been a little time-consuming and I would have to change all my projects. However, with the role-based security, this takes three minutes tops.

Go to **Manage Roles** and start with creating a new global role and naming it user. Give this user only the **Overall Read** permission. Then, create a project role and name it CSharp Web Shop (or something). The awesome (and tricky) thing here is that this job role has a regular expression pattern that is used to match items for which the role is valid. That also means that when a project title changes, you may not have permission to view it anymore. So, in our case, the pattern should be (CSharp Web Shop)(.*). Add the role and check every permission (no (un)check all button here, very annoying). So, we now have a global user role and a project **CSharp Web Shop** role.

To assign these roles, we need to go to the **Assign Roles** screen. First, add a user to the global roles and assign the **user** role. Then, add the user to the project roles and assign the **CSharp Web Shop** role:

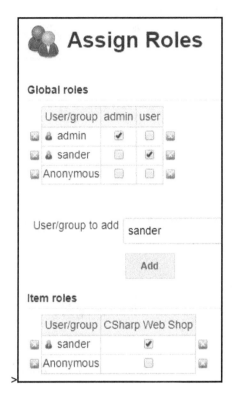

When you save your changes and log in as this user, you will now find that the user only has access to all the projects starting with **CSharp Web Shop**. That was fast and easy and adding new users is fast and easy as well! Just give them the role(s) you want and you are good to go; no project configuration necessary.

Summary

In this chapter, we have taken a look at various Jenkins features and plugins. Next to various plugins, we have discussed some security considerations, both on your network and in Jenkins. With the Blue Ocean plugin, we have taken a look at the future of Jenkins, both visually and functionally through code. The Blue Ocean plugin is also our prelude to pipelines, which will be discussed in great detail in the next chapter.

11
Jenkins Pipelines

So far, we have worked with the classic Jenkins. We have created projects and pipelines of projects, created views to visualize the dependencies, and used various plugins to aid us with this task. In the previous chapter, we also got a taste of the Jenkins projects in code using the new Blue Ocean pipeline editor. We are not going to use Blue Ocean in this chapter, but we are going to take a better look at these pipelines using configuration as code. Just to be clear, the Blue Ocean plugin is not required to run any sample in this chapter. You can use pipelines, multibranch pipelines, and Jenkinsfiles without Blue Ocean.

Using code for your configuration has a couple of advantages. First of all, you can write your own code according to the latest standards and best practices, which allows for optimization, parameterization, and reuse. Second, code is easy to store in source control, so you can apply versioning to your Jenkins projects. Code moves easy, so copying a project to another Jenkins server is easy. The best part is that you can keep your code with the project you are building, so you have everything in one place (which is probably Git).

Of course, using code has some disadvantages as well. For some people, it may be easier to click a bit in a (somewhat intuitive) user interface than it is to code. You will not get any intellisense for your Jenkins code, so it is not always clear what you can write. The biggest downside with the Jenkins pipeline, for me, is that not every plugin supports this newer style of configuring projects. And if a plugin does not support it, you cannot use it. Luckily, there is still the Windows batch or Linux shell command, so by far, most things can be achieved using the code pipeline. The worst case scenario is that you create a classic project for the few plugins that are not supported and trigger it from your pipeline code.

In this chapter, we are going to write these pipelines and learn how to run them using Jenkins.

Groovy

First things first, we have seen the pipeline syntax in the previous chapter when we used the Blue Ocean pipeline editor. The language that is used in these pipelines is called Groovy (`http://groovy-lang.org/`). Groovy is not unlike JavaScript and JavaScript would actually be a more appropriate name because Groovy is a scripting language for the Java platform. You can download Groovy from their website, `http://groovy-lang.org/download.html`, in case you want to practice locally. For Windows, simply download Groovy, unzip it, and add an entry to the `PATH` variable to `[unpack folder]\groovy-[your.version]\bin`. You can add a `PATH` variable by going to the computer's **Control Panel**, then **System**, and then the **Advanced System** settings on the left-hand side menu. In the popup is an **Environment Variables...** button, which will take you to another popup where you can edit your PATH.

Now, create a file somewhere and put some Hello World code in it:

```
System.out.println("Hello Java");
println "Hello Groovy"
```

As you can see, from the first line, Java code is valid in Groovy. The second line is more Groovy-ish. You can save the file as `myfile.groovy`, `.gvy`, `.gy`, or `.gsh`, all are valid Groovy file extensions. You can now run the script by simply running `groovy myfile.groovy` in a Command Prompt. If you did not add the path to the `PATH` variable in Windows, you will have to reference `groovy-[version]\bin\groovy.bat` manually every time. Here is a little shortcut: if your file has the `groovy`, `gvy`, `gy`, or `gsh` extension, then you do not have to type the extension, just `groovy myfile` will suffice.

So now, you have Groovy running locally. I am not going to discuss the entire Groovy syntax here. Instead, I am going to discuss little bits throughout the examples in the remainder of the chapter. The Groovy website has some learning materials as well. Rest assured, you do not need to be a Groovy aficionado to get this stuff working in Jenkins.

Pipeline projects

So, let's continue on to Jenkins, where we are going to create our first Pipeline project. Go to **New Item** and pick the **Pipeline** project template. This will take you to the configuration screen, which looks a little different from what you are used to. For example, you are missing some options in the **General** section of the configuration. The **Source Code Management** section is missing. But most important of all, you get a brand new **Pipeline** section:

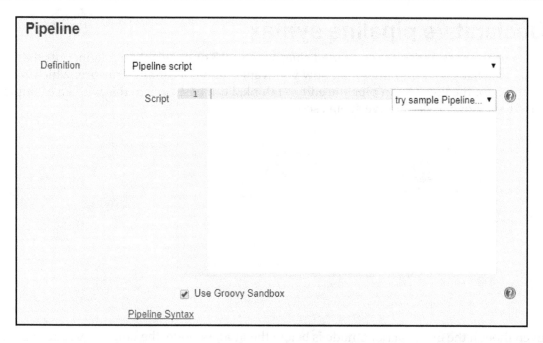

In this **Pipeline** section, you get a choice to pick your pipeline definition, **Pipeline script** or **Pipeline script from SCM**. For now, we are going to leave it on the **Pipeline script**, but later, we will see that the other option is actually way more practical. Below the definition field is a large **Script** field where your pipeline goes. Remember that this script will run inside the Jenkins environment, so you get various environment variables and functions that would not otherwise be available in Groovy. On the other hand, because you are running in Jenkins, your actions are limited. For example, you do not have sufficient permissions to save a file somewhere to disk. Under the **Script** field is a checkbox where you can enable or disable the Groovy Sandbox. Disabling it gives you more privileges than you would normally have in Jenkins, so from a security perspective, it is best to leave it enabled.

We will get to the script, the most important part of this entire configuration, in a bit. You can already read more about it on the Jenkins website (`https://jenkins.io/doc/book/pipeline/syntax/`). It is going to look a bit different from the pipeline we generated using the Blue Ocean pipeline editor. The pipeline editor generated the so-called **Declarative Pipeline Syntax**, which is a more recent addition to Jenkins, while we are going to use the scripted pipeline syntax. Scripted syntax is basically what you would expect from a script; it just runs code from top to bottom. Before we continue, let's focus on the differences between the two a little bit.

Declarative pipeline syntax

Declarative syntax, which is supported since version 2.5 of the Pipeline plugin, puts the focus on what you want rather than how you want it. It has a certain structure, which is required for the Blue Ocean pipeline editor. I think, I can best explain this with an example. Take the following declarative syntax script:

```
pipeline {
  agent any
  stages {
    stage('Greet') {
      steps {
        echo env.greetings
      }
    }
  }
  environment {
    greetings = 'Hello'
  }
}
```

Even though the `environment` node is below the `stages` node, the `echo env.greetings` line prints `Hello`. Obviously, the `environment` node was interpreted before the stages were executed. This is because we are describing what we want rather than how we want it. We want an environment variable named `greetings`. We want `stages` and `steps`. We do not really care how Jenkins or Groovy assigns the `greetings` variable and reads the value or how it injects it into our steps; we just describe that we want it. A declarative script always starts with a `pipeline` block, that is how Jenkins, and we, know that it is declarative.

Since we have the pipeline editor that can generate this for us, let's not go deeper into this style. A lot of the syntax still has overlap with the scripted pipeline syntax.

Scripted pipeline syntax

The scripted pipeline syntax is probably a little easier to grasp. It is just code like you are used to. As such, it does not really need a lot of explanation. The previous example can be rewritten in *regular* scripted syntax:

```
def greetings = 'Hello'
stage('Greet') {
    echo greetings
}
```

Groovy is an *optionally typed* language, so you may be more comfortable with the following alternative:

```
String greetings = 'Hello'
[...]
```

That is A LOT shorter than the same code in declarative style. As you can see, we still use the `stage('Greet') { ... }` block, but we do not wrap it in a `stages { ... }` block and it does not contain a `steps { ... }` block. In fact, `stages` and `steps` are not even allowed in this context. Jenkins will not recognize them and will throw an error.

Pipeline stages

At this point, you may be wondering what this `stage` block is about anyway. Put either the declarative or the scripted pipeline example in the **Script** field of your pipeline project, save it, and run it. On your project page, you should now see your first build and your first stage:

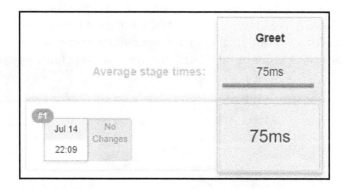

You can add another stage and Jenkins will visualize that one too:

```
def greetings = 'Hello'
stage('Greet') {
    echo greetings
}
stage('Say goodbye') {
    echo 'Goodbye'
}
```

The output of the script looks as follows:

		Greet	Say goodbye
Average stage times:		61ms	30ms
#2 Jul 14 22:10	No Changes	47ms	30ms
#1 Jul 14 22:09	No Changes	75ms	

As you can see, in the second picture, build #1 did not have the **Say goodbye** stage yet. If you add stages at the end like that, Jenkins just leaves them blank for builds that did not have that stage yet. However, if you change a stage name completely, or you remove a stage, Jenkins cannot show older builds. Furthermore, if a stage fails, this will be indicated by a red square:

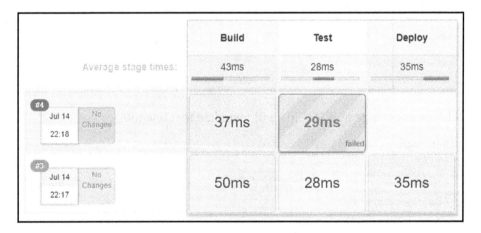

		Build	Test	Deploy
Average stage times:		43ms	28ms	35ms
#4 Jul 14 22:18	No Changes	37ms	29ms failed	
#3 Jul 14 22:17	No Changes	50ms	28ms	35ms

For now, we have no source control in our pipeline yet, but when you do, the block that now says **No changes** shows the number of new commits included in the current build.

Clicking on a square enables you to view the logs for that stage and even for separate steps, including how much time it took to complete. The following screenshot contains the logs of the test steps we generated in the previous chapter (we will run them later in this chapter):

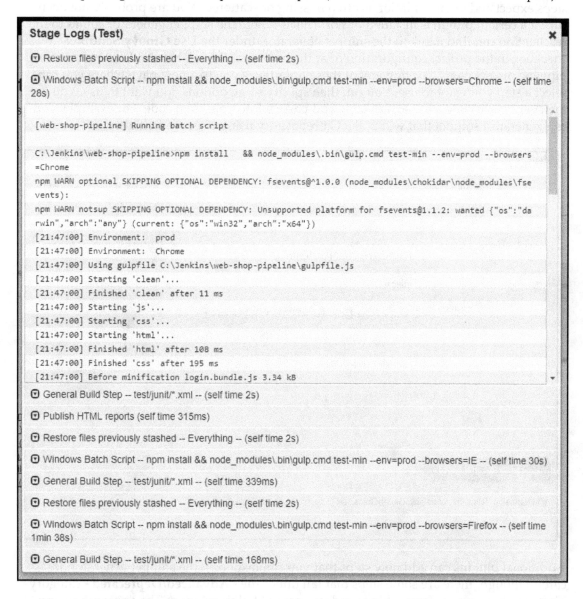

Of course, you can still view the complete console output. All in all, these are some pretty sweet features and we are going to see them live in this chapter.

The snippet generator

Another useful feature is the snippet generator. It is very hard to guess what syntax some steps expect and documentation is often missing or scattered. You are probably not even sure if a certain plugin is installed or not. This is where the snippet generator comes to the rescue. You can find a link to the snippet generator under the **Use Groovy Sandbox** checkbox in the project configuration or at the bottom of the left-hand side menu on a pipeline project page. Clicking any of those links takes you to a new page where you can select a step you want to use. You can then specify some options you want to use. You can then generate a code snippet and copy and paste it into your own code. For example, you can generate a snippet that will poll a Git repository using your credentials:

Additional plugins can add new steps that you can inspect in the snippet generator. Be careful though, there are some steps that fall under the **- Advanced/Deprecated -** category. Those are two very different things and you cannot tell them apart. The one you can and probably want to use, while the other is better not used. Personally, I try to avoid steps in this category altogether. A very weird design choice, but at least, you have been warned.

Building the web shop

Now that we know how to run pipelines, we can test the script that we created in the previous chapter using the Blue Ocean pipeline editor. Simply copy the script (found in the GitHub repository) and copy it into the **Script** field. A little warning here, pipelines can cause deadlocks! A pipeline needs a node to run on, but then spawns separate builds for the individual stages. So when your pipeline is running on the Linux node and a stage requires the Linux node as well, but the Linux node is configured to only run one build at a time, the stage will wait indefinitely for the Linux node to become available again. Make sure you always have at least one more executor on your nodes than you have pipelines. Unfortunately, it is currently not (yet?) possible to trigger pipelines on a specific node, so you can have a node specifically for building pipelines. That way, you can build stages on other slaves and you would be sure stages would never be waiting on their host pipelines to finish.

We can now run the script from the previous chapter. You will notice that there are indeed two builds triggered. Too bad you cannot see which build is the pipeline and which build is the stage:

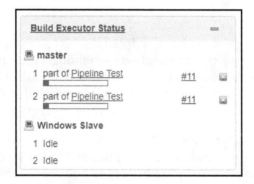

Funny thing, this script runs three test stages in parallel. The script still only has one test stage node though, so the stage view will still only show one stage, but this will show as completed as soon as one of the tests completes.

You can still see the three different test stages running in the Jenkins build overview though:

The script should run fine. Since we have scripted the GitLab trigger, you should now also see that configured in the project configuration even though you only pasted the script. For this trigger to work properly, you still need to create a webhook in GitLab by the way. Once you do that, you will even see that your build status is updated in GitLab. If you script anything like a Git trigger or polling, you need to run the script at least once to enable it:

A funny thing happened while I was writing this chapter. I was testing some scripts and noticed several plugins needed updating. Being a good civilian, I updated my plugins only to find my builds failing with some weird Java `NullPointerException`. Turns out there was a bug in the new version of the GitLab plugin. Reverting to the previous version fixed the problem. It happens with new versions of plugins that introduce bugs (you think they are practicing CI?) or are incompatible with your current version of some other component.

The Jenkinsfile

Putting your script in the Jenkins configuration is fine, but there is an alternative, the Jenkinsfile. The Jenkinsfile is simply a file in your Git repository that contains the pipeline script you want to run. So, copy the pipeline script and place it in a file named `Jenkinsfile` (no extension) in the root of your repository and commit it to Git. Now, go to the configuration of your pipeline project and change the definition from **Pipeline script** to **Pipeline script from SCM**. You must now pick your SCM, which is Git, and then configure the connection to your repository. This works exactly the same as in freestyle projects. Additionally, there is a **Script Path**, which defaults to **Jenkinsfile** and **Lightweight checkout**, which you can leave checked. Again, save and run the project and, basically, everything will be like before, except your script is now in your repository.

That is really all there is to the Jenkinsfile. However, the Jenkinsfile is a prerequisite for the next step in our pipeline adventure, the multibranch pipeline.

Multibranch pipeline

The Multibranch pipeline is the next step from the *regular* pipeline. It is pretty much the same, except it can run your script on every branch that has it. Any new branches are automatically scanned and build. Add a new item in Jenkins and pick the **Multibranch Pipeline** project type. The configuration requires you to specify your Git repository, but this time, you cannot specify a specific branch. The build configuration mode is set to by Jenkinsfile which, in this case, means your Jenkinsfile from source control. We can leave all the other settings for now. Save your configuration and you will be taken to the Scan Multibranch Pipeline Log. You should see Jenkins checking your repository for branches and Jenkinsfiles:

```
Getting remote branches...
Seen branch in repository origin/master
Seen 1 remote branch
Checking branch master
    'Jenkinsfile' found
Met criteria
Scheduled build for branch: master
Done.
```

The project page for the multibranch pipeline project looks very different from other projects. That is because it does not show latest build information, but branches that can be build using the Jenkinsfile. The project will scan for new branches regularly and add them to the project page if a Jenkinsfile is found. Alternatively, you can trigger a scan manually by clicking the **Scan Multibranch Pipeline Now** on the left-hand side menu:

On the project page, you can see which branches are currently passing the build, when branches were last built, and how long that took. Clicking on a branch takes you to the branch page, which looks more like the project page that you are used to. You can configure branches and specify build triggers, how many builds to keep, and so on, but it is advised to keep as much configuration in your script as possible. For example, you can keep up to five builds by calling the `properties` function in your script:

```
properties([buildDiscarder(logRotator(numToKeepStr: '5',
artifactNumToKeepStr: '5')), gitLabConnection('Local GitLab'),
pipelineTriggers([])])
```

In the declarative syntax, you can add this to the `options` node:

```
options {
  gitLabConnection('Local GitLab')
  buildDiscarder(logRotator(numToKeepStr: '5', artifactNumToKeepStr: '5'))
}
```

For more options, you can check out the snippet generator for `properties: Set job properties`.

One thing that is currently very confusing about multibranch pipeline projects is that you have no way of seeing if any branch fails when you are on the main page:

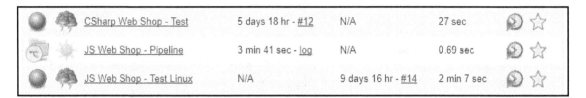

Instead of a blue or red ball, the multibranch pipeline shows a folder with no status information. So you have no idea whether everything builds or does not. The weather icon does show the cumulative status of your branch builds though, but even when it is cloudy, your branches can all currently pass the build. The last build times are also not build times of your branches, but the last time your repository was scanned for branches. Finally, the build button triggers a branch scan and not a build of your branches. The Blue Ocean plugin does this a lot better already because it shows whether all the builds are passing or if one or more builds are failing.

Likewise, it shows when a build fails:

Another very nice feature of the multibranch pipeline is the replay function. It often happens that you want to try out some script in Jenkins, but you are not sure on the syntax or what works best. Having to commit your Jenkinsfile for each small change you make just to test whether it works is rather tiresome and really pollutes your commit log. With replay, you can simply click on a build and hit the replay button. You are allowed to change the script before you replay the the build, so you can correct whatever you want until it works. When everything works, you can copy the script from your replay window and into your Jenkinsfile and you will commit a working script right away. When you have multiple scripts, you can edit each one of them. Replay only works when the previous build had valid syntax though. So, you can replay failed builds unless there was a syntax error in your script.

Branch scripts

We have talked about branching before, but it is not until now that its use becomes apparent. Using multibranch pipelines, you can have a different build strategy per branch. For example, you probably want to build, test, report, and SonarQube your development branch, but you want to build, minify, test, and release your production branch. One option is to have a different Jenkinsfile in each branch. However, that makes it a little harder for Git to merge branches and you will always have an additional merge branch.

Another method is checking out what branch you are working in using the BRANCH_NAME environment variable and act based on that:

```
stage('Test Script') {
    echo env.BRANCH_NAME
    if (env.BRANCH_NAME == 'master') {
        echo 'This is the master branch'
    } else {
        echo 'This is not the master branch'
    }
}
```

Having a couple of if-else branches in your Jenkinsfile may be fine, but when your build logic is already complicated or completely different for each branch, you may be better off by writing a Groovy script per branch and loading that into your Jenkinsfile. Create two new files in the root of your project, jenkins.master.groovy and jenkins.Development.groovy. We are going to create a different test routine for both the files. In the jenkins.master.groovy file, we are going to test our minified script and, in jenkins.Development.groovy, we are going to test the source code and analyze it using SonarQube (or for simplicity, we are just going to echo some lines of text):

```
// jenkins.master.groovy
def test() {
    echo 'Testing the minified software...'
    echo 'Minified software tested.'
}
return this

// jenkins.Development.groovy
def test() {
    echo 'Testing the source code...'
    echo 'Source code tested.'
    echo 'Running SonarQube analysis.'
}
return this
```

In both scripts, we are simply defining a function and returning the body. Returning the body is important if we want to use the test function in our Jenkinsfile. In the Jenkinsfile, we can load any of these scripts based on the env.BRANCH_NAME variable. We need to run this inside a node block or the load function will fail because Required context class hudson.FilePath is missing:

```
node('linux') {
    stage('Build') {
        // Same logic for every branch.
        checkout scm
        echo 'Building the software.'
    }
    stage('Test') {
        // Logic is different for every branch.
        def script = load 'jenkins.' + env.BRANCH_NAME + '.groovy'
        script.test()
    }
}
```

Finally, create a Development branch if you did not already have one; make sure everything is committed to Git and scan the multibranch pipeline for branches. You can now build your master and development branches and you should see two separate builds. Of course, you will now need to add an additional script for every new branch so we can add a default:

```
def fileName = 'jenkins.' + env.BRANCH_NAME + '.groovy'
if (!fileExists(fileName)) {
    echo 'Branch specific script not found, using Development default.'
    fileName = 'jenkins.Development.groovy'
}
def script = load fileName
script.test()
```

Now, when you add a new branch, it will build using the Development script by default.

Speaking of which, when we commit to a branch, we want that branch to build and not all the others. Using the GitLab trigger with a webhook, we should be sure our webhook works. You can create a webhook for the project, such as [...]/project/JS%20Web%20Shop%20-%20Pipeline, or you can specify a branch, such as [...]/project/JS%20Web%20Shop%20-%20Pipeline/master. Testing the first webhook will trigger all the branches, but will still only trigger the current branch when committing.

Completing the script

So far, we know how to utilize the multibranch pipeline and we have most of a working script, but it is not completely what we configured earlier in classic Jenkins. So, let's complete the script so we have pretty much everything. We can now also easily differentiate between different branches. Basically, I want to get everything up and running as though we were building an actual product. We will fill in the final details on releasing the software in the final chapters of this book.

First, we are going to make a few edits to our gulpfile. It was fine earlier, but now that we are going to trigger three builds at the same time, it makes no sense to use PhantomJS every time. Also, we want to be able to trigger the `test-min` task without also triggering the regular `test` task. The change is pretty simple. Just change the `browsers` Karma configuration in the gulpfile. You can find the changed gulpfile in the GitHub repository for this book in the code samples for this chapter:

```
.task('test', ['build'], function (done) {
    new karma({
        configFile: __dirname + '/test/karma.conf.js',
        singleRun: true,
        browsers: browsers ? browsers : ['PhantomJS']
    }, [...]
})
.task('test-min', ['build'], function (done) {
    new karma({
        configFile: __dirname + '/test/karma.min.conf.js',
        browsers: browsers ? browsers : ['PhantomJS']
    }, [...]
})
```

We can now either specify the browsers when starting Gulp or we do not, in which case Karma will use PhantomJS. You may also want to change your default task so that it tests only your source code and not the minified code:

```
.task('default', ['lint', 'test', 'test-node']);
```

We can now continue with the Jenkinsfile that we had in the previous chapter. We can also rewrite it using the scripted syntax. Since we have the declarative script already, let's just continue to use that. The change we just made to our gulpfile actually plays very nice with our current script, so we do not have to change anything for that to work.

One thing that bothers me in the current setup is that we need to unstash *Everything* and run `npm install` for every browser test. Unfortunately, there is nothing we can do about that. Jenkins runs every stage in its own workspace and, when a workspace is already in use, it creates `workspace@tmp` or `workspace@2` workspaces. So, instead of sharing the workspace, parallel builds need to run in their own context entirely. We can run the browser tests in sequence, but let's leave it like it is.

Node.js tests

The first thing we can add to the script are our Node.js tests. We can place this between the Build stage and the Test stage. It is fine to run these tests on Linux and they are pretty lightweight. And we should also not forget to publish our reports except, of course, the Cobertura report, which we cannot publish using the pipeline:

```
stage('Test NodeJS') {
  steps {
    node(label: 'linux') {
      ws(dir: 'web-shop-pipeline') {
        gitlabCommitStatus(name: 'Test NodeJS') {
          sh 'node_modules/.bin/istanbul cover node_modules/jasmine-
node/bin/jasmine-node -- --junitreport --output node-junit test/spec'
          junit 'node-junit/*.xml'
          publishHTML target: [
            allowMissing: false,
            alwaysLinkToLastBuild: false,
            keepAll: false,
            reportDir: 'coverage/lcov-report',
            reportFiles: 'index.html',
            reportName: 'NodeJS Coverage Report'
          ]
        }
      }
    }
  }
}
```

SonarQube

The next thing we will want to do is run a SonarQube scanner. First, let's fix our `sonar-project.properties` file, which still has `chapter7` for `projectKey` and `projectName`:

```
sonar.projectKey=jswebshop
sonar.projectName=JS Web Shop
```

```
sonar.projectVersion=1.0
[...]
```

To invoke the SonarQube scanner, we are going to use a `script` block. Using the script block, we can define variables and assign them values. In this case, we are going to use the `tool` command to get the `SonarQube` location. You can generate the `tool` command using the snippet generator. After that, we can invoke `SonarQube` using a shell command. Since it is the `PhantomJS` tests that will generate the LCOV report, we can run this stage on the Linux node again:

```
stage('SonarQube') {
  steps {
    node(label: 'linux') {
      ws(dir: 'web-shop-pipeline') {
        gitlabCommitStatus(name: 'SonarQube') {
          script {
            def sonar = tool name: 'Local', type:
'hudson.plugins.sonar.SonarRunnerInstallation'
            sh sonar + '/bin/sonar-scanner'
          }
        }
      }
    }
  }
}
```

We probably also want to fail the build if the quality gate fails. To do this, we must run our SonarQube runner inside a Sonar environment and, after that, we can wait for SonarQube to report the status of the scan back to Jenkins. We can wait for SonarQube by using the `waitForQualityGate` function. You should know that these steps do not need to be in the same stage and that `waitForQualityGate` pauses the current build and waits for SonarQube to finish the scan, which might take a while. A good setup, for example, would be to run your SonarQube analysis, then do your tests, and finally, report the SonarQube status. That way, you are making the most out of the asynchronous nature of SonarQube. Our projects scans within seconds though, so there really is no need for such a setup:

```
script {
  def sonar = tool name: 'Local', type:
'hudson.plugins.sonar.SonarRunnerInstallation'

  withSonarQubeEnv {
    sh sonar + '/bin/sonar-scanner'
  }
  def qg = waitForQualityGate()
  if (qg.status != 'OK') {
    error "Pipeline aborted due to quality gate failure: ${qg.status}"
```

```
    }
  }
```

There is just one more thing we need to do to get this to work. We need to set up a webhook in SonarQube. So go to SonarQube, then **Administration**, and then the **General Settings** under **Configuration**. There is a page for webhooks. Name your webhook Jenkins or something similar and give it the URL `http://127.0.0.1:8080/sonarqube-webhook/` (or `<your Jenkins instance>/sonarqube-webhook/`). The trailing backslash is mandatory! Test her out and see if it works. If your build hangs on something like `SonarQube task 'AV1NaMZ99HRZ_Yq5jAH6' status is 'PENDING'`, your webhook probably is not configured correctly. You could wrap `waitForQualityGate()` in a timeout block just to be sure your build will not hang forever:

```
timeout(time: 10, unit: 'SECONDS') {
   def qg = waitForQualityGate()
   [...]
}
```

Selenium tests

Next, are the Selenium tests. This is really just a batch command on the Windows slave. We can `unstash 'Everything'` and run `npm install` again, but we can also just save one from our tests. While not all tests can use the same workspace, it is perfectly fine to give them their own workspaces. Since we are already using the `Test Chrome` node to publish our reports, let's build that one in a workspace that we can also use for our Selenium tests:

```
[...]
 "Test Chrome": {
           node(label: 'windows') {
              ws(dir: 'web-shop-pipeline') {
                 gitlabCommitStatus(name: 'Test Chrome') {
[...]
```

After that, it is just a matter of running the batch. We are going to run the script a little different than before though. First, for clarity, we will just run four batch scripts rather than appending them with `&&`. Second, because we are running in a script, and this is only possible in a `script` block, we can have a `try-catch-finally` block. A `try-catch` block catches any errors, which we do not really need, but a `finally` block executes always, even when there is an error, which is pretty handy! That way, we can always delete our running instance from PM2, even if Protractor fails:

```
stage('Selenium') {
   steps {
```

```
    node(label: 'windows') {
      ws(dir: 'web-shop-pipeline') {
        gitlabCommitStatus(name: 'Selenium') {
          script {
            try {
              bat 'node_modules\\.bin\\webdriver-manager.cmd update'
              bat 'node_modules\\.bin\\pm2.cmd start --name=jenkins
index.js -- --port=1234'
              bat 'node_modules\\.bin\\protractor.cmd --baseUrl
http://localhost:1234 test\\protractor.conf.js'
            } finally {
              bat 'node_modules\\.bin\\pm2.cmd delete -s jenkins'
            }
          }
        }
      }
    }
  }
```

Archiving artifacts

The next step is pretty easy, we want to archive our artifacts so we can put them in production later. We are building our web shop on Linux, so that is where we are going to archive our artifacts as well:

```
stage('Archiving Artifacts') {
  steps {
    node(label: 'linux') {
      ws(dir: 'web-shop-pipeline') {
        archiveArtifacts 'prod/,
node_modules/bootstrap/dist/css/bootstrap.min.css,
node_modules/angular/angular.min.js,
node_modules/bootstrap/dist/js/bootstrap.min.js,
node_modules/jquery/dist/jquery.min.js'
      }
    }
  }
}
```

We do not need to commit the status to GitLab for this one. If this fails, Jenkins fails and obviously not our commit, because we tested those thoroughly at this point. The archiveArtifacts step can easily be created using the snippet generator by the way. You need the archiveArtifacts step near the top of the dropdown and not the **archive** step under **Advanced/Deprecated** (because that one is deprecated).

You can find the artifacts on your build page or on the branch overview at the front of the build bar between the time and Git commits and your first stage.

Build failure

No matter how well you write your code, your build will fail once in a while (and probably more often), so it is a good idea to send an email when this happens. The declarative pipeline has a `post` node that lets you act on a certain build status, for example, failure. The `post` block can be placed in the top node of your pipeline or in a `stage` block (that way, we could have omitted the `try-finally` block earlier). The post conditions are `always`, `changed`, `failure`, `success`, and `unstable`. We are going to use `failure` and send an email:

```
pipeline {
  agent any
  [...]
  stages {
    [...]
  }
  post {
    failure {
      mail body: """FAILED: Job '${env.JOB_NAME} [${env.BUILD_NUMBER}]':
            Check console output at ${env.BUILD_URL}""",
            subject: """FAILED: Job '${env.JOB_NAME}
[${env.BUILD_NUMBER}]'""",
            to: 'sander.rossel@gmail.com'
    }
  }
}
```

You can make the body whatever you want, but using some environment variables is pretty handy, so you can quickly go to the specific build from your email. You may want to send an email on `unstable` as well. What is also really handy is an email when your build goes from whatever state to success. You are probably not interested in every successful build, but you do want to know when a build recovers from a previous failure. Unfortunately, this is not currently easily possible; you could have a `variable`, `buildFailed`, and add a `post` block with a `failure` block to every stage and set the `buildFailed` variable. Then, send an email in the `changed` block of the global `post` block. This is quite a hassle; it is better to just send an email every time the build stage changes:

```
pipeline {
  agent any
  [...]
```

```
    stages {
      [...]
    }
    post {
      failure {
        [...]
      }
      changed {
          mail body: """STATE CHANGED: Job '${env.JOB_NAME}
[${env.BUILD_NUMBER}]':
              Check console output at ${env.BUILD_URL}""",
              subject: """STATE CHANGED: Job '${env.JOB_NAME}
[${env.BUILD_NUMBER}]'""",
              to: 'sander.rossel@gmail.com'
      }
    }
  }
}
```

That is it for the Jenkinsfile for now. In the next chapters, we are going to add to the Jenkinsfile just a bit more. For now, you can find the complete Jenkinsfile for this chapter in the GitHub repository for this book.

Summary

In this chapter, we explored multibranch pipelines. Multibranch pipelines offer a lot of flexibility through scripted and declarative style Groovy scripts. Unfortunately, writing a script is not even half as easy as creating a project using the classic projects. Next to increased flexibility, the script offers an advantage in that it is just code and is committed to Git, giving you easy backups and version management. Multibranch pipelines also make it easy to build every branch in your Git repository automatically, even as you add them. In the next chapter, we are moving away from Jenkins again to create and test a web API.

12
Testing a Web API

At this point, you are probably hoping we are getting to the delivery and deployment part, right? Almost, so hang on. There is just one more thing I would like to discuss, which is Web API testing. There are plenty of application types, such as desktop applications, embedded applications, and web applications like we created in this book. And, of course, all those applications can be created using a ton of languages and at least a gazillion frameworks. All of them take a different approach to testing and have their own testing frameworks. Throughout this book, we have used Jasmine, xUnit, and Selenium, to name but a few. In this day and age, companies want web services, though, be they JSON services or XML/SOAP services. And there is one thing I really like about those kinds of applications; they all operate on HTTP, no matter their underlying language or framework. That means testing is completely language agnostic!

In this chapter, we are going to build a simple web service using Node.js. No worries; it will be really simple and we do not need the whole Gulp circus this time. I will even leave out the database because we are really not interested in all that. After we have built this simple service, we are going to test it using Postman. Postman is an application for making and testing web requests. I mostly like it because it is easy, lightweight, and uses JavaScript for scripting.

There are two alternatives I would like to mention really quickly up-front: SoapUI, and Apache JMeter. Both SoapUI and JMeter are obviously (a little ugly and clunky) Java applications. They do not really fit in with your other Windows applications. Anyway, they are quite powerful, which is their strength and weakness. Both SoapUI and JMeter support the testing of HTTP, HTTPS, SOAP, REST, and even more. SoapUI even generates endpoints and requests from any WSDL you specify, making testing really quick and easy. The learning curve for both applications is a little steep, though, because they can do just about anything.

I have a little more experience with SoapUI than I have with JMeter and I know SoapUI uses Groovy for custom tests. It also has built-in functionality for various tests, such as schema compliance, (not) SOAP fault, and HTTP status codes. JMeter, on the other hand, is great for stress testing and timing. You can easily set multiple calls to the same API in a loop. The best part is that both are free to use.

Building a REST service

The first thing we have to do is create a little REST service. **Representational State Transfer (REST)** basically means that a service is stateless and makes use of the standard HTTP verbs like GET, PUT, POST, and DELETE. That makes it a bit easier for us to write. We can create a RESTful service using Node.js and Express, pretty much like we did before. So, create a new folder and name it `web-api` or some such. Next, we need our `package.json` file, so start up a command prompt and use the `npm init` command. You can leave all the defaults, as we are not really going to do anything with them anyway. Next, we can install Express, the `body-parser`, and the `command-line-args` package:

```
npm install express --save
npm install body-parser --save
npm install command-line-args --save
```

We can now set up our bare bones script that allows us to at least run the application:

```
var express = require('express'),
    bodyParser = require('body-parser'),
    commandLineArgs = require('command-line-args'),
    app = express();

app.use(bodyParser.json());

var options = commandLineArgs({ name: 'port', defaultValue: 80 });
var server = app.listen(options.port, '127.0.0.1');
console.log('Server running at http://127.0.0.1:' + options.port);
```

We can now decide what we want with our Web API. How about we create a little to-do list? We can insert items we need to do, update the status, and delete items when they no longer need to be done. Let's create a little in-memory list (as said, we are not going to use a database) and return it on GET. Sending an `id` parameter in the URL is optional to return a single item from the list:

```
var todos - [{
    id: 1,
    description: 'Write a book.',
    status: 'In progress'
}, {
    id: 2,
    description: 'Celebrate finishing the book.',
    status: 'New'
}];

app.get('/todo', function (req, res) {
    if (req.query.id) {
        res.json(todos.find(t => t.id === +req.query.id));
    } else {
        res.json(todos);
    }
});
```

As you can see, we can access URL parameters using `req.query.parameterName`. This is an Express utility and not vanilla Node.js. When we have an `id`, we return the item with that `id` from the list or, otherwise, we return the entire list. You can test this by running the application (using `nodemon index.js`, which you can install using `npm install nodemon -g` if you don't already have it) and browsing to `localhost/todo` or `localhost/todo?id=1` using your favorite browser.

Next, we want to be able to insert new items. Inserting is usually done using the POST verb. We really only require one thing in the body, which is a `description` of the to-do item. We can, optionally, allow a `status` to be set, but use a default of `New`:

```
app.post('/todo', function (req, res) {
    if (req.body.description) {
        var newId = Math.max.apply(null, todos.map(t => t.id)) + 1;
        var newItem = {
            id: newId,
            description: req.body.description,
            status: req.body.status || 'New'
        };
        todos.push(newItem);
        res.json(newItem);
    } else {
```

```
                res.status(400).send('Description field is required.');
        }
});
```

When the description is not set, we return a 400 code, Bad Request, with the message that the description field is required. If the description is set, we get the max `id` in the current to-do list and add 1, which will be the new `id` (it is also not thread safe, but that does not really matter for our example). We push the new item into the to-do list and return the new item to the client.

We currently have no way to test this method because our browser does not allow easy POSTing. We could write a small JavaScript script and do an AJAX call, but we are not going to do that. We are first going to write the PUT and DELETE methods, and then we are going to test this thing. Then, we are going to run actual E2E tests and automate them!

With a PUT request, we should be able to update items. Based on the `id`, we can set the `description` and the `status` of an item. If `id` is not set in the request, we can return a 400, like before, and when `id` is set, but not found, we can return a 404. When all is well, we return the (updated) element:

```
app.put('/todo', function (req, res) {
    if (req.body.id) {
        var item = todos.find(t => t.id === +req.body.id);
        if (item) {
            item.description = req.body.description || item.description;
            item.status = req.body.status || item.status;
            res.json(item);
        } else {
            res.status(404).send('No such todo item.');
        }
    } else {
        res.status(400).send('Id field is required.');
    }
});
```

As you can see, both `description` and `status` are optional. If neither is set, we just do not update anything and the request is sort of equal to a GET with `id`.

Last, we need a DELETE method to delete items from the list. Like with PUT, we need `id`. When `id` is not set, we return a 400 code. When `id` is set, but we cannot find the element, we return a 404 code. When an item with `id` is found, we can remove it from the array and return the deleted element:

```
app.delete('/todo', function (req, res) {
    if (req.body.id) {
        var item = todos.find(t => t.id === +req.body.id);
        if (item) {
            todos.splice(todos.indexOf(item), 1);
            res.json(item);
        } else {
            res.status(404).send('No such todo item.');
        }
    } else {
        res.status(400).send('Id field is required.');
    }
});
```

We now have GET, POST, PUT, and DELETE methods to read, create, update, and delete our to-do items. We have no state and everything is done using regular HTTP verbs, so we are completely RESTful. In the remainder of this chapter, we are going to test the API using Postman.

Postman

I have already mentioned Postman in the introduction of this chapter. Postman comes in three flavors: **free**, **Pro**, and **Enterprise**. The free version already gives us more than we need for this project and it is really great for most projects, really. You may find a Postman Chrome plugin, but there is no need to bother with it. It is limited, and last I heard, they will deprecate it by the end of 2017. You can download Postman for the platform you are using on their website, `https://www.getpostman.com/`. Simply install Postman, nothing to worry about there, and start it. When you start Postman, you will see a loading screen with a text like `Distorting space-time continuum` or `Moving satellites into position`.

Be really careful here, or you will mess up reality as we know it for all of us! Just kidding; it is just a funny message and will not actually do anything. When Postman is started, it should look something like this:

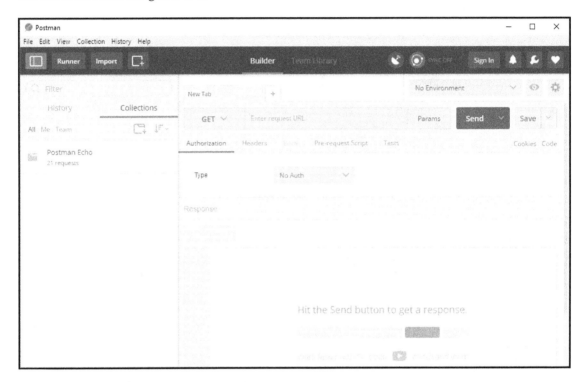

In here, you can enter a URL, verb, headers, cookies, payload data--pretty much anything. Make sure your API is running. Now try to GET the `localhost/todo` and `localhost/todo?id=1` URLs. Just enter the URLs and hit the **Send** button. You should get the result in the large response field at the bottom. Notice there are a couple of tabs. You can, for example, view all headers that were returned in the response.

On the left-hand side, you can find your collections and history. Your history is automatically saved and enables you to quickly redo previous web requests. You can save requests and tests in collections, which we will do later in this chapter. If your history and collections are not showing, try making your Postman screen a little bigger. You can also show it using the button at the top left of the screen.

First, we are going to create a new to-do item to check whether it all works as expected. You can leave the request URL on `localhost/todo`. Since everything relies on the HTTP verbs, we do not have URLs, such as `localhost/todo/create` or `localhost/createtodo`. Now put the verb on POST. Once you put the verb on POST, the **Body** tab should become available. On the **Body** tab, you can specify the type and payload of the body. We need the **raw** type and, from the dropdown that appears, you need to select **JSON (application/json)**. This will actually add a `Content-Type` header on the **Headers** tab. We can now specify our payload, which must be a valid JSON:

```
{
    "description": "Add a new item to the TODO list."
}
```

If you have done everything correctly, this is what it looks like:

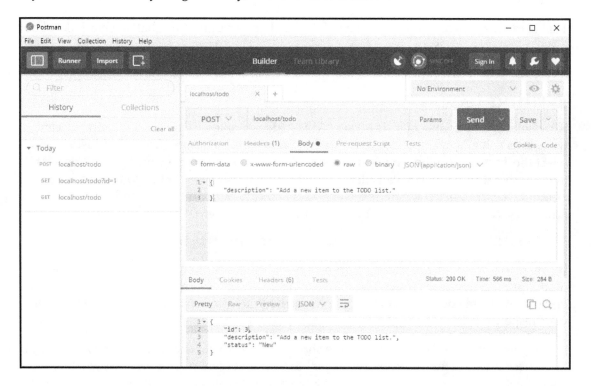

After that, we can update the item we just inserted. Put the verb on `PUT` and set `id` and a new `description` and `status` in your body:

```
{
    "id": 3,
    "description": "Add a new item to the TODO list using Postman.",
    "status": "Done"
}
```

You can check whether everything is as you expect it to be by re-running your GET request from your history.

And last, we are going to delete the item, simply by switching the verb from the PUT request to DELETE. You can remove the description and status from your request body, but leaving them there will not have any effects, either.

That is really how easy Postman can be. It is small and intuitive and that is what I like about it.

Writing tests

Now, let's write a couple of tests for our API. As I mentioned in the introduction, we can write tests using JavaScript. Get your GET `localhost/todo?id=1` from your history and select the **Tests** tab (in the request, not the response). You will see a couple of snippets on the right-hand side that you can click after which they will be added to your script. For example, we can use the `Response body: Contains string` snippet and change it a little so we can verify that somewhere in our response we get `id` 1:

```
tests["Body contains id 1"] = responseBody.has('"id":1,');
```

We need to test for the raw response (which has no spaces or new lines) rather than the pretty, printed response (which has spaces and new lines). When you send the request now, Postman will run your tests as well. You can see the status of your tests in the **Tests** tab of your response section.

We can make this test better, though. We should be able to parse our response to JSON and then check whether the `id` property is equal to `1`. In that scenario, we also test whether we are not getting, for example, an array in our response. We can use the `Response body: JSON value check` snippet:

```
var jsonData = JSON.parse(responseBody);
tests["Id equals 1"] = jsonData.id === 1;
```

And now that we have the JSON data as a JavaScript object, we can easily test all kinds of things, such as the status.

We can also time our call. While that may be good practice, I have found it very hard to test. Ideally, you want your request to be handled as quickly as possible, but that also depends on your server and how busy it is. For example, I am getting response times of 500 to 600 milliseconds, which is actually a bit slow (only on the first request, though). I once had such a test on a crappy test server and the response times ranged from less than 200 milliseconds to over a second, depending on what else that server was doing (like running other Jenkins jobs). However, we can test that it never takes longer than a second. There is a `Response time is less than 200ms` snippet:

```
tests["Response time is less than a second"] = responseTime < 1000;
```

Another useful test is to check the HTTP status that is returned. We can use the snippet `Status code: Code is 200` as is:

```
tests["Status code is 200"] = responseCode.code === 200;
```

End the request and check whether your tests succeed (I have made one fail deliberately):

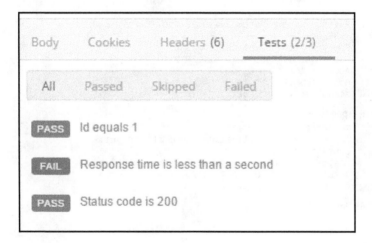

As you can see, it is quite easy to write tests using Postman, as it is just JavaScript. The snippets help, too. However, there comes a time when your tests fail on some unexpected value. Maybe an invalid cast or a null reference. At such times, it can really come in handy if you have some extra tools to inspect values of objects. Postman has just that. In the top menu, go to **View** and then **Show Postman Console** (shortcut keys *Cmd + Alt + C* or *Alt + Ctrl + C* on Windows). This opens up the console and shows your requests, responses, and anything you log to the console:

```
var jsonData = JSON.parse(responseBody);
console.log(jsonData);
```

The console should show you what's in the `jsonData` object:

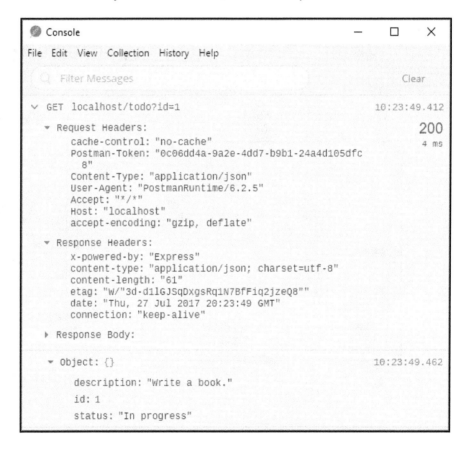

Testing XML

Personally, I am not a fan of XML. Like Linus Torvalds, creator of Linux, once said: *XML is crap. Really. There are no excuses. XML is nasty to parse for humans, and it's a disaster to parse even for computers. There's just no reason for that horrible crap to exist.* However, for some reason, there are still people who just love XML. In my experience, it is especially *enterprise* businesses who rely on XML a lot. So, whether you like it or not, you will probably have to work with XML at some point during your career. When working with XML, the earlier mentioned SoapUI is probably your go-to API test solution. However, Postman can test XML just fine. So, let's set up a little test using XML. We can easily turn our GET method into an XML variant.

First, we need an XML parser, like `js2xmlparser`:

```
npm install js2xmlparser --save
```

After that, we can copy/paste the GET method and send XML back instead of JSON:

```
var js2xmlparser = require('js2xmlparser');

app.get('/xml/todo', function (req, res) {
    if (req.query.id) {
        var item = todos.find(t => t.id === +req.query.id);
        if (item) {
            var xml = js2xmlparser.parse('todo', item);
            res.setHeader('content-type', 'text/xml');
            res.end(xml);
        } else {
            res.status(500).send('No such todo item.');
        }
    } else {
        var xml = js2xmlparser.parse('todo', todos);
        res.setHeader('content-type', 'text/xml');
        res.end(xml);
    }
});
```

So, we parse the object to XML using `js2xmlparser.parse`. After that, we set the `content-type` header to `text/xml` and then we send the XML back using `res.end`.

It is not very hard to test XML in Postman, but there are a few gotchas. We can test this method using the URL `localhost/xml/todo?id=1`. We can use the same tests as before, so we check whether `id` really equals 1. First, we must parse our response to JSON using `xml2Json`. After that, you should remember that XML has a parent node, (in our case, that is `todo`), so we get an object with a `todo` property:

```
var jsonData = xml2Json(responseBody).todo;
```

Also, JSON has strings enclosed in double quotes while numerics are kept as they are. XML has no such thing, so everything becomes a string. Because of this, we must cast our `id` property to a numeric before we can test it for value and type equality with ===:

```
var jsonData = xml2Json(responseBody).todo;
tests["Id equals 1"] = +jsonData.id === 1;
```

Other than that, it is really pretty much the same as with regular JSON. If you are having problems finding out how, exactly, Postman parsed your XML to JSON, you can always use the Postman Console.

Collections

Now that we have a request with some tests, we probably want to save it somewhere and also add other requests with their own tests. You can save multiple requests in a collection. Simply hit the **Save** button next to the **Send** button. You will have to specify your request name, which defaults to the URL, but you can name it something like `Get TODO 1`. You can add an optional description, such as `Gets TODO item 1 and tests whether we got the correct item back`. And finally, you have to either save it to an existing collection or create a new collection. We are going to create a new collection named `Web API`. Hit **Save** and your collection will be saved. You can view it in the **Collections** tab on the left-hand side (if your screen is wide enough). Collections are not fully supported only if you have a Postman account in the free version, and there are also some features that are supported, such as mocking and publishing documentation. Whether you want an account to play with these features is up to you. For this chapter, you do not need an account. Other than that, you can, of course, edit your collection and your separate requests and you can run your collections.

There is already a preinstalled collection named **Postman Echo** that you can use as an example:

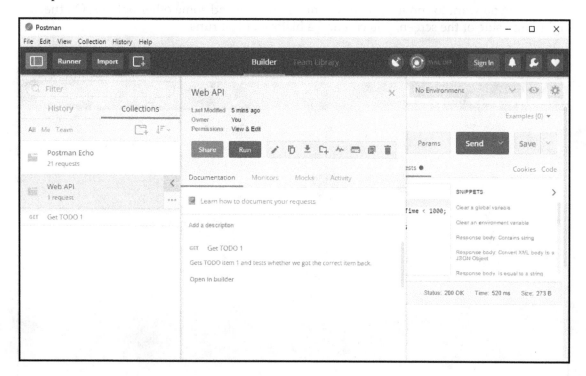

When you run your collection, Postman will open a new screen called a **Collection Runner**. In this runner, you can specify the collection to run (which is now defaulted to Web API) how often you want to run it, what environment to use, and some other options. On the right-hand side of the screen, you can find a history of test runs:

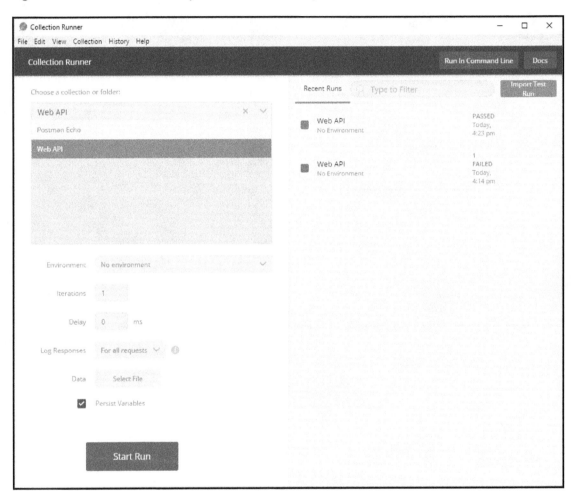

Just hitting **Start Run** will run your requests and present you with the overall status of your tests:

Now, let's add some additional tests to the collection. First, let's add the POST action with and without a default status. You know how to do the requests, so let's focus on the test scripts. In the first request, we are not going to give the new item a default status, so we should check for the given description and status New:

```
var jsonData = JSON.parse(responseBody);
tests["Description equals request description"] = jsonData.description ===
"Add a new item to the TODO list.";
tests["Status equals 'New'"] = jsonData.status === "New";

tests["Response time is less than a second"] = responseTime < 1000;
tests["Status code is 200"] = responseCode.code === 200;
```

Save this request and name it Create TODO default status. This time, do not create a new collection, but add it to our existing collection.

It would be cool if we could do another GET next, to check whether the item was really added to the list. We can do this using either global variables or environment variables. Both global and environment work pretty much the same, except that we currently do not have an environment. So let's go with global for now. Somewhere in your POST test script, you can set `id`:

```
postman.setGlobalVariable("createdId", jsonData.id);
```

You can now use this variable pretty much everywhere. To use it, use the `{{variable_name}}` syntax. So, create a new GET request with the URL `localhost/goto?id={{createdId}}`. In the test script, you can now also verify that you really get the correct ID from the server:

```
var jsonData = JSON.parse(responseBody);
tests["Id equals " + globals.createdId] = jsonData.id ===
+globals.createdId;

tests["Description equals request description"] = jsonData.description ===
"Add a new item to the TODO list.";
tests["Status equals 'New'"] = jsonData.status === "New";

tests["Response time is less than a second"] = responseTime < 1000;
tests["Status code is 200"] = responseCode.code === 200;
```

Just keep in mind that all your global variables are stored as strings. In the upper-right corner is a button with an eye symbol. Clicking this button lets you view, add, delete, and change global variables. Be aware that your tests are now dependent upon each other, though. You need to run the POST before you can run the GET, because POST sets the variable that GET needs. Add the new GET request with tests to your collection as well. If you run your collection now, you should have three requests with a total of twelve tests.

You can create something like that for the POST with a default status as well. You can easily copy requests, by the way. Just click the three-dotted menu next to a request in your collection and choose **Duplicate**. The request will be added to your collection right away. Here is another tip; do not forget to save! You may be used to editors auto-saving or, at least, saving when you hit run/debug. Postman does no such thing. You really have to explicitly hit the save button. Annoying, but that is how it works.

When we have our two POST and two corresponding GET requests, we are moving on with the PUT, or update, request. You can use the global variable in the request body:

```
{
    "id": {{createdId}},
    "description": "Add a new item to the TODO list using Postman.",
    "status": "Done"
```

```
}
```

The test script is almost exactly the same as before, save for our updates, of course:

```
var jsonData = JSON.parse(responseBody);
tests["Id equals " + globals.createdId] = jsonData.id ===
+globals.createdId;
tests["Description equals request description"] = jsonData.description ===
"Add a new item to the TODO list using Postman.";
tests["Status equals 'New'"] = jsonData.status === "Done";

tests["Response time is less than a second"] = responseTime < 1000;
tests["Status code is 200"] = responseCode.code === 200;
```

You can then create another GET request to make sure everything was really updated. After that, we create a DELETE request. The body is almost the same as the PUT request:

```
{
    "id": {{createdId}}
}
```

And the test script is exactly the same.

Lastly, we want to test if the deleted item was really deleted. This is interesting. We expect 404, no such item found:

```
tests["Response time is less than a second"] = responseTime < 1000;
tests["Status code is 404"] = responseCode.code === 404;
```

However, when we now run our tests, this one fails. Instead, we get an empty response and a status code of 200. So, we should really change our code and it will return what we expect. The problem is that we just try to find the item and return whatever is found, even if we do not find anything. So, we should change the code to return a 404 when we have no such item:

```
app.get('/todo', function (req, res) {
    if (req.query.id) {
        var item = todos.find(t => t.id === +req.query.id);
        if (item) {
            res.json(item);
        } else {
            res.status(404).send('No such todo item.');
        }
    } else {
        res.json(todos);
    }
});
```

I could think of a few more tests, such as the 404 with PUT and DELETE and a test for the entire list, but let's keep it at this. We really have more than enough tests to make an interesting example.

When you have an API with many endpoints, you may want to organize your collections a bit better. It is possible to create folders in your collections and then folders in those folders. Using folders, it is easier to keep all your tests together. For example, you can have a `todo` folder that tests all your calls to `localhost/todo` and you can have a `users` folder that tests all calls to `localhost/users`.

Environments

I have already mentioned environments, and now we are going to take a closer look at them. Environments are an invaluable tool when testing. For example, all our URLs are now targeting localhost, but when we are going to run our API on a server (test, production, whatever), we probably want to run our tests on that server, too. Manually changing all URLs is not really an option, especially when you have lots of tests. This is where environments come in. An environment is basically a set of variables like global variables, except environments can be easily interchanged, while global variables cannot. You can manage your environment by clicking the gear button in the top right corner of Postman and clicking the **Manage environments** button.

In the environments management, simply click the **Add** button to add an environment and name it `Local`. In your environment, add a key `baseUrl` and a value `localhost`. You can now change your URLs to `{{baseUrl}}/todo`. Postman will probably still give you a warning that there is no such variable in the current environment. Somewhere in the upper right corner is a dropdown that says **No Environment**, but you can now select your **Local** environment from the dropdown and everything will work again.

You can now easily create a new environment (for example, `Test`) and also specify the key `baseUrl`, but with the value `test.mycompany.com`. Now all you have to do to target your company's test server is change the environment in the upper right corner. We can now also use our environment for the `createdId` variable instead of the globals. In your POST test scripts, change the `setGlobalVariable` function to `setEnvironmentVariable`:

```
postman.setEnvironmentVariable("createdId", jsonData.id);
```

And in your other tests scripts, you replace `globals.createdId` with `environment.createdId`:

```
tests["Id equals " + environment.createdId] = jsonData.id ===
+environment.createdId;
```

Again, both global and environment variables are stored as strings, so be sure to use `JSON.stringify` and `JSON.parse` on arrays and objects if you want to store those.

Newman

Now that we have our Postman tests, complete in a collection with environments, we probably want to automate our tests. In Jenkins, this works pretty much the same as our Selenium tests; make sure your web service is running somewhere and run the tests using the command line. The problem is that Postman is a desktop application and we cannot run it from the command line. Not without Newman, that is (`https://github.com/postmanlabs/newman`). You can install Newman using `npm`:

```
npm install newman --save-dev
npm install newman -g
```

Before we can use Newman, we must do two things: export our collection and export our environment(s). We can start with the collection. Go to your collections in Postman and click the button with three dots. From the menu, choose **Export**. You will now get a popup asking if you want to save as **v1** or **v2**; choose **v2** (as recommended by the popup). I have saved the file in the `web-api\tests` folder and I have chosen the name suggested by Postman, `Web API.postman_collection.json`.

Next, we can export our environment. In Postman, go to your environments. Every environment has four options: Share (a Pro feature), Duplicate, Export, and Remove. So, choose Export and save the environment with your collection. Again, I have kept the name suggested by Postman, `Local.postman_environment.json`.

The collection and environment files are just JSON files, so you can view and edit them in any text editor. It also works great with your source control, because you can easily see who changed what and when.

You can also import your collections and environment. The collection import button is at the top left in Postman, the big button that says **Import** (next to **Runner**). You can import environments through the environment management window. That way, you can import, edit, and export your collections and environment on different computers (or in a team).

Now that we have our collection and environment in JSON files, we can run them using Newman:

```
cd web-api\tests
newman run "Web API.postman_collection.json" -e
Local.postman_environment.json
```

The -e variable is short for --environment, of course. It really is that easy:

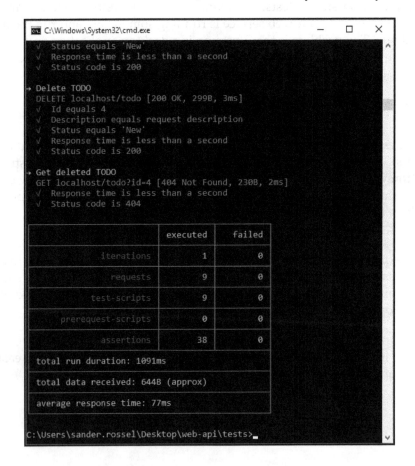

Create an error in your code and verify that it works:

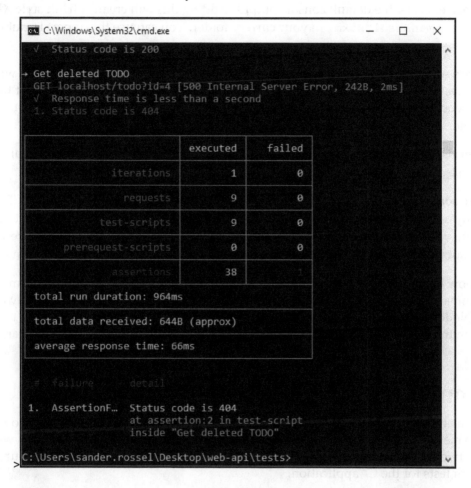

One of the most important things, especially when you are going to use Postman and Newman in Jenkins, is your reporting. And as we know, Jenkins prefers JUnit format reports. Luckily for us, Newman has this functionality built in. It is just a matter of adding the `--reporters` options to the command line:

```
newman run "Web API.postman_collection.json" -e
Local.postman_environment.json --reporters "cli,junit" --reporter-junit-
export PostmanResults.xml
```

We need to specify the `--reporter-junit-export` options for the `junit` reporter. The `cli` reporter is just the default console output. Adding this will create a JUnit style XML file named `PostmanResults.xml` in your current folder. You can use this report to publish in Jenkins.

There are some additional parameters you may want to use. You can specify a file with your global variables. This is also a JSON file. You can export it from Postman (but for some reason, you cannot import it, only copy and paste it). You can use the `-g` or `--global` parameters for your global file.

Another useful parameter is `-n`, or `--iteration-count`, for when you want to run some stress tests.

Because some platforms do not display colors properly, you can use `--no-color`. To not have any output at all, use `--silent`. To not get blacklisted by your server (or just plain DDoS it), you can set a delay between requests (in milliseconds) using `--delay-request` and to not wait too long for the result, you can set a timeout with `--timeout-request`.

You know how to get this working in Jenkins. Run the API using PM2 and then simply post the command in a Windows batch script or a Linux shell script. Because we already have an entire Node.js website, we are not going to reproduce those steps, and we are also not going to do anything else with this example. So, this was it for both Postman and Newman.

Summary

Postman and Newman are invaluable tools in testing your web APIs. I probably do not have to mention this, but they can be used to test your regular web applications as well. In the last two chapters, we are going to release our web shop and also, finally, run our Selenium tests for the C# application.

13

Continuous Delivery

We are finally getting into the next portion of this book, Continuous Delivery and Deployment. But, before we continue, let's have a brief recap of what we have learned so far. When we start working on a new project, the first thing we need is some source control repository. In this book, we have used Git. Using Git, we can create multiple branches to keep different environments and features apart. In this chapter, we are going to see why this is so important. While we write the software, we want to create automated tests, such as unit tests, E2E tests, and database tests. The more useful tests you have, the more reliable your software becomes. Upon each Git commit, we want to automatically test our software using continuous integration software, in our case, Jenkins. When our tests and, optionally, static code analyzers such as JSLint and SonarQube pass, we know our software is probably in pretty good shape. So good a shape, in fact, we can release our software to the customer.

The way I see it, we basically have three types of deployment: manual or automated and, when automated, there is deployment that depends on human interaction and there is full automatic deployment that requires no further human intervention. The automated deployment that still needs some human interaction is what we call Continuous Delivery. Basically, when you have your release files ready to be deployed at any time, you are practicing Continuous Delivery. In this chapter, we are going to set up an environment using Continuous Delivery. The next step, continuous automated deployment, or simply Continuous Deployment, will be discussed in the next, and final, chapter.

Let's take another look at the picture from Chapter 1, *Continuous Integration, Delivery, and Deployment Foundations*, but slightly different, to visualize the difference between Continuous Delivery and Deployment:

As you can see Continuous Delivery and Continuous Deployment end with the software being deployed, the main difference is that the deployment is still manually triggered (and sometimes manually executed as well) in Continuous Delivery. The takeaway is this, with continuous delivery we should always have a release package that is ready to be deployed at any time, but the deployment step itself is still manual or manually triggered. Whether that deployment step is copying some files, clicking a button or clicking a few buttons (well, not too much I guess) doesn't matter all that much. Continuous Delivery always requires a manual trigger. The difference with "traditional" deployment, however, is that the trigger can take place at any time because we have that release package ready and updating should be easy. Often as easy as clicking a button!

In this chapter we are going to start with a fully manual deployment and make sure we can easily release our software at any time after that first setup. In the next chapter we are going to completely automate this process and make the step to continuous deployment. At the end of this chapter we'll be left with a release package that can be manually deployed at any time, but after the next chapter it shouldn't be too difficult to implement a single button click strategy for your continuous delivery process.

Branching

We have discussed branching using Git in Chapter 3, *Version Control with Git*. We have discussed how your code should go from a commit on a development environment to a test environment, be it automatically tested and manually tested if necessary; then an acceptance environment where the customer can have a look at it and finally, a production environment where customers can use the software pretty much fully automated. So, you will have to set up a complete DTAP street (Development, Test, Acceptance, and Production), but still be able to differentiate between them all.

Perhaps you may have more or fewer environments, but you still want to know what commits are on what environment. We are going to set up one of those environments in this chapter. First, we are going to look at the process of branching your software so it can be distributed to the different (fictional) environments.

We want our code to go from our development environment to our test environment. Any commit can be deployed to test as soon as it is available. After all, test is where we test if our software is ready for the real world. So, we can have this fully automated. We can create new Git branches now, **Acceptance** and **Production**. Ultimately, we want an environment that looks something like the following screenshot:

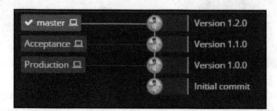

In this branching model, we have our local master branch, which we use for development. Everything from master is deployed directly to our test server and tested. When the tests succeed, we can manually merge master into **Acceptance** (in this example, I used a fast-forward). A commit to the Acceptance branch will deploy everything to the acceptance environment, where the customer can test whether they are satisfied with the changes. When the customer is satisfied with the changes, we can merge the Acceptance branch into the **Production** branch and, again, a commit to **Production** will deploy the software to the production environment. If everything goes well, everything, except the commits and merges, happens in a fully-automated way and there is little to no downtime.

Unfortunately, no matter how well everything is tested, there will be bugs on production. It can be a technical bug, but it can also be some functional bug--something everyone overlooked.

Whatever the case may be, the bug needs to be fixed. It is now easy to branch from the Production branch, fix the bug, and merge the fix into master, **Acceptance**, and **Production** (in whatever order is appropriate given the situation).

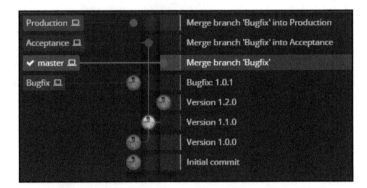

The example is a bit hard to read, but you can clearly see that the **Bugfix** branch was branched from **Production**, then merged into master, then **Acceptance** and, after customer confirmation (implied), merged in to the **Production** branch. Meanwhile, **Production** is still on version 1.0.0 and the fix did not have to wait for version 1.1.0, or worse 1.2.0, to be accepted and deployed. Since the **Bugfix** was also merged to **Acceptance** and master, it is fixed in all the current versions and we can delete the **Bugfix** branch.

We are now going to create our own branch to finally put this to practice. We need to pick either the JavaScript project or the C# .NET Core project. You may do both, of course. Since our JavaScript project already has a complete Jenkins files, let's go with that one. It is custom to keep your master branch for your production code and create a separate Development branch. However, I have found that people often check out the master branch and start working on that, so you may want to keep the master branch as your Development branch and create a separate Production branch. Whatever you do, it is all about agreeing with your team on what branches you can commit changes. Now that we have two branches, we are going to create separate Jenkins files for each branch. We have already explored the possibilities for this in Chapter 11, *Jenkins Pipelines*. I am going to have one branch build and test the software, and the other make a deployable package. You should decide whether you want to test the software on your production branch again. In theory, it is not necessary because it has been already tested. So, two branches, two separate Jenkins files.

The one on Development does the building and testing:

```
pipeline {
  agent any
  options {
    gitLabConnection('Local GitLab')
    buildDiscarder(logRotator(numToKeepStr: '5', artifactNumToKeepStr:
'5'))
  }
  triggers {
    gitlab(triggerOnPush: true, branchFilterType: 'All')
  }
  stages {
    stage('Checkout') {
      // ...
    }
    stage('Build') {
      // ...
    }
    stage('Test NodeJS') {
      // ...
    }
    stage('Test') {
      // ...
    }
    stage('SonarQube') {
      // ...
    }
  }
  post {
    // ...
  }
}
```

And the master Jenkinsfile creates the deployable package:

```
pipeline {
  agent any
  options {
    gitLabConnection('Local GitLab')
    buildDiscarder(logRotator(numToKeepStr: '5', artifactNumToKeepStr:
'5'))
  }
  triggers {
    gitlab(triggerOnPush: true, branchFilterType: 'All')
  }
  stages {
    stage('Checkout') {
```

```
        // ...
      }
      stage('Build') {
        // ...
      }
      stage('Archiving Artifacts') {
        // We only need production packages here.
        sh 'rm -rf node_modules'
        sh 'npm install --production'
        archiveArtifacts 'index.js, config.*.js, prod/, node_modules/'
      }
    }
    post {
      // ...
    }
  }
```

With multiple branches, you will quickly find that Jenkins runs out of available executors and that your nodes have to wait for each other and that you have got yourself a Jenkins deadlock. I have mentioned this earlier in Chapter 11, *Jenkins Pipelines*, but the only way we can really fix this is by having a lightweight master node that only runs the scripts, but does all the actual work on separate nodes. Because setting up such an environment is a lot of work for us now, we can minimize the damage by disabling concurrent builds in the Jenkinsfile, which is good practice anyway:

```
options {
    [...]
    disableConcurrentBuilds()
}
```

Also, keep in mind that we used a custom workspace for our build. The separate branches now use the same folder, which can have unexpected side effects such as files being locked or deleted by the other build. Of course, we can fix this as well: remember, we know what branch we are currently building on. Simply create an environment variable and use it in all instances of ws. You could append env.BRANCH_NAME in the ws nodes directly, but by using an environment variable, you keep your code a little cleaner. Note that the ${something} syntax (called string interpolation) only works when you use double quotes (if you use single quotes, your workspace will literally be named ...${env.BRANCH_NAME}):

```
pipeline {
  [...]
  environment {
    ws = "web-shop-pipeline-${env.BRANCH_NAME}"
  }
  [...]
```

```
ws(dir: env.ws) {
```

You can find the full Jenkinsfiles in the Git repository for the book on the same branch. I have named them Jenkinsfile (master) and Jenkinsfile (Development).

When everything is stable and your website is running, try committing something to your Development branch that will break the build. For example, a change in some HTML file, such as `index.ejs`. Break the build by omitting a closing bracket (in `div`) and change the text by adding `Any product!`, so you know whether the change was deployed:

```
<div class="col-lg-12"
    <h2>Search for products... Any product!</h2>
</div>
```

When you commit this change, you will find the Development branch in Jenkins starts building and fails. We can still merge this to master (which will also fail, but only because we did not break an actual unit test), but we would have to be stupid to merge a broken build. What is important here is that our master branch is still correct and ready for deployment at any time. Jenkins will send an email to us (and our team) to say that something is not well in the Development branch and we can fix our error. Once it is fixed and the build succeeds, we can manually merge (or cherry-pick) to master and Jenkins will deploy the new software.

Manual deployment

Before we can automatically deploy our software, we must first manually deploy our software. Or, at least, make sure everything is in place before we can automate it. Deploying is a bit hard because we do not really have anything to deploy to, but at least we can deploy to either our Linux VM or our Windows host.

In this chapter we are going to work with some dependencies that are required to run our software, like NGINX and our database software. The installation and configuration of such tools can be automated, but this is outside the scope of this book. You will also often find other teams, such as network administrators, are responsible for delivering necessary (virtual) servers with the necessary installed software.

Installing NGINX

The first thing we need to do before we can do anything else is install NGINX (https://www.nginx.com/). NGINX is an HTTP server, reverse proxy, and IMAP/POP3 proxy server. With NGINX, we can host our Node.js application using PM2 and use NGINX as a reverse proxy to make it available to our host Windows system. We can also run our .NET Core application using NGINX.

So, on your Linux VM, install NGINX:

```
sudo apt-get update
sudo apt-get install nginx
sudo systemctl restart nginx
sudo systemctl enable nginx
```

Then, install NGINX and make sure that it gets started on start up. I am going to do a fast-forward here; we are going to run PM2 on port 8889 internally and make it available on port 8888 externally. We are going to do the same for our .NET application using ports 9998 and 9999. So, what we have to do is configure NGINX so it reroutes 8889 to 8888 and 9998 to 9999. We can add that in the file /etc/nginx/sites-available/default:

```
cd /etc/nginx/sites-available
sudo vi default
```

Now, in the default file, add the following nodes at the bottom:

```
server {
    listen 8888;
    server_name _;

    location / {
        proxy_pass http://127.0.0.1:8889;
        proxy_http_version 1.1;
        proxy_set_header Upgrade $http_upgrade;
        proxy_set_header Connection 'upgrade';
        proxy_set_header Host $host;
        proxy_cache_bypass $http_upgrade;
    }
}

server {
    listen 9999;
    server_name _;

    location / {
        proxy_pass http://127.0.0.1:9998;
        proxy_http_version 1.1;
```

```
        proxy_set_header Upgrade $http_upgrade;
        proxy_set_header Connection 'upgrade';
        proxy_set_header Host $host;
        proxy_cache_bypass $http_upgrade;
    }
}
```

Then, restart NGINX. You may have to restart your server before the changes can take effect (because we just installed it):

```
sudo systemctl restart nginx
sudo reboot
```

This sets up NGINX. Now, if you browse to your server ports 8888 and 9999, you should see a NGINX **502 Bad Gateway** page.

Node.js web shop

Next, we want to run our JavaScript web shop. We will need at least PM2, which we already used to run our Selenium tests in Jenkins. This time, we will need to install PM2 globally:

```
sudo npm install pm2 -g
```

The easiest way to test if everything, including NGINX, works is by going directly into our Jenkins workspace and starting our index.js file from there. I am assuming you have the entire pipeline example on your Linux VM:

```
cd /var/lib/jenkins/web-shop-pipeline
pm2 start index.js --name=webshop-js -- --port=8889
pm2 ls
```

Try browsing to `ciserver:8888` in your Windows host again and you should now see your web shop!

Of course, we do not want to run our application from a Jenkins folder. Instead, we should get our files from Jenkins to somewhere else on our machine. Luckily, we have our artifacts in Jenkins. Simply download the generated zip file; it should have all the files we need (and quite a few unnecessary `node_modules`--you can remove them and use `npm install --production` if you want to). We now need to get the files from our host to our VM. We can do this using WinSCP (`https://winscp.net/eng/index.php`). Just head over to the downloads page and get the installation package of the latest version. Install it and go for the default options.

When you open WinSCP, you will be presented with the login screen. Simply log in with the SCP protocol (Secure Copy Protocol, `https://en.wikipedia.org/wiki/Secure_copy`), which uses SSH (Secure SHell, `https://en.wikipedia.org/wiki/Secure_Shell`) to copy files. You can save your session so you have a shortcut next time you need to connect.

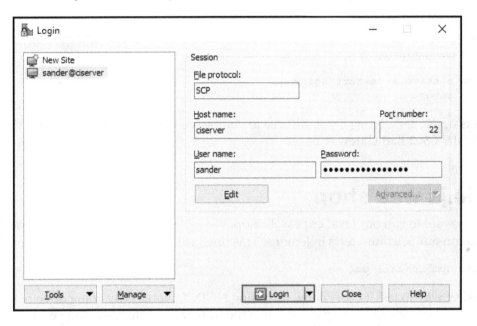

Once you are logged in, you will see a split screen showing your local computer on the left-hand side and your remote Linux VM on the right-hand side. Using WinSCP, browse to `/var/www` on your VM and create two folders, `webshop-js` and `webshop-net`. On the right-hand side, browse to your unpacked Jenkins archive.

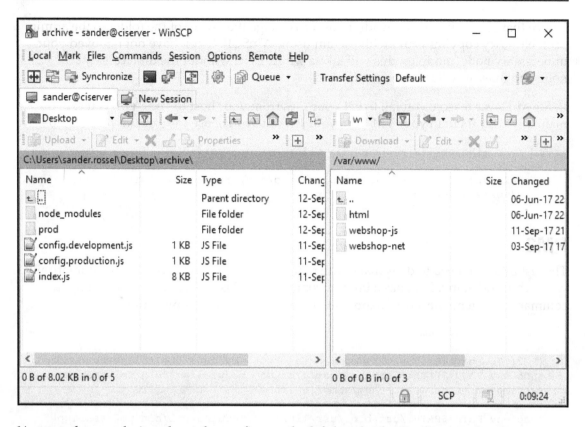

You may be wondering about the configs on the left-hand side--I will get to that in a minute. For now, it will suffice to drag all your files from the left-hand side into the webshop-js folder on the right-hand side. Unfortunately, you will be presented with a Permission Denied exception. You will need to give your user sufficient privileges to write to the folder.

Go into your VM (the actual one, not WinSCP) and make your user the owner of /var/www/webshop-js:

```
su sander
sudo chown -R sander:sander /var/www/webshop-js
ls -l /var/www
```

Notice that I am using my own admin user to change the owner of the folder to the admin user. Now, try copying your archive again using WinSCP. If you have not removed your unnecessary node_modules, this will take a while. Even without the unnecessary node_modules, it will take about a minute.

If, for whatever reason, you fail to get your files from your host to your VM, you can manually copy them in your VM from your Jenkins workspace to /var/www/webshop-js:

```
cd /var/lib/jenkins/web-shop-pipeline-master/artifacts
sudo cp -rf
{index.js,config.*.js,node_modules,prod/css,prod/scripts,prod/views}
/var/www/webshop-js
```

PM2

The last thing we need to do is make sure that PM2, and our webshop, starts automatically when your VM starts. PM2 has a built-in command for just that, startup. Running this command will generate a command that you have to run. Just copy it and run it:

```
pm2 startup systemd

[PM2] You have to run this command as root. Execute the following command:
sudo env PATH=$PATH:/usr/bin /usr/lib/node_modules/pm2/bin/pm2 startup
systemd -u [username] --hp /home/[username]

sudo env PATH=$PATH:/usr/bin /usr/lib/node_modules/pm2/bin/pm2 startup
systemd -u [username] --hp /home/[username]
```

systemd is for Ubuntu 16 and higher and CentOS, Arch, and Debian. There are other supported systems, such as Darwin, MacOSx, Gentoo, and FreeBSD. It is pretty well documented actually (http://pm2.keymetrics.io/docs/usage/startup/). Alternatively, you can omit the system variable and let PM2 figure it out.

We can now run some processes in PM2 and save them, so they will automatically be started when the VM boots. Make sure you run the index.js file from /var/www/webshop-js and not from your Jenkins workspace:

```
pm2 start /var/www/webshop-js/index.js --name=webshop-js -- --port=8889
pm2 save

[to disable startup]
pm2 unstartup systemd
```

What this command basically does is creates, modifies, or deletes the file
`/etc/systemd/system/pm2-[username].service` and adds the PM2 process
somewhere.

MongoDB

So, you should have your web shop running now, but we are currently running on the
database that we used to develop our software. We need a separate instance for our
development environment and our current environment. So, first let's create a new database
and give our current user rights to that database. We will need to create a new database and
user that we can use for our new environment.

Since we have not yet created an admin user, this was not really necessary until now. We
kind of locked ourselves out of the database. Not a smart thing to do, but easy to fix. First,
we need to disable authentication in the config file and restart MongoDB:

```
sudo vi /etc/mongod.conf

[...]
#security:
#   authorization: 'enabled'
[...]

sudo service mongod restart
```

After that, we can enter the MongoDB shell and create our admin user:

```
mongo
use admin
db.createUser({
user: 'admin',
pwd: 'admin',
roles: [{ role: 'root', db: 'admin' }]
})
exit
```

The role `root` gives a user all privileges on a database. By giving the user the role on the
`admin` database, the user effectively becomes a super user. You can now re-enable
authorization and restart MongoDB again.

We can also create a new database and user this way:

```
mongo
use admin
db.auth('admin', 'admin')
use webshop-prod
db.createUser({user: 'prod', pwd: 'prod', roles: [{ role: 'readWrite', db:
'webshop-prod' }] })
exit
```

And now, we can also log in to this database with the new user using **Robomongo**. Doing all this using Robomongo did not work for me, probably because MongoDB changes its API and Robomongo is not up to the latest version yet.

We also need to copy the data from one database to the other. For now, it is a lot easier to just copy the database altogether:

```
use admin
db.auth('admin', 'admin')
use webshop-prod
db.dropDatabase()
db.copyDatabase('webshop', 'webshop-prod')
```

So now that we have the new database and the data, we can configure the password in our software. Create two files named `config.development.js` and `config.production.js`. We are going to put our Mongo URLs in these files:

```
// config.development.js
module.exports = {
    dbConnection: 'mongodb://username:password@ciserver:27017/webshop'
};

// config.production.js
module.exports = {
    dbConnection: 'mongodb://prod:prod@ciserver:27017/webshop-prod'
};
```

We now have to change our `index.js` file, so it reads the correct config file:

```
var config = require('./config.' + (process.env.NODE_ENV || 'development')
+ '.js'),
    mongoUrl = config.dbConnection;
```

We are using the development configuration file as a default. To use the production file, or any other configuration you might have, you can set the NODE_ENV variable from your console:

```
// Windows
set NODE_ENV=production
nodemon index.js

// Linux
NODE_ENV=production nodemon index.js
```

Do not forget to add the configuration you want to your Jenkins artifact.

Run

Now that we have all our files built and ready, along with a production database and an environment-specific configuration file and our archive copied, we are finally ready to launch the application:

```
cd /var/www/webshop-js
NODE_ENV=production pm2 start index.js --name=webshop-js -- --port=8889
pm2 save
```

You are now running all the minified code on the production database automatically on start up. Once again, browse to ciserver:8888 and verify that everything works. Try changing something in your production database and see that it reflects on the website.

E2E testing

At this point, you can add an additional Jenkins project that tests whether your production website is running properly. Since we do manual deployments at this point, there is no way for Jenkins to know when you are done deploying, and the Selenium tests could be triggered manually.

Of course, you should be careful with such tests. For example, you need to make sure you are using a test account and that you do not send any emails to actual customers (would not be the first time someone accidentally sends test data to real users!). However, doing some automated smoke testing on your production environment is more than worth it! Most things are covered by unit tests, but if something obvious is amiss, such as the database, this is the way to notice it before your customers do. It is worth it to deploy a version of the software to a local server as well. It gives you the ability to test a production deployment without any risk of messing up real data.

C# .NET Core web shop

And now, we can do the same for our .NET Core application. Of course, we are using different tools to deploy .NET Core applications. For .NET Core, we cannot use PM2, which is a Node.js tool. Instead, we will create a service (script that executes on start up) that starts the cross-platform web server Kestrel, which is used to run the ASP.NET Core software. It is the same web server that is used when you run your web shop from Visual Studio Code. Again, we will need NGINX as a reverse proxy, but we already set that up when we installed NGINX, so that part is covered.

To create the service that will start Kestrel and run our .NET Core application, we can simply create a new file under `/etc/systemd/system` named `kestrel-webshop-net.service`:

```
sudo vi /etc/systemd/system/kestrel-webshop-net.service
```

In the service file, place the following script:

```
[Unit]
Description=A .NET Core Webshop

[Service]
WorkingDirectory=/var/www/webshop-net
ExecStart=/usr/bin/dotnet /var/www/webshop-net/web-shop.dll
Restart=always
RestartSec=10 # Restart service after 10 seconds if dotnet service crashes
SyslogIdentifier=webshop-net
User=www-data
Environment=ASPNETCORE_ENVIRONMENT=Production
ASPNETCORE_URLS=http://localhost:9998

[Install]
WantedBy=multi-user.target
```

We now need to get the web-shop.dll into the `/var/www/webshop-net` folder, just like we did with the JavaScript web shop.

For a quick see-if-it-works solution, you can simply go to your Jenkins workspace folder. We should still have a classic Jenkins project. Build it and run it from there:

```
cd /var/lib/jenkins/workspace/CSharp\ Web\ Shop\ -\ Build
sudo dotnet publish -o ../prod web-shop/web-shop.csproj
cd prod
ASPNETCORE_URLS="http://*:9998" web-shop.dll

[Browse to ciserver:9999 in your host]
[Ctrl+C to close]
```

As you can see, we need to publish our .NET Core application before we can run it. The `-o` parameter specifies the output of the built files. The value of the output parameter is relative to the `csproj` file you are building, not to your current location, hence, `../`. We can also copy everything to our `www` folder and check whether the service can run correctly:

```
cd /var/lib/jenkins/workspace/CSharp\ Web\ Shop\ -\ Build
sudo cp -rf prod/ /var/www/webshop-net
```

We can now enable and start the service and make sure it is running correctly:

```
sudo systemctl enable kestrel-webshop-net
sudo systemctl start kestrel-webshop-net
sudo systemctl status kestrel-webshop-net
```

Now, on your host, browse to `ciserver:9999` and you should see your .NET Core web shop running.

In Jenkins, we should fix our project and make sure it creates a build as well as an artifact. Perhaps, this is a good time to create a Jenkinsfile for the C# .NET Core project as well. We will start with the Development Jenkinsfile. A lot is just copied and pasted from the JavaScript Jenkinsfile, so I am just showing the differences here.

First of all, the checkout stage is slightly different because we also have to do a Bower install:

```
stage('Checkout') {
  steps {
    node(label: 'linux') {
      ws(dir: env.ws) {
        checkout scm
        sh '''cd web-shop
            npm install
            node_modules/.bin/bower install'''
```

```
            }
        }
    }
}
```

The triple quotes are used with `sh` when it is multiline.

In the build phase, we need to build the project using `dotnet` as well as run `gulp`:

```
sh '''cd web-shop
    dotnet restore
    dotnet build
    dotnet bundle
    node_modules/.bin/gulp'''
stash(name: 'Everything', excludes: 'node_modules/**', includes: '**/**')
```

Again, we stash everything so that we can use it in the test phase on our Windows slave. This one is a bit tricky, especially with the very long and complex OpenCover command. It was explained in Chapter 9, *A C# .NET Core and PostgreSQL Web App*, though, so it should be familiar:

```
unstash 'Everything'
bat 'cd web-shop-tests && dotnet restore && (if not exist TestResults mkdir
TestResults) && "C:\\Program Files (x86)\\OpenCover\\OpenCover.Console.exe"
-target:"C:\\Program Files\\dotnet\\dotnet.exe" -targetargs:"test -l
"trx;LogFileName=result.trx"" -register:user -filter:"+[web-shop]* -[web-
shop-tests]*" -output:"TestResults\\OpenCover Coverage.xml" -oldStyle &&
OpenCoverToCoberturaConverter.exe -input:"TestResults\\OpenCover
Coverage.xml" -output:TestResults\\Cobertura.xml &&
ReportGenerator\\ReportGenerator.exe -reports:"TestResults\\OpenCover
Coverage.xml" -targetDir:TestResults\\CoverageHTML'

bat 'msxsl -o JUnitResults.xml web-shop-tests\\TestResults\\result.trx trx-
to-junit.xsl'
junit 'JUnitResults.xml'

publishHTML target: [
    allowMissing: false,
    alwaysLinkToLastBuild: false,
    keepAll: false,
    reportDir: 'web-shop-tests/TestResults/CoverageHTML',
    reportFiles: 'index.htm',
    reportName: 'Coverage Report'
]
step([$class: 'CoberturaPublisher',
    autoUpdateHealth: false,
    autoUpdateStability: false,
    coberturaReportFile: 'web-shop-tests/TestResults/Cobertura.xml',
```

```
        failUnhealthy: false,
        failUnstable: false,
        maxNumberOfBuilds: 0,
        onlyStable: false,
        sourceEncoding: 'ASCII',
        zoomCoverageChart: false
])
```

So, a few things are going on here. First is the weird batch script with the `msxsl` command. Unfortunately, it is not possible to publish TRX files to Jenkins using the pipeline script, so we need to get creative. One way to get around this limitation is by transforming the TRX, which is just XML, to the JUnit format, which is just slightly different XML. You can download the msxsl tool from Microsoft at `https://www.microsoft.com/en-us/download/details.aspx?id=21714`. Download it and put it in the root of your C# .NET Core project. The XSL file describes the translation from one format to another. It is quite big so I will not post it here, but it is in GitHub. I used this approach for the full .NET test framework as well. I got the current xslt from a GitHub Gist (`https://gist.github.com/cdroulers/510d2ecd6ff92002bb39469821a3a1b5`) and it seems to work well enough.

Then, there is a Cobertura Publisher step. Pipeline support for the Cobertura plugin was actually added while writing this book, so you guys are in luck! You can simply generate it from the pipeline snippet generator by selecting "step: General Build Step" in "Sample Step" and then "Publish Cobertura Coverage Report" in "Build Step".

Last is the database test. You can generate the code for the TAP Publish step the same way you can generate the code for the Cobertura report:

```
unstash 'Everything'
sh 'pg_prove -d webshop -v web-shop/test/sql/*.sql | tee tap.txt'
step([$class: 'TapPublisher',
    testResults: 'tap.txt'
])
```

Next, we can create a Jenkinsfile for the master branch too. Of course, this is also not very different from what we already had. The only thing we need to add is basically a `dotnet publish` command:

```
sh 'rm -rf node_modules'
sh 'npm install --only=production'
sh 'dotnet publish -o ../prod web-shop/web-shop.csproj'
archiveArtifacts 'prod/'
```

To run the Jenkinsfile, you need to create a multibranch pipeline in Jenkins. You can copy the existing multibranch pipeline for our JavaScript web shop and simply change the Git URL. Last, be sure to create a webhook in GitLab, so your branches are automatically triggered when you make a commit to a branch.

Run

Again, we can copy the files from our Jenkins artifact using WinSCP, but we need to make the root user the owner of the `/var/www/webshop-net` folder, so we have sufficient permissions to copy the files:

```
sudo chown -R jenkins:jenkins /var/www/webshop-net
```

Now, try copying the artifacts using WinSCP and browse to ciserver:9999 to see that everything works as it should. You can run your Selenium tests against ciserver:9999 to see if everything still works!

PostgreSQL

The last thing that remains is our production database. We can quite easily set up our new database as we still have all the scripts we need to set it up. Do not worry about all the pgTap scripts. We are not going to test this database; we already did that on our development database after all. Simply run the `CREATE DATABASE` script in pgAdmin, but be sure to rename the database to something such as `"webshop-prod"` (quotes necessary):

```
CREATE DATABASE "webshop-prod"
    [...]
```

Now open the query tool on the new database and execute the rest of the scripts.

To configure our database connection string in .NET Core, we will need to do a little refactoring (and do things the correct way). We can add the connection strings to the `appsettings.json` file. Each environment has its own `appsettings.json` file, for example, `appsettings.Development.json` and `appsettings.Production.json`. Default values can be set in the `appsettings.json` file, while specific values can be overwritten per environment file. You should have `appsettings.json` and `appsettings.Development.json` already. Add `appsettings.Production.json` as well.

Add a `ConnectionStrings` node to `appsettings.json` and to
`appsettings.Production.json`:

```
// appsettings.json
{
  "Logging": {
    [...]
  },
  "ConnectionStrings": {
    "WebShopDatabase":
"Host=ciserver;Database=webshop;Username=sa;Password=sa"
  }
}

// appsettings.Production.json
{
  "ConnectionStrings": {
    "WebShopDatabase": "Host=ciserver;Database=webshop-
prod;Username=sa;Password=sa"
  }
}
```

The next part is a bit tricky. We can read the configuration at start up, pass it to `DbContext`,
and inject it to our classes using constructor injection. The configuration has already been
read and stored in the `Configuration` property of the `Startup` object. We can add
`DbContext` to `IServiceCollection`, so it is injected into our classes.
`IServiceCollection` passes `DbContextOptionsBuilder` that we can use to initialize
our context, pretty much like we already did. So, add the `serves.AddDbContext` line
under `services.AddMvc();` in Startup.cs:

```
services.AddMvc();
// Add this line.
services.AddDbContext<WebShopContext>(
    optionsBuilder => optionsBuilder.UseNpgsql(
        Configuration.GetConnectionString("WebShopDatabase")
    )
);
```

To make this work, we need to modify `WebShopContext` as well. Add a constructor that
takes `DbContextOptions<TContext>` as a parameter and pass it to the base constructor.
Also, remove the `OnConfiguration` method:

```
public class WebShopContext : DbContext
{
    public WebShopContext(DbContextOptions<WebShopContext> context)
        : base(context)
```

```
    { }

    [...]

    // Remove this method.
    //protected override void OnConfiguring(DbContextOptionsBuilder
optionsBuilder)
    //{
    //
optionsBuilder.UseNpgsql("Host=ciserver;Database=webshop;Username=sa;Passwo
rd=sa");
    //}
}
```

Last but not least, we can inject our context to our controllers and use that instead of creating a new context every time we need it. Here is an example for `HomeController`. Notice that I removed the `using (var context = new WebShopContext())` code:

```
public class HomeController : Controller
{
    private readonly WebShopContext context;
    public HomeController(WebShopContext context)
    {
        this.context = context;
    }
>
    [...]

    public IActionResult GetTopProducts()
    {
        var products = context.Products
            [...]
        return Json(products);
    }

    [...]
}
```

Once you have refactored all the controllers, you should be ready to go. You can run your software and see it take the connection string from `appsettings.json`. When you run in the `Production` mode, you will see the connection string from `appsettings.Production.json`. You can run in the `Production` mode by changing the `ASPNETCORE_ENVIRONMENT` variable in `launch.json`.

Of course, we will need to release our software again for this to take effect. However, since we set everything up in Jenkins to automatically create a new build that we can simply copy and paste using WinSCP, this should not be a problem. After the next chapter it won't be difficult to implement a single button click strategy for your continuous delivery process. Any changes to the database will have to be manually deployed though! You can run your Selenium tests again to see if the new database works as expected.

Setting up all these tools and databases is a real drag. You could probably automate it using Jenkins, but that is probably pretty difficult and time-consuming. However, there are plenty of situations where you need multiples of these kinds of servers. Maybe you want to put a load balancer between your customer and your server or maybe you just have a lot of websites running.

Of course, there are tools that greatly speed up this process, either through virtualization or containerization. Using tools, such as Puppet (`https://puppet.com/`) or Chef (`https://www.chef.io/chef/`), the so-called Infrastructure-as-Code solutions, you can deploy new (virtual) servers on the fly.

Containerization is a little different in that it runs an isolated runtime environment on your host machine. You can easily spin up a container that contains all the necessary software and run some program in it. Docker (`https://www.docker.com/`) is the most popular alternative by far. Docker is also a very popular tool for testing purposes.

These tools are outside the scope of this book. They belong to the Ops in DevOps, while this book has a focus on the Dev in DevOps.

Summary

In this chapter, we have deployed both our JavaScript web shop and our C# .NET Core web shop. While both applications require a different setup, the process is more or less the same. We could relatively easily initiate a deployment using the artifacts that Jenkins already archived for us. A final small step awaits in the next and last chapter of this book--go from a commit to a production update that is completely automated.

14
Continuous Deployment

In this last chapter of the book, we will look at Continuous Deployment and its difference from Continuous Delivery. We have already set up Continuous Delivery in the last chapter. In this chapter, we will use our new branch to build and test our software and change the master branch to actually deploy and test the software fully automated. As explained in the last chapter, simply merging those branches, or cherry-picking specific commits, can lead to a more-or-less automated deployment. With Continuous Deployment, we want everything to be fully automated. In both cases, it is very important that your software is always deployable, but continuous deployment takes that statement a step further by actually deploying the software to a production environment.

As mentioned before, and I want to stress this again and again, continuous deployment is not always an option. Especially databases make this fully automated process a risk for many customers. However, you can still automatically deploy a version of their product to your local environment for testing purposes.

JavaScript Deployment using SSH

The first thing we need to do is get out artifacts from our Jenkins build to where we want them fully automated. Usually, this will be some remote server, but we do not have that. However, what we will do is to pretend that our local Linux machine is some other remote Linux machine and transfer the files using SSH.

First, in our master Jenkinsfile, we will need to unpack our artifacts so that we can copy them at all. Jenkins will mention that `unarchive` is deprecated and replaced for most purposes by `stash` and `unstash`. As far as I know, `stash` and `unstash` are temporary for the duration of the build, while `archive` keeps your artifacts even when the build is complete. We need the archive because we always want to know what is currently running on production and maybe because we want to be able to manually deploy files as well. The only way to get your files back using the pipeline is using `unarchive`, so I am not sure why it is deprecated or what *most purposes* means, but it seems perfectly fine to use it here:

```
unarchive mapping: ['**/**' : './artifacts']
```

This means we are unarchiving everything (`**/**`) and placing it in our current workspace in the `artifacts` folder (which will be created). Alternatively, we can just copy the files directly, without unarchiving first. It is a bit more work, but faster and certainly not deprecated.

We can now copy these files using SSH. Since we will use SSH using Jenkins, and we want to connect using Jenkins, we need to give the Jenkins account, that is, the user on which Jenkins is running, remote access to our server. You can log in to the Jenkins user using the `su` command (switch user). However, the user needs a password first:

```
sudo passwd jenkins
Enter new UNIX password: [your password]
Retype new UNIX password: [your password]
passwd: password updated successfully

su jenkins
Password: [your password]
```

Now that we are logged in as Jenkins, we can generate a key to be used by SSH and add our key to the known hosts:

```
ssh-keygen -t rsa
[Enter]
[No passphrase, so enter again]
[Again, no passphrase, enter]
ssh-keyscan -t rsa ciserver >> ~/.ssh/known_hosts
ssh-copy-id jenkins@ciserver
[Jenkins password]
```

Your key files will be placed in the `~/.ssh` hidden folder:

```
cd ~/.ssh
ls
```

We can now use SSH to connect to the server, but we do not have writing permissions to
`/var/www/webshop-js` yet. Instead of giving permissions, we will make Jenkins the owner
of the folder. First, switch back to your root user so that we can switch the user:

```
sudo chown -R jenkins:jenkins /var/www/webshop-js
```

Keep in mind that we set the owner of this folder to your root user in Chapter 13,
Continuous Delivery. Now that the root user is not the owner anymore, their permissions
have been revoked and logging in using WinSCP is no longer possible with that user. You
can, however, log in using the jenkins user now.

Finally, we can copy the files using the scp command, which uses SSH to copy files. Before
we do so, we can, optionally, clear out the webshop-js folder so that we do not get stuck
with old files and we know for sure that our build does not rely on some old files:

```
unarchive mapping: ['**/**' : './artifacts']
sh 'rm -rf /var/www/webshop-js/*'
sh 'scp -r artifacts/* jenkins@ciserver:/var/www/webshop-js'
```

The complete code for the Archiving Artifacts and Deployment stages in the
Jenkinsfile looks as follows:

```
stage('Archiving Artifacts') {
  steps {
    node(label: 'linux') {
      ws(dir: env.ws) {
        sh 'rm -rf node_modules'
        sh 'npm install --only=production'
        archiveArtifacts 'index.js, config.*.js, prod/, node_modules/'
      }
    }
  }
}
stage('Deployment') {
  steps {
    node(label: 'linux') {
      ws(dir: env.ws) {
        unarchive mapping: ['**/**' : './artifacts']
        sh 'rm -rf /var/www/webshop-js/*'
        sh 'scp -r artifacts/* jenkins@ciserver:/var/www/webshop-js'
      }
    }
  }
}
```

If you are not cleaning out your workspace before or after building, ensure that you add the `artifacts` folder to the `sonar.exclusions` in the `sonar-project.properties` file:

```
sonar.exclusions=[...], artifacts/**
```

If you run your Jenkins pipeline now, your files should be automatically copied to `/var/www/webshop-js`. Try making some text change in an HTML file, commit it, and wait for a few minutes; you should see your change appear on that page.

E2E testing

We can now add a new step in our master Jenkinsfile. When the web shop is automatically deployed, we can run some Selenium tests to check whether everything works. We have a bug production if this does not work, and we should fix it asap! It is highly unlikely that we get issues at this stage though, especially since the Development branch also has a Selenium step:

```
stage('Selenium') {
  steps {
    node(label: 'windows') {
      ws(dir: env.ws) {
        gitlabCommitStatus(name: 'Selenium') {
          script {
            unstash 'Everything'
            bat 'npm install'
            bat 'node_modules\\.bin\\webdriver-manager.cmd update'
            bat 'node_modules\\.bin\\protractor.cmd --baseUrl
http://ciserver:8888 test\\protractor.conf.js'
          }
        }
      }
    }
  }
}
```

C# .NET Core Deployment using SSH

Next up is the C# web application. We have already done most of the work; now set up SSH.

Fixing our Jenkinsfile so that it copies our archived files automatically should not be a problem. We can do this again using SSH. First, we need to make Jenkins the owner of the webshop-net folder:

```
sudo chown -R jenkins:jenkins /var/www/webshop-net
```

Again, this means that your root user loses privileges, and if you want to copy using WinSCP, you should use the jenkins user.

After that, it is pretty much the same as for the JavaScript webshop:

```
sh 'rm -rf /var/www/webshop-net/*'
sh 'scp -r prod/* jenkins@ciserver:/var/www/webshop-net'
```

The complete code for the Archive Artifacts and Deployment steps looks as follows:

```
stage('Archiving Artifacts') {
  steps {
    node(label: 'linux') {
      ws(dir: env.ws) {
        sh 'rm -rf node_modules'
        sh 'npm install --only=production'
        sh 'dotnet publish -o ../prod web-shop/web-shop.csproj'
        archiveArtifacts 'prod/'
      }
    }
  }
}
stage('Deployment') {
  steps {
    node(label: 'linux') {
      ws(dir: env.ws) {
        unarchive mapping: ['**/**' : './artifacts']
        sh 'rm -rf /var/www/webshop-net/*'
        sh 'scp -r artifacts/prod/* jenkins@ciserver:/var/www/webshop-net'
      }
    }
  }
}
```

Again, try changing some text in an HTML file, commit it, and see that it is automatically deployed.

E2E testing

Now that we have our .NET Core application running, we can add our Selenium tests to our Jenkins build. Ensure that you add them after you have deployed the software. Speaking of which, it may be worth it to deploy a version of your software before everything is minified, uglified, and bundled to some local company server, and run your tests on that environment as well. It will be a lot easier to debug any problems, and the setup can more closely match your ultimate production environment than your local development machine does.

To fix our Selenium tests, we first have to make some minor code changes. Unfortunately, .NET Core unit test projects are a little more limited than MVC Core projects, so we do not have any app settings or other configuration files. It is probably possible somehow, but since it is not supplied out of the box and we do not really need it, we will hardcode our URL into the code:

```
public SeleniumTests()
{
    server = new TestServer(new WebHostBuilder()
        .UseStartup<Startup>());
    client = server.CreateClient();
    client.BaseAddress = new Uri("http://ciserver:9999");
}

[...]

// Change the GoToUrl to use the base address.
driver.Navigate().GoToUrl($"{client.BaseAddress}");

[...]

// No slash between BaseAddress and page.
driver.Navigate().GoToUrl($"{client.BaseAddress}ShoppingCart");
```

You can already run them locally, using `dotnet test`, and see whether everything still works. If you need to test locally, you can just manually change 9999 to 5000, but that should not be necessary all that often. Keep in mind that you are currently testing the minified source, so when you do this on a test server first, you can be pretty sure that your code works on production as well.

Changing your Jenkins build is now pretty easy; whether you are using the classic Jenkins projects or the Jenkinsfile, just execute the `dotnet test` command. Of course, we want some reporting too. We can, again, use the msxsl tool in the Jenkins file:

```
stage('Selenium') {
  steps {
    node(label: 'windows') {
      ws(dir: env.ws) {
        gitlabCommitStatus(name: 'Selenium') {
          script {
            unstash 'Everything'
            bat 'dotnet test -l "trx;LogFileName=result.trx" web-shop-
selenium\\web-shop-selenium.csproj'
            bat 'msxsl -o JUnitResults.xml web-shop-
selenium\\TestResults\\result.trx trx-to-junit.xsl'
            junit 'JUnitResults.xml'
          }
        }
      }
    }
  }
}
```

Database

Databases are really difficult to update automatically. As I have mentioned somewhere earlier in this book, you will often face customers or database administrators who flat out forbid you to do any updates on a database, let alone do so automatically. It is not uncommon that developers deliver their scripts to a person, typically the DBA, who then manually checks them and runs them on the database. For good reason, the database stores what a business is all about or what it needs to run properly--data. Losing or damaging it can put a company out of business (but, of course, you have backups).

Less severe, but potentially damaging to the business, are scripts that lock tables, update live data, or change business rules. You can imagine that some scripts, such as updating a 1,000 GB table, can potentially lock an entire system. Such updates should happen outside of business hours (if possible) and in controlled environments.

It is probably a good bet to not do continuous deployment on a database, but it may still be a valid option when you are in control of the software and database or when the database has non-critical data.

When you are certain you can do database updates automatically without problems, there are various tools that can help you with this task. One such tool is the Entity Framework when you are doing .NET (Core) development. We have chosen a database-first approach, but you might as well go for a code-first approach for new projects or switch from database-first to code-first halfway. A code-first approach, using Migrations (`https://docs.microsoft.com/en-us/aspnet/core/data/ef-mvc/migrations`), means you can code your classes and your object context, and .NET will generate or update your database when you next run your application. This means that any new version of your software will check your database schema and update it, if necessary, when it is executed. One cool feature is that you can also downgrade your database to a previous version. Well, this is cool in theory, but personally, I have never downgraded a production application. Migrations add a little startup time to your application, but it is potentially worth it. There are other .NET tools that can do more or less the same, such as FluentMigrator (`https://github.com/fluentmigrator/fluentmigrator`), which is based on Ruby on Rails Migrations. I have written about Entity Framework Migrations in a previous book of mine--*SQL Server For C# Developers Succinctly* (`https://www.syncfusion.com/resources/techportal/details/ebooks/sql_server_for_c_sharp_developers_succinctly`)--that you can download for free. Anyway, it is not in the scope of this book, so I am not discussing it any further here.

If you are working with scripts, there are some possibilities as well. Flyway (`https://flywaydb.org/`) is one such possibility; it supports many SQL databases, such as SQL Server, MySQL, Oracle and, of course, PostgreSQL. Flyway is incredibly easy to use. We can start by using the command-line tool from Windows just to see what it is and does. So, download the latest command-line tool from the Flyway website (`https://flywaydb.org/getstarted/download`). Simply unzip the `tool` folder to somewhere on your computer; I have placed it on my desktop for easy access. Next, simply create a new database and name it whatever you want, such as `flyway_demo`:

```
CREATE DATABASE flyway_demo
    WITH
    OWNER = sa
    ENCODING = 'UTF8'
    CONNECTION LIMIT = -1;
```

Now, let's create a new folder in the same folder that you put the `Flyway` folder in; in my case, it is the desktop. It does not really matter what you name it, but I named it `Flyway demo`. Now, create a new folder within that folder and name it `Migrations`. In the `Migrations` folder, we will put our first migration script, which is just a `CREATE TABLE` statement. So, create a file and name it `V1_0__Create table.sql` (with a double underscore between `0` and `Create`). In the file, put the following SQL statement:

```
CREATE TABLE public.some_table
(
```

```
        id integer NOT NULL,
        name text COLLATE pg_catalog."default" NOT NULL,
        CONSTRAINT some_table_pkey PRIMARY KEY (id)
)
WITH (
    OIDS = FALSE
)
TABLESPACE pg_default;

ALTER TABLE public.some_table
    OWNER to sa;
```

We now need to tell Flyway where it can find its migrations, how it can recognize them, on what server and database to execute them, and how to log in. We can use a configuration file for this. Put a file named `flyway.conf` in the same folder as the `Migrations` folder. Put the following contents in the file:

```
flyway.driver=org.postgresql.Driver
flyway.url=jdbc:postgresql://ciserver:5432/flyway_demo
flyway.user=sa
flyway.password=sa
flyway.locations=filesystem:Migrations
flyway.sqlMigrationPrefix=V
flyway.sqlMigrationSeparator=__
flyway.sqlMigrationSuffix=.sql
flyway.validateOnMigrate=true
```

It is really quite self-explanatory. We specify the driver, the URL to the database, our credentials (obviously `sa`/`sa` is not very secure!), the `locations` parameter specifies where Flyway can find its SQL scripts, the `sqlMigrationPrefix`, `sqlMigrationSeparator` and `sqlMigrationSuffix` tell Flyway how to recognize migration files and, lastly, `validateOnMigrate` adds an additional validation. We can now open up a command prompt, browse to the folder containing our `flyway.conf` file and `Migrations` folder and run `flyway migrate`. Flyway will pick up the configuration file and use those options:

```
..\flyway-4.2.0\flyway migrate
```

Optionally, you can add additional parameters in the Command Prompt or overwrite parameters from the configuration:

```
..\flyway-4.2.0\flyway -url=jdbc:postgresql://ciserver:5432/another_db
migrate
```

The output is as follows:

```
C:\Windows\System32\cmd.exe                                          —    □    ×

Microsoft Windows [Version 10.0.15063]
(c) 2017 Microsoft Corporation. All rights reserved.

C:\Users\sander.rossel\Desktop\Flyway demo>..\flyway-4.2.0\flyway migrate
Flyway 4.2.0 by Boxfuse

Database: jdbc:postgresql://ciserver:5432/flyway_demo (PostgreSQL 9.5)
Successfully validated 1 migration (execution time 00:00.011s)
Creating Metadata table: "public"."schema_version"
Current version of schema "public": << Empty Schema >>
Migrating schema "public" to version 1.0 - Create tables
Successfully applied 1 migration to schema "public" (execution time 00:00.058s).

C:\Users\sander.rossel\Desktop\Flyway demo>
```

When you check out the database now, it has two new tables: the `some_table`, as per our migration, and the `schema_version` table that Flyway added in order to keep track of migrations. Do not change migrations that have been migrated; create another migration instead:

installed_rank [PK] integer	version character	description character var	type charac	script character varying (1000	checksum integer	installed_by character var	installed_on timestamp wi	execution_time integer	success boolean
1	1.0	Create tables	SQL	V1_0__Create tables.sql	332611729	sa	2017-09-06 2...	5	true

If you run `flyway migrate` again, you will find that nothing happens; you will get a `No migration necessary` message. You can add new migrations, and they will all be executed on a single `flyway migrate`. Try it by copying our first migration and naming it `V1_1__Another table`, and change `some_table` to `other_table` in the script.

We can now try to use flyway migrate on our `webshop` database. Unfortunately, you will get the `ERROR: Found non empty schema(s)!` message. Flyway is saying that there is no `schema_version`, but the database is not empty either. We can add a baseline by adding one to our configuration file and running `flyway baseline`:

```
[...]
flyway.baselineVersion=0.9
flyway.baselineDescription=Base Migration
```

Now, run `flyway baseline`, followed by `flyway migrate`:

```
..\flyway-4.2.0\flyway baseline
..\flyway-4.2.0\flyway migrate
```

The baseline version is quite important. We have two scripts: `V1_0__*` and `V1_1__*`. If we put our baseline on version 1.0 or 2.0, then the `V1_0` and, possibly, the `V1_1` scripts will not be executed.

So, now you can put Flyway on your Windows or Ubuntu machine, or commit it with your project, and use it in your Jenkins build to update your databases. Just ensure that you properly version and write your migrations.

Next, to automate tools and keep track of database scripts, you can opt for a third option-- database compare tools. There are plenty of tools out there that can compare database schemas and generate update scripts that you can run as you see fit.

As MongoDB is schemaless, updates are a lot easier. Just update the software with a new table or field, and MongoDB will just insert it or return a default value for the already existing records that do not have the new field yet.

Summary

In the final chapter of the book, we went from committing some code to seeing it live on another environment without any further human intervention. We copied files using Jenkins and SSH, and we also looked at database deployment with Flyway.

This concludes the book. We saw various methods to guarantee a certain level of code quality, ranging from linting to unit tests. Other than that, we have used various tools, such as SonarQube, Karma, Gulp, and Jenkins. However, there is more to see. I have mentioned tools such as Puppet, Chef, and Docker, but we did not discuss them at length. CI is hot and the field is ever going forward, so keep yourself updated. With this book, you should have a solid theoretical knowledge and the necessary practical skills to put any new tool to good use.

Index

www.ingramcontent.com/pod-product-compliance
Lightning Source LLC
Chambersburg PA
CBHW060645060326
40690CB00020B/4522